David Fallon

CAMBRIDGE STUDIES IN EIGHTEENTH-CENTURY
ENGLISH LITERATURE AND THOUGHT 13

Richardson's *Clarissa* and the eighteenth-century reader

Written as a collection of letters in which very different accounts of the action are unsupervised by sustained authorial comment, Richardson's novel *Clarissa* offers an extreme example of the capacity of narrative to give the reader final responsibility for resolving or construing meaning. It is paradoxical then that its author was a writer committed to avowedly didactic goals. Tom Keymer counters the tendency of recent critics to suggest that *Clarissa*'s textual indeterminacy defeats these goals, arguing that Richardson pursues a subtler and more generous means of educating his readers by making them 'if not Authors, Carvers' of the text.

Discussing Richardson's use of epistolary form throughout his career, Keymer goes on to focus in detail on the three instalments in which *Clarissa* was first published, drawing on the documented responses of its first readers to illuminate his technique as a writer, and set the novel in its contemporary ethical, political and ideological context.

CAMBRIDGE STUDIES IN EIGHTEENTH-CENTURY ENGLISH LITERATURE AND THOUGHT

General Editors: Dr HOWARD ERSKINE-HILL, Litt.D., FBA, *Pembroke College, Cambridge*
and Professor JOHN RICHETTI, *University of Pennsylvania*

Editorial Board: Morris Brownell, *University of Nevada*
Leopold Damrosch, *Harvard University*
J. Paul Hunter, *University of Chicago*
Isobel Grundy, *University of Alberta*
Lawrence Lipking, *Northwestern University*
Harold Love, *Monash University*
Claude Rawson, *Yale University*
Pat Rogers, *University of South Florida*
James Sambrook, *University of Southampton*

This series is designed to accommodate monographs and critical studies on authors, works, genres and other aspects of literary culture from the later part of the seventeenth century to the end of the eighteenth. Since academic engagement with this field has become an increasingly interdisciplinary enterprise, books will be especially encouraged which in some way stress the cultural context of the literature, or examine it in relation to contemporary art, music, philosophy, historiography, religion, politics, social affairs and so on.

Titles published

The Transformation of The Decline and Fall of the Roman Empire
by David Womersley

Women's Place in Pope's World
by Valerie Rumbold

Sterne's Fiction and the Double Principle
by Jonathan Lamb

Warrior Women and Popular Balladry, 1650–1850
by Dianne Dugaw

The Body in Swift and Defoe
by Carol Flynn

The Rhetoric of Berkeley's Philosophy
by Peter Walmsley

Space and the Eighteenth-Century English Novel
by Simon Varey

*Reason, Grace, and Sentiment: A Study of the Language of Religion and Ethics
in England, 1660–1780*
by Isabel Rivers

Defoe's Politics: Parliament, Power, Kingship and Robinson Crusoe
by Manuel Schonhorn

Sentimental Comedy: Theory & Practice
by Frank Ellis

Arguments of Augustan Wit
by John Sitter

Robert South (1634–1716): An Introduction to his Life and Sermons
by Gerard Reedy, S.J.

Richardson's Clarissa *and the Eighteenth-Century Reader*
by Tom Keymer

Frontispiece   'Reflections on Clarissa Harlowe', engraved by G. Scorodomow after Sir Joshua Reynolds's portrait (exhibited at the RA in 1771) of his niece Theophila Palmer reading 'Clarissa'. Windsor Castle, Royal Library. © 1991 Her Majesty The Queen.

Richardson's Clarissa
and the Eighteenth-Century Reader

TOM KEYMER

Lecturer in English
Royal Holloway and Bedford New College
University of London

CAMBRIDGE
UNIVERSITY PRESS

PUBLISHED BY THE PRESS SYNDICATE OF THE UNIVERSITY OF CAMBRIDGE
The Pitt Building, Trumpington Street, Cambridge, United Kingdom

CAMBRIDGE UNIVERSITY PRESS
The Edinburgh Building, Cambridge CB2 2RU, UK
40 West 20th Street, New York NY 10011–4211, USA
477 Williamstown Road, Port Melbourne, VIC 3207, Australia
Ruiz de Alarcón 13, 28014 Madrid, Spain
Dock House, The Waterfront, Cape Town 8001, South Africa

http://www.cambridge.org

First published 1992
Reprinted 1993
First paperback edition 2004

A catalogue record for this book is available from the British Library

Library of Congress cataloguing in publication data
Keymer, Tom.
Richardson's Clarissa and the eighteenth-century reader / Tom Keymer.
p.   cm.
Includes bibliographical references and index.
ISBN 0 521 39023 0 (hardback)
1. Richardson, Samuel, 1689–1761.   Clarissa.   2. Authors and readers – Great Britain –
History – 18th century.   3. Reader – response criticism.   I. Title.
PR3664.C43K49   1992
823'.6 – dc20   91–4225 CIP

ISBN 0 521 39023 0 hardback
ISBN 0 521 60440 0 paperback

To the memory of Maggie Warburton 1895–1990

Contents

x Contents

Preface

On publishing his *Life of Samuel Johnson, LL.D.* in 1787, Boswell's rival biographer Sir John Hawkins was widely attacked for the rancorous tenor of his work. Boswell himself alluded sourly to 'the ponderous labours of solemn inaccuracy and dark uncharitable conjecture'; 'Philo Johnson' sneered that 'Sir John Hawkins, with all the humanity and very little of the dexterity of a Clare-Market butcher, has raised his blunt axe to deface the image of his friend.'[1] But Hawkins could at least claim to have been consistent in his iconoclasm, as his remarks on the novelists of the period, and Richardson in particular, show. 'Those who were unacquainted with Richardson, and had red his books, were led to believe, that they exhibited a picture of his own mind, and that his temper and domestic behaviour could not but correspond with that refined morality which they inculcate', he reports; 'but in this they were deceived.' The sorry truth was that Richardson's conduct bespoke a sullenness wholly at odds with 'that philanthropy which he laboured to inculcate'. 'He was austere in the government of his family, and issued his orders to some of his servants in writing only'; his wife and daughters 'appeared to have been taught to converse with him by signs' (which he reciprocated, in the main, with 'frowns and gesticulations, importing that they should leave his presence'); he refused (or was unable) to converse himself. Hawkins could speak from experience:

I once travelled with him in the Fulham stage-coach, in which, at my getting in, I found him seated. I learned, by somewhat he said to the coachman, who he was, and made some essays towards conversation, but he seemed disinclined to any. There was one other passenger, who being a female, I was, in common civility, bound to take notice of; but my male companion I left to indulge himself in a reverie, which neither he nor I interrupted by the utterance of a single word, and lasted till he was set down at his house on Parson's green. He had the courtesy to ask us in, but as our acquaintance had but lately commenced, and had received but little improvement in our journey, the civility was declined.[2]

[1] *St James's Chronicle* (12–15 May 1787); *European Magazine* (May 1787), 313. Both passages are quoted at length by Bertram H. Davis (who suggests that 'Philo Johnson' was the pseudonym of George Steevens), *Johnson before Boswell: A Study of Sir John Hawkins' Life of Samuel Johnson* (New Haven, 1960), pp. 24, 21–2.

[2] *The Life of Samuel Johnson, LL.D.*, 2nd edn (1787), pp. 384–5.

For the biographer, the story of Hawkins's frustrated 'essays towards conversation' is of mild but limited interest (and has no place in Eaves and Kimpel's compendious modern life): it tells us little of Richardson's mind beyond the fact of its inaccessibility. For the critic, however, the anecdote has a curious aptness – albeit an aptness unnoted by Hawkins himself, who thought the novel an empty genre, Richardson's novels 'flimsy and thin, and his style mean and feeble', and Fielding's 'seemingly intended to sap the foundation of . . . morality'.[3] In his eagerness to belittle the novelists, Hawkins had failed to see that his own preoccupation with the practice of 'conversation' between an author and his audience (a preoccupation displayed not only here but in the *Life of Johnson* as a whole) was a concern they fully shared. Where his interests were confined to the colloquial arts of the assembly ('Familiar discourse; chat; easy talk'),[4] however, the novelists extended the term to embrace literary as well as oral modes, and found in the language of dialogue and sociability a powerful metaphor through which to explore the more complex patterns of communication and interaction made possible in the novel itself. Perhaps the most famous example comes in Sterne's *Tristram Shandy*, where Tristram ponders the consequences for the reader of the fractures, ellipses and lacunae that pepper his reports:

Writing, when properly managed (as you may be sure I think mine is), is but a different name for conversation. As no one, who knows what he is about in good company, would venture to talk all; – so no author, who understands the just boundaries of decorum and good-breeding, would presume to think all: The truest respect which you can pay to the reader's understanding, is to halve the matter amicably, and leave him something to imagine, in his turn, as well as yourself.

By leaving meanings uncertain, incoherent or simply incomplete, Tristram suggests, his text instigates a newly reciprocal form of communication, in which meaning is constructed not by the author alone but by the collaboration of two increasingly equal participants, author and reader: 'For my own part, I am eternally paying him compliments of this kind, and do all that lies in my power to keep his imagination as busy as my own.'[5]

It is in *Tom Jones*, however, that the analogy between narrative and

---

[3] *Ibid.*, p. 214.

[4] Samuel Johnson, *A Dictionary of the English Language* (1755), 'Conversation'.

[5] *The Life and Opinions of Tristram Shandy, Gentleman*, ed. Ian Campbell Ross (Oxford, 1983), p. 87. Despite playful apostrophes elsewhere to 'Madam' as well as 'Sir', it will be noted that Sterne's practice in this and other abstract references to *Tristram Shandy*'s reader is to use the pronouns 'he' and 'his'. In the absence of a simple, concise and unobtrusive alternative, I have followed suit. The attention drawn in this study to the activities of many women readers is enough to make clear, I hope, that in this matter such pronouns are not to be taken as gender-specific, except at those points where reference is explicitly made to the implications of gender for reading.

conversation comes closest to Sir John Hawkins's experience on the road
to Parson's Green. The passage in question looks back to a related moment
in *Joseph Andrews*, where Fielding invites his reader to regard the blank
leaves that separate the novel's books 'as those Stages, where, in long
Journeys, the Traveller stays some time to repose himself, and consider of
what he hath seen in the Parts he hath already past through'.[6] In *Tom
Jones*, however, the image is adjusted to stress not the visibility of a
narrated world so much as the *audibility* of a narrating voice – a shift that
enables Fielding to register with greater precision the situation and experience of his reader. 'We are now, Reader, arrived at the last Stage of our
long Journey', in the opening words of Book XVIII. Throughout this
journey, 'like Fellow-Travellers in a Stage-Coach, who have passed
several Days in the Company of each other', reader and author have been
engaged in what amounts to familiar 'Conversation', the latter entertaining the former with his narratives, commentaries and explanations.[7]

As the image suggests, Fielding's method as a novelist is not to involve
his readers directly in the represented world and leave them to understand
its workings for themselves. Instead he filters his story through the reports
of an assertive authorial persona (in Wayne Booth's famous terms, the
dramatised 'Fielding' or 'second self' constructed in the text),[8] whose
mediation works to guide, inform and even at times control the reader in
his understanding of the action. The insistence of this authorial voice, of
course, does not entirely preclude a conversation of *Tristram Shandy*'s kind,
for the guidance is not without its lapses, and in its moments of silence,
obliquity and even occasional misdirection it gives the reader too a
constructive role to play. 'Bestir thyself therefore on this Occasion', as the
narrator urges in Book XI:

for tho' we will always lend thee proper Assistance in difficult Places, as we do not,
like some others, expect thee to use the Arts of Divination to discover our
Meaning; yet we shall not indulge thy Laziness where nothing but thy own
Attention is required; for thou art highly mistaken if thou dost imagine that we
intended ... to leave thy Sagacity nothing to do, or that without sometimes
exercising this Talent, thou wilt be able to travel through our Pages with any
Pleasure or Profit to thyself.[9]

Clearly, the reader must keep on his toes, and cannot always expect the
simple reliability of the novel's final book (where 'All will be plain
Narrative only', just as in the final stage of a journey 'all Jokes and

---

[6] *The History of the Adventures of Joseph Andrews and An Apology for the Life of Mrs Shamela Andrews*, ed.
  Douglas Brooks (1970), p. 78.

[7] *The History of Tom Jones, A Foundling*, ed. Martin C. Battestin and Fredson Bowers, 2 vols.
  (Oxford, 1974), II, 913.

[8] See *The Rhetoric of Fiction*, 2nd edn (Chicago, 1983), pp. 71–6, 215–18.

[9] *Tom Jones*, II, 614.

Raillery are at this Time laid aside; whatever Characters any of the Passengers have for the Jest-sake personated on the Road, are now thrown off, and the Conversation is usually plain and serious'). For all his addiction to jest, however, Fielding's authorial persona remains an eloquent and persuasive interpreter of the novel's action, and establishes in even the most playful of his reports an explicit and determinate framework for response. Dramatic presentation is accompanied at every point by discursive commentary; and while Ian Watt may have overstated the case when he wrote that Fielding's 'conception of his role is that of a guide who, not content with taking us "behind the scenes of this great theatre of nature", feels that he must explain everything which is to be found there',[10] it is impossible to miss the influence of the overt authorial 'Assistance' to which the text itself alludes. George Eliot's celebrated allusion to Fielding as a novelist 'who seems to bring his arm-chair to the proscenium and chat with us'[11] exactly describes the combination (and priority) of effects.

But what of Richardson, and what of Richardson's reader? In the preface to *Clarissa*, Richardson writes of having resisted the arguments of readers of his manuscript who had urged him to dispense with the novel's epistolary form and throw it 'into the narrative way' (I, vi; p. 36). Images of conversation or guidance, as a result, could hardly be less apt. Where in *Tom Jones* what might be called the raw material of the novel, the hypothetical reality it reports, is consistently organised and mediated by an ever-present 'Fielding', there is no comparable 'Richardson' to supervise the reader's experience of *Clarissa* or *Sir Charles Grandison*. The author remains almost entirely an absence,[12] and each novel's raw material remains, in a sense, raw: the reader is presented not with a detached, third-person assessment of experience, but with something as diffusive and multifarious, and as intractable in its meanings, as experience itself. For these reasons, Richardson too is often likened to a dramatist, but one who denies his audience the voice from the proscenium, and instead stays silent in the wings. By refusing to reduce his work to 'a pattern perceived and articulated with hindsight and by an author', Mark Kinkead-Weekes has written, Richardson causes the reader 'to experience directly for oneself rather than through an authorial filter'. He thereby achieves what Kinkead-Weekes calls 'the equivalent in the novel of the experience of drama'.[13] It might be added that this reticence lends him a striking resemblance to the negligent 'others' described by Fielding, who withhold

[10] *The Rise of the Novel: Studies in Defoe, Richardson and Fielding* (1957), p. 285.

[11] *Middlemarch*, ed. W. J. Harvey (Harmondsworth, 1965), p. 170.

[12] In *Clarissa*, the nearest equivalent to an authorial commentary comes in a peripheral apparatus of editorial footnotes and abstracts which, though largely absent from the original edition of 1747–8, is of significant effect in the second and third: see below, pp. 246–8.

[13] Kinkead-Weekes, *Samuel Richardson: Dramatic Novelist* (1973), p. 395.

authorial 'Assistance' and expect the reader 'to use the Arts of Divination
to discover [their] Meaning'. He seems, indeed, to 'halve the matter' of
understanding more equally even than Sterne. By requiring the reader to
make his own sense of the novel's world, unguided by anything remotely
like a single authorial voice, he taxes the reader's understanding to what,
in the context even of these other very demanding texts, is an exceptional
extent.

It is here that the happiness of Sir John Hawkins's anecdote lies. If
Fielding's model of novel-reading as conversation is at all applicable to
Clarissa, it must take very much this form; for 'Richardson' in the novels,
like Richardson in the Fulham stage-coach, remains obstinately withdrawn. Sterne's version of the image, likewise, is here aptly recast; for if in
Richardson's novels' 'the just boundaries of decorum and good-breeding'
expected in conversation come under strain (and Hawkins's feeling, in his
own case, is clearly that they do), it is not because the author tries to 'talk
all', but because he declines to utter a word. Rebuffed in his 'essays
towards conversation' and left to his own devices, Hawkins's experience
mirrors the situation of Richardson's reader with an exactness that could
only have been improved if Richardson had told him to get out and walk.
'Something . . . must be left to the Reader to make out', Richardson once
wrote;[14] and in the absence of authorial commentary almost everything is.

Yet it would be wrong to assume from Richardson's elimination of this
intervening voice that the reader's access to each novel's basic facts of
character and action therefore becomes direct. The reader's situation is
not completely analogous to that of the audience at a play, for Richardson
too places intermediaries between reader and story. These intermediaries
are rarely detached and managerial like Fielding's narrators, however,
and their interference is more easily forgotten. Pursuing the case for
Richardson as dramatic novelist, for example, Kinkead-Weekes identifies
Richardson's 'new Manner of Writing – to the Moment'[15] as an attempt
above all 'to catch living voices in a dramatic present', and he has little
time for the specifically epistolary foundation of the method. In the novels
'the experience of living from moment to moment . . . is more important
than the letter convention', he insists: what is significant is not that
Richardson's narrators *write*, or that they write *letters*, but that their
letter-writing coincides in time with events which as a result are represented with unique fulness and immediacy. Here, Kinkead-Weekes contends, is the difference between the dramatic Richardson and the more
genuinely epistolary Laclos. 'Richardson is an "epistolary novelist" cer-

---

[14] To Lady Bradshaigh, 25 February 1754, Carroll, p. 296.
[15] The phrase (Richardson to Lady Bradshaigh, 9 October 1756, Carroll, p. 329) denotes
   Richardson's method of simultaneous or periodic narrative, in which narrating time and
   narrated time approximately coincide: see Kinkead-Weekes, *Samuel Richardson*, p. 395.

tainly', he concedes, 'but to lay the emphasis there is to mistake a technical means, however central, for the formal end itself: the novel as drama.'[16]

This disinclination to see more in Richardson's narrative form than an ingenious means of collapsing the space between the telling and the told is deeply ingrained in criticism. The tone was set in Ian Watt's influential *Rise of the Novel*, where Richardson's 'formal realism' is applauded for providing 'a more immediate imitation of individual experience set in its temporal and spatial environment than do other literary forms', and these emphases survive largely intact in the work even of critics concerned to take issue with Watt's larger thesis: 'What was significant and unique in this new method of spontaneous writing', writes Lennard Davis, 'was the ability to recapture recent time past' and 'to fashion language and narrative so as to cleave closer to the real in terms of time and space.'[17] Yet to think of epistolary narrative as purely and simply transparent, delivering 'the real' to the reader unmediated and entire, is to consider only one of a range of effects made available to Richardson by the letter form, and exploited by him in it. It is also to miss the reasons which made Laclos himself describe *Clarissa*, in separate contexts, as 'celui des Romans où il y a le plus de génie' and 'le chef-d'œuvre des romans'.[18]

This study begins by questioning the assumption that Richardson turned to letters simply as a convention for achieving dramatic immediacy. By restoring to view the many aspects of his narrative method that qualify or interfere with effects of this kind, it attempts to reinstate him as an epistolary novelist in the fullest possible sense. The first chapter makes a detailed analysis of the epistolary form, arguing that in Richardson's hands letter-narrative focuses attention only indirectly on 'the experience of living from moment to moment', and that its emphasis falls first and foremost on the experience of *writing* – on the efforts of engaged parties to describe, make sense of, and often advance particular purposes in, their world. The novels show no bland confidence in the capacity of writing to replicate the fulness of experience, whether inner or outer, I shall argue. They are preoccupied by the inevitability of slippage between world and word, and in particular by the deformations that arise from the rhetorical or performative tendencies of first-person discourse. Fielding too was a subtle analyst of these tendencies, and he may well have had *Clarissa* in mind when he wrote in *Tom Jones*:

For let a Man be never so honest, the Account of his own Conduct will, in Spite of himself, be so very favourable, that his Vices will come purified through his Lips, and, like foul Liquors well strained, will leave all their Foulness behind. For tho' the Facts themselves may appear, yet so different will be the Motives, Circum-

---

[16] Kinkead-Weekes, *Samuel Richardson*, pp. 396–7.
[17] Watt, p. 32; Davis, *Factual Fictions: The Origins of the English Novel* (New York, 1983), p. 183.
[18] *Œuvres complètes*, ed. Laurent Versini (Paris, 1979), pp. 469, 440.

stances, and Consequences, when a Man tells his own Story, and when his Enemy tells it, that we scarce can recognize the Facts to be one and the same.[19]

In *Clarissa*, where a woman tells her own story, and where her enemy tells it, the letter form provided Richardson with an ideal medium in which to explore such distortions and interferences to the full (as Fielding, for all his alertness, never did). The result is very far from an effect of pure transparency. It amounts instead to a uniquely complicated unreliability – even a kind of opacity.

In making this analysis, I am concerned not simply with the formal properties of Richardson's narrative but with its consequences, again, for the reader – and from this perspective the epistolary form can be seen to intensify the difficulties of reading still further. Now it is not simply that the form excludes a detached, objective voice, and requires the reader to judge on his own initiative. The effects of this absence are further compounded by the profusion of involved, subjective voices which rise in its place and which, though ready enough to urge analyses or judgments on the reader, do so only in highly questionable and often irreconcilable ways. Far from placing the reader in immediate possession of each novel's story, Richardson's method complicates his access to it to an unprecedented degree, confronting him with problems of interpretation and response which in the end go far beyond those of a spectator left to reach his own understanding of a play – for here one sees not the action itself, only a tangle of unreliable and adversarial versions of it, each compromised and limited (among other conditions) by the rhetorical situation of the reporter. Meanings remain vexed, controversial, even indeterminate; and in the absence of synthesis, or of any objective guidance in matters of evaluation and judgment, the reader is pushed into the most exacting and creative of roles. He must make sense, for himself, of all the text's confusions, complexities and quarrels.

To make these emphases on the intricacy of Richardson's narrative form and the intensity of the demands made by it on the reader is not an unprecedented move. Writing in the heyday of deconstruction, both William Beatty Warner and Terry Castle have explored the literariness of Richardson's writing, dwelling on its tendency to vest final responsibility for the construction of meaning with the reader alone.[20] Where I part company with these more recent critics is in attributing this 'authorising' of the reader to a considered strategy on Richardson's part rather than to an accident of textuality or form, and in resisting the assumption that it necessarily entails the collapse of his didactic project. Few have time these days for Richardson's didacticism, and there is certainly reason enough to

---

[19] *Tom Jones*, I, 420.
[20] Warner, *Reading Clarissa: The Struggles of Interpretation* (New Haven, 1979); Castle, *Clarissa's Ciphers: Meaning and Disruption in Richardson's Clarissa* (Ithaca, 1982).

hesitate before embracing, lock, stock and barrel, his attitudes and beliefs.
Yet what many of Richardson's contemporaries saw when they considered
this didacticism was not the naive attempt to enforce banal warnings
against misconduct so often derided in modern criticism, but a far more
intelligent, extensive and dynamic endeavour (in the words of one) to
'new-Model [the] Affections' of the reader, and 'to inform the Understanding'[21] – an endeavour closer in motivation if not in form to Fielding's
attempts to exercise and empower the 'Sagacity' of his reader than either
novelist was ever prepared to admit. This project should not, I think, be
dismissed as the debilitating obsession of a writer whose real achievement
was at root unconscious, and whose refusal to subject readers to explicit
authorial direction led inevitably to self-defeat. By withholding any
presiding authorial voice, or by dissolving it instead into a multiplicity of
competing epistolary voices, Richardson knowingly fostered the active
participation of his readers, whom he expected to become 'if not Authors,
Carvers' of the text.[22] The instructiveness of the novels, I shall argue,
derives precisely from this method of putting readers, morally and intellectually, on their mettle. It is by an active encounter with difficulties, and
not by the passive reception of lessons, that Richardson's reader may
learn.

This book, then, is not simply an account of Richardson's narrative
form, or of the role in which it casts the reader. It is an attempt to explain
the reader's role within the terms of Richardson's aim of enhancing,
through the mental experience of reading, the reader's competence to
understand, judge and negotiate the actual experience of living in the
world – a world that is itself, as Clarissa reminds us, 'a state of temptation
and tryal, of doubt and uncertainty' (VII, 241; p. 1377). Following a lead
suggested by Johnson's *Rambler*, I shall argue that the novels educate their
reader by involving him in instructive 'mock encounters' with difficulties,
challenges and dilemmas closely related in kind to those he will encounter
in life itself: they inform his capacity to make sense of the world by first
requiring him to make sense, from his own resources, of a correspondingly
exacting text. By approaching Richardson in this way, I hope to show that
much of the complexity of form, debatability of meaning and urgency of
implication for which we value the novels today is not only consistent
with, but in great measure attributable to, the conscious didactic purposes
which moved their author to write them. At the same time, I hope to
explicate and amplify the sense which many of Richardson's astutest

[21] Philip Skelton to Richardson, 10 June 1749, FM XV, 2, f.47; Skelton's contribution to
    Richardson's MS *Hints of Prefaces*, reprinted in *Samuel Richardson, Clarissa: Preface, Hints of
    Prefaces, and Postscript*, ed. R. F. Brissenden, Augustan Reprint Society No. 103 (Los Angeles,
    1964), p. 8.
[22] Richardson to Lady Bradshaigh, 25 February 1754, Carroll, p. 296. A carver is one who
    chooses or decides: see below, p. 74.

contemporaries shared of the novels' power not only to represent the world mimetically but to equip the reader for life within it – their power, in Johnson's words, 'not only to show mankind, but to provide that they may be seen hereafter with less hazard'.[23]

The main body of the book pursues this analysis by a close study of *Clarissa*. In three chapters corresponding to the three instalments in which the novel first appeared, I focus in particular on the difficulties and challenges with which the reader is confronted, and on the activities required of him in the process of reading. The emphasis falls recurrently on the underlying complexities of the multiple epistolary form, which offers the reader conflicting points of access to the story and leaves him to measure and judge them for himself; but the novel's difficulty of course extends far beyond this basic formal problem. The need to measure and judge the novel's rival reports takes on its urgency only because of the vexedness of the story itself, the vexedness of the ethical, religious, social and political questions that arise around it, and their vexedness in particular for the reader of Richardson's day. Each chapter therefore focuses on a particular crux in the text, which in each case is also a crux in both eighteenth-century and modern criticism. The first approaches the conflict between Clarissa and her father from the point of view of technical casuistry, and relates Richardson's intensification of this conflict in the letter-exchanges at Harlowe Place to the central and controversial place held by the father–child topos in eighteenth-century discussions of familial, social and political relations. The second approaches the depiction of Lovelace in the light of Richardson's earlier writings about dramatic representations of criminality and transgression, examining the reader's exposure to Lovelacean ways of seeing in the central volumes and the threat thereby posed to 'moral' interpretation of the novel as a whole. The third discusses Clarissa's death and the protection of her memory in the context of literary, theological and jurisprudential debates about justice, focusing in particular on the implications for reading of the analogies between narrative and forensic practice with which the novel closes. As well as pursuing a close reading of the text, these chapters accordingly devote much space to matters of historical and ideological background, with a view to restoring a sense of the contexts against which the novel was written and originally read.

In both these matters, textual and contextual, I have been lucky in the sources available. Critics concerned to stress the creative or participatory activities of readers are often taken to task for lapsing into stories about a hypostatised or ideal reader, and stories, moreover, in which this reader is in fact manipulated and constrained by the text, forced into a preordained

---

[23] *The Rambler*, ed. W. J. Bate and Albrecht B. Strauss, *The Yale Edition of the Works of Samuel Johnson* (New Haven, 1969), III, 23; III, 22 (No. 4, 31 March 1750).

sequence of responses.[24] Richardson's case, however, provides a rare opportunity to combine theoretical recognition of the text's openness with empirical observation of the diverse responses activated by it at the time of its first appearance. The surviving records of early reception are unusually copious and rich, offering intriguing evidence not only of particular responses arrived at by particular readers but also of the larger terms of reference within which their readings were typically framed. Where appropriate, I draw on these documented responses to illustrate the kinds of activity in which *Clarissa* involves its reader, the kinds of challenge and choice with which the reader is faced, and the variety of ways in which actual historical readers came to terms with the demands of their role as 'Carvers'. In part, the abundance of this evidence arises from the difficulty and contentiousness I describe: it is clear that many readers felt compelled by the vexedness of the text and the urgency of its matter to work out their responses in writing, or to enter into debates with other readers which in some cases were extraordinarily detailed and closely argued. The evidence also arises in part from Richardson's own anxiety to monitor the reception of the text, both before publication when he circulated manuscript copies among a quorum of sample readers, readjusting the text in the light of their responses, and also afterwards, when he carried into his personal correspondence his concern to stimulate and provoke, involving his correspondents in further debates about particular cruxes in the text. Many of his records, including a substantial file of letters on *Clarissa* compiled during and immediately after the year of its publication, survive in the Forster Collection at the Victoria and Albert Museum, which has provided an important source for this study.

In his laborious processes of composition and revision, Richardson often solicited advice, rarely found it worth taking, and shortly before publishing *Clarissa* mournfully wrote: 'I wish I had never consulted any body but Dr. Young, who so kindly vouchsafed me his ear, and sometimes his opinion.'[25] I have been luckier in ears and opinions. Ian Jack supervised the dissertation on which this book is based with generosity and wisdom, and I have also been helped, at various stages and in various ways, by Gillian Beer, Paul-Gabriel Boucé, Roger Bowdler, Edward Copeland, Margaret Anne Doody, Howard Erskine-Hill, Rita Goldberg, Mark Kinkead-Weekes, J. H. Prynne, Angus Ross, Peter Sabor, Barry Windeatt, the readers for Cambridge University Press, and many others. A British Academy Studentship held at Gonville and Caius College, a Research Fellowship at Emmanuel College and a Lectureship at Royal

---

[24] See Jonathan Culler's critique, *On Deconstruction: Theory and Criticism after Structuralism* (1983), pp. 64–83.

[25] 19 November 1747, *The Correspondence of Edward Young*, ed. Henry Pettit (Oxford, 1971), p. 289.

Holloway and Bedford New College enabled me to bring the project to completion, and I am grateful for the encouragement of friends, colleagues and students in all three places. Carol Plazzotta was tireless in her support throughout the most difficult stages of my work, and I cannot thank her enough for all her help. Many thanks also to Virginia Cox and Tim Crane, to Pru Robey, to my parents, and to the dedicatee, who would have been this book's most generous reader.

A note on references and abbreviations

With the publication of Angus Ross's modernised reprint of the first edition (Harmondsworth, 1985) and Florian Stuber's facsimile edition of the third (New York, 1990), critics now have access to good texts of *Clarissa* in its two most important variant states. I have chosen to follow the first edition, published in three instalments in 1747–8 (vols. I and II on 1 December 1747; vols. III and IV on 28 April 1748; vols. V, VI and VII on 6 December 1748). I do so because this edition, by presenting *Clarissa* in three separately published instalments, most clearly shows the three-part structure also observed in the organisation of this study; because it was on this text (or its immediate MS precursors) that many of the early responses cited below were based; and because the first edition, while it omits some valuable material, is unmarred by the sometimes heavy-handed editorial interventions of 1751. Unless otherwise indicated, references are therefore made directly to the first edition, and are supplemented by the corresponding page-number in Ross's text, thus: VI, 322; p. 1169. Occasional references to whole letters are by letter-number, and follow the numbering of Ross's text (see his tables of letters, pp. 1500–12).

Other abbreviations are as follows:

Barbauld	*The Correspondence of Samuel Richardson*, ed. Anna Lætitia Barbauld, 6 vols. (1804)
Carroll	*Selected Letters of Samuel Richardson*, ed. John Carroll (Oxford, 1964)
FM	Victoria and Albert Museum, Forster Collection, 48E5–48E10 (vols. XI–XVI)
Familiar Letters	*Familiar Letters on Important Occasions*, ed. J. Isaacs (1928)
Grandison	*The History of Sir Charles Grandison*, ed. Jocelyn Harris, 3 vols. (1972)
Pamela	*Pamela: or, Virtue Rewarded*, ed. T. C. Duncan Eaves and Ben D. Kimpel (Boston, 1971)
Sentiments	*A Collection of the Moral and Instructive Sentiments, Maxims, Cautions and Reflections, Contained in the Histories of Pamela, Clarissa, and Sir Charles Grandison* (1755)

In citing from Richardson's papers, I have tried to avoid cluttering the text with complete records of his many deletions, alterations and corrections. Unless otherwise indicated, a quotation from a letter or other manuscript source will simply follow whatever appears to be its writer's own final revised version. In dating letters, I observe the suggestions of T. C. Duncan Eaves and Ben D. Kimpel in their checklist of the correspondence: see *Samuel Richardson: A Biography* (Oxford, 1971), pp. 620–704.

1

Reading epistolary fiction

In a Man's Letters you know, Madam, his soul lies naked, his letters are only the mirrour of his breast, whatever passes within him is shown undisguised in its natural process. Nothing is inverted, nothing distorted, you see systems in their elements, you discover actions in their motives.

Johnson to Mrs Thrale, 27 October 1777[1]

Very few can boast of hearts which they dare lay open to themselves, and of which, by whatever accident exposed, they do not shun a distinct and continued view; and certainly what we hide from ourselves we do not shew to our friends. There is, indeed, no transaction which offers stronger temptations to fallacy and sophistication than epistolary intercourse.

Johnson, *Life of Pope*[2]

Familiar letters and the language of the heart

The classic period of the epistolary novel was also, in the writings of Pope, Horace Walpole, Lady Mary Wortley Montagu and others, the heyday of the familiar letter. For Howard Anderson and Irvin Ehrenpreis, the letter is 'the exemplary form of the period', which in its characteristic tones of candour and spontaneity 'reflects the profoundly social quality of the age'.[3] Other critics ground similar claims in the intimacy associated with the form. Keith Stewart has found in eighteenth-century epistolary prose an informality of style and substance which at its best made possible 'the immediate representation of felt experience', 'suffused with the character, the personality, of the writer'.[4] Bruce Redford, most recently, has traced the vigour and interest of what he terms 'a specifically Augustan epistolary mode' to a new sense of vocation on the part of its exponents, 'a feeling

---

[1] *The Letters of Samuel Johnson*, ed. R. W. Chapman, 3 vols. (Oxford, 1952), II, 228.

[2] *Lives of the English Poets*, ed. George Birkbeck Hill, 3 vols. (Oxford, 1905), III, 207.

[3] 'The Familiar Letter in the Eighteenth Century: Some Generalizations', in *The Familiar Letter in the Eighteenth Century*, ed. Howard Anderson, Philip B. Daghlian and Irvin Ehrenpreis (Lawrence, 1966), p. 282.

[4] 'Towards Defining an Aesthetic for the Familiar Letter in Eighteenth-Century England', *Prose Studies*, 5 (1982), 189.

that letter-writing is not merely a stopgap enterprise, but rather a campaign for intimacy with the other'.[5] For all these commentators alike, the familar letter is a form of major literary significance, and one distinguished by an expressive potential all of its own. In the hands of its most celebrated eighteenth-century practitioners, it opened the way to writing of an immediacy, eloquence and frankness unmatched in more established or prestigious literary genres.

Emphases such as these find what is perhaps their classic expression in Thomas Sprat's 'Account of the Life and Writings of Mr. Abraham Cowley' (1668), in which Sprat takes the then unusual step of submitting to critical attention not only the essays, poems and plays of his subject but also his familiar letters. 'In these he always express'd the Native tenderness and Innocent gayety of his Mind', Sprat writes. With this consistent note of intimacy and unreserve, moreover, Cowley had demonstrated to perfection the proper character of familiar letters as a whole. 'They should not consist of fulsom Complements, or tedious Politicks, or elaborate Elegancies, or general Fancies', Sprat goes on: avoiding formality in both their manner and their matter, letters instead 'should have a Native clearness and shortness, a Domestical plaines, and a peculiar kind of Familiarity'.[6]

This, in Sprat's usage, is language of some weight. Only a year earlier, in his *History of the Royal Society*, he had written nostalgically of 'the primitive purity, and shortness, when men deliver'd so many *things*, almost in an equal number of *words*': writers should seek to recover this state, he had urged, by use of 'a close, naked, natural way of speaking; positive expressions; clear senses; a native easiness; bringing all things as near the mathematical plainness, as they can'.[7] The link between these celebrated prescriptions and the 'Life of Cowley' is evident enough; and Sprat's return in the later text to the same key terms makes clear the special value he attaches to familiar letters as a representational mode. In the plainness of their language, and in the candour of expression which is the natural counterpart of that plainness, he suggests, familiar letters bring us uniquely close to their writer's private self. So close, in fact (and here is the paradoxical point of Sprat's discussion), that to expose their contents to public view would be an unthinkably indecorous act. 'In such Letters the Souls of men should appear undress'd', he concludes: 'And in that negligent habit they may be fit to be seen by one or two in a Chamber, but not to go abroad into the Streets.'[8]

[5] *The Converse of the Pen: Acts of Intimacy in the Eighteenth-Century Familiar Letter* (Chicago, 1986), pp. 2, 10.
[6] 'An Account of the Life and Writings of Mr. Abraham Cowley' (1668), in *Critical Essays of the Seventeenth Century*, ed. J. E. Spingarn (Oxford, 1908), II, 137.
[7] *The History of the Royal Society* (1667), ed. Jackson I. Cope and Harold Whitmore Jones (1959), p. 113.
[8] 'Life and Writings of Mr. Abraham Cowley', II, 137.

Needless to say, Sprat's enthusiasm for the peculiar intimacy of the letter form held greater appeal than his accompanying strictures against publication. Cowley's own 'undress'd Soul' did in fact largely escape the public gaze (although an initial group of fourteen letters reached print as early as 1702).[9] But in subsequent decades the immediacy of access to the interior lives of the great cited by Sprat as an argument forbidding publication began to present less fastidious editors with just the reverse idea. The 1690s saw a spate of epistolary miscellanies, each quietly tempting its readership with the illicit pleasures of the peep-hole.[10] The trend gained further ground in the following century, sustained by the familar letter's reputation for offering (as an editor of Rochester's letters put it) 'the Delight that constantly results from looking into human Nature, and examining the Recesses of the Mind'.[11] At the same time, many letter-writers themselves grew increasingly explicit in hailing the form's capacity to make available, above established genres, an authentic discourse of the self. Lady Mary Wortley Montagu's letters to Sir James Steuart showed her 'mind undressed', she wrote, while Thomas Rundle described his correspondence with Bishop Talbot in the following terms: 'When absent, our letters were the pictures of our souls, and every post we conversed.'[12] Sprat's terminology had entered common currency, and could be wittily exaggerated in the words of Samuel Johnson to Mrs Thrale: 'In a Man's Letters you know, Madam, his soul lies naked, his letters are only the mirrour of his breast.'

Here, in sum, is the standard, traditional view of the familiar letter. Addressed as it is to a specific recipient (or group of recipients) with whom the writer is on terms of confidence and ease, the letter encourages a candour of expression unlooked for in other, more formal or more public, literary genres. It attests its frankness, moreover, in its very mode of expression: as a passage cited in Johnson's *Dictionary* prescribes, 'the stile of letters ought to be free, easy, and natural; as near approaching to familiar conversation as possible'.[13] Private in context and colloquial in style, the

---

9 See M. R. Perkin, *Abraham Cowley: A Bibliography* (Folkestone, 1977), pp. 87–90.

10 See James Sutherland, *English Literature in the Late Seventeenth Century* (Oxford, 1969), p. 231. One very successful example of the genre was *Familiar Letters: Written by Right Honourable John Late Earl of Rochester, and Several Other Persons of Honour and Quality* (1697), which in its prefatory matter deals at some length (though evasively) with Sprat's objections. For the relevant passages, see *The Letters of John Wilmot, Earl of Rochester*, ed. Jeremy Treglown (Oxford, 1980), pp. 259–62.

11 Editor's preface, *The Museum; or, The Literary and Historical Register*, 31 (23 May 1747), also reprinted in Treglown, p. 264.

12 Lady Mary Wortley Montagu to Sir James Steuart, 18 October [1758]. *The Complete Letters of Lady Mary Wortley Montagu*, ed. Robert Halsband, 3 vols. (Oxford, 1965–7), III, 182–3; letter from Thomas Rundle in *Epistle Elegant, Familiar, and Instructive* (1791), p. 526; both cited by Stewart, 'The Familiar Letter in Eighteenth-Century England', 186, 180.

13 *A Dictionary of the English Language* (1755), 'Letter'. The passage in question comes from the preface to William Walsh's *Letters and Poems, Amorous and Gallant* (1692), 'pages of inanity' cited

letter is thus uniquely placed to reproduce the intimacy of familiar speech: as in conversation, the analogy suggests, barriers fall away and gaps close, to leave on the page an unusually unguarded view of the writer's mind and of his immediate responses to the world.

But what of the novel in letters? Are we to expect of epistolary fiction too something equivalent to the 'free, easy, and natural' disclosures of the form from which it borrows its basic narrative unit? That, certainly, is an assumption often made in discussions of familiar letter and epistolary novel alike. 'It is this candour, this note of spontaneous veracity – and not merely the advantage of a consistent point of view – that led the epistolary novelist to base his structure on the familiar letter', Anderson and Ehrenpreis suggest.[14] For centuries before them, readers and critics have begun from the same position, expecting fictional epistolary narrative to be marked, above all, by a peculiarly full and intimate exposure of its narrator's inner life. As James Beattie noted in his pioneering taxonomy of narrative types, Richardson's chosen form provided the perfect medium for psychological investigations of this kind, and enabled him to 'delineate ... the operation of the passions' with new profundity and force.

That author has adopted a plan of narrative of a peculiar kind: the persons, who bear a part in the action, are themselves the relaters of it. This is done by means of letters, or epistles; wherein the story is continued from time to time, and the passions freely expressed, as they arise from every change of fortune, and while the persons concerned are supposed to be ignorant of the events that are to follow.[15]

By making his characters their own narrators, Beattie saw, Richardson had eliminated the interferences characteristic of third-person forms, in which an external voice mediates between the world of the novel and the reader he invites to view it. Moreover, Richardson's narrative method was not retrospective (as in the memoir novel of Defoe) but continuous or periodic, bringing the narrator closer to the experience he describes in tense as well as person. In effect, the gap between each novel's underlying facts of character and action and their discursive presentation in narrative had been reduced to the barest minimum, leaving Richardson's characters ideally placed to report their lives, both inner and outer, in uniquely intimate detail. 'And thus', Beattie goes on, 'the several agents are introduced in their turns, speaking, or, which is the same thing in this case, writing, suitably to their respective feelings, and characters.' By these

elsewhere by Johnson to illustrate the banality of contemporary epistolary theory: see *The Rambler*, ed. W. J. Bate and Albrecht B. Strauss, *The Yale Edition of the Works of Samuel Johnson*, III–V (New Haven, 1969), V, 44 (No. 152, 31 August 1751).

[14] 'The Familiar Letter in the Eighteenth Century', p. 282.

[15] 'On Fable and Romance', in *Dissertations Moral and Critical* (1783), p. 567. For a fuller discussion of *Clarissa*, see also Beattie's letter to John Ogilby of 20 August 1759, in Sir William Forbes, *An Account of the Life and Writings of James Beattie*, 2nd edn, 3 vols. (Edinburgh, 1807), I, 46–57.

means, they seemed to place their fictive addressees, and by extension actual readers, in full possession of their own interior lives.

As a model for the analysis of epistolary narrative, this general approach has much to recommend it. The intimate, confessional qualities identified by Beattie as the distinctive province of the novel in letters did indeed make available to Richardson a psychological realism unprecedented in prose fiction, and it is for this achievement above all that his novels have always been known. Early criticism abounds with eulogies on his ability to lay bare the inmost depths of the soul: Johnson's contrast between Fielding's 'characters of manners' and Richardson's 'characters of nature, where a man must dive into the recesses of the human heart', is only the most memorable of many.[16] During the later eclipse of Richardson's reputation, even so hostile an assessment as Coleridge's famous objection to his 'morbid consciousness of every thought and feeling in the whole flux and reflux of the mind'[17] could dwell on similar characteristics. And with the longer view of twentieth-century literary history, these same aspects of Richardson's epistolary form made possible its identification as the pioneering precursor of interior monologue and the stream of consciousness – a precursor too unwieldy to be of lasting usefulness, perhaps, but in its day a brilliantly innovative means of catching in narrative the complexity of the inner life. For novelists and critics of the 1920s, Richardson's affinity was above all with James: Forster links the two, Ford finds Richardson in essence 'a modern novelist', 'an eighteenth-century Henry James', while in his seminal study *The Craft of Fiction* Percy Lubbock suspends his account of *The Ambassadors* to credit *Clarissa* with a like capacity 'to show a mind in action, to give a dramatic display of the commotion within a breast'.[18] In a later survey, Walter Allen names Richardson as the earliest identifiable exponent of the stream of consciousness technique, noting that 'for anything like his direct rendering of the minds of his characters in the very moment of thinking and feeling, we have to wait for more than a century, for the appearance of Henry James ... James Joyce, Dorothy Richardson, and Virginia Woolf'.[19]

Nowhere is this approach to Richardson better expounded, however, than in Ian Watt's *The Rise of the Novel*, a study in which the various strands of argument sketched out above are definitively linked. Drawing first on Johnson's definition of letters as 'the mirrour of [the] breast', Watt begins by identifying the form as 'the most direct material evidence for the

[16] *Boswell's Life of Johnson*, ed. George Birkbeck Hill, rev. L. F. Powell (Oxford, 1934–50), II, 49.

[17] *Biographia Literaria*, ed. James Engell and W. Jackson Bate, *The Collected Works of Samuel Taylor Coleridge*, VII, 2 vols. (Princeton, 1983), II, 211.

[18] E. M. Forster, *Aspects of the Novel* (1927), pp. 26–7; Ford Madox Ford, *The English Novel, from the Earliest Days to the Death of Joseph Conrad* (1930; rpt. Manchester, 1983), p. 75; Percy Lubbock, *The Craft of Fiction* (1921), p. 152.

[19] *The English Novel* (1954), pp. 332, 49.

inner life of their writers that exist[s]' and 'the nearest record of ...
consciousness in ordinary life'. He then goes on to argue (in characteristically circumspect terms) that in fiction too 'the epistolary method impels
the writer towards producing something that may pass for the spontaneous
transcription of the subjective reactions of the protagonists to the events as
they occur'. Related chapters develop these suggestions by close reading of
Pamela and *Clarissa*, and prepare the way for a conclusion in which Watt
looks forward to James, Proust and the Joyce of *Ulysses*'s closing pages as
Richardson's heirs in exploring 'the subjective and psychological direction'. The result is a coherent and persuasive account of Richardson's
significance as a novelist whose epistolary form made possible a newly
exhaustive report of private experience, thereby laying foundations for a
whole tradition of psychological realism in the novel.[20]

Yet, for all its usefulness, this line of argument has one unfortunate
effect. By stressing the immediacy of access to consciousness facilitated by
the epistolary form, it does indeed succeed in linking Richardson's narrative technique with later methods of indicating the flux of the inner life.
But it does so only by neglecting (or excusing as a regrettably clumsy
means to other ends) one significant feature of letter-narrative unshared
by the stream of consciousness – a feature which in fact makes the
epistolary novel much more than simply a primitive precursor form, while
also giving its psychological realism a complexity all of its own. For
although Clarissa Harlowe may indeed prepare the way for Clarissa
Dalloway and the like, she does so only incidentally, and by virtue of an
activity peculiar to the letter form. She *writes* her story; she writes it as it
happens; and she writes it to a particular reader: during the period
documented by the novel, indeed, writing is (with reading) her prime
activity. Critics who see Richardson as primarily concerned with the
minute-by-minute impulses of thought and feeling, rather than with the
business of writing itself, are of course not entirely blind to this obvious
condition. Drawing as they do on prevailing notions of the letter as
spontaneous and transparent, however, they find little significance in it.
Writing 'in this case' is 'the same thing' as speaking, James Beattie
assumes, and shows 'the passions freely expressed'; while for Ian Watt
Richardson's narrative form offers a direct representation of internal
processes, 'a short-cut, as it were, to the heart'.[21] Since the familiar letter is
simply an undesigned (and undesigning) transcription of raw consciousness, what Richardson's narrators turn out at their escritoires has the
status of something *un*written. Their confessions remain uncomplicated,
and uncompromised, by the deliberateness of the literary act.

Yet there remain many reasons for questioning the widespread view

---

[20] *The Rise of the Novel: Studies in Defoe, Richardson and Fielding* (1957), pp. 191, 192, 295.
[21] *Ibid.*, p. 195.

that the epistolary novel is quite so blind as this to its own inherent literariness, or that it uses the familiar letter simply as a conventional means of making legible the inner life. Indeed, whether the familiar letter can even be thought to lend itself to such uncomplicated purposes is questionable enough. For Thomas Sprat's approach to the form is not the only one available, and even within the period itself the reputed transparency of familiar letters came under increasingly sceptical examination. Something of the change can be seen in the uneasy tone of Hugh Blair's *Lectures on Rhetoric and Belles-Lettres* (1783), where, even as the orthodox view is endorsed, significant caveats are added. 'It is childish indeed to expect', Blair warns,

that in Letters we are to find the whole heart of the Author unveiled. Concealment and disguise take place, more or less, in all human intercourse. But still, as Letters from one friend to another make the nearest approach to conversation, we may expect to see more of a character displayed in these than in other productions, which are studied for public view. We please ourselves with beholding the Writer in a situation which allows him to be at his ease, and to give vent occasionally to the overflowings of his heart.[22]

Here Blair's conclusion is to uphold the traditional distinction between the formal, public genres of literature and the intimate, spontaneous disclosures of the familiar letter. Epistolary prose, he suggests, is a peculiarly artless medium: eschewing the sophisticating adornments of poetry or rhetoric, it offers a chance to penetrate the usual veneer of public self-presentation and glimpse the writer's true nature, unhindered by affectation or disguise. Even as he reiterates this view, however, Blair hedges it about with qualifying phrases: letters constitute 'the nearest approach' to conversation, not Beattie's 'same thing'; rather than simply displaying character, they allow us only to '*expect* to see *more* of a character displayed'; rather than beholding the overflowings of the heart, we merely behold the writer 'in a situation which *allows* him ... to give vent *occasionally* to the overflowings of his heart'. One cannot look to the letter for anything like unqualified self-revelation, as Blair's previous sentences more explicitly affirm: the unveiling, at best, will be only a relative matter.

No eighteenth-century writer did more to throw in question the conventional view of epistolary discourse as an artless report of the heart than its most aggressive proponent, Alexander Pope. Pope's correspondence turns frequently on the related themes of spontaneity and sincerity in letters, echoing the terminology of Thomas Sprat with an insistence in which even the limited sense of reserve conveyed by the key term 'undress'[23] eventu-

---

[22] *Lectures on Rhetoric and Belles-Lettres* (1783), II, 298.

[23] Not nudity, of course, but 'a loose or negligent dress', signifying informality (Johnson, *Dictionary*, 'Undress'). The letter cited above, in which Lady Mary Wortley Montagu applies the term to her own writing, makes clear the usual sense. Steuart's criticisms on her letters, she

ally seems to be lost. When Richardson's future friend and literary adviser Aaron Hill was rumoured to have acquired a collection of Czar Peter the Great's epistolary manuscripts, Pope addressed him in just this vein. 'There is a Pleasure in seeing the Nature and Temper of Men in the plainest Undress', he wrote, expecting Peter's letters to show a 'perfect Likeness, without Art, Affectation, or even the Gloss of Colouring, with a noble Neglect of all that Finishing and Smoothing, which any other Hand would have been obliged to bestow on so principal a Figure'. Where Sprat had found artless self-revelations of this kind indecorous, however, Pope drew from the same analysis an opposite conclusion, and expressed to Hill his eagerness 'to see the Great Czar of *Muscovy* . . . drawn by himself, like an antient Master, in rough Strokes, without heightening, or shadowing'. Precisely the qualities which made Sprat recommend the suppression of private letters now argued for their publication. By reducing the biographer's role to one of faithful editorship and allowing Peter to speak in his own authentic voice, Pope suggests, the letters would enable Hill to overcome the usual misrepresentations and interferences of historiography. Not a single phrase should be refined, however, since to do so could only damage a self-portrait all the more genuine for its inattentiveness to formal literary constraints. 'There will be no Danger of your dressing this *Mars* too finely', he predicts (perhaps with a dig at the ornate bombast of Hill's verse encomium to Peter, *The Northern-Star*), 'whose Armour is not Gold, but Adamant, and whose Stile in all Probability is much more strong, than it is polish'd.'[24]

Pope makes many similar claims for his own epistolary self-portraiture. His earliest letters repeatedly invoke the convention of epistolary negligence, as though to convince their recipients that each contains little less than the pure transcription of his own authentic self. Even his lapses in grammar, spelling and handwriting are adduced as emblems of sincerity. 'You see my letters are scribbled with all the carelessness and inattention imaginable', he assures John Caryll in November 1712: 'my style, like my soul, appears in its natural undress before my friend.'[25] Within a month he is marvelling again at the abundance in his letters of 'thoughts just warm from the brain without any polishing or dress, the very *déshabille* of the understanding', and at his tendency to set down 'so fairly and faithfully' in

wrote, were 'worse than surprising a fine lady just sat down to her toilet. I am content to let you see my mind undressed, but I will not have you so curiously remark the defects in it. To carry on the simile, when a Beauty appears with all her graces and airs adorned for a ball, it is lawful to censure whatever you see amiss in her ornaments, but when you are received to a friendly breakfast, 'tis downright cruelty or (something worse) ingratitude to view too nicely all the disorder you may see . . . [N]ever forget that I do not write to you and dear Lady Fanny from my head but from my heart' (Halsband, III, 182–3).

24 To Hill, [September 1726?], *The Correspondence of Alexander Pope*, ed. George Sherburn, 5 vols. (Oxford, 1956), II, 405.
25 To Caryll, 19 November 1712, Sherburn, I, 155.

correspondence 'the true and undisguised state of my mind'.[26] In more whimsical vein he makes similar professions to Lady Mary Wortley Montagu, promising

the most impartial Representations of a free heart, and the truest Copies you ever saw, tho' of a very mean Original. Not a feature will be soften'd, or any advantageous Light employd to make the Ugly thing a little less hideous, but you shall find it in all respects most Horribly Like.[27]

Only much later, when an edition of letters pirated by Edmund Curll in 1735 had begun to expose this 'Thinking aloud ... or Talking upon paper'[28] to an inquisitive world, does Pope alert his readers to a new reticence. He continues to refer to the letters in the same terms, describing them in 1736 as 'the markes of a plain mind, & undesigning heart'.[29] But in the same year he also warned the Earl of Orrery (who 'would draw out one's most naked Sentiments, without any Care about the cloathing them') that his natural candour must henceforth be restrained: 'such an Exposal of my private Thoughts as has befallen me in the publication of my freest Letters', he laments, 'had given me a check that will last for life'.[30] As though in covert enactment of his meaning, Pope combines this revocation of epistolary candour with a passage of obvious dissimulation, in which he denies responsibility for the Curll edition – an edition he had in fact instigated himself, probably to prepare the way for his own authorised *Letters* of 1737.[31] Far from giving a check for life, indeed, publication of the letters had provided him with a perfect opportunity to replace his public reputation for waspish misanthropy with a happier image of benign and generous good nature.[32] To secure the impression, Pope not only revised and rewrote the letters for publication, but also larded the 1737 text with allusions to the convention of epistolary undress, thereby confirming the status of the letters as receptacles of intimate truth. In particular, his preface to this edition presses readers to agree that the contents to follow, as 'every judge of writing will see, were by no means Efforts of the Genius but Emanations of the Heart'. They are 'a proof what were his real Sentiments, as they flow'd warm from the heart, and fresh from the occasion; without the least thought that ever the world should be witness to them'.[33]

[26] To Caryll, 5 December 1712, Sherburn, I, 160; I, 161.
[27] To Lady Mary Wortley Montagu, 18 August [1716], Sherburn, I, 352–3.
[28] Pope to Lady Mary Wortley Montagu, 18 August [1716], Sherburn, I, 353.
[29] To Hugh Bethel, 2 November 1736, Sherburn, IV, 39.
[30] To Orrery, 10 May 1736, Sherburn, IV, 16.
[31] For an account of the elaborate transactions that led to these two publications, see James Anderson Winn, *A Window in the Bosom: The Letters of Alexander Pope* (Hamden, 1977), pp. 29–41 and 203–21.
[32] See Maynard Mack, *Alexander Pope: A Life* (New Haven, 1985), pp. 657–62.
[33] Preface to the quarto edition of Pope's *Letters* (1737), in Sherburn, I, xxxvii; I, xxxviii–ix. It should be added that Pope's notorious tampering with the text of this edition, including the

A reader need not be aware of ulterior motives such as this, however, to see complications in the theory of letter-writing that Pope officially espoused and claimed to have practised himself. His insistent identification of letters as careless 'Emanations of the Heart' is a questionable one, obscuring as it does the element of conscious and wilful self-projection necessarily at work in any autobiographical act. No amount of harping on the themes of negligence and unreserve can quite banish from mind what in *Clarissa* Lovelace calls 'the *premeditation of writing*' (VII, 74; p. 1269) – the inescapable fact that writing is an act of the intelligence. That, nonetheless, is Pope's attempt. On examination, indeed, his insistence on the spontaneity of his letters seems an attempt to prove them not just artless but *author*less – authorless in the sense, at any rate, that he thereby seeks to pre-empt any charge of fraudulent self-projection, endowing the self of the letters instead with the status of objective fact. It is as though (to take at face value the notion of epistolary negligence) the letter-writer falls into a state of suspended consciousness while his unwitting fingers move cardiographically along the page; better still, as though he is temporarily occupied by some impersonal intelligence, who writes with all the advantages of the subject's self-knowledge but with no corresponding temptation to adjust, conceal, or improve. The fragility of the illusion is nowhere more apparent than where Pope himself burlesques it: 'If Momus his project had taken of having Windows in our breasts', he tells Lady Mary, 'I should be for carrying it further and making those windows Casements: that while a Man showd his Heart to all the world, he might do something more for his friends, e'en take it out, and trust it to their handling.'[34]

It would of course be perverse to argue, against Pope, that the letter's inherent literariness makes it simply worthless as evidence of the writer's inner life. In comparison with public literary genres, it can indeed claim to be informal, and thus at least potentially candid. Ungoverned as it is by any very highly developed conventions, nothing need obstruct its expressive function: it need not engage in political controversy, advance a philosophical argument, or even scan. Perhaps more important, the simple fact that letters are written for a limited audience, and that an audience presumably both familiar and friendly, may well make for the greater intimacy so often celebrated in the eighteenth century by correspondents and theorists alike. But these conditions, while they may encourage disclosure, may also encourage less uncomplicated kinds of representation. Many questions are begged by the language of negligence and

reallocation of letters to new recipients, may have involved political expediency as well as personal vanity – a factor at which Pope himself hints in the preface, where he hopes that the letters will give the lie to his reputation as 'a dangerous member of Society, a bigotted Papist, and an enemy to the Establishment' (Sherburn, I, xxxviii).

[34] To Lady Mary Wortley Montagu, 18 August [1716], Sherburn, I, 353.

transparency, and by the assumptions about epistolary self-revelation to which this language gives voice. Can it be assumed that a unitary and describable self is in place prior to its articulation in language, or that the relation between writing and the self is simply descriptive (rather than also constitutive)? Can it be assumed, equally, that the conscious mind is ever in full possession of its own internal processes, or that the individual's response to the evidence of his unconscious will involve no measure of resistance, suppression or displacement? Above all, given the prominence of the *tertium quid* in epistolary discourse, the reader, can it be assumed that the letter is governed solely by the relation between writer and referent (as opposed to that between writer and addressee)? Will not the context of intentions, attitudes and expectations in which the epistolary transaction takes place interfere, at least to an extent, with the letter's fidelity to the real?

There is no need of deconstruction, psychoanalysis or speech-act theory to open up such issues. For Samuel Johnson, the manifest fraudulence of Pope's epistolary self-fashioning compelled a commonsense interrogation of both his confessional stance and the conventions that underwrote it. Not that Johnson had never before thought to question the prevailing view of the letter. In a *Rambler* paper of 1751 he had called not for artlessness but on the contrary for careful deliberation in familiar letters on the grounds that 'words ought surely to be laboured when they are intended to stand for things'.[35] Years later, even as he repeated to Mrs Thrale the usual pieties about the power of letters to show the soul 'undisguised', his sceptical tone is most clearly heard in the irony with which he goes on:

Of this great truth sounded by the knowing to the ignorant, and so echoed by the ignorant to the knowing, what evidence have you now before you. Is not my soul laid open in these veracious pages? do not you see me reduced to my first principles?[36]

Yet it was only when faced by the need, four years later, to consider the reliability of Pope's letters as sources for his 1781 *Life of Pope* that Johnson undertook a more direct examination of the form. 'Of his social qualities', he begins,

if an estimate be made from his Letters, an opinion too favourable cannot easily be formed; they exhibit a perpetual and unclouded effulgence of general benevolence and particular fondness. There is nothing but liberality, gratitude, constancy, and tenderness. It has been so long said as to be commonly believed that the true characters of men may be found in their letters, and that he who writes to his friend lays his heart open before him. But the truth is that such were the simple friendships of the *Golden Age*, and are now the friendships only of children.[37]

[35] *Rambler*, V, 47 (No. 152, 31 August 1751).
[36] To Mrs Thrale, 27 October 1777, Chapman, II, 228.
[37] *Lives of the English Poets*, III, 206–7.

Shifting from particular to general, Johnson develops his critique. Self-analysis is in any case a suspect enterprise, he suggests, but the epistolary form only redoubles the problem: in it, the inevitable deliberateness of writing combines with the constraining presence of the particular reader addressed to rule out the possibility of pure disclosure. The letter, in fact, is a rhetorical act, and one more likely to exaggerate than minimise the deformations inveterate in all autobiographical texts:

Very few can boast of hearts which they dare lay open to themselves, and of which, by whatever accident exposed, they do not shun a distinct and continued view; and certainly what we hide from ourselves we do not shew to our friends. There is, indeed, no transaction which offers stronger temptations to fallacy and sophistication than epistolary intercourse. In the eagerness of conversation the first emotions of the mind often burst out before they are considered; in the tumult of business interest and passion have their genuine effect; but a friendly letter is a calm and deliberate performance in the cool of leisure, in the stillness of solitude, and surely no man sits down to depreciate by design his own character.[38]

Least of all, Johnson adds, to a friend. Indeed, the letter is in this respect still more to be distrusted than public forms, for two particular reasons. It addresses a reader whose predispositions are well enough known to the writer for his letter to play upon them; and at the same time it makes such manipulation likely – 'for by whom can a man so much wish to be thought better than he is as by him whose kindness he desires to gain or keep?'

It would be hard to imagine a more succinct or effective demystification of standard assumptions than this. Johnson's analysis restores to view all that Pope had obscured. Far from being *undressed*, it now seems, the letter is likely in the first place to be *dressed* or adorned in conformity with the writer's chosen image of himself, and moreover to be *addressed* to a reader on whom it will pursue specific designs.[39] The notion of authentic self-portraiture must be discarded: in place of the letter as disclosure Johnson offers a new model, the letter as transaction or performance. Consideration of this rhetorical context alters everything, and throws new light in particular on Pope's tireless reiteration of the letter's capacity to undress the soul. Considered expressively, the 'undress' image simply expounds a theory. Considered rhetorically, it becomes a more cynical device, aimed at persuading the reader to overlook the fundamental conditions of the letter and read it instead as what it could never be – as pure and faithful representation, the flawless image, here, of an unflawed man.

Earlier in the *Life*, Johnson identifies as a prime case of Pope's insincer-

---

[38] *Ibid.*, III, 207.

[39] For an investigation of these distinctions in the French epistolary novel, see Janet Gurkin Altman, 'Addressed and Undressed Language in *Les Liaisons dangereuses*', in *Laclos: Critical Approaches to Les Liaisons dangereuses*, ed. Lloyd R. Free (Madrid, 1978), pp. 223–57.

ity a famous epistolary duel he held over the *Dunciad* with Aaron Hill.[40]
The exchange usefully illustrates the discrepancy between Pope's theory of
epistolary candour and his actual practice, and shows in particular the
coincidence in his letters of professions of truth with occasions of dissimulation. In January 1731 Pope received from Hill a letter complaining at his
depiction in the *Dunciad* of a diving poet identified in the 1728 texts as
'H—' and in 1729 as '* *' (suggesting 'Aaron').[41] His reply is a careful
exercise in equivocation, and unleashes on the aggrieved Hill a torrent of
disclaimers. The 'A. H.' which had offended Hill in another work,[42] he
protests, did not refer to any one individual, these being initials 'set at
Random to occasion what they did occasion, the Suspicion of bad and
jealous Writers, of which Number I could never reckon Mr. *Hill*'. As for
the *Dunciad* itself, the poem meant Hill 'a real Compliment' in the passage
of 'oblique *Panegyric*' to which his complaint referred. In any case, the
notes to the poem (one of which had made clear the application to Hill)
were not even written by Pope; and the particular note in question was not
a piece of ridicule but 'a Commendation', such as he himself would be
proud to have received. Throughout this catalogue of denials, repeated
professions of sincerity keep up a parenthetical covering fire. The first
excuse is made 'in Truth'; the substance of the second 'has been thought by
many'; the third is 'a great Truth'; and Pope has grown so weary of telling
it that he can only bring himself to tell the fourth because he 'love[s] Truth
so well'. 'Therefore, believe me', he sums up, 'I never was other than
friendly to you, in my own Mind.' The remaining paragraphs go on to
offer his own example as an object lesson in the dignified endurance of
detraction ('I do faithfully assure you, I never was angry at any Criticism,
made on my Poetry, by whomsoever'), a proper sense of moral perspective
('I only wish you knew, as well as I do, how much I prefer Qualities of the
Heart to those of the Head'), and the humility appropriate to a mere
versifier ('I vow to God, I never thought any great Matters of my poetical
Capacity'). In conclusion, he makes his usual hint at the artlessness of
what he has written ('This is a silly Letter') and, again as usual, links its
negligence with its authenticity ('but it will shew you my Mind
honestly').[43]

When Hill, unconvinced by these explanations and irritated by the
accompanying rhetoric, replied with ironic allusions to Pope's 'Love of

---

[40] *Lives of the English Poets*, III, 151.

[41] See *The Dunciad*, ed. James Sutherland, *The Twickenham Edition of the Poems of Alexander Pope*, V, 3rd edn (1963), 136–7 (*Dunciad A*, Book II, lines 283–6).

[42] See chapter 6 of *Peri Bathous* (1728), which numbers Hill among the '*Flying Fishes* ... who now and then rise upon their fins, and fly out of the Profund; but their wings are soon dry, and they drop down to the bottom' (*The Prose Works of Alexander Pope, 1725–1744*, ed. Rosemary Cowler (Oxford, 1986), p. 196).

[43] Pope to Hill, 26 January 1730/1, Sherburn, III, 165–6.

Truth' and reminded him that 'To be *Honest* is the Duty of every *plain Man*',[44] Pope was undeterred. Giving an ingenious twist to the negligence theme, he found in the offence taken by Hill only further confirmation of his own epistolary artlessness: a less 'silly', more carefully considered letter might better have served his purpose, which was not to offend his addressee but 'to shew him a better Thing, Sincerity; which I'm sorry should be so ill express'd as to seem Rudeness'.[45] Effective rhetoric, he implies, is beyond his reach: his letters are capable only (though most profoundly) of confession.

Looking back on the letters, Hill found their insistence on their own sincerity and truthfulness not only grossly inaccurate but a positive invitation to read them as the reverse. Over two years (and in a correspondence of which Richardson's side, unfortunately, is incomplete) he repeatedly complained to Richardson of Pope's epistolary dissimulation. His greatest mistake, Hill wrote, was 'that unnecessary noise he used to make in boast of his morality', a point so arrestingly repeated as to subvert its own meaning: 'It seemed to me almost a call upon suspicion, that a man should rate the duties of plain honesty, as if they had been qualities extraordinary!'[46] Clearly recalling his own experience at the wrong end of Pope's pen, Hill also suggested to Richardson a new way of seeing the link between heart and text in the epistolary form. Letters may not actively *un*cover the heart of their writer, he contends – but they can never prevent the *dis*coveries of the perceptive reader:

The heart of man is said to be inscrutable: but this can scarce be truly said of any writing man. The heart of such still shews, and needs must shew itself, beyond all power of concealment; and, without the writer's purpose, or even knowledge, will a thousand times, and in a thousand places, start up in its own true native colour, let the subject it is displayed upon bend never so remotely from the un-intended manifestation.[47]

Paradoxically, Hill suggests, the letter retains its capacity to unveil, but through the vigilance of its reader more than any supposed negligence in its writer. For this reason, Pope's enterprise could only have been self-defeating. In later correspondence with Richardson Hill even suggested that, in the case of his 'Letters ... writt in controversial Clashes between him and me', Pope had acknowledged as much: 'he begg'd me to conceal his Letters: after being stung into Sense of the gross Openings he had left in 'em against Himself.'[48]

[44] Hill to Pope, 28 January 1730/1, Sherburn, III, 167; III, 168.
[45] Pope to Hill, 5 February 1730/1, Sherburn, III, 169–70.
[46] Hill to Richardson, 10 September 1744, Barbauld, I, 106.
[47] Hill to Richardson, 10 September 1744, Barbauld, I, 105.
[48] Hill to Richardson, 10 July 1746, FM XIII, 3, f. 45; 21 July 1746, FM XIII, 3, f.47.
    Reluctantly, Hill did conceal the letters: they were published only after his death, in *A*

Both Hill and Johnson, of course, had axes to grind. More balanced assessment of Pope's letters would place them between the two extremes proposed by Pope himself and by his two antagonists, to recognise within them the interplay of those 'contradictory and powerful impulses toward self-exposure and imaginative disguise' (in a more recent commentator's words)[49] to which they owe their interest and vigour. The controversy in which Hill and Johnson were engaged, however, is significant not only for its bearing on Pope, but also for its more general expansion of the terms in which epistolary writing can be understood. By emphasising the rhetorical situation of the letter-writer, by preferring a self-reliant scepticism to unthinking acquiescence in convention, and by circumventing the twin perversions of 'fallacy and sophistication' with reference to other means of knowing their perpetrator, both Hill and Johnson develop subversive accounts of the letters. In so doing, they suggest the need to read not only Pope's but all epistolary writing critically, keeping perpetually in view the letter's habitual drift away from the spontaneity of talking and the negligence of undress. Hill, in correspondence, was unsystematic; but Johnson's *Life of Pope* articulates a cogent theory of epistolary discourse that is quite opposite to Pope's own. Where Pope stresses representational fidelity, Johnson dismisses the notion of the epistolary window as a prelapsarian dream, and finds in letter-writing instead an inevitable gravitation towards disguise. Taken together, their rival explanations mark the two extremes between which all epistolary discourse may be supposed to lie – on one hand, the pure, *un*dressed, expressive ideal; on the other, its impure, *ad*dressed, manipulative antithesis. Confessional and rhetorical impulses vie within a form which, whatever the extremity of Johnson's position, must at least be credited with very much greater complexity and range than Pope himself makes out.

A short account of God's dealings with Pamela Andrews

For the novel in letters, and in particular for any assumption that the form tends inherently towards narrative reliability and immediacy, the Pope controversy has significant implications. In its light, the familiar letter can be seen to offer the novelist a much greater variety of possibilities than those traditionally attributed to it, opening the way to a kind of fiction which might focus as much on the action of writing itself as on the underlying processes of consciousness and plot.

To approach the epistolary novel with this expectation, however, is to encounter a major difficulty. Familiar letters themselves can be hard

Collection of Letters, Never before Printed: Written by Alexander Pope, Esq; and Other Ingenious Gentlemen, to the Late Aaron Hill, Esq (1751).
[49] Winn, *A Window in the Bosom*, p. 41.

enough to read, a fact vividly illustrated by the conflicting readings of the
Pope correspondence arrived at within Richardson's circle alone. Where
Johnson and Hill claimed to explode the image of 'general benevolence
and particular fondness' constructed in the letters, others proved ready to
accept it: Ralph Allen (a model, aptly enough, for Fielding's credulous
Squire Allworthy)[50] was reportedly moved to contract a friendship with
Pope 'on the sight of his Letters, which gave [him] the highest opinion of
the other's general benevolence and goodness of heart'; Lady Bradshaigh
too found that Pope's letters 'shewed him an excellent good man' (thereby
leaving herself exposed to Richardson's teasing scepticism).[51] Even when
faced with ambiguity as acute as this, however, the doubtful reader can
always turn for confirmation to other sources. As Johnson explains, 'Pope
confesses his early letters to be vitiated with "affection and ambition": to
know whether he disentangled himself from these perverters of epistolary
integrity his book and his life must be set in comparison'.[52] Johnson is then
able to contrast external evidence of Pope's vanity with his epistolary
claims to humility, thereby exposing a basic discrepancy between 'book'
and 'life', and finding in the former, if not outright fraud, then a very clear
case of nature to advantage dressed. 'When Pope murmurs at the world',
Johnson concludes, 'when he professes contempt of fame, when he speaks
of riches and poverty, of success and disappointment, with negligent
indifference, he certainly does not express his habitual and settled sentiments, but either wilfully disguises his own character, or, what is more
likely, invests himself with temporary qualities, and sallies out in the
colours of the present moment.'[53] By comparisons such as this, the self of
the letters can be proved, in effect, a fiction.

'Epistolary integrity', however, is not so easily verifiable in the novel,
where 'book' and 'life' are one and the same, and no ulterior world is
available against which to measure the reliability of narrative. Here
interpretation must depend on the letters alone; and if these letters are of a
kind to throw up only very questionable versions of what in the first place
is only a hypothetical reality, the problem of indeterminacy could hardly
be more acute. As a result, any novelist bold enough to exchange Popean
for Johnsonian theories of the letter risks simply baffling his readers – and
while that risk may happily suit a postmodernist writer like John Barth in
his 'old-time epistolary novel' *Letters* (1979), its appeal to earlier novelists

---

[50] See Martin C. Battestin, *Henry Fielding: A Life* (1989), pp. 453–6.

[51] William Warburton's note (from his 1751 edition of Pope's *Works*), Sherburn, IV, 19n.; Lady
Bradshaigh to Richardson, 25 November 1750, Barbauld, VI, 45. Richardson's response to
Lady Bradshaigh's judgment does not survive, but its tone is evident from her own words: 'I
only said Mr. Pope's Letters shewed him an excellent good man, and so they certainly do. Of
which you are glad, with all your heart. Now I do not think you are glad, for you seem not to
think him so good.'

[52] *Lives of the English Poets*, III, 208.   [53] Ibid., III, 212.

is hardly likely to have been wide. It is no surprise, then, that most eighteenth-century epistolary novels stage a cautious retreat from the potential complexity of their own form, preferring safer theories of epistolary transparency to any more troubling recognition of the letter's capacity to distort, transform or conceal. It is no surprise, equally, that such novels are now unread. One example is the anonymous *Geraldina* (1798), a multiple-correspondent novel which entirely failed to present its letters as anything more than the most straightforward vehicle of story. As the *Monthly Review* complained:

> The reader ... will have to encounter the labour of extracting the plot and incident from the raw material; and he must read the same story related by each person in drama, with the addition of a large portion of sentiment, advice, and opinion, corresponding with the character of those respective personages. This done, he will be rewarded with *three elopements* and a *suicide*.[54]

Here, it would seem, the novel trusted wholly for its interest to the fashionable excesses of its plot: its epistolary manner was no more than a transparent, cumbersome and highly repetitive means of conveying incident and sentiment to the reader.

Yet there remains a demonstrable alternative to redundancy and tedium of this sort. As Janet Altman has shown in her pioneering study *Epistolarity* ('working definition: the use of the letter's formal properties to create meaning'), more enduring contributions to the genre have taken their own narrative method more seriously. Drawing in particular on the French tradition from *Lettres portugaises* (1669) to *Les Liaisons dangereuses* (1782), Altman contests any relegation of the epistolary novel to the category of a primitive precursor form. Instead she describes a narrative genre with distinctive properties of its own, which flourishes in particular 'at those moments when novelists most openly reflect upon the relation between storytelling and intersubjective communication and begin to question the way in which writing reflects, betrays, or constitutes the relations between self, other, and experience'.[55] From this viewpoint, Laclos's *Liaisons dangereuses* represents perhaps the fullest exploitation of the form, and has indeed been widely recognised as a novel in which letters act not only as a record of the action but also as its very substance, as the primary medium in which the plots and sieges with which Laclos is concerned take place.[56]

---

[54] *Monthly Review* (August 1798), 457, partly quoted by Frank Gees Black, *The Epistolary Novel in the Late Eighteenth Century* (Eugene, 1940), p. 51.

[55] *Epistolarity: Approaches to a Form* (Columbus, 1982), p. 4, 212.

[56] Laclos's novel is evidently a major influence on the two earlier attempts to define a poetics of the epistolary novel on which Altman builds, François Jost's 'Le Roman épistolaire et la technique narrative au XVIIIe siècle', *Comparative Literature Studies*, 3 (1966), 397–427, and Jean Rousset's 'Une Forme littéraire: le roman par lettres', in *Forme et signification* (Paris, 1962). See also John Preston, '*Les Liaisons dangereuses*: Epistolary Narrative and Moral Discovery',

While they illuminate Laclos, however, analyses of this kind have
brought little change to the standard view of Richardson's own epistolary
technique as no more than a short cut to dramatic and psychological
immediacy. Indeed, Altman herself finds Richardson's novels paradoxically lacking in epistolarity. In his hands, she suggests, the letter is simply
a means of delivering, in all its fulness, the narrated world, and his novels
show little interest in the more disruptive possibilities of their form. The
Richardsonian letter-writer 'faithfully record[s] both the events and their
psychological effect on him at the time', she writes: 'We rarely question his
reliability as a narrator.'[57] Even critics more alert than this to slippages
between event and report in Richardson's novels prefer to attribute such
interferences more to the intractability of language itself than to any
authorial design. Terry Eagleton describes a Richardson who is unprepared to countenance the opening of even the smallest gap between
experience and expression, and who entrusts his novels instead to 'the
fiction that "experience" can be conveyed in all its living immediacy by
language, the faith that writing and reality may be at one'.[58] Terry Castle
too finds him staunchly resistant to the vagaries of his narrative medium:
her own account of the letter form as obstinately non-representational,
'primarily responsible for the disruption of the mimetic illusion', is one, she
writes, with which 'Richardson ... would not have agreed'.[59] And in an
earlier attempt to draw from Richardson's personal correspondence a
coherent theory of epistolary discourse, Malvin Zirker attributes to him
the usual naive assumption 'that letters are artless, that they reflect the
unpremeditated outpourings of an agitated soul, that they are rich in
sincerity and allow the reader to confront directly his correspondent's
personality'. As Zirker himself notes, Richardson's remarks to this effect
are very infrequent, and also betray signs of ulterior motive: all occur
where he is in effect researching his novels in correspondence with young
women, and arguing that letters are unpremeditated outpourings for the
evident reason that unpremeditated outpourings are what he wants in
reply. The unusual context of these remarks, however, does nothing to
deter Zirker from finding in them a statement not only of Richardson's
theory of the letter, but also of his intention as a writer of epistolary
narrative. Indeed, he even allows his assumed intention to countermand
the evidence of the texts themselves. 'If we are to read Richardson's novels
as he intends us to', Zirker writes, 'we must accept his convention for the

French Studies, 24 (1970), 23–36; Ronald C. Rosbottom, Choderlos de Laclos (Boston, Mass.,
1978); and essays by Rosbottom and Altman in Laclos: Critical Approaches to Les Liaisons
dangereuses, ed. Lloyd R. Free (Madrid, 1978).
[57] Altman, 'Addressed and Undressed Language in Les Liaisons dangereuses', pp. 224, 225.
[58] The Rape of Clarissa: Writing, Sexuality and Class Struggle in Samuel Richardson (Oxford, 1982),
p. 40.
[59] Clarissa's Ciphers: Meaning and Disruption in Richardson's Clarissa (Ithaca, 1982), p. 152.

letter; if we insist on retaining our real-life expectations for letters, we inevitably find that even Richardson's good characters are calculators.' We should do the former, he concludes, and 'grant Richardson his unrealistic theory about letters for the purposes of his novelistic art' – an art that now seems gloriously blind, for thousands of pages, to the fundamentals of its own form.[60]

Much in Richardson's first novel, it must be said, would seem to bear out such views. Where the preliminary matter to *Les Liaisons dangereuses* warns that the disclosures of its letter-writers are often 'feints ou dissimulés',[61] the puffs used by Richardson to introduce *Pamela* direct the reader to find only the confessional within. Analogies with Pope's preface of 1737 are striking. The first commendation, by the Grub Street translator Jean Baptiste de Freval, describes Pamela's letters as 'written under the immediate Impression of every Circumstance which occasioned them, and that to those who had a Right to know the fair Writer's most secret Thoughts'. As a result, 'the several Passions of the Mind must ... be more affectingly described, and Nature may be traced in her undisguised Inclinations with much more Propriety and Exactness, than can possibly be found in a Detail of Actions long past'.[62] The second puff, by William Webster (perhaps best known, like Aaron Hill, for his undistinguished role in the *Dunciad*),[63] urges Richardson to 'let us have *Pamela* as *Pamela* wrote it; in her own Words, without Amputation, or Addition'. Pamela's letters, he writes, are 'Soliloquies', in which 'She pours out all her Soul ... without Disguise; so that one may judge of, nay, almost see, the inmost Recesses of her Mind. A pure clear Fountain of Truth and Innocence, a Magazine of Virtue and unblemish'd Thoughts!' (p. 7). With such images, both accounts lay heavy emphasis on the transparency of the letter form, and work in combination to foreclose the possibility that Pamela, in her conduct or in her writing, is anything other than artless.

Within the text that follows, Pamela draws on similar assumptions herself. Her letters propose an utterly uncomplicated view of the relation between self and text, and ask to be read as little less than her own interior life displayed in conveniently legible form. Rebuked by Mr B. for her hostile representations of him, she repeatedly defends herself with reference to standard explanations of the letter as a form of spontaneous overflow. In her letters to her parents, she simply 'broke my Mind freely to them ... and poured forth my Griefs' (p. 41); of her journal, she has 'no Reason to be afraid of being found insincere, or having, in any respect,

[60] 'Richardson's Correspondence', in *The Familiar Letter in the Eighteenth Century*, ed. Howard Anderson, Philip B. Daghlian, and Irvin Ehrenpreis (Lawrence, 1966), pp. 77, 78–9, 79.

[61] 'Préface du rédacteur', in Laclos, *Œuvres complètes*, ed. Laurent Versini (Paris, 1979), p. 7.

[62] *Pamela*, p. 4. Further references are given in brackets in the text.

[63] With the Methodist George Whitefield (q.v.), Webster is a champion brayer: see *The Dunciad*, V, 308 (*Dunciad B*, Book II, line 258).

told you a Falsehood; because, tho' I don't remember all I wrote, I know I wrote my Heart; and that is not deceitful' (p. 200). Unpremeditated, honest, and above all intensely felt, her writings constitute a faithful reproduction of reality: as she tells her parents, 'I have only writ Truth' (p. 206). The point is conceded in the end even by Mr B., who comes to value the letters precisely for their confessional quality, and for what seems an innocence of rhetorical intent – 'because they are your true Sentiments at *the Time*', he tells her, 'and because they were *not* written for my Perusal' (p. 237).

It is undoubtedly the case that *Pamela* draws much of its power from this confessional strain, and must have done so all the more strikingly for readers unaccustomed to the methods of psychological exposure developed in novels of later date. Whether the heroine's mind and heart are to be read simply at the most manifest or superficial level of her letters, however, is another matter. One might argue, on the contrary, that *Pamela* is most fully known not to the reader who uncritically accepts the image of uncomplicated purity, innocence and piety with which she presents her parents, but rather to one who approaches her letters as acts of writing which may work instead to modify or even perhaps screen out important aspects of the experience they seem to disclose. To some extent, readers have always done just this, finding in Pamela unconscious motivations for which her own official image of herself is unable to find room; and such scepticism is clearly solicited at those critical points where the undeceitful heart she claims to transcribe so faithfully seems to stray beyond her control. If Pamela's 'inmost Recesses' are to be known, on such occasions, they can be known only by a reader alert to possible discrepancies between actual inclination and discursive explanation. As Mark Kinkead-Weekes notes, Richardson's is 'an art that encourages reading between the lines. One is constantly discovering things about his characters that they do not know themselves.'[64] What one discovers about Pamela, when she delays observing her parents' advice to 'flee this evil Great House and Man' with the bathetic explanation that she must first finish flowering his waistcoat (pp. 38, 51), or when she muses 'To be sure, he is a handsome fine Gentleman! – What pity his Heart is not as good as his Appearance!' (p. 171), is an attitude towards Mr B. that is considerably more ambivalent than she thinks.

To read between the lines in this way, nonetheless, is to remain within the conventional view of the epistolary novel as a form of interior monologue – as the artless transcription of a heart that may at times be opaque and recalcitrant, but remains essentially undisguised. In this view, Pamela deceives her readers only to the extent that she deceives herself. There are

---

[64] *Samuel Richardson: Dramatic Novelist* (1973), p. 484.

times, however, when even this more limited faith in her letters is hard to sustain, and when the doubtful reliability of the portrait they paint seems more than simply unconscious. If her oddly insistent harping on the sincerity of her letters does not itself sound warning bells, her later meditations on the difficulty of casting her experience in acceptable narrative form make the problem inescapable. 'Now, my dear Father and Mother, what shall we say of this truly diabolical Master!', she writes, finally acknowledging a complication that her writing can no longer hold at bay. 'O how shall I find Words to paint my Griefs, and his Deceit! I have as good as confessed I love him; but indeed it was on supposing him good' (p. 196). What to say, how to find words simply for her own condition, become increasingly hard as Pamela strives in her letters to fortify an image of perfect rectitude against the awareness of illicit impulse. Her confessional manner, at such points, comes to seem at once more troubled and more selective than first appeared. When she turns from her own 'Griefs' to 'his Deceit', moreover, the illusion of pure and artless representation becomes virtually unsustainable. Far from being a neutral and unquestionable account of events, it becomes clear, her narrative carries with it the most insistent of moral glosses, and is shaped at every point by a simple, polarised model of struggle between black and white. Here, in fact, Pamela has precious little difficulty in finding words: in the extravagant language of her letters, Mr B. is rarely less then 'the worst Heart in the World' (p. 65), a 'black, perfidious Creature', 'an Implement ... in the Hands of *Lucifer*, to ruin the innocent Heart' (p. 86), 'a wicked Violator of all the Laws of God and Man' (p. 94). The only question is whether these words are the right ones. Since Pamela's viewpoint presides, the novel can only hint at reasons for dissent by offering fragmentary alternatives, such as her own initial view of Mr B. as 'the best of Gentlemen' (p. 26: a view, of course, to which she returns), or Mrs Jervis's subtler view of a man caught between passion and convention, who 'has try'd to overcome [his love], because he knows you are so much his Inferior; and ... finds he can't' (p. 49). Whatever one chooses to make of Pamela's master, however, little room is left to doubt the reductiveness with which she herself defines him.

As the narrative progresses the problem of Pamela's tendentiousness only grows, the conflict between Mr B.'s evil and her own good taking on ever more religious overtones to the point where the desire to construct a tale of providential care seems to supersede all other concerns. 'I will continue my Writing still', she tells her parents, even as she prepares to rejoin them, 'because, may-be, I shall like to read it, when I am with you, to see what Dangers God has enabled me to escape; and tho' I bring it in my Pocket' (p. 85). No longer is her narrative motivated by any mere need to convey news. Instead it becomes an interpretative tool, a means by which Pamela, in recording her experience, can suffuse its every aspect with the gratifying clarity of a familiar Puritan myth – a myth in which she herself is cast as the righteous sufferer guided by God's hand. Her appropriation and revision of Psalm 137 mark a stage at which she retains some inhibitions about such daring gestures: 'I remembering the 137th Psalm to be a little touching, turn'd to it, and took the Liberty to alter it to my Case more; I hope I did not sin in it', she writes (p. 127). But in later pages she makes her claims with growing conviction, so that as events draw towards their happy close she is able to find within her letters a luminous and coherent account of her own divinely managed protection and reward. They prove 'the Goodness of that Providence, which has, thro' so many intricate Mazes, made me tread the Paths of Innocence, and so amply rewarded me' (p. 232); incidentally, they demonstrate the fallacy of any irreligious belief 'that we are absolutely to direct for ourselves' (p. 261).

For all their professions of spontaneous veracity, then, Pamela's letters also betray at least the symptoms of rhetorical design: as well as simply reporting events, they also interpret and persuade. What remains uncertain is whether the great extent to which these supposedly unconsidered scribblings turn out to serve Pamela's cause should be seen as a matter of chance alone, or whether the letters should be seen instead as false in their confessional pose, and carefully contrived to acquit her of the particular charges to which she has become so very vulnerable. One effect of Richardson's method of writing 'to the Moment' is to eliminate the question of retrospective organisation: unlike the memoir novel, letter-narrative precludes any speculation that events have been realigned and reinterpreted to fit a thesis determined after the fact. One can see, all the same, that the structure of explanation imposed by Pamela on her own life is at the very least highly schematic, and that her narrative, with its repeated invocations of Providence and its associated oppositions between her own pure innocence and the absolute evil of her adversary, turns out to do her nothing but good. For if Providence itself does not win Pamela a rich husband and rapid social acceptance, then its literary invocation clearly does. When Mr B. reads her narrative, the impression it gives him plays a significant part in his resolution to marry its pious writer: as she exults, 'the Contents of my Papers, have, as I hope, satisfy'd all his Scruples, and been a Means to promote my Happiness' (p. 261). Even the recalcitrant Lady Davers is won over by letters which Pamela prudently asks her to consider 'as the naked Sentiments of my Heart ... deliver'd to those, whose Indulgence I was sure of; and for whose Sight, only, they were written' (p. 375). Almost immediately, she prepares to endorse her brother's socially transgressive marriage, and joins a swelling chorus in praise of Pamela's artlessness of deed and pen:

There is such a noble Simplicity in thy Story, such an honest Artlesness in thy Mind, and such a sweet Humility in thy Deportment, notwithstanding thy present Station, that I believe I shall be forced to love thee, whether I will or not: And the Sight of your Papers, I dare say, will crown the Work, will disarm my Pride, banish my Resentment ... and justify my Brother's Conduct; and, at the same time, redound to your own everlasting Honour.   (p. 375)

Yet this extraordinary power in Pamela's papers, their power to 'disarm', 'banish', and 'force' a reader to relinquish all suspicions about her conduct, is not the product of artlessness alone. The letters have an explanatory force of which their writer is fully aware, and can replace Lady Davers's cynical assumptions about the marriage with the most winning of interpretations. As Pamela predicts, 'when she sees them all, she will be quite reconcil'd; for she will see it is all God Almighty's Doings; and that a Gentleman of his Parts and Knowledge was not to be drawn in by such a poor young Body as me' (p. 388). That, precisely, is what her narrative argues from start to finish. By casting Pamela herself as insignificant and incompetent, incapable of mercenary design, it can dismiss from view some very awkward facts. It will put right any reader inclined to suspect that the chambermaid, and not the squire, was the real predator, and with an explanation that defies reply. 'It is all God Almighty's Doings.'

Subsequent readers have been less ready than Lady Davers to take Pamela's letters at face value. At publication the world was divided, reports one contemporary, between 'two different parties, *Pamelists* and *Antipamelists*'. The first were loyal readers, happy to accept Pamela's word, but the second gleefully subverted the surface explanations of her narrative to discover instead just what she hopes to preclude – 'the Behaviour of an hypocritical, crafty Girl, in her Courtship; who understands the Art of bringing a man to her Lure'.[65] The Antipamelists were a vocal group. In parody after parody (and according to a note of Richardson's the novel 'gave Birth to no less than 16 Pieces, as Remarks, Imitations, Retailings of the Story, Pyracies, &c.'),[66] Pamela became a 'Fair Impostor' and a 'young Politician', her story one of 'Feign'd Innocence' and 'Mock-Modesty', her narrative the deceitful literary counterpart of her triumphantly deceitful behaviour. Though it appears (in a phrase from one Antipamelist verse) 'innocently told',[67] it is, the Antipamelists allege,

---

[65] [Peter Shaw], *The Reflector* (1750), p. 14. The passage plagiarises Ludwig Holberg's *Moral Thoughts* (1744): see A. D. McKillop, *Samuel Richardson: Printer and Novelist* (Chapel Hill, 1936), pp. 101–2.

[66] FM XVI, 1, f. 56.

[67] 'Remarks on *Pamela*. By a *Prude*', *London Magazine*, 10 (May 1741), 250. The preceding phrases are taken from the title pages of J— W—, *Pamela; or, The Fair Impostor* (1744), [Fielding], *Shamela* (1741), and the title- and half-title-pages of [Eliza Haywood], *Anti-Pamela; or, Feign'd Innocence Detected* (1741).

the very reverse, a sustained act of dissimulation in which Pamela beguiles her unsuspecting readers, lures them to repeat the basic interpretative error of her booby husband. What the Pamelists had praised in their heroine was merely a clever mask: in the words of perhaps her dourest critic, 'She may be compar'd to one of the fair Apples of *Sodom*, beautiful for the Eye to behold, but Stains and Rottenness within.'[68]

It would of course be futile to follow the Antipamelists too far into the question of what Pamela is 'really' like. But it is important to note the relation between their position and a narrative technique which makes it, on the basis of the text alone, quite as tenable as that text's explicit thesis. Because epistolary narrative can be read as a wholly candid undressing of the soul, a wholly designing address to its reader, or anything between these two extremes along a scale of conscious and inadvertent misrepresentation, the novel can plausibly be explained in the most subversive of ways. For the Pamelist Webster, who explicitly draws the familiar parallel between negligent dress and negligent discourse, Pamela's letters could be compared to the homespun clothes with which she signifies her pious rejection of Mr B.'s evil great house. Urging the case for the first-person *Pamela*, he asks Richardson: 'Produce her to us in her neat Country Apparel, such as she appear'd in, on her intended Departure to her Parents; for such best becomes her Innocence and beautiful Simplicity' (*Pamela*, pp. 7–8). But an appearance of simplicity, the Antipamelists reply, can just as well be the product of art. Citing Pamela's own strangely incautious words on the subject ('I trick'd myself up as well as I could in my new Garb ... To say Truth, I never lik'd myself so well in my Life': p. 60), the author of *Pamela Censured* protests that these homespun clothes are very far from signifying her innocent rejection of the evil great house, and represent instead her most ingenious gambit at winning it. She 'dresses herself in the most alluring Habit that her Circumstances will afford', parading herself before Mr B. as 'a beautiful young Rustic, each latent Grace, and every blooming Charm ... called forth to wound, not in affected Finery, but in an artful Simplicity'. Now the affectation of negligence appears the subtlest ruse of all – the ruse of one who 'instead of being artless and innocent sets out at first with as much Knowledge of the Arts of the Town, as if she had been born and bred in *Covent* Garden, all her Life Time'.[69]

Unlike Webster's puff, *Pamela Censured* fails to pursue its interpretation of Pamela's dress as far as the analogy with her letters. Only the first and most damaging of the Antipamelist critiques, in fact, moves successfully beyond this kind of assault on Pamela's morals and motives to deal in

---

[68] Charles Povey, *The Virgin in Eden*, 2nd edn (1741), p. 70.

[69] *Pamela Censured* (1741), ed. Charles Batten, Jr, Augustan Reprint Society No. 175 (Los Angeles, 1976), pp. 35, 36, 21–2.

detail with the status of her narrative. Fielding's satire, however, more than makes up for the limitations of its successors. For *Shamela* is not merely (if at all) the patrician attack on the implicit social radicalism of Richardson's plot that it is sometimes alleged to be. Fielding may indeed have shared the anxieties that inform his cousin Lady Mary's distaste for the novel ('the Joy of the Chambermaids of all Nations', she loftily calls it, and later scoffs at a levelling marriage she hears of in Italy as 'exactly ressembling and, I beleive, copy'd from Pamela').[70] It is worth recalling, however, that Fielding was later happy to commit Mr B.'s solecism himself and marry (in Smollett's words) 'his own cook-wench'[71] – a foray into the carnivalesque that sets evident limits to his much derided social bigotry. If *Shamela* has a political motive at all, indeed, it can far more credibly be seen not as a reactionary attack on plebeian adventurism but as a further satire, continuous with his later plays and *Jonathan Wild*, on the dubious ethos of Walpole's enterprise culture: Shamela is presented as the very type of the corrupt and pharisaical entrepreneur, and Fielding explictly links her manoeuvres with Wildian '*Pollitricks*' and the worldly success fraudulently achieved 'by Men, who are notorious for Luxury, Pride, Cruelty, Treachery, and the most abandoned Prostitution; Wretches who are ready to invent and maintain Schemes repugnant to the Interest, the Liberty, and the Happiness of Mankind, not to supply their Necessities ... but to pamper their Avarice and Ambition'.[72]

What animates *Shamela* in particular, though, is a desire not simply to excoriate the avaricious and ambitious but also to undermine the grounds of their success – the methods, above all rhetorical, which enable them to screen their motives behind a mask of public spirit, virtuous indifference or simple piety. Fieldings' subject, in short, is what he elsewhere calls 'that detestable Fiend, Hypocrisy'[73] – and hypocrisy, beyond this, in its specifically literary incarnation. Here the vulnerability of Pamela's letters gave a perfect opportunity to satirise such impostures as practised in the culture at large. Accordingly, Fielding first links his primary target with other unlikely panegyrics of recent date – Colley Cibber's *Apology*, Conyers Middleton's *Life of Cicero*, and the life of '*his Honour* himself' (i.e. Walpole) which 'John Puff' envisages in one of *Shamela*'s preliminary letters.[74] Having indicated this more general scope, Fielding then concentrates his

[70] Lady Mary Wortley Montagu to Lady Bute, 25 October 1750, Halsband, II, 470; to Lady Bute, 8 December 1754, Halsband, III, 70.

[71] See Battestin, *Henry Fielding: A Life* (1989), p. 423.

[72] *Joseph Andrews and Shamela*, ed. Douglas Brooks (Oxford, 1970), pp. 353, 323. For a stimulating (though sometimes questionable) account of the politics of *Shamela*, see Hugh Amory, '*Shamela* as Aesopic Satire', *ELH*, 38 (1971), 239–53.

[73] 'An Essay on the Knowledge of the Characters of Men', in *Miscellanies, Volume One*, ed. Henry Knight Miller (Oxford, 1972), p. 156.

[74] *Joseph Andrews and Shamela*, pp. 315–18, 319.

fire directly on *Pamela*, treating its text as an exemplary case of discursive speciousness and masking. *Shamela* thus combines a general attack on dissembling rhetoric with a more detailed attempt to lay bare all that is most questionable in Pamela's narrative in particular, and in the conventions and strategies on which it rests. The result, in this more immediate matter at least, was instant and ruinous. As a verse in the *London Magazine* reports, *Shamela* disabused an audience previously beguiled by Pamela's fair words:

> Admir'd *Pamela*, till *Shamela* shown,
> Appear'd in ev'ry colour – but her own:
> Uncensur'd she remain'd in borrow'd light,
> No nun more chaste, few angels shone so bright.
> But now, the idol we no more adore.[75]

For these first readers at least, Fielding's *travesty* of Pamela's letters (the term means, initially, a new-dressing) was Pamela's undoing. By inviting them to resist what now seemed mere illusion, it created the conditions and defined the terms in which the ensuing controversy could flourish. It showed (as the verse continues) 'our chaste nymph a w—'.

Beyond the various allusions of *Shamela*'s preliminary matter, Fielding's concern with the rhetorical masking of avarice and ambition can be seen in the care he takes to specify Shamela's reading. In Letter 5 Shamela's mother expresses pleasure that she is reading 'good Books', and encloses two more – 'one of Mr. *Whitefield*'s Sermons, and also the Dealings with him'. No further mention is made of the sermon, but the next letter finds Shamela reading 'that charming Book about the Dealings' – a charming book her master then mistakes for '*Rochester*'s Poems', the very byword in the period for corrupting literature. The same confusion of categories returns in Letter 12's inventory of Shamela's library, an incongruous mix of the devotional and the pornographic in which '*Venus in the Cloyster: Or, the Nun in her Smock*' rubs shoulders with, again, '*God's Dealings with Mr. Whitefield*'.[76]

The book thus highlighted, *A Short Account of God's Dealings with the Reverend Mr. George Whitefield*, is the spiritual autobiography of a leading early Methodist, published, like *Pamela*, in 1740. An improving enough text, one might assume, perhaps flaunted by Shamela to advertise her piety or to conceal her interest in erotica. Yet Fielding means much more than this by citing *God's Dealings*, as he does by having Shamela note at the same point that her copy of the ubiquitous conduct manual *The Whole Duty of Man* has 'the Duty to one's Neighbour, torn out'. Charity, or duty to one's neighbour, is for later Fielding heroes like Parson Adams or Tom

[75] 'To the Author of *Shamela*', *London Magazine*, 10 (June 1741), 304.
[76] *Joseph Andrews and Shamela*, pp. 328, 344.

Jones the supreme virtue. For more enthusiastic Christians, however, it could seem of only marginal importance. This, at any rate, is the charge repeatedly levelled in Fielding's journals and novels against Whitefield and his followers, whose emphasis on justification by faith alone offered instead (as Martin Battestin writes) 'a comfortable and licentious doctrine, a convenient rationale for hypocrisy ... making salvation a matter of credulity and confidence rather than the practical exercise of virtue and charity'.[77] This is also the charge levelled by *Shamela* against *Pamela*, first in an ironic preliminary description of the novel as one in which 'the useful and truly religious Doctrine of *Grace* is every where inculcated', and later in wry allusions to the doctrine's convenience to Shamela: the 'good Books' she reads will somehow sanction her conduct or 'make amends', she tells her mother, and later she reminds herself, arrestingly, that 'doing good to one another ... is one of the greatest Sins we can commit', while ''tis not what we do, but what we believe, that must save us'.[78] Fielding had clearly detected in Pamela's spiritual self-absorption and in her readiness to explain her own successes as marks of divine favour the same refusal to take full responsibility for one's conduct and the same convenient relegation of practical virtue that characterise Whitefield's doctrine (and make it, the hint is, the appropriate theology of the age). The self-serving 'Vartue' which in *Shamela* replaces practical virtue is at one, Fielding suggests, with what in a later allusion to Whitefield he calls 'the pernicious principles of Methodism'.[79] (He was not the only reader to see a link: in a letter of 1741 Richardson complains that many had found him, on *Pamela*'s evidence, 'too much of a Methodist'.[80])

Shamela's emphasis on Whitefield's autobiography rather than on his sermons (as in *Joseph Andrews* and the *Champion*), however, shows the extent to which Fielding's concern here is as much narratological as theological, though still concerned with accountability for one's own behaviour. For in *God's Dealings* the rationale for hypocrisy to be found in Whitefield's theology is embodied in narrative form. In its very title the book attributes the course of its subject's life more to divine superintendence than to any human agency, while the rigid determinism of the text itself ostentatiously minimises his role in contriving the events he records. *God's Dealings*, in fact, is that seeming contradiction, an autobiography in which the autobiographer himself is more often object than subject, and little more than the witness to another's deeds. By the simple device of making Whitefield the mere puppet of a divinely arranged plot, it acquits him of any suspicions that might arise from his own worldly success.

---

[77] Martin C. Battestin, *The Moral Basis of Fielding's Art: A Study of Joseph Andrews* (Middletown, Conn., 1959), p. 97; see also pp. 81–4.

[78] *Joseph Andrews and Shamela*, pp. 321, 327, 336.   [79] *Tom Jones*, I, 430.

[80] Richardson to Cheyne, 31 August 1741, Carroll, p. 47.

Indeed, it adduces his success instead as evidence of special election. And since God has guided not only the life but the writing of it too (Whitefield even cites 'the Assistance I have had from the Holy Spirit, in bringing many Things to my Remembrance, which otherwise I would have forgotten'), he is acquitted as well of responsibility for the claims of his own text. Should any subversive reader allege the convenience of his explanatory scheme, he has his answer ready: 'Although the following Account of what God has done for my Soul, will undoubtedly be differently judged of by different People; yet, since I believe a single Eye to God's Glory moves me to write, and I find myself much pressed in Spirit to publish it at this Time, I am not in the least sollicitous about the Reception it will meet with in the World.' Later (and perhaps with more solicitude) he derides those who 'thro' Ignorance, Prejudice, and Unbelief, when they read this, will contradict and blaspheme'.[81]

In the body of the narrative itself, blanket use of the divine third person casts Whitefield as almost entirely passive, and attributes his every achievement not simply to the purest of motives but to an apparent *absence* of motives. At first, to be sure, he is capable of self-criticism. His purpose, he says, is to tell 'what I was by Nature, as well as what I am by Grace', and in the opening account of his unregenerate youth confession and extenuation are engagingly interwoven: 'Part of the Money I used to steal from my Parents I gave to the Poor, and some Books I privately took from others, (for which I have since restored four-fold) I remember were Books of Devotion.' Once Grace has been extended to this notably Defoean free-trader, however, the tendency of money (along with livings and other honours) to stick to Whitefield's fingers comes to demand more careful explanation. One particular crux comes where he wins the distinction (at an unprecedentedly young age) of election to the clergy, despite his own pious refusal to push himself forward. 'I still continued instant in Prayer against going into Holy Orders', he writes, 'and was not thoroughly convinced it was the divine Will, till God, by his Providence, brought me acquainted with the present Bishop of *Gloucester*.' Neither ambition, avarice nor even accident can be allowed as factors in bringing about the interview that follows, which has a single luminous meaning – that Whitefield has been called by God. As always, he simply bows to the inevitable, which here involves not only speedy ordination but also (as he cannot resist recalling) a tidy sum to boot: 'Thus God dealt with my Soul. – At the same Time, by his gracious Providence, he supplied me with all Things needful for my Body also. – For he inclined the Bishop's Heart to give me five Guineas more, and, by this Time, a Quarter's Allowance was due to me from Sir *John Phillips*.'[82]

[81] *A Short Account of God's Dealings with the Reverend Mr. George Whitefield* (1740), pp. 6, 5, 72.
[82] *Ibid.*, pp. 7, 11, 62, 70.

One sees, at such points, why Fielding has Shamela refer to the book as simply 'the Dealings'. One sees, as well, the scope it provides for reflections on *Pamela* itself – for here too virtue is handsomely rewarded, and by no apparent intention or effort of the narrator's own. As Whitefield concludes, 'thus did GOD, by a Variety of unforeseen Acts of Providence and Grace, train me up for, and at length introduce me into the Service of his Church.'[83] With these insistent invocations of the divine will, and the disclaimers about his own will implied by them, the similarity with Pamela's method becomes clear. Like hers, Whitefield's relation of events is in no way pure or neutral, but instead works to pre-empt the suspicions to which his actions are most likely to expose him. What links the two writers, Fielding hints, is not simply the wealth or status mysteriously achieved by both, but also the rhetorical prowess with which they explain it away. Like Pamela, Whitefield scores great worldly success; and like Pamela he uses the motif of providential direction to deny his own pursuit of it.

Fielding's allusion to *God's Dealings* is just one of many details that make clear the intense literariness of his critique, the strength of his concern with discursive as well as more straightforwardly practical hypocrisy. Indeed, there is a sense in which *Shamela*'s most damaging charge is not against Pamela's claim that Mr B. 'was not to be drawn in by such a poor young Body as me' so much as against *Pamela*'s prefatory account of itself as a novel in which 'She pours out all her Soul ... without Disguise.' The true ridiculous, Fielding writes in the preface to *Joseph Andrews*, is 'to discover any one to be the exact Reverse of what he affects';[84] and *Shamela* does just this to Pamela in her capacity, above all, as a narrator. Her letters, the title-page alleges, are a medium of 'notorious FALSHOODS and MISREP-RESENTATIONS', which the parody to follow will leave 'exposed and refuted'.[85] The whole letter-collection, in fact, is an imposition on the reader, in which Pamela/Shamela's clever design on Mr B. is translated, with redoubled fraudulence, into a celebration of virtue's reward: *Shamela* will reverse the process, so that 'this little Jade may not impose on the World, as she hath on her Master'.[86] To secure this goal Fielding makes little change to the novel's surface action, which (as Bernard Kreissman notes in his account of the *Pamela* controversy) 'is so closely duplicated that were only the action dramatized, an onlooker would believe he was viewing identical stories – one in a condensed version'.[87] Instead, he retains *Pamela*'s primary events but reverses their narrative interpretation, positing the rediscovery of the original (and, it would seem, truly candid)

---

[83] *Ibid.*, p. 71.   [84] *Joseph Andrews and Shamela*, p. 7.   [85] *Ibid.*, p. 313.

[86] *Ibid.*, p. 325.

[87] Bernard Kreissman, *Pamela-Shamela: A Study of the Criticisms, Burlesques, Parodies and Adaptations of Richardson's Pamela* (Lincoln, Nebr., 1960), p. 11.

letters as they stood before their revision into *Pamela* by an editor who '*can make black white, it seems*'.[88] As published, the suggestion is, Pamela's letters were simply lies – albeit lies adroitly enough contrived to fool all but the wariest reader.

This final matter – the matter of *Pamela*'s reception – is most directly addressed in the epistolary frame-tale that surrounds Fielding's re-reading of the novel. For at its beginning and end *Shamela*'s most immediate concern is neither with Mr B.'s persecution of Pamela nor with its shadowy antithesis, Pamela's drawing-in of Mr B.: instead the focus is on the interpretative activities of two fictive readers, Parson Tickletext and Parson Oliver, whose prefatory letters expound opposing readings of the text. The tale as a whole records the education in scepticism of Tickletext, the more gullible of the two, who had at first been drawn in by Pamela's explanations to repeat the usual Pamelist platitudes. He is disabused at last by Oliver's demonstration that these explanations are in fact wholly specious: Pamela, he finally learns, has 'endeavoured by perverting and misrepresenting Facts to be thought to deserve what she now enjoys', while her published narrative displays at every point such an 'excellent Knack of making every Character amiable' as to constitute a wholesale 'Perversion of Truth'. With this explicit attention to the perils of the unwary reader, *Shamela* completes its claim to have become 'an Antidote to this Poison', curing Tickletext's (and, Oliver hopes, the public's) susceptibility to fraudulent rhetoric of the kind on which *Pamela* depends.[89]

It would be foolish to conclude by adjudicating between *Pamela* and *Shamela*. Fielding's demonstration is not that there is a real story whitewashed in *Pamela*, simply that its narrative cannot escape challenge, and remains open to a reading quite opposite to the one it explicitly invites. Pamela as 'w[hore]', his parody suggests, is as valid a reading of the original text as Pamela as 'chaste nymph'. In this sense, *Shamela* is not a satire on mercenary servant girls but a satire on writing, and it should not send us back to *Pamela* with hopes of discovering its heroine's 'true' character or with the intention of asking (as Kreissman asks) 'But are they really so different?'[90] Instead *Shamela* reminds us, disconcertingly, that Pamela exists nowhere but in her own words – words which work hard, but eventually fail, to confirm their writer's proposals about herself. Pamela the angel and Shamela the jade could hardly be *more* different; but both are equally possible.

It is tempting to argue that Fielding's deconstruction of Pamela's letters alerted Richardson to complications of which he was initially unaware, and thus prepared the way for the more self-conscious and sophisticated

---

[88] *Joseph Andrews and Shamela*, p. 354.   [89] *Ibid.*, pp. 324, 325, 356.
[90] Kreissman, *Pamela–Shamela*, p. 15.

narrative patterns of his later novels. Certainly, Fielding would appear to have wrecked the foundations of Richardson's writing very much as Johnson was to damage Pope's, challenging and subverting the basic assumptions about 'epistolary integrity' on which his fiction was based. Yet to return from *Shamela* to *Pamela* is to see that Fielding's satire merely makes plain an ambivalence that had preoccupied Richardson all along. Not only is the action of *Shamela* the same as *Pamela*'s; its allegations are the same. *Pamela*, in fact, anticipates its own parody at every point. It is not simply that Richardson has his heroine give such obvious hostages to fortune as her gleeful report that Mr Longman the steward 'wish'd he was a young Man for my sake, I should be his Wife, and he would settle all he had upon me on Marriage; and you must know, he is reckon'd worth a Power of Money' (p. 51). More significant still is Richardson's explicit inclusion within Pamela's narrative of something like its Antipamelist antithesis. *Shamela*'s 'new' plot (of Pamela's mercenary ambitions, of faints that are feints, of her affair with Parson Williams) is in fact entirely derived from the accusations of Mr B., who complains at 'her Intrigue with the young Clergyman' (p. 90) and her 'lucky Knack at falling into fits, when she pleases' (p. 68). He also protests, in a passage of obvious relevance to her remarks on Mr Longman's 'Power of Money': 'she is an artful young Baggage; and had I a young handsome Butler or Steward, she'd soon make her Market of one of them, if she thought it worth while to snap at him for a Husband' (p. 39). Most damaging of all, however, is the presence within the novel of a sustained critique of its narrator's rhetorical skill. Mr B. continually complains that Pamela is 'a mighty Letter-writer', able in her writing to transform the complex events and motives of experience into an unfairly polarised manifesto, 'in which she makes herself an Angel of Light, and me, her kind Master and Benefactor, a Devil Incarnate!' (p. 45). His accusations are quite specific, and lead him to consider the smallest details of Pamela's writing and speech. When she uses the phrase 'good Mr. *Longman*', for example, he protests that 'All your confederates are good, every one of them: But such of my Servants as have done their Duty, and obey'd my Orders, are painted out, by you, as black as Devils' (p. 202). With colouring of this kind, he alleges, Pamela's narrative deforms experience almost beyond recognition: as he warns her parents, 'Something, possibly, there might be in what she has wrote from time to time; but, believe me, with all her pretended Simplicity and Innocence, I never knew so much romantick Invention as she is Mistress of' (p. 90).

Richardson's intention, very probably, was to raise the problem of Pamela's reliability in order to make way for its dramatic resolution, which comes when Mr B. at last retracts his complaints and, with his confession that 'your white Angel got the better of my black one' (p. 231), even converts to Pamela's interpretative scheme. Richardson, after all, was a Pamelist himself. But *Pamela* is by no means the untroubled tract it at first appears to be: clearly enough, the Antipamelists could tell its author nothing new about the ambivalence of his heroine's text.

Richardson's correspondence with Eusebius Silvester, 1754–1759; or, How to do things with letters

If anything, *Pamela*'s guarded invocations of the theory of epistolary transparency marked a new departure for Richardson. In his earliest writings the letter is more often rhetorical than simply expressive, a tool with which to influence or persuade. His first works of epistolary fiction were written when, in boyhood, he ghosted love-letters on behalf of three local women. Faithful representation was only a low priority and, as he later told his Dutch translator Johannes Stinstra, the letters in question were far more complex than simple transcriptions of the heart. 'I have been directed to chide, and even repulse', he writes, '... at the very time that the Heart of the Chider or Repulser was open before me, overflowing with Esteem and Affection; and the fair Repulser dreading to be taken at her Word, directing *this* Word, or *that* Expression, to be softened or changed.'[91] Stinstra's response was to point the link between these letters and those of Richardson's heroines. Richardson's early experience as 'Secretary in Love-matters' must have let him 'come to the full knowledge of the woman's heart, and his deepest recesses' (*sic*), preparing him 'to paint with lively colours the most internal thoughts, deliberations, and affections of a Clarissa, an Anna Howe, a Miss Biron'.[92]

More often cited as the precursor of the novels is the model letter-writer *Letters Written to and for Particular Friends, On the Most Important Occasions* (usually known as *Familiar Letters*) on which Richardson was at work when the idea of *Pamela* took root.[93] The work consists of short, fictionalised cases of conscience, and in this context again the letter is presented not as a spontaneous transcription of the heart but rather as a tool, an instrument put carefully to work by each fictive correspondent to advance an analysis or urge a course of action. Little attempt is made at purely expressive writing; instead what one writer aptly calls 'the force of a *letter*'[94] is turned always to particular rhetorical ends, each correspondent's purpose being above all to influence the judgment or conduct of his addressee. In Richardson's eyes, such carefully weighted letters might serve as models

---

[91] 2 June 1753, *The Richardson–Stinstra Correspondence and Stinstra's Prefaces to Clarissa*, ed. W. C. Slattery (Carbondale, 1969), p. 27.

[92] Stinstra to Richardson, 24 December 1753, Slattery, p. 61.

[93] See Richardson's letter to Aaron Hill on the genesis of *Pamela*, c.1 February 1741, Carroll, pp. 40–1.

[94] *Familiar Letters*, p. 64.

for readers to adapt in cases of similar need in their own personal lives: in one instance, intended effects are so finely calculated that Richardson offers six different replies to a clandestine address, varying in subtle ways according to the response desired.[95]

Richardson's personal correspondence too shows a continuing interest in epistolary rhetoric and suasion, which here comes to seem less benign in its effects. A good example comes in two letters written to Sarah Wescomb during the period of *Clarissa*'s composition and early revision, in which he expresses a troubled awareness of the potential duplicity of the form. The passages in question are sometimes cited to demonstrate Richardson's naive idealisation of letters, and at first sight they do indeed look like simple effusions on the usual themes of conversation and negligence. 'What charming advantages, what high delights … flow from the familiar correspondences of friendly and undesigning hearts!', one letter begins, going on to detail the ways in which 'the converse of the pen' embodies the subtlest impulses of the heart, unlocks the bosom, 'makes distance, presence', and seals the ties of friendship. A letter's style, Richardson suggests, is 'indicative, generally beyond the power of disguise, of the mind of the writer' – and nowhere more so than in the letter to which he now replies, 'every line of it flowing with that artless freedom, that noble consciousness of honourable meaning, which shine in every feature, in every sentiment, in every expression of the fair writer!'[96]

Even as he voices these very familiar views, however, Richardson shows considerable uneasiness with them. The letter, he adds, can attain this privileged status not because of its innate spontaneity but on the contrary 'because of the deliberation it allows, from the very preparation to, and action of, writing'. And as his talk of '*un*designing hearts' and 'the power of disguise' already begins to imply, there are always more sinister purposes to which 'deliberation' can be put. Elsewhere he becomes more explicit about one such extreme alternative – for the letter, he warns, may also be a medium of deception, seduction and peril. 'If of our Sex an artful, a designing … Heart endeavour to obtrude itself upon Hearts so diffident, so modest, so worthy', he writes, '… Then let him be treated with Contempt and shunned and avoided.' Men, in fact, should be more or less ruled out as correspondents (with the exception, of course, of the undersigned 'undesigning scribbler'): 'Writing to your own sex I would principally recommend; since ours is hardly ever void of design, and makes a correspondence dangerous.'[97] Here he elaborates no further; but Anna

---

[95] *Ibid.*, pp. 129–32.
[96] [Late September 1746?], Carroll, pp. 64–5. 'Artless freedom' in fact puts it mildly. Many of the young women with whom Richardson corresponded were accomplished writers – but not Sarah Wescomb.
[97] 15 September 1746, Carroll, pp. 68–9; [late September 1746?], Carroll, p. 66.

Howe has relevant points to make about such dangerous liaisons when in *Clarissa* she detects an unequal struggle between exponents of the two epistolary types, confession and manipulation. 'I knew it to be a dangerous thing', she tells Clarissa, 'for two single persons of different sexes, to enter into familiarity and correspondence with each other; since, as to the latter, must not a person be capable of premeditated art, who can sit down and write, and not write from the heart? – And a woman to write her heart to a man practised in deceit ... what advantage does it give him over her?' (IV, 337; p. 748).

This very ambivalent view of the letter as a form that lends itself equally to candid expression and insincere design is nowhere more evident than in Richardson's last writings, and in one text explicitly concerned with the difficulties of interpretation posed by epistolary writing. At the end of his life he envisaged, and went some way towards executing, a fifth epistolary history to add to the two *Pamela* novels, *Clarissa*, and *Sir Charles Grandison*. The result survives in the Forster Collection at the Victoria and Albert Museum as a sequence of forty-five letters intended, according to Richardson's draft of the last, as 'a Warning Piece to Posterity';[98] and though never published the text bears much evidence of preparation for a wider readership. Richardson has arranged the letters in chronological order, indicated italics (with his usual freedom) by underlining in lighter ink, made minor alterations for the sake of style and clarity, added explanatory notes, and inserted short narrative accounts of meetings between the two correspondents. Thus the text has been to a great extent made ready for a larger public, and has some claims to be considered as Richardson's last significant literary work.

Of course, Richardson gave up novel-writing after *Grandison*, gloomily announcing that he would write no more until his existing novels were 'generally understood'.[99] The 'Warning Piece', however, was not exactly a novel. The letters it contains were real, recording a correspondence conducted in the later 1750s between Richardson himself and an attorney of Warwick named Eusebius Silvester.[100] Yet the manuscript cannot for

---

[98] FM XV, 1, f.57.   [99] To Susanna Highmore, 31 January 1754, Carroll, p. 275.

[100] Euseby, son of Nicholas and Susanna (née Dormer) Sylvester, was baptised in Tamworth, Staffs., on 19 January 1714 (*International Genealogical Index*, 1988). In the early 1730s he became an articled clerk to his uncle Thomas Harris, a solicitor of Dorking, with whom he remained for two and a half years before joining George Garnett of Tooks Court, Holborn, in the same capacity and for a similar period. He was then able, at Serjeants Inn on 11 May 1738, to swear an affidavit designed to secure his recognition as a qualified attorney, in which he describes himself as 'Euseby Silvester of Tooks Court, London, Gentleman' (Public Record Office, CP 5/5 [3]). He duly appears in the Rolls of the Common Bench Attorneys, which give his place of residence as Middlesex, but in the Roll for Michaelmas 1745 the addition 'now Warwick' appears against his name (PRO, CP 11/12). In a Memorial to the Lords Commissioners of the Treasury dated 27 November 1758 (a document in which he 'most Humbly hopes, he shall meet with Your Lordships ffavour and Encouragement' for drawing to their attention frauds and evasions of duty allegedly practised by tanners and curriers) he is still

this reason simply be dismissed to the secondary category of 'correspondence', divorced from Richardson's more properly 'imaginative' works.
Indeed, there is a sense in which, by improvising an epistolary history from
genuine materials, it carries to a logical culmination the project of a writer
who had always obscured the fictionality of his novels, preferring to
present them instead as authentic collections of letters. It brings to a
logical culmination, as well, the intense self-consciousness about the processes of writing and reading with which all the novels are imbued. For
writing and reading, specifically the writing and reading of letters, are
what its warning is all about. The work questions, in unusually direct
manner, the special claims to authenticity of expression and representation conventionally made for the epistolary form, and it slowly but
surely subverts the complacent assumption that to read a letter is to
converse with the sender's soul. Like *Les Liaisons dangereuses*, it tells a
cautionary tale of manipulative writers and manipulated readers; and like
Les Liaisons dangereuses it does so in letters which not only report the action
but also embody and advance it. Its story, moreover, can be understood
only by a reader prepared to see the letter not as a transparent unbosoming of the soul's recesses, but as a rhetorical act in which the writer in fact
obscures the heart he pretends to disclose. Or so Richardson, outraged at
the fraud apparently practised on him by his silver-tongued correspondent, eventually came to assume.

The correspondence opens with an unsolicited letter, in which Silvester
introduces himself to Richardson by praising the recently published
Grandison. He had found in its pages a sublime expression of what, coincidentally, were his own moral convictions: the novel had 'not only Proved
too in the most evident, but illustrated in the most engaging man[ner]
what I have long been contending for, That if Mankind would take but
half [the] trouble to correct & improve their Minds on Natural and
Rational Principles, as [they] do to viciate & debase them, by unnatural &
irrational ones, deceit, fraud & rap[ine] in their various & direful shapes
& all their baleful consequences, wou'd immediately vanish; and Sincerity, Peace, Harmony, & Universal-Benevolence & all their Happy consequences, succeed!' Silvester continues in the same vein at length, but
even so finds opportunity to introduce what would become a recurrent
and central theme: his ineffective command of language, and in particular
his pen's inability to do justice to the fulness of his heart. Praise of *Grandison*
'is not in the Power of any Pen directed by the most able Head, therefore
highly absurd in me who have no abilitys that way to attempt it', he
confesses; 'but however defective or incapable my Head may be, my Heart
wou'd not let me rest, 'till it had vented some honest tho' homely

---

'Eusebius Silvester of the Borough of Warwick in the County of Warwick Gentleman' (British
Library, Add. MS 32886, f.92). His date of death remains untraced.

Encomiums & Thanks to You for the exquisite Pleasure both, particularly
the latter, has received from the perusal of Your Works: which certainly
contain the most perfect, beautiful & amiable Portraits of the Humane
Mind that was ever yet drawn, or even conceived by any Mortal Being'.[101]

Whether honest or not, the praise is certainly far from plain (though
perhaps unexceptional by the unctuous standards of the day). Richardson
may have had doubts, and made private enquiries about Silvester;[102] but
when reassured that his correspondent was indeed both genuine and of
'a Good Caracter & ... very Sober'[103] he accepted its sincerity, and wrote
back to suggest a continued correspondence. Silvester obliged with 'a
short history of my situation', a sorry tale of honesty beleaguered in a
world conducive only to ruthless ambition (and 'short' by no standard but
that of *Grandison* itself). His life, he wrote, had been 'a confused Scene of
Advers Perplexitys almost from my Cradle'. His patrimony had been lost
through the worldly failure of a father 'defeated by those very Qualitys
which ought rather to have merited success; an open frankness and
generosity of Heart, which led him, to place too much Confidence in those,
who by an abuse of it, were the occasion of a series of Misfortunes which at
length ... weighed him down & deprived him of his life!'[104] His own
career, begun under such difficult conditions, inevitably continued the
pattern: for the same reason of personal integrity, which made the profession of attorney almost impossible to pursue, he was perpetually beset
by financial troubles. In a passage perhaps aimed at Richardson's own
well-known distrust of the legal professions[105] he explains his difficulty:

I have no great reason to believe, that I have or ever shall attain to any great
Eminence in my Profession; because, I cannot think it my Duty to prosecute my
Clients Affairs with so much Rigour as to Ruin & drive to the last Extremitys,
Unfortunate & Distressed ffamilys, when by more moderate measures my client
might apparently Recover his whole Demand & Charges, instead of a part or
perhaps none at all; the Ruin of such unhappy ffamilys prevented & an oppor-

---

[101] Silvester to Richardson, 22 August 1754, FM XIV, 4, f.1.
[102] Richardson's note, FM XIV, 4, f.2. His uncertainty was also heightened by his correspondent's name, which he at first suspected to be a pseudonym designed to associate Silvester
with a minor worthy in *Grandison*, 'honest Mr. Sylvester, the attorney' (*Grandison*, II, 667).
[103] Thomas Wilmot to Richardson, 22 September 1754, FM XIV, 4, f.2.
[104] Silvester to Richardson, recd 12 October 1754, FM XIV, 4, f.4. Whatever his qualities of
heart or causes of death (his burial on 9 September 1745 is recorded in the Parish Register of
Hints, Staffs.), Silvester's father Nicholas does indeed seem to have been chronically indebted,
as well as (in his own eyes at least) ill-used. He was also incurably litigious. Between 1724 and
1744 his name appears frequently in the records of the Court of Chancery, and when not
fending off suits for the recovery of debt he seems to have had a particular fondness for
contesting wills. As to the real cause of his financial troubles, it may be worth considering the
implications of his father-in-law Euseby Dormer's will of 1728: in leaving his daughter £140,
Dormer pointedly and (in light of events) very prudently stipulates that 'no part may be at the
disposal or control of Nicholas Silvester her husband' (PRO, Prob. 11/632/245).
[105] See, for example, *Sentiments*, pp. 147–8, 305.

tunity given them to retrieve their Circumstances; nor can I think it my Duty to
tamper with or corrupt Evidence to declare more or less than the Truth, in order
to carry a point for my Client against Law, Justice or Equity; by which a Man
obtains the good Opinion of all Wealthy Suitors & his very Name strikes Terror in
the minds of all the needy, distressed, & unfortunate; which are the primary
fundamentals on which modern Eminency is founded: besides, the Old-Style-
notions abovementioned, have taught me to be so squeamishly sc[r]upulous, as to
think it a fault to undertake any Suit for my Client 'till all prudent & reasonable
means have been used to settle the Affair in an Amicable way, especially where the
Defend:' is in needy Circumstances; by which I not only foolishly give up my own
Profits & the Reputation of being concerned in a larger share of Business, but also
the like Advantages that wou'd otherwise accrue to some Worthy Brother, who
wou'd of necessity have been employed on the other side, whereby I not only
incurr his displeasure, but the Censure of the whole ffraternity, as a Dastardly
Unnatural Brother, & perhaps looked upon as a sheepish, stupid & indolent
ffellow by my Client; nor can I multiply or protract Suits for the benefit of Self &
Brotherhood.[106]

And so he goes on, for half as many lines again before the next full-stop.
Here perhaps is writing from the heart at last, a garrulous and tangled
outpour as near to Molly Bloom as to the elegantly crafted prose of
Alexander Pope. Yet for all this breathlessness, the disorderly surface of
Silvester's style belies a very deliberate pattern of emphasis. With its
accumulated protestations, the letter strains to keep perpetually before its
reader three salient and closely related points. Silvester, it insists, is an
honest man; Silvester's profession rewards only the dishonest; Silvester is
not the wealthy man he deserves to be – themes that would return.

There follows a break of slightly over a year in the sequence, during
which time the correspondents met twice, once in London and once at
Parson's Green. Silvester then allowed the correspondence to lapse, but
abruptly reopened it six months after the second visit in a letter of thanks
to Richardson for a copy of *Pamela* presented to him on that occasion.
Most of the letter is given over to encomium, focused in particular on
Pamela's theories of education, but the praise is now less obviously
unmotivated. His real purpose in writing (as he defensively puts it, in
'neglect[ing] to return Thanks for one ffavour 'till one has occasion to
solicit another') is to request Richardson to print a manuscript of his
'containing some Observations on Agriculture', which he has been urged
by 'Persons of considerable abilitys' to publish – 'in justice to the Publick',
he hastens to add, 'as well as myself'.[107] A month later he writes again,

---

[106] Silvester to Richardson, recd 12 October 1754, FM XIV, 4, f.5.
[107] Silvester to Richardson, 12 November 1755, FM XIV, 4, f.7. Richardson seems to have
complied (Richardson to Silvester, 24 November, f.8; Silvester to Richardson, 15 December,
f.9), but I have been unable to trace the work. Later letters make clear that it outlined a
scheme for reclaiming or improving 'excellent Lands, now lying waste and uncultivated'

introducing an unsolicited statement of his financial predicament by
lamenting, at some length, his inability to 'do something more than
profess' his admiration for Richardson: 'And This, notwithstanding the
difficultys I have hitherto labour'd under in life, I do not quite despair
of doing.' Despite his crippling honesty he retains 'a tolerable prospect'
in his profession, as well as 'many considerable Reversionary Expectancys
from numbers of Wealthy Kindred'. Better still, he dreams of one day
securing 'an acquisition of ffortune, that wou'd appear too romantick to
mention' from the land-reclamation scheme outlined in his agricultural
work: this would enable him to found a sentimental community living
'in mutual and Virtuous Harmony' after the example of Grandison Hall
– 'A Knott of Worthys, with The Real Sr Cha:^{s} Grandison at their
Head'.[108]

From this point on, the letters are almost exclusively concerned with the
parlous state of Silvester's finances, which early in 1756 approach the first
of many critical points. The next letter, in February, returns to the theme
of corrupt lawyers and the penury that accompanies Silvester's high-
minded refusal to join their ranks. The impasse can be evaded by the
land-reclamation project which, if he can hold out long enough to secure
its adoption by the Ministry, promises unimaginable (and honest) returns.
But that 'if' is a big one, for Silvester bears 'a load that might have wrent
the Heart or turn'd the Head of any Mortal Being but me, long e're this',
and now even he is weakening – 'for I begin to find Twenty Years almost
ffriendless opposition to the most adverse ffortune, Too much for me!'
Without some assistance, certainly, he will fail – and then how unjust it
would be 'if, just in the very Crisis & turn of my ffortune, I sho'd, after so
many Years Painful Struggles, be dashed down & sunk again to the
Extremitys I have been, thro' my ffathers Misfortunes, & I must fall a
sacrifice to adversity & unhappy times, for want of that small Assistance,

(Richardson to Silvester, 22 February 1756, f.13). Bearing in mind this subject, as well as
Silvester's talent for hyperbole, a likely candidate is the anonymous *A New System of Agri-
culture: or, A Plain, Easy and Demonstrative Method of Speedily Growing Rich: Proving, by Undeniable
Arguments, That Every Land-Owner, in England, May Advance His Estate to a Double Value, in the
Space of One Year's Time ... By a Country Gentleman ... Printed for A. Millar, in the Strand* (1755).
But this work has no printer's ornaments to identify it and seems to bear the wrong date, given
Richardson's usual practice of attaching the following year's date to books printed in
November or December. It is also much terser in style and more learned in reference than
either Silvester's letters or the later work to which (in the dedication) he puts his name, *The
Causes of the Present High Price of Corn and Grain, and A State of the Abuses and Impositions Practised
upon the Publick in General, and the Poor in Particular, by the Millers or Meal-men* (1757). This is
certainly the work which Silvester asked Richardson to print in a letter of 27 December 1756
(FM XV, 1, f.38); Richardson, by now guarded, replied by proxy 'that it does not suit him to
print or to be concerned with the little Piece about Corn' (William Richardson to Silvester, 31
December 1756, FM XV, 1, f.38).
[108] Silvester to Richardson, 15 December 1755, FM XIV, 4, ff.9, 10.

which might perhaps be given to me, not only with safety to a ffriend but with advantage too'.[109]

The rest of the story should by now be becoming clear. What is surprising is that Richardson himself failed to foresee it. He wrote back a week later to ask the extent of the wanted 'small Assistance'; Silvester, in a reply heavily larded with professions of his integrity and complaints at his affliction, named his price, going on to add the helpful suggestion that Richardson might choose to raise a subscription among his wealthier friends. Unfortunately, he has 'no Security to offer but that of personal, and that depending on a continuance of my life & my success in it; the first from an happiness of constitution seems not unlikely to be long, & the latter, I think, I cou'd not miss of, if I had 100l. to pay off some demands that now press hard upon me'. But long life, otherwise, cannot be guaranteed – 'ffor if I cannot raise a Friend to assist me with a [sum] to enable me to keep up my Credit here, all my future Views in life will soon, in all humane probability, be for ever blasted! ffor I have had so fatal an instance in an unfortunate ffather, of what treatment a reduced man must expect to meet with from the World, that after such a disaster, I cou'd never raise my hopes any more!'[110]

Richardson replied sympathetically (though with no particular haste). He had tried to raise a subscription on Silvester's behalf, and although unsuccessful in this and unable to meet such a large demand himself he was ready to offer a loan of £25. Moreover, Richardson seems at this point to have been quite without suspicion: he fails, at any rate, to recognise even the possibility that Silvester's seemingly undesigning exposure of his heart's (and his pocket's) inmost recesses had all along been calculated to draw from him precisely the response he now delivered. Instead he read Silvester's letters in just the way that Silvester invited him to read them: he took them, explicitly, for transcripts of the heart, ungoverned by any design more complex than one of candid self-expression and communication. The original letter on *Grandison*, he wrote, was 'an Approbation so warm, that it does as much Honour to the Heart that gives it, as to the Work'. 'You must have an excellent Heart', he repeats later in the same letter, and having received Silvester's remarks on *Pamela* a year later he adds: 'I love you for that good Heart which so visibly dictates to y^r Pen.'[111] Even where he alludes most directly to the performative powers of letters which had moved him, after all, to the tune of £25, he fails to draw what later was to seem the only possible conclusion. If there is a hint of guardedness in his confession that he is 'very much affected, my dear Mr

[109] Silvester to Richardson, 15 February 1756, FM XIV, 4, f.11.
[110] Silvester to Richardson, 28 February 1756, FM XIV, 4, f.15.
[111] Richardson to Silvester, 24 September 1754, FM XIV, 4, f.3; 24 November 1755, FM XIV, 4, f.8.

Silvester, w[th]: y[e] Contents of yr last now before me', and with 'y[e] Despond-
ency y[t] seems to sadden every too well painted Line', it is not yet more
than a hint. He remains confident enough, instead, to credit his afflicted
correspondent with 'Comforts in your own Breast which Millions cannot
purchase'.[112]

Like the letters of Pope and Pamela, however, Silvester's letters are
open to subversive interpretation, and even at this stage the 'Warning
Piece' makes strong hints to that effect. It is able to do so by virtue of the
double role that Richardson allows himself within it, not only as protagonist but also as editor. Initially, his role is that of the naive addressee who
reads each letter at face value, thereby allowing himself to be manipulated
by a writer for whom letters are a means of influencing opinion and thus,
by extension, action. He suspects nothing, even when alerted to the
possibility of fraud by 'a wealthy and benevolent Man' to whom, armed
with Silvester's letter of 28 February 1756, he had appealed on Silvester's
behalf: 'He attributed to me an Easiness & Credulity', Richardson rue-
fully reports, 'on reading to him y:[t] Part of yr letter w:[ch] mentions yr
Inability to give any better Security than you own you can give; & yr
Confession of yr suffering Health, &c—.'[113] Elsewhere, however, Richardson is far less credulous than this. Not only the reader *within* the text,
gulled by Silvester's continuing tale of woe, he also takes on the more
knowing role of reader (and editor) of the text as a whole, who has read
(and lived) to its end. In this capacity he reaches a new and much more
hostile interpretation of Silvester's letters, a fact made apparent in his
underlining of their most extravagant phrases, his marginal comments,
and in particular his connecting notes. By a particularly effusive passage
in the February letter, where Silvester laments that 'tho' my Immortal
part my Mind, may stand this severe Test! ... the Mortal or Perishable
part the Body, may languish even to Death', the elderly Richardson's
unsteady hand notes: 'What flightly, contradictory Nonsense!'[114] With
still more striking contrast, he adds the following note between Silvester's
first two letters (and between his own original replies in praise of
Silvester's heart):

May, 1755. He came to Town again. Visited me; May 4. at Parson's Green. His
seeming Modesty, good Behaviour, and specious Address, confirmed in me the
high Opinion which his Letters and Professions gave me of his Integrity and
Worthiness of Heart.[115]

---

[112] Richardson to Silvester, 22 February 1756, FM XIV, 4, f.13.
[113] Richardson to Silvester, 16 March 1756, FM XIV, 4, f.16.
[114] Silvester to Richardson, 28 February 1756, FM XIV, 4, f.14.
[115] Richardson's note, FM XIV, 4, f.6. Before 'high Opinion' Richardson appears to have
deleted the word 'imprudent'.

With hindsight, Silvester's letters could come to seem more suspect than at first appeared. It is clear enough, all the same, that even after the first loan they could still move Richardson to set aside whatever misgivings he had by then begun to feel. Just when his tolerance and trust seemed near their end, Silvester was able to quell his suspicions by citing the loss of 'that good Opinion I flatter'd myself I had been so happy to have obtained with You' as 'the greatest Calamity, deep as my Distresses are, that cou'd possibly befal me'.[116] Richardson wrote back immediately, quoting the emotive phrase: '"Deep as your Distresses ARE!" Dear Sir, what Words are these! They afflict me. Not the shadow of a Distress should my worthy Mr. Silvester have, if I could remove it, with any tolerable Convenience to myself.'[117] A new tone of reserve, bordering on reproach, has entered Richardson's writing; but he is still far from the scepticism which later made him, as editor, simply underline in Silvester's letter the same offending phrase.

Silvester's luck, however, was now beginning to run out, and as the correspondence continues his ever more intense rhetoric of suffering innocence fights a losing battle with the hard evidence of events. In August 1756 he successfully extracted another £25 from a reluctant Richardson (who this time insisted on security and the repayment of both loans within a year). But his renewed suggestions for a subscription 'among the most benevolent and wealthy of your Acquaintance' got the shortest shrift. 'I am truly amazed!', Richardson replied: 'Give me leave to say, that in this Instance, I have some Doubts of your Head – Of your Heart I can have none.'[118] Perhaps realising that just such doubts might now soon arrive, Silvester then allowed the correspondence to lapse again, breaking silence only to offer Richardson the opportunity to 'contribute to the Publick Utility' by printing his latest piece, 'on a Popular Subject now under the Consideration of our Legislators'.[119] This time Richardson curtly declines, and after waiting for the year to elapse he was forced to complain, in his tersest letter to date: 'I know not how to account for your Silence, Sir, consistently with the Professions made to / Your Friend & Servant / S. R.'[120] From then on, he accounted for the inconsistency in the obvious way, and not without justification – by assuming Silvester's professions to have been simply fraudulent. Silvester never repaid the money, and the correspondence ended in recrimination. 'You knew your own Circumstances', Richardson wrote.

[116] Silvester to Richardson, 12 May 1756, FM XIV, 4, f.21.
[117] Richardson to Silvester, 15 May 1756, FM XIV, 4, f.22.
[118] Silvester to Richardson, 12 August 1756, FM XV, 1, f.35; Richardson to Silvester, 13 August 1756, FM XV, 1, f.36.
[119] Silvester to Richardson, 27 December 1756, FM XV, 1, f. 38. For details of the work see above, note 107.
[120] Richardson to Silvester, 28 August 1757, FM XV, 1, f.39.

I depended upon the Professions you made me; a mere Stranger to you, but by those Professions, and by that scrupulous Love of Virtue which you boasted of in every Letter You should not have sought to involve in your Uncertainties a Man labouring under Bodily Infirmities and Weight of Years, and to whom you even officiously pretended Love and Esteem on the purest Motives.[121]

Silvester continued to insist, in response, on 'that Veracity & Integrity which, however appearances may be construed, I hope I shall live no longer than I shall hold most Sacred'[122] – but in vain. Richardson had moved from one extreme to another: no longer trusting all, he now believed nothing, and re-read the whole correspondence to find cynical motives even at its inception. The first letter, he now saw, was designed to influence him 'from the Vanity you might hope to excite in me by your undesired and officious Applauses of Writings which Applauses I attributed more to the Goodness of your own Heart, than to any Merit in me. (This wounds me not a little, when I think of it, and look back upon the Beginning of our Correspondence!)'[123] Where Silvester defends himself against charges of dissembling and specious rhetoric by protesting 'I have neither the abilities or pen of Mr. Richardson', Richardson exclaims, in the margin, 'Nonsense!!!' Where he apologises that he had 'undesignedly or inadvertently fallen into a too warm defence against accusations I cou'd not think myself deserving of', Richardson simply remarks 'Facts are agt. him.' And where he concludes that events 'may perhaps furnish some appearances against me, but conscious of the integrity of my own intentions, I ... cou'd wish that the most inward recesses of my heart were exposed to the whole World' ('this may perhaps seem like boasting', he adds), Richardson adds another welter of marginal exclamation marks and protests: 'No, no! It cannot look like that. It is capable of a much worse Look!'[124]

Richardson's letter of 17 July 1759 was his last. He continued the correspondence only by proxy, and seemed in the end to attach more importance to a statement of Silvester's finances needed for completion of the 'Warning Piece' than to the debt itself. The last letter in the sequence, dated 21 August, reproaches Silvester for his 'parading Epistles' and for having 'attacked' his correspondent 'in so artful and designing a Manner, as now appears on Proof'. 'More than *some* Appearances are against you', accuses Richardson's amanuensis, John Douglas, 'and therefore he wishes you not to surfeit him, with the Repetition of such gross Pretensions to *Integrity* of *Heart*, as you abounded with in every Letter, and continue thro'

[121] Richardson to Silvester, 5 August 1758, FM XV, 1, f.44.
[122] Silvester to Richardson, 30 June 1759, FM XV, 1, f.50.
[123] Richardson to Silvester, 17 July 1759, FM XV, 1, f.52.
[124] Silvester to Richardson, (annotated by Richardson), 13 August 1759, FM XV, 1, ff.56–7. Richardson's annotations were subsequently scored through.

Detection.'[125] Richardson's reading of the letters had at last settled at a new and opposite extreme: no longer the emanations of the heart, they were now its screen.

Doubtless Richardson realised that, published as a cautionary epistolary novel, what in one sense was merely a squabble about money would have bordered too closely on farce. His plan to publish the 'Warning Piece to Posterity' may have been no more than a last threat to Silvester, or may indeed never have been conveyed: in the later copy of the final letter the phrase 'to Posterity' has been scored out and replaced by 'to his Friends and Family'.[126] Beneath its hints of the absurd, however, what Richardson here assembled and thought (however fleetingly) of publishing carries serious implications for the epistolary novel, and can no more be dismissed as a mere warning against lending money than *Clarissa* can be dismissed as a warning against running off with young men. At another level, the 'Warning Piece' is a drama of disguise and deception, a burgherly *Liaisons dangereuses*. In its pages, Richardson records (and invites the reader to repeat) his own experience as a reader at first beguiled by specious rhetoric masquerading as writing from the heart, and at last aware that what he took for a window was all along a mask. In so doing, he perfectly illustrates the peculiar ambivalence of the letter form, and challenges in particular the special claims to authenticity of disclosure with which it comes equipped. He calls, in effect, for a new approach to epistolary narrative on the reader's part, in which attention shifts away from what the letters say to focus instead on what they are intended to do. At first, of course, Silvester's narrative letters are presented in the usual way, as a plausible vehicle of truth: they relate, minutely enough, a story about a worthy man's struggles and sufferings in a world fit only for the dishonest. But the principal story with which Richardson is concerned lies not here, in what the letters tell, but rather in what they *show* – a story of epistolary stratagems and plots, in which a trusting reader falls victim to a cunning writer. To read the letters for their surface content alone would simply be to fall again for Silvester's confidence trick, and miss Richardson's warning. The one safe way to read them, as Richardson finally makes clear, is to abandon theories of epistolary transparency for something more like the alternative model that Johnson was later to propose. In this sense the 'Warning Piece' is a warning, above all, against *misreading*, and one all the more dramatic and vivid for any reader who (like Richardson himself) is at first deceived by Silvester's seemingly undressed heart.

[125] John Douglas to Silvester, 21 August 1759, FM XV, 1, f.58. Though signed by Douglas the letter was evidently composed by Richardson, whose draft survives at the bottom of Silvester's previous letter. If anything, the draft is sterner. 'More than *some* Appearances are ag.^t you', it reads. 'All Appearances, and all *Facts*, are against you' (FM XV, 1, f.57).
[126] FM XV, 1, f.58.

The last irony of this monument to epistolary indeterminacy is that from these two stories (Silvester's tale of suffering innocence, Richardson's warning against epistolary fraud) emerges a third and equally plausible story, in which a feckless projector, capable of art but no more than averagely devious, makes the mistake of borrowing money from a vain and increasingly querulous old man, who later reacts to non-repayment by forming an opinion as extreme and far from the mark as the high opinion it replaces. In the eyes of Richardson's biographers, Silvester 'had indeed been guilty of deceit in the sacred matter of pecuniary obligation, obviously because he was unable to avoid deceiving himself';[127] and their generosity is not unreasonable. Certainly, Silvester's apparent confidence that the Ministry would make over to him huge tracts of waste land to improve (so making him, in Richardson's words, 'ye richest, & of consequence, ye most considerable private Man in the British Dominions')[128] says little for his grasp on reality. Perhaps Richardson was nearest the mark midway through the correspondence, when he questions not Silvester's heart so much as his head. It is hard not to sympathise, at any rate, with Silvester's final protests at the extremity and vehemence of the accusations in which Richardson ended, and with his hint that if his letters really had been fraudulent then *Clarissa*'s author, of all readers, should at least have been ready to spot it. 'Surely I must have been a long premeditated and weak Villain too', his penultimate letter points out, 'to have entred into a feigned Correspondence, in order to extort ffavours from a Man whose Works publickly declared him, to have the greatest knowl[edge] of Human Nature & the World too, of perhaps any Man in it! What my motives were in beginning that Correspondence, let my Letters speak for me!'[129]

Yet that, of course, is a task the letters can no longer perform – not, at least, with a single voice. Read once by Richardson as signs of integrity and once as agents of deceit, they remain obscure, ambiguous, and even in a sense illegible: beneath their surface Eusebius Silvester can be seen in a variety of ways, but remains in the end unknown.

---

[127] T. C. Duncan Eaves and Ben D. Kimpel, *Samuel Richardson: A Biography* (Oxford, 1971), p. 470.

[128] Richardson to Silvester, 22 February 1756, FM XIV, 4, f.13. According to Richardson's later note (f.26), Silvester's 'principal Project ... was to obtain Grants to himself of many Hundred Thousands of Acres of which the Forests, Chaces, Commons, belonging to the Crown ... consist, that he might break up the Ground, and turn it into Farms, and let them out to his Under-Servants, and to be cultivated according to a method invented by himself, and Father, he being a great Schemer in Agriculture'.

[129] Silvester to Richardson, 21 July 1759, FM XV, 1, f.53.

Epistolary form in *Clarissa*: some preliminaries

In these examples from either end of his literary career, something of Richardson's preoccupation with the vagaries of his medium can be seen. Narrative reliability is a significant topic even in the relatively naive *Pamela*, and in the manuscript 'Warning Piece' of the Silvester correspondence the ambivalence of the letter comes to the very forefront of the text. But nothing can prepare the reader for the elaborate and perplexing interplay of confession, casuistry, apology and dissembling presented in the narrative of *Clarissa*, or for the novel's sustained exploration of the vexed processes through which experience is reformulated in words. These questions are more fully investigated in the chapters to follow; first, however, it may be useful to make some general remarks about *Clarissa*'s multiple epistolary form, and in particular about the emphatic demystification of 'writing from the heart' that results from it.

It is sometimes noted that Richardson returned in *Clarissa* to the thematic conflicts first addressed in *Pamela*, but that he did so in newly unblinking mood, pursuing to their troubling conclusions all the problems from which the wish-fulfilling reconciliations of the earlier work had shied away.[130] Something very similar can be said of the novel's form: all the questions begged by *Pamela*'s confident epistolary monologue are directly confronted in *Clarissa*, which in its very structure refuses to recognise the adequacy or completeness of any single account. The novel's organisation is labyrinthine and defies simple description, but several complementary patterns can be picked out. In place of *Pamela*'s almost unbroken monologue, which is never far from (and at one stage becomes) a soliloquising diary or journal, *Clarissa* is genuinely dialogic in form, giving not only the heroine's letters to her addressee Anna but also a commentary on these letters in Anna's replies. Anna is a friendly examiner but an examiner nonetheless, and her responses enable Richardson to incorporate in the text a sustained and explicit interrogation of its own main narrative (an innovation that sets *Clarissa* apart from the majority of epistolary novels, and makes it unique in Richardson's own work).[131] Anna's viewpoint, moreover, is not the only available alternative. Where in *Pamela* Antipamelist objection is voiced only in occasional allegations quoted by Pamela herself, what Richardson calls *Clarissa*'s 'double, yet separate,

---

130 See William M. Sale, Jr, 'From *Pamela* to *Clarissa*', in *The Age of Johnson*, ed. Frederick W. Hilles (New Haven, 1949), pp. 135–6; Eagleton, *Rape of Clarissa*, p. 39.

131 Explaining the formal structure of *Grandison*, Richardson noted its divergence from that of *Clarissa*, in which 'there is a twofold Correspondence necessary – one between her and Miss Howe; the other between Lovelace and Belford. The Subject of one Letter arose often out of another. It was necessary it should. In the new Work, (Except one or two Letters of each of the Respondents ...), the Answers to the Letters of the Narratist are only supposed, and really sunk ...' (to Stinstra, 2 June 1753, Slattery, pp. 31–2).

Correspondence' (I, iii; p. 35) gives the heroine's antagonist more or less equal time. In Lovelace's letters an eloquent alternative to Clarissa's version of the story is proposed, so that the narrative as a whole oscillates between parallel yet in many ways antithetical accounts of the same events. Then, to complete the symmetry, these letters themselves receive the same treatment as Clarissa's, and are subject to discussion and dispute in the increasingly critical commentary of their recipient, Belford.

The neat symmetry of this basic scheme is complicated by a third structural feature, most clearly seen in the eventual reversal of roles (and power) that takes place between Belford and Lovelace in the final volumes. As Richardson notes in a draft preface, each of the novel's three original instalments corresponds roughly with the primacy of a particular narrator:

The Two first Volumes chiefly written by the Two ladies.
Two next .... by Lovelace.
Three last .... by the reforming Belford.[132]

This, in fact, is to simplify a more complex distribution: narrative is equally divided between Lovelace and Clarissa in the third volume, for example, while the fifth is almost entirely Lovelace's. But it takes only a glance at the 'Table of Letters' appended to Angus Ross's recent Penguin edition of the novel to see the approximate validity of Richardson's note. Nor is the advantage held by each of these temporarily presiding narrators a simply statistical matter. The role carries with it the opportunity to project on the instalment in question a particular view of events, the result being that the three distinct phases through which the text moves invite readers to perceive their story in widely divergent ways.

Superimposed on one another, these three patterns of dialogue, parallelism and shifting perspective create an intricate enough effect. Yet to think in such schematic terms is still to underestimate the disorienting, kaleidoscopic variety of the text, which rarely allows one narrator an unbroken run of more than half a dozen letters (the significant exception being the oppressive dominance of Lovelace's viewpoint before the rape), and which juxtaposes over thirty distinct voices in at least fifty separate correspondences. Perspectives accumulate, compete and disperse, creating an effect close to the kind of narrative polyphony defined by Mikhail Bakhtin, in which the single authorial voice is dissolved into a multiplicity of autonomous and coequal voices and consciousnesses, each marked by its own idiolect and informed by its own world view.[133] The novels' universe

---

[132] *Samuel Richardson, Clarissa: Preface, Hints of Prefaces, and Postscript*, ed. R. F. Brissenden, Augustan Reprint Society No. 103 (Los Angeles, 1964), p. 4.

[133] See Mikhail Bakhtin, *Problems of Dostoevsky's Poetics*, trans. Caryl Emerson (Minneapolis, 1984), pp. 6–7. It might be noted that Bakhtin's exemplary practitioner of the polyphonic novel began his career with *Poor Folk*, an epistolary work which makes explicit reference to

becomes multifarious, plural. Yet for all the applicability of this model to a work rightly praised by contemporaries for its fine discriminations of narrative voice (and one moreover in which these various voices articulate not simply differences of personality but collisions of ideology) polyphony is hardly the word.[134] There is little sign of any harmonious convergence or counterpoint between the novel's adversarial narratives, which instead of combining to present from every angle an amplified reality are recurrently and irreconcilably at odds. More aptly, Terry Castle describes 'a *cacophony* of voices, a multiplicity of exegetes struggling to articulate different "constructions" of the world'; for William Beatty Warner, the text is a battleground, 'a vast plain where Clarissa and Lovelace ... and the two ways of interpreting the world they embody, collide and contend'.[135] It is as though *Clarissa* represents the fullest and most dramatic exploration of a phenomenon that the other great novel of the period, Fielding's *Tom Jones*, was able only to describe: 'For let a Man be never so honest', as Fielding's narrator explains,

the Account of his own Conduct will, in Spite of himself, be so very favourable, that his Vices will come purified through his Lips, and, like foul Liquors well strained, will leave all their Foulness behind. For tho' the Facts themselves may appear, yet so different will be the Motives, Circumstances, and Consequences, when a Man tells his own Story, and when his Enemy tells it, that we scarce can recognize the Facts to be one and the same.[136]

The effect of *Clarissa* could hardly be better defined. In its very organisation the narrative is in conflict with itself, with results so discordant that at times one is driven to think not of competing versions of an identical reality, but of reality's displacement by the force of competing fictions.

Clarissa's very length attests this primacy of discourse over story, the elevation of writing to the thematic centre of the book. There is a huge disproportion between the novel's basic plot and the seemingly endless proliferation of letters in which it is represented, interpreted, debated, and

Clarissa. See Joseph Frank, *Dostoevsky: The Seeds of Revolt, 1821–1849*, 2nd edn (Princeton, 1977), p. 150.

[134] For early comment on 'the specific Difference of Stile preserved by every Writer' in the novel, see Sarah Fielding, *Remarks on Clarissa* (1749), ed. Peter Sabor, Augustan Reprint Society Nos. 231–2 (Los Angeles, 1985), p. 39; Diderot, 'Eloge de Richardson', in *Œuvres esthétiques*, ed. Paul Vernière (Paris, 1960), p. 39. On the question of polyphony, it is worth noting that Richardson considered but then rejected a similar image himself when revising *Clarissa*'s preface. Contrasting the multiple epistolary method with authorial narration, he adds that the latter 'may not unfitly be compared to the dead Tolling of a single Bell, in Opposition to the wonderful Variety of Sounds, which constitute the Harmony of a Handel' (*Hints of Prefaces*, p. 13).

[135] Castle, *Clarissa's Ciphers*, p. 21 (italics mine); William Beatty Warner, *Reading Clarissa: The Struggles of Interpretation* (New Haven, 1979), p. viii.

[136] *The History of Tom Jones, A Foundling*, ed. Martin C. Battestin and Fredson Bowers (Oxford, 1974), I, 420.

eventually all but consumed. And while this disproportion is due at least in part to Richardson's famous circumstantial realism, it is due still more to the studious prolixity with which each narrative segment is weighed (and weighted) by its writer, and then again is carefully analysed in the reply of its addressee. 'There *is* no Story', wrote Hester Thrale Piozzi, responding to James Beattie's complaint at the need for readers to 'disentangle themselves' of the narrators' reflections to get at the events themselves: 'A Man gets a Girl from her Parents – violates her Free Will, & She dies of a broken heart. That is all the Story.'[137] Better known is Samuel Johnson's rebuke to those who, by seeking to 'read Richardson for the story', risk hanging themselves with impatience;[138] and certainly Richardson's method makes reading for plot alone an almost impossible task. The novel buries what is told, its hypothetical ulterior reality, beneath a collection of discontinuous, variously reliable and often downright contradictory acts of telling, and thus invites the reader to find not one but two stories within its pages. There is the story of events, the elemental myth of abduction, violation and death dismissed (yet at the same time so evocatively described) by Mrs Piozzi. And there is a second story, which in many ways outgrows the first – a story of characters at writing-desks, struggling to fix their experiences adequately in prose and so define and assert their own conflicting senses, psychologically, epistemologically and above all morally, of what is happening in their world. As John Preston succinctly puts it, letters '*replace* the narrated events; it is the act of writing them that forms the action of the novel'.[139]

Yet these two stories are of course intertwined, for the letters are never independent, but work to reiterate and extend, in the very form of the novel, the fundamental contentions of its plot. The link between them is ingeniously suggested by a draft title at one stage considered by Richardson, '*The Lady's Legacy*'.[140] With inspired ambiguity, the title anticipates two of the novel's great concerns – the exchange of property, and the exchange of texts. As critics concerned with *Clarissa*'s socio-economic implications have noted, it refers at the level of plot to Grandfather

---

[137] Beattie to John Ogilvie, 20 August 1759, in Sir William Forbes, *An Account of the Life and Writings of James Beattie*, 2nd edn, 3 vols. (Edinburgh, 1807), I, 49; Piozzi's marginalia (British Library, 10856.ee.9), I, 48.

[138] *Boswell's Life of Johnson*, II, 175.

[139] Preston, 'Epistolary Narrative and Moral Discovery', p. 24.

[140] Richardson discusses this title in a letter to Aaron Hill of 5 January 1746/7, Carroll, p. 77. The title itself, followed by a long subtitle, is transcribed on a separate page in the correspondence with Hill (FM XIII, 3, f.66; also in Carroll, p. 77n.). It was probably Hill's own suggestion, occurring as it does during a phase of the correspondence in which Hill was arguing against the title *Clarissa* (Hill to Richardson, 5 November 1746, FM XIII, 3, f.65). It is not impossible, however, that it was Richardson's own more subtle revision of Hill's original suggestion, *The Lady's Remembrancer: Or, The Way of a Young Man, with a Maid*, to which Richardson's only recorded response is a marginal '!!!' (f.65).

Harlowe's bequest to Clarissa of his estate, a breach in conventional patterns of inheritance she later identifies as 'the original cause of all my misfortunes' (IV, 349; p. 754).[141] Yet the title also has another and perhaps more important meaning, as is suggested by Richardson's remark that '*The Lady's Legacy*, it cannot now be properly called, as it might at first, because in the last Revisal, I have made the Sollicitude for the Publication, to be rather Miss Howe's than hers.'[142] '*The Lady's Legacy*', it would appear, meant not only the estate, the grandfather's bequest to Clarissa, but also the 'History' itself, Clarissa's bequest to the reader. 'Published' (as the draft title continues) 'in Compliance with the Lady's Order on her Death-Bed', this second bequest was one in which the misfortunes arising from the first would be recorded and Clarissa's own conduct through them vindicated.[143] Even after the revision in which this plan was reattributed to Anna, Richardson continues to stress the rhetorical motivation of the text, notably in Anna's own longing for a history that would definitively prove 'the villainy of the worst of men, and the virtue of the most excellent of women' (VI, 83; p. 1017). Also stressed, however, is the fact that the letter-collection eventually compiled to serve this end is far less coherent and single in its rhetorical charge than Anna intends, if only because it also represents voices at odds with Clarissa's own: as Belford tells Lovelace, 'thou must fare better from thy own pen, than from hers' (VI, 329; p. 1174). Instead of telling a simple story from a single viewpoint (Anna's original intention), *Clarissa*'s collection of letters allows the various antagonists to perpetuate their antagonisms in writing. As a result, the only access to Clarissa's story available to the reader comes through a maze of pleas and accusations, blackenings and whitenings, which recapitulate, in discursive form, the struggles of her life.

Central to this complex and controversial narrative structure is the complexity of the letter itself. Quite apart from its questionable validity as a receptacle of narrative information, Richardson insists on its instability in practical ways, thereby reinforcing the need to treat it warily. In *Clarissa*'s world the exchange of letters is fraught with real hazard, in ways that do little to inspire confidence in the form. Letters are sent as decoys and written in code; they are hidden, stolen, doctored and forged; there are clandestine letters, allegorical letters, threatening letters, pseudonymous letters, and hints even of treasonable letters. Letters, moreover, not only record but in large part propel the plot. For Lovelace, they provide a means of drawing Clarissa beyond the walls of her father's house: he

---

141 See Christopher Hill, 'Clarissa Harlowe and her Times', *Essays in Criticism*, 5 (1955), p. 318; Janet Todd, *Women's Friendship in Literature* (New York, 1980), p. 9.
142 To Aaron Hill, 5 January 1746/7, Carroll, p. 77.
143 For a fuller account of the way in which Richardson attributes the original compilation of *Clarissa* to the editorial activities of its own characters, see below, pp. 220–36.

entangles her in a clandestine correspondence, using it to play on her fears and convince her of his own benign intentions. For Clarissa, they soon become the only medium in which she can plead her cause: she addresses to her family a stream of casuistical letters, carefully marshalling her evidence and arguments in the hope of persuading them to retract their commands. Both characters, significantly, are perceived as accomplished and therefore potentially dangerous writers, and according to their antagonists the letter becomes, in their hands, an ominous and powerful tool. Clarissa and Anna are alarmed at Lovelace's reputation as 'a great plotter, and a great writer' (I, 23; p. 50) and anxiously ponder the seditious connotations of the cipher in which 'the great correspondence by letters which he holds' with Belford is disguised (I, 68; p. 74). The Harlowes, for their part, are always reminding Clarissa of her 'knack at writing' (VI, 337; p. 1179), a knack they find so forceful that they eventually forbid her its exercise. They present themselves as disadvantaged competitors in the face of her affective skill (her 'power of painting her distresses so as to pierce a stone': VI, 301; p. 1156) and her manipulative rhetoric (her expertise, as Bella tells her, in 'making every one do what you would, when you wrote': VI, 337; p. 1179).

Letters, clearly, must be handled with care, and by the reader of *Clarissa* as well as by the inhabitants of its world. At the outset, to be sure, they seem to promise the purest transcription of reality, which Anna and Clarissa seem to see between them as itself a kind of text, already inscribed with meaning. Anna opens the novel by asking Clarissa to 'write ... the whole of your story' (I, 3; p. 40), and Clarissa responds by undertaking to 'recite facts only, and leave you to judge of the truth' (I, 6; p. 41): her reports, it would seem, will merely give voice to an inherently legible world, and will do so with completeness and neutrality. Yet these disavowals of partiality (and the conventional assumptions about the immediacy and transparency of letters on which they rest) are soon exposed as wishful myths, invoked only to be challenged. One such occasion comes in the novel's third edition, where Lovelace reminds Clarissa that he 'loved Familiar-letter-writing ... above all the species of writing: It was writing from the heart (without the fetters prescribed by method or study) as the very word *Cor-respondence* implied. Not the heart only; the *soul* was in it'.[144] The passage is sometimes cited to show Richardson's unquestioning faith in 'writing from the heart',[145] and at first view he does indeed seem to have placed in Lovelace's mouth a restatement of what by this time the reader might with reason have forgotten – that letter-narrative is spontaneous and natural, giving unimpeded view of the writer's inner life. Yet it would be rash to take as an objective statement even of Lovelace's theory, let

[144] *Clarissa*, 3rd edn (1751; rpt. New York, 1990), IV, 269.
[145] See Warner, *Reading Clarissa*, p. 97; Watt, *Rise of the Novel*, p. 216.

alone Richardson's, a celebration of the letter's candour and reliability that is itself so subtle and calculating. In context, Lovelace's professions are clearly no more than an attempt to persuade Clarissa to grant him access to her correspondence with Anna, while at the same time lulling her suspicions at the subject and character of his own with Belford. His etymological fraud alone should prompt at least a second thought about the convention it is concocted to uphold; and even Clarissa finds his effusions hard to swallow. There are crucial distinctions between letters and conversation, she reminds him, and it would be foolish to read the characteristic informality of the epistolary style as a guarantee of careless or unthinking composition. She finds it 'impossible, be the Letters written in as easy and familiar a style as they would, but that they must have that advantage from sitting down to write them which prompt speech could not always have'.[146] Writing, she adds, is an act of '*premeditation*', and must always be judged as such. When, volumes later, she herself makes telling use of the advantage of sitting down to write by contriving in her allegorical letter to Lovelace a text designed above all to mislead, Lovelace finds himself bitterly concurring with her views: 'one would not expect, that she should set about deceiving again; more especially by the *premeditation of writing*', he complains (VII, 74; p. 1269).[147]

Elsewhere Clarissa is at once more scrupulous and less successful in her preoccupation with the hazards of the letter and the difficulties involved in reliable epistolary self-presentation. She reads Lovelace's early letters with extreme (though undiscerning) care to assess whether each is 'the genuine product of his heart' (II, 116; p. 269), and she applies the same rigour to her own, finding within them two potential areas of misrepresentation. The first concerns the limits of her own self-knowledge, and thus the limits of any first-person account as a reliable explication of her own interior life. The problem is first opened up by the sceptical readings of Anna who, as the correspondence develops, frequently alleges Clarissa's letters to betray meanings quite distinct from (and even opposite to) their surface content, notably on the question of her avowed indifference to Lovelace. Challenged on one such occasion for failing to represent her true inclinations,

---

[146] *Clarissa*, 3rd edn (1751; rpt. New York, 1990), IV, 271.

[147] In his influential article '*Clarissa* Restored?', Mark Kinkead-Weekes casts doubt on Richardson's claim that the many new passages included in the third edition of the novel were 'Restored from the Original Manuscripts of the History of Clarissa', and suggests instead that most were newly written in an attempt to reassert control over the novel's wayward reception (*Review of English Studies*, NS 10, No. 38 (1959), 156–71). The fact that in the passage quoted here from the *first* edition Lovelace recalls and alludes to a word used by Clarissa only in the *third* would seem to suggest that here at least the material newly included in 1751 was indeed a genuine restoration from an earlier draft. It follows that the third edition cannot be interpreted *simply* as a later revision of *Clarissa*, just as it cannot be interpreted simply as a return to the pre-publication original. Doubtless it combines both functions – and in ways which, in the absence of documentary evidence, will never be wholly disentangled.

Clarissa protests the sincerity of her narrative, but is forced to acknowledge its provisional and possibly fallible nature. 'But of this I assure you', she writes, 'That whatever interpretation my words were capable of, I *intended not* any reserve to you. I wrote my heart, at the time' (I, 256; p. 176). As time goes on, however, awareness of her own involuntary misrepresentations becomes harder to dismiss, and Clarissa begins to recognise Anna's second person as paradoxically more authoritative than her own first. 'The heart is very deceitful', she later concedes, alarmed at her failure to detect and describe its secret impulses: 'do you, my dear friend, lay mine open (but surely it is always open before you!), and spare me not, if you find or think it culpable' (IV, 56; p. 596). How the heart can be at once deceitful and open is a contradiction Clarissa is at this point unable to resolve. But as the dual impulses to confession and equivocation in her prose come increasingly into conflict, she reaches a disquieting answer. In the mad papers written immediately after the rape she dismisses as misleading 'the knowlege I thought I had of my own heart', and looks for a truer analysis to her 'penetrating sister' Bella (who represents perhaps the most hostile perspective on Clarissa in the entire text). Addressing Bella with a repeat of what in context is the most disturbing of puns, she confesses: 'You penetrated my proud heart with the jealousy of an elder sister's searching eye. / You knew me better than I knew myself' (V, 236–7; p. 891).[148]

Here, it would seem, is more than enough to undermine a reader's faith in the reliability of Clarissa's letters. Yet the problems raised by her narrative go far beyond the relatively simple matter of the narrator's own capacity for self-awareness. Again Clarissa gives the lead herself, when lamenting the impossibility of transcending her own subjective stance to arrive at genuinely impartial judgments. She knows that 'where *Self* is judge, matters, even with *good people*, will not always be rightly judged of' (VI, 333; p. 1176), and she applies the point to her own epistolary practice, lamenting its recurrent lapses into special pleading. Her efforts at objective documentation, she finds, are subverted by 'self-partiality, that strange misleader' (VI, 34; p. 987), and compromised by a presumptuous moral gloss – by her tendency, as she elsewhere puts it, 'to make *my* sake, *God's* sake', in her analyses of events (II, 286; p. 359). Such insights lead her far from her early claim to offer a neutral recitation of 'facts only', and with good reason. It is impossible, after all, for even the most prolix writer to write referentially without first making selections from the infinite raw material of experience and then, in the process of organising each sentence, also interpreting the chosen evidence. Completeness and neutrality

---

[148] See Leo Braudy's investigation of this term, 'Penetration and Impenetrability in *Clarissa*', in *New Approaches to Eighteenth-Century Literature: Selected Papers from the English Institute*, ed. Phillip Harth (New York, 1974), pp. 177–206.

will always be beyond reach: as the narrator of a more recent epistolary novel puts it, 'Une lettre, même la plus longue, force à simplifier ce qui n'aurait pas dû l'être';[149] and it is on these inevitable conditions that Clarissa's antagonists seize. Turning to the forensic language that pervades the final instalment,[150] Lovelace tells Hickman that 'tho' the lady will tell the *truth*, and nothing *but* the truth, yet, perhaps, she will not tell the *whole* truth' (VI, 206; p. 1095). And in her uncle's eyes the slippage between this hypothetical ideal of 'the *whole* truth' and Clarissa's efforts to 'recite' it seems a matter not simply of narrative mediation but rather of narrative mendacity. '*He that is first in his own cause*, saith the wise man, *seemeth just: But his neighbour cometh, and searcheth him*', he warns. 'And so, in this respect, will I be your *neighbour*; for I will search your heart to the bottom; that is to say, if your letter be written from your heart' (I, 214–15; p. 154).

Writing from the heart, it should be clear, is by no means the straightforward matter it might at first appear, even in Clarissa's own obtrusively conscientious narrative. As with Pope, the very situation of the autobiographical letter-writer invites suspicions, and the novel does nothing to discourage a sceptical approach. Indeed, it is noteworthy that Pope's two most aggressive critics read Clarissa's letters with almost the same misgivings, finding in them a similar deficiency in transparency and truth. Drawing a contrast between the novel's original draft and an early revision in which Richardson seems to have been accentuating the slightly suspect air of Clarissa's narrative, Aaron Hill complained that she had now lost the traditional epistolary virtues: he found in her letters 'an elegant Propriety, or Stiffness, where, before, there shone a native negligence of undress'd Loveliness, and picturesque Simplicity'.[151] More forthrightly, Johnson identified Fielding's *Amelia* as a 'more perfect' heroine than Richardson's Clarissa, supporting his criticism of the latter's character with the charge (tantalisingly undeveloped) that 'there is always something which she prefers to truth'.[152] Nor were they alone in their complaints at Clarissa's sophistications. Another reader within Richardson's circle, Sarah Chapone, took up Hill's theme to criticise the heroine's letters by contrast with those of Anna, who 'excels her in one, and but one Perfection; namely, Simplicity' – simplicity being

that Rectitude of Mind which suppresses all useless Reflections upon itself and the Actions which spring from it. It differs from Sincerity, but is more excellent. Many Persons are sincere, who are not simple: They are ever at the Glass to study and

149 Marguerite Yourcenar, *Alexis*, in *Œuvres romanesques* (Paris, 1982), p. 9.
150 See below, pp. 218–44.
151 Hill to Richardson, March 1745/6, FM XIII, 3, f.29.
152 Hester Lynch Piozzi (Mrs Thrale), *Anecdotes of the Late Samuel Johnson* (1786), in *Johnsonian Miscellanies*, ed. G. B. Hill, 2 vols. (1897), I, 297.

adjust themselves: They are in continual Fear of being taken for what they are not; whereas the simple Person forgets that Self of which the other is so jealous: And provided the Actions be right, makes no further Reflection upon it.[153]

For this reader, clearly enough, the relentless anxiety of Clarissa's epistolary self-fashioning was not suspect, merely regrettable. Less indulgent readers, however, found simplicity and sincerity less easy to separate, and saw in the kinds of study and adjustment described by Sarah Chapone a hint of more fraudulent effects. A good example is provided by the early reviewer who challenged Clarissa's explanation that she corresponds with Lovelace 'to prevent ill consequences' as 'apparently no more than a pretence', alleging instead that she continues it 'more by inclination'.[154] For this reader at least, her letters seemed to disguise as much as they disclosed.

Lovelace's narrative, of course, only compounds the problem; and it is here that Richardson most directly undermines the myth of writing from the heart. 'As much of my heart, as I know of it myself, will I tell thee' (V, 279; p. 915) is perhaps the nearest Lovelace comes to endorsing it with any sincerity, and even here it is not the standard formula so much as the qualification made to it that is arresting. More often, he presents the intimate revelation of the heart and the immediate transcription of reality conventionally associated with the letter form as no more than a clever illusion. 'Thou'lt observe ... that tho' this was written afterwards, yet (as in other places) I write it ... as if I had retired to put down every sentence as spoken', he notes immediately before the rape, choosing perhaps the most unsettling moment possible to remind Belford that what he reads is not a recital but a creation, a work of artifice and wit: 'I know thou likest this lively *present-tense* manner, as it is one of my peculiars' (V, 221; p. 882). There are various such 'peculiars' up Lovelace's sleeve, but all offer only wilful exaggerations of processes at work in every letter of the novel. His narrative is inventive, playful, and in the end strangely autonomous: he boasts in an early letter of his ability to write 'as well without a subject, as with one' (I, 193–4; p. 142), and representational fidelity is rarely his first concern. A telling analogy likens the letter not to the heart but to the face, when 'the pen and the countenance assume airs of levity', and so disguise an actual state of gloom (VII, 339; p. 1439). One thinks again of Fielding's melancholy view of the world as 'a vast Masquerade, where the

---

[153] Chapone to Richardson, [March 1752], FM XII, 2, f.55. Her own epistolary practices were very different. 'I never stand ballancing upon Words', she told Richardson: 'They all serve as Volunteers; for I never press any into the Service, and all the Duty I exact from them is plainly and fully to deliver my Meaning' (ff.56–7).

[154] Albrecht von Haller, 'A Critical Account of *Clarissa*', *Gentleman's Magazine*, 19 (1749), reprinted in *Novel and Romance, 1700–1800: A Documentary Record*, ed. Ioan Williams (1970), pp. 137, 134.

greatest Part appear disguised under false Vizors and Habits';[155] writing from the heart, certainly, is not in question. Engaged, like every narrator in the book, in the contentious (and endlessly contended) enterprise of fixing the moral significance of its struggles, Lovelace is happy to acknowledge all the narratological problems posed in Clarissa's letters, and concludes that glossing, that necessary accompaniment to any literary rendition of the world, is all. As Johnson's *Dictionary* notes, to gloss is not only 'To explain by comment' but also 'To palliate by specious exposition or representation' and 'To embellish with superficial lustre';[156] and for Lovelace the drift from the first of these activities to the second and third is not just inevitable but also to be desired. His theory is simple enough: 'It is much better . . . to tell your own story, when it *must* be known, than to have an adversary tell it for you' (VI, 116; p. 1038) – better because of the opportunities to select, order, and couch to advantage available to the teller. 'It is but glossing over *one* part of a story, and omitting *another*, that will make a bad cause a good one at any time' (VII, 102; p. 1287), he later boasts.

One need not wholly embrace the baffled relativism to which Lord M. is reduced at this point, with his remark that '*one story was good, till another was heard*' (VII, 100; p. 1286), to see what far-reaching implications such passages have for the novel as a whole. Lovelace is not the only one to gloss and gloss over, only the readiest to admit it; and his further reminders that he is not the novel's only rhetorician sound important alarms. When he finds the same processes at work in Clarissa's writing, 'the whole letter so written, as to make *herself* more admired, *me* more detested' (VI, 322; p. 1169), or when he challenges the supposed neutrality of the epistolary history envisaged in Clarissa's will by complaining that he is 'to be *manifestoed* against' (VII, 336; p. 1437), he merely makes explicit within the text itself anxieties that have preoccupied generations of readers, from Hill and Johnson to the deconstructionists of recent years. *Clarissa* makes available no such thing as a neutral text, no writing that does not in the first place serve its writer.

Clarissa herself has an early skirmish with the problem when, during her confinement at Harlowe Place, Lovelace meets the rest of the family at church. There is no doubt, at one level, about what happens: Lovelace, sitting in front of the Harlowe pew, turns and engages the family in conversation. But beyond this basic information the illusion of direct access to events is impossible to sustain. The affair is narrated twice and on both occasions is relayed in Clarissa's letters, the first version originating with the servant Shorey and the second with Lovelace himself. But their rival accounts, she soon finds, entirely fail to converge. Shorey applauds

---

[155] *Miscellanies, Volume One*, p. 155.   [156] Johnson, *Dictionary*, 'To Gloss'.

the Harlowes' forbearance in the face of Lovelace's arrogant and provoca-
tive behaviour; Lovelace, on the other hand, tells a story of pride swal-
lowed and deferential courtesy on his part, provocatively spurned by the
Harlowes; and both these heavily glossed accounts are themselves buried,
as Clarissa passes them on, beneath her own efforts to ascertain and
understand an already irrecoverable truth. Confronted with the problem
of reconciling the two conflicting reports, she despairs 'that there would
hardly be a guilty person in the world, were each *suspected* or *accused* person
to tell his or her own story, and be allowed any degree of credit' (I, 250;
p. 172). All might be resolved, she assumes, by the impartial account of an
uninvolved spectator, Dr Lewen – 'But, alas! I am debarred from seeing
that good man, or any one who would advise me what to do in my present
difficult situation! –.'

There is in this episode an epitome of the novel itself, which exactly does
allow its suspected or accused persons to tell their own stories, and in so
doing confronts the reader with a welter of charges, counter-charges and
pleas. It thus refuses to establish what in its first letter it initially seems to
promise, a 'whole' story. Or rather, in its accumulation of so many
different efforts to fix and define such a story, it only shifts the ideal of
wholeness further beyond reach. Nor is there any 'good man' to hand to
set the record straight: no authoritative voice rises above the various
narratives to adjudicate between them (and the reductiveness of the
notorious interpretative footnotes appended by Richardson to later
revisions of the text shows how inadequate any such single voice would
have to be). Clarissa's story is vexed, complex and irreducible; and by
giving voice to such contradictory versions of it Richardson only redoubles
its remoteness. In this respect, the multiple epistolary form of his novel
problematises the very notion of a definable core of meaning, of a coherent
'*whole* truth' at its centre, and focuses attention instead on the only events
to which our access is reliable or direct – the epistolary acts in which the
novel's most interested parties create and communicate their various
conflicting tales. It is only by the closest attention to these primary events,
to *Clarissa*'s story of story-telling, that the novel's reader will understand
anything at all.

Richardson's reader

It is hardly surprising, when the novel was in its formative stages and
narrative of this intricacy a complete innovation, that *Clarissa*'s first readers
were more often simply bemused. Writing in the *Jacobite's Journal* a
month after publication began, Fielding (no longer the instigator but now
the witness of interpretative struggle) gives early evidence of problems
caused by the proliferation, within the first instalment alone, of contend-

ing points of view. Readers failed to converge on a single definitive understanding of the text; the coffee-houses ring with misreading. 'Clarissa is undutiful; she is too dutiful', he reports. 'She is too cold; she is too fond. She uses her Father, Mother, Uncles, Brother, Sister, Lover, Friend, too ill, too well. In short, there is scarce a Contradiction in Character, which I have not heard assigned from different Reasons to this poor Girl.'[157] And the next instalment only aggravated the problem, as Sarah Fielding adds:

The Objections now arose so fast, it was impossible to guess where they would end. *Clarissa* herself was a Prude – a Coquet – all the Contradictions mentioned some Time ago in a printed Paper, with the Addition of many more, were laid to her Charge. She was an undutiful Daughter – too strict in her Principles of Obedience to such Parents – too fond of a Rake and a Libertine – her Heart was as inpenitrable and unsusceptible of Affection, as the hardest Marble.[158]

In response to the difficulties of the text, each reader seems to have cut through its interplay of conflicting views by adopting and endorsing the perspective of a single voice. Nor was the voice always Clarissa's. The authoritarian defended the Harlowes and the libertine defended Lovelace, each judging the novel from a position already defined within it. As Sarah Fielding saw, their criticisms of Clarissa were anticipated by, and could only reiterate, 'the Reproaches cast on her in her Lifetime' – as though the text had been reading its readers, not vice versa:

She has been called perverse and obstinate by many of her Readers; *James Harlowe* called her so before them. Some say she was romantic; so said *Bella*; disobedient; all the *Harlowes* agree in that; a Prude; so said *Sally Martin*; had a Mind incapable of Love; Mr. *Lovelace's* Accusation ... I verily think I have not heard *Clarissa* condemned for any one Fault, but the Author has made some of the *Harlowes*, or some of Mrs. *Sinclair's* Family accuse her of it before.[159]

Where Mr B.'s alternative account of Pamela's conduct had given rise to a single Antipamelist objection, the diverse and far more highly developed perspectives of Clarissa's antagonists produced within the novel's readership an equivalent diversity of objection. Already, *Clarissa's* reception had proved as controversial and various as the text itself.

It is tempting to conclude, having observed the instability of the multiple epistolary form and at least a hint of the interpretative chaos to which it seems, almost immediately, to have led, that *Clarissa* must remain obstinately indeterminate in its meanings, and that reading can end only in impasse. It is undeniable, at any rate, that the novel is *difficult* to read.

---

[157] *The Jacobite's Journal and Related Writings*, ed. W. B. Coley (Oxford, 1975), p. 120 (No. 5, 2 January 1748).

[158] *Remarks on Clarissa* (1749), ed. Peter Sabor, Augustan Reprint Society Nos. 231–2 (Los Angeles, 1985), p. 13.

[159] *Ibid.*, p. 41.

Yet to see the confusion that results from these early readers' failure to recognise that no single viewpoint provides an adequate key to *Clarissa*, and that all viewpoints alike are implicated in (even contaminated by) its conflicts, is not necessarily to find the text in the last resort illegible. It is instead to see the extent of the task with which Richardson confronts his reader; for it is on the reader's active involvement, given the openness and incoherence of the text itself, that the onus of interpretation falls. Unguided by any objective voice and assailed instead by a babble of partisan voices, the reader must judge independently of them all (yet at the same time in the light of them all), and so make sense of the underlying 'History' on his own initiative. Acknowledging the gulf that separates him from immediate possession of Clarissa's story, he must be ready to read against the grain, in continual awareness of possible discrepancies between each narrative segment and the 'truth' it pretends to deliver. Finally, he must seek to bridge that gulf by efforts of judgment and interpretation very much more careful than those with which, according to these shrewdest of witnesses, the novel was originally met.

A contemporary memoir novel by Richardson's French translator Prévost makes such demands explicit. At its opening, the narrator announces his love for the 'fair Greek' who is the novel's subject, and then considers the implications of that announcement for the status of his own account: 'Shall I not render myself suspected by the confession with which I set out? ... Who will not mistrust my descriptions and encomiums? Will not the violence of my passion change the nature of every thing which I see or do?' The narrator's conclusion, and the novelist's invitation, are challenging: 'These are reasons', he continues, 'which shou'd keep the reader upon his guard.'[160] The reader of *Clarissa*, likewise, must be 'upon his guard', and will find many more such reasons for vigilance built into the structure of the text. Prévost's memoir novel, after all, is simple in organisation, and affords only limited scope for questioning the reliability of its narrative: there is only one narrator, and the impulse of his writing is unmistakably confessional. Richardson's epistolary novel, however, introduces a new complication by involving its narrators in various kinds of self-justification (addressed always to particular readers) and then compounds the complication by multiplying the number of narrating voices. Even as they complicate the novel, however, these features also make available ways of addressing the resulting problems. For while the text cannot supply its reader with any pure unmediated reality against which to measure the deficiencies of its reports, it does offer the next best thing: it

---

[160] I quote from the English translation (1741–2) of Prévost's *Histoire d'une grecque moderne*: 'Abbot Provost', *The History of a Fair Greek*, 2nd edn (1755), p. 5. On unreliability in Prévost's original see Jean Rousset, *Narcisse romancier: essai sur la première personne dans le roman* (Paris, 1973), pp. 139–57.

first provides explanations for narrative distortion, and then juxtaposes accounts which differ in all but the most basic facts, thereby enabling the reader to gauge the shortcomings of each by comparison and contrast as well as by purely internal evidence. The very multiplicity of the narrative makes possible (and indeed requires) a wary consideration of what happens to events in the process of narration, impressing on the reader the remoteness of what he is asked to interpret, and throwing him on his own resources to pursue the perpetually deficient '*whole* truth'. To the extent that the main narratives are carefully analysed within the text by their initial addressees, it even starts the process itself. Readers *in* the novel provide models for readers *of* it; and while Anna and Belford are by no means perfect exegetes, both have the right idea. 'A stander-by is often a better judge of the game than those that play', Anna twice tells Clarissa, explicitly claiming for the reader a higher level of awareness than the narrator's own (I, 66; pp. 73–4; see also III, 68–9; p. 407). Belford has a similar view of reading as a matter of independent and rigorous effort, exercised this time in resistance of narrative palliation: if Lovelace is an equivocating lawyer, 'throwing dust in the eyes of his judges', he, the reader, must be at pains to detect 'a partial whitener of his *own* cause, or blackener of *another*'s' (VII, 114; p. 1295).

It is here that Richardson makes what is perhaps his most innovative and daring gesture as a novelist, relinquishing control over a complex and multifarious text left open instead to the determination of the reader. A problem, however, remains. Can Richardson really have expected or intended to delegate his authorial prerogative in such ways? To find the reader enlisted as final arbiter of textual meaning is unsurprising enough in the work of his more playful successors, Sterne and Diderot, but it squares ill with our image of Richardson himself, puritan didact, jealous guardian of meanings. Here instead would seem to be another instance of a phenomenon familiar in modern criticism, Richardson's blindness to the most basic tendencies of his writing; for ever since Coleridge distinguished his admiration for Richardson's fiction from his loathing of Richardson's mind[161] a disparity between the achievement of the novels and the apparent banality of their didactic motivation has been regularly alleged. Much of the most illuminating Richardson criticism is largely dismissive of Richardson himself; instead, it is standard practice to give a quick pat on the head to one version or another of Coleridge's 'oozy ... praise-mad, canting' prig before getting down to the serious analysis of what he failed to see he meant. A commonplace of humanist criticism is the distinction between 'Richardson' the pioneering artist and 'Mr Richardson' the London merchant – a distinction first developed by Mark Kinkead-

---

[161] See *Anima Poetae*, ed. Ernest Hartley Coleridge (1895), p. 166.

Weekes to express his sense of a man whose 'deepest moral convictions run clean counter to the drama that gives his fiction its most vivid life'.[162] From a psychoanalytic perspective, Morris Golden finds the novels still more at odds with their superficial manifesto, and attributes the gap to a conflict between conscious ideologue and unconscious fantasist within the author's mind: 'despite his reputation as a conventional moralist', Golden writes, '... the persistent reader feels that conventional morality is irrelevant to Richardson's achievement.'[163] And in recent years poststructuralism, most relevantly for the matter to hand, has affirmed the inherent unruliness of each text in the face of didactic control. Terry Castle, for example, brilliantly describes the relation between the adversarial structure of *Clarissa*'s narrative and the intensification of the reader's role demanded by it, but discounts Richardson's own contribution to the process: 'Though committed ostensibly to "Instruction" – an ideal transfer of meaning from author to reader – Richardson chose in *Clarissa* the form least suited to didactic ultimatum. Authorial "Instruction" cannot coexist happily with readerly "construction" – yet it is this last operation that the multiple-correspondent epistolary novel requires.' Earlier she writes that he 'does not seem to have intended or foreseen this "birth" of the reader – the very liberation his choice of form entails. Indeed, every claim he made for his "History" during and after its first publication suggests just the opposite: that he assumed it remained within the power of the epistolary novelist to pursue a great "end" – the moral indoctrination of the reader.'[164]

Not only a slave to the debilitating aesthetic of the sugared pill, Richardson would appear to have been its most incompetent practitioner as well: wherever we stand, we seem to see not what the author would have us see but a proliferation of subversive meanings – whether from the triumph of the creative imagination, the deepest wells of the unconscious or the lawless plurality of language being the only matter in question. And at first sight there is indeed little room to demur. Only the most short-sighted reader could deny that *Clarissa* is too complex and too fiercely contested in its meanings to make possible the communication of simple didactic messages; while only the most short-sighted scholar could deny the strength of Richardson's commitment to instruction as a final goal. He was, as Eagleton writes in his trenchant (and refreshingly unpatronising) discussion of Richardson's purposes, 'a properly didactic, propagandist writer';[165] and he gave voice to the social, moral and religious concerns of his City milieu too insistently to leave the matter in any doubt. The writer of *Clarissa* was also the writer of *The Apprentice's Vade Mecum*, 'the first

[162] *Samuel Richardson*, p. 453; see also p. 456.
[163] *Richardson's Characters* (Ann Arbor, 1963), p. 192.
[164] *Clarissa's Ciphers*, pp. 172, 170.   [165] *Rape of Clarissa*, p. 24.

English novelist' also the ninety-eighth Master of the Worshipful Company of Stationers; and his writings, without exception, are enmeshed in the political and rhetorical contexts suggested by these facts. He took to his pen with the largest expectations, setting out to reform his readers in the most ambitious of ways. 'Rather instruct, than divert or amuse' reads a motto in his manuscript *Hints of Prefaces*:[166] as he always insisted, his novels were aimed not at the entertainment of his readership but at its education. He expected his writings to exert discernible influence on the mind, heart and life of each individual reader, and through an accumulation of such effects to contribute in the end towards securing what he anxiously called 'the Bonds of Human Society'.[167]

These intentions and priorities on Richardson's part are unmistakable (and, it might be added, more interesting in themselves than is very often supposed). Whether he set about fulfilling them with either the innocence or the dogmatism that is usually assumed, however, is less clear. One might expect that such ambitious and complicated designs on the reader as those to which he was committed would give rise to texts themselves more ambitious and complicated than the banal receptacles of moral imperatives that he is so often taken to have intended. Yet such attempts as have been made to reconstruct Richardson's theory of fiction in more sympathetic terms and prove it adequate to the novels themselves tend only to support the theories of unconscious achievement they explicitly contest. The most systematic example, and also the most bathetic, is Donald Ball's *Samuel Richardson's Theory of Fiction*, where Richardson is credited with a project of just the sort which (as Castle shows) could only be subverted by the nature of the texts themselves. In Ball's view, Richardson's epistolary form is designed simply to provide 'a sense of the present unobtainable in narrative writing', enabling him to bring the reader into immediate and unproblematic contact with a story that is itself entirely lucid and unequivocal in its offer to the reader of examples to be adopted, warnings to be heeded, and edifying morals to be drawn. Vivid representation and romantic interest work in combination 'to attract the reader's attention and direct it to useful goals':[168] the reader, in effect, is to be kept sitting still by the entertainment value of the novels while the good author slyly injects him with regular doses of edification. No account is taken of the fiction's inherent resistance to the simplicity of didactic messages, and no satisfactory explanation of the all-important relation between narrative method and moral purpose is found. Far from explaining our experience of intricate novels in terms of a comparably intricate strategy of education on the part of their author, Ball's version of Richardson's theory simply ignores the complexities of his actual perform-

---

[166] *Hints of Prefaces*, p. 6.   [167] *The Apprentice's Vade Mecum* (1734), p. 83.
[168] Donald L. Ball, *Samuel Richardson's Theory of Fiction* (The Hague, 1971), pp. 29, 56.

ance, thereby leaving the Richardson/Mr Richardson dichotomy apparently as necessary as ever.

Where Richardson's theory seems least adequate to his practice, however, it is worth at least questioning our understanding of that theory – an understanding that has foundered, in this case and others, on the poverty of available sources. For there is, despite Richardson's notorious prolixity, surprisingly little reliable evidence to go on. The prefaces are short, formulaic and derivative; the letters, though substantially devoted to the novels, focus mainly on details within them, rarely generalising from the particular; and the novels themselves make few forays into the realm of narrative theory. All these sources, furthermore, are complicated by contexts that to a great extent deny them the status of objective statement. Passages within the novels themselves present the most obvious case. As Richardson made clear when dissociating himself from the tone and attitude with which Lovelace reports the fire-scene, he kept too strictly to his narrative method of '*personating* (in order to describe the more naturally)' for us to be able to attribute any passage to anyone except the personated narrator in question.[169] Indeed, when abstracting from the novels *A Collection of . . . Moral and Instructive Sentiments* he explicitly noted as a result of his ventriloquising method the novels' resistance to the requirements of a wisdom manual, and took particular pains to prevent readers confusing his characters' opinions with his own: as he told Thomas Edwards, 'many of ye Sentiments are Characteristical; & . . . wou'd have sounded strange, laid down, or propos'd, for general Imitation, as from a moral Writer'.[170] Elsewhere he writes, 'It is not fair to say – I, identically I, am any-where, while I keep within the character.'[171] The lesson is clear. If (to return to an example cited above) Clarissa or Lovelace defines letters as straightforward reports of the heart, the definition can be interpreted in a number of ways (most obviously as evidence of Clarissa's vulnerability to, or Lovelace's expertise in, writing *not* from the heart). What it cannot be taken for is a reliable statement of Richardson's own position.

The prefaces pose greater problems still. In the first place, one can hardly expect a writer whose consistent method most centrally involves the absence of any authorial voice, and at least the pretence of being merely the editor or printer of 'found' works, to open each text with a comprehensive explication of his aesthetic as a novelist. Unfortunately for our purposes, but understandably for his, Richardson never does. Of course, the prefaces do make a number of general pronouncements about

---

[169] *Answer to the Letter of a Very Reverend and Worthy Gentleman* (1749), reprinted in T. C. D. Eaves and B. D. Kimpel, 'An Unpublished Pamphlet by Samuel Richardson', *Philological Quarterly*, 63 (1984), 404.

[170] August 1755, FM XII, 1, f.145.

[171] To Lady Bradshaigh, 14 February 1754, Carroll, p. 286.

the novels, many of which show little enough sensitivity to the distinctive potentialities of the genre. One of *Pamela*'s claims to discover 'under the modest Disguise of a *Novel*, all the *Soul* of Religion, Good-breeding, Discretion, Good-nature, Wit, Fancy, Fine Thought, and Morality'; one of *Clarissa*'s offers its reader an unenticing choice in the pages to follow between '*Directions for his Conduct*, or *Employment for his Pity*'; while before *Sentiments* we learn, more dishearteningly still, that 'under the gay air, and captivating semblance of a *Novel*' the author has tempted the public 'to the perusal of many a persuasive *Sermon*'.[172] Yet these sources too must be handled with care. In the first place, they represent precisely the blend of apology and justification that had to be (and was) concocted by almost any author who had turned to what in contemporary eyes was a low and suspect genre: they are so conventional, in fact, as to be almost without meaning. More important, Richardson himself wrote none of them: the first was written by Aaron Hill, the second by William Warburton, and the third by Benjamin Kennicott. Richardson went to great lengths to avoid writing prefaces, and when he did write his own he drew heavily on other sources: his manuscript *Hints of Prefaces* for the 1751 *Clarissa*, for example, shows his laborious efforts to patch together passages from Warburton, Joseph Spence, Philip Skelton, and his own correspondence with Lady Bradshaigh.[173] At about the same time he asked David Graham, a young Cambridge scholar he knew only on the evidence of a single letter, to do the job for him and write a replacement for all the novel's existing prefaces – which, he said, were 'temporary only'. 'But of all the Species of Writing, I love not Preface-Writing', he confesses.[174]

One might suspect as the cause of this dislike an inability on Richardson's part to consider theoretical questions about the structure and rhetoric of his fiction, or at least the lack of any language in which to do so. It is certainly the case that existing criticism was ill equipped to tackle the 'new Species of Writing' that he claimed to have introduced: as one reader pointed out, 'Your Plan is new, entirely your own, not thought of by the Antients, not treated of by Aristotle; so that I know not by what Rules we shall go about to judge you.'[175] Yet if contemporary readers and critics felt themselves bereft of theoretical scaffolding, Richardson's own many coinages ('Writing – to the Moment', 'personating', 'narratist', 'respondent' and 'Characteristical' have already been quoted) show his own single-handed development of precisely the sort of concepts and terms that were needed. His failure to extend this innovative critical language in prefaces

---

172 *Pamela*, p. 9; *Clarissa*, III, vi (sometimes IV, vi: not in Ross); *Sentiments*, pp. vi–vii.
173 See *Hints of Prefaces*, pp. 1–14.
174 To David Graham, 3 May 1750, Carroll, p. 159.
175 John Read to Richardson, 5 December 1748, FM XV, 2, f.28. For Richardson's use of the term 'new Species of Writing' see Carroll, pp. 76, 78.

to the novels probably has more to do with the limited function a preface was expected to perform than with Richardson's own aptitude for the task. 'I am not resolved whether a Preface should be put to it at all. If there were, it should be but a Page or two, apprizing the Reader of the Diffusiveness of the Piece, and pretending to nothing but Simplicity and Nature, in Characters New and Uncommon', he airily writes to Aaron Hill a year before *Clarissa*'s publication.[176] In contemporary conditions a preface's role was not to muse on formal and moral complexity in the manner of Henry James but to offer the reader a succinct, defensive justification for resorting to the genre at all, before propelling him as soon as possible into the text itself – a task his brief prefaces to *Clarissa* and *Grandison* admirably perform.

The correspondence presents perhaps the most difficult area of all. It runs to thousands of pages and deals extensively with literary matters; yet Richardson's presence within it is in many ways as evasive as in the novels themselves. His epistolary voice is strangely chameleon-like, adapted always to the particular context of each exchange. Often he clearly plays devil's advocate, shifting his position from one letter to the next, and his arguments as well as his tone vary markedly according to the character and status of each recipient. As a result, our sense of his attitudes is determined by the fact that a large proportion of his surviving letters were written to women considerably younger than himself, to whom his approach is at once inhibited and patronising. It is to these letters, and in particular to the undue prominence given them by Anna Lætitia Barbauld in her 1804 edition of Richardson's *Correspondence*, that his reputation for fatuous and condescending authoritarianism is largely owing. Had he corresponded more extensively with Fielding (or had the correspondence survived),[177] we should doubtless have a different view of his thinking; as it is, his occasional letters to such other writers as Sarah Fielding and Edward Moore greatly complicate the usual picture. It seems, however, that even with contacts such as these Richardson may well have felt that he had no intimates fully capable of understanding his purposes and methods. When Aaron Hill's attempted abridgment of *Clarissa* at the turn of 1746–7 finally brought home to him the resolute impercipience of his principal literary consultant, he suspended the correspondence, and later wished that he 'had never consulted any body but Dr. Young'.[178] Yet the Young correspondence is considerably more formal,

[176] To Aaron Hill, 5 January 1746/7, Carroll, pp. 77–8.
[177] Despite the *Pamela* quarrel and an evident resurgence of ill-feeling in the early 1750s, the two were close enough in 1748 for Richardson to send Fielding, at least two months before publication, the fifth volume of *Clarissa*. Fielding's glowing response of 15 October is all that survives; there must have been more.
[178] See T. C. D. Eaves and B. D. Kimpel, 'The Composition of *Clarissa* and Its Revision before Publication', *PMLA*, 83 (1968), 425.

reticent and undetailed than that with Hill, the result being that there
remains almost no significant evidence of Richardson's thinking about
Clarissa in the crucial last year before publication began.

Thus the reasons for hesitating before attributing to Richardson any
particular and firmly held theory of fiction are almost overwhelming.
Confronted by his usual paradoxical combination of prolixity and evasiveness, we are thrown back, in great measure, on inference. But to
suppose a radical discontinuity between purpose and practice is by no
means the only inference available, nor even the most plausible. Indeed,
there is much in the letters to suggest that the characteristic difficulty and
complexity of Richardson's narrative method, far from subverting his
didactic project, may be directly attributed to it – may, in fact, be credited
as its primary enabling means. On this matter, his very reluctance to
explain is itself a revealing habit. Typically, each letter takes issue with
views expressed in the letter to which it replies, but rarely in a dictatorial
way: instead it challenges the reader's opinion, puts questions, and above
all sends him back to re-examine the text. It is geared not to explanation
but to interrogation, and rather than correcting readers it invites them to
correct themselves – an extreme case occurring when, having received
from one woman a letter accusing Clarissa of coquetry and from another a
letter accusing her of prudery, Richardson declined to write any direct
answer to either and chose instead 'to send each the other's letter for a full
answer of her's'.[179] This addiction to the question-mark certainly frus-
trates efforts to collate from the letters a stated theory of fiction, but it does
usefully demonstrate a procedure common also to the novels, in which the
reader is offered no definitive answers and is instead required to confront
problems and resolve ambiguities himself. 'I must question your attention'
and 'Be pleased to reperuse' are two of the letters' most characteristic
phrases: they take up where the fiction ends, continuing its insistence on
the reader's own final responsibility for the production of textual meaning.

At such points, where Richardson's concern is not to spell out for his
readers a single and definitive reading of the text but instead to enhance
still further the text's capacity to put them on their mettle and make them
work, his much-derided didacticism takes on a very different aspect. It
becomes possible to see in his writing forms of 'authorial instruction' that
could not only coexist with, but could actually require, 'readerly construction' of very much the kind that Castle describes; it becomes possible to
see, in fact, that on the all-important question of the reader's role the
aesthetic of the novelist and the strategy of the didact were to a great
extent one and the same. For Richardson was not simply the blinkered
dogmatist of modern caricature, and indeed knew well enough (if only

---

[179] Richardson to Lady Bradshaigh, [February–March 1751], Barbauld, VI, 82.

from the study he made of Locke's *Some Thoughts Concerning Education* in writing *Pamela II*) that a successful teacher will not be 'dogmatical, positive, or overbearing'.[180] It is entirely in keeping with this recognition, and with Locke's more general insistence on the need to enlist the active co-operation of the pupil, that his approach in the novels should be to withhold the simplicity of didactic imperatives and refuse to dictate a series of straightforward, uncontested meanings. His aesthetic is above all an aesthetic of difficulty, in which 'dogmatical, positive, or overbearing' techniques of authorial explication have little or no part. Complexity and openness take the place of simplicity and closure; and while this refusal on Richardson's part to reduce, clarify or explain the intricate matter of his fiction does indeed frustrate banal attempts at indoctrination and control of the kind with which he is usually associated, it also opens the way to far more subtle and dynamic processes of education – processes arising not from authorial insistence, but from the very considerable activities and efforts demanded of the reader by virtue of its very absence.

That Richardson consciously saw the experience of reading as most beneficial when most exacting, and that he attached special value to forms of literature which cast the reader as much more than a passive recipient of meaning, begins to emerge in a number of letters written to Aaron Hill as the publication of *Clarissa* neared completion. In them he discusses not his own work but Hill's; of greatest interest, however, are his accompanying remarks on Milton, Pope, and the different approaches adopted by each towards their respective audiences. Having first praised the effect of the *Spectator* on public taste (an allusion, seemingly, to Addison's popularisation of Milton), one of these letters goes on to lament the 'Stupidity' into which readers had subsequently fallen. Readers should 'exert themselves', Richardson writes, yet 'Indolence' was now the rule; and matters had only been made worse by the readiness of Pope to acquiesce in these conditions. By accompanying his poetry with obtrusive authorial directions as to how it should be understood, Pope had left his readers with little or nothing to do. He 'could not trust his Works with the Vulgar', Richardson sardonically complains, 'without Notes longer than the Work . . . to tell them what he meant, and that he *had* a Meaning, in this or that Place. And thus every-one was taught to read with his Eyes.'[181] By contrast, Milton's refusal to make this easy offer of authorial 'Eyes' provided what for Richardson was clearly a healthier alternative, albeit one to which modern readers of both Milton and also Milton's followers like Hill himself were ill disposed to rise. In an earlier letter he tactfully explains the sinking of Hill's own work by analogy with *Paradise Lost*, a poem that resists easy understanding and demands from the reader a correspondingly

---

[180] *Sentiments*, p. 26.   [181] To Hill, 7 November 1748, Carroll, p. 100.

more strenuous involvement: 'Your writings require thought to read, and to take in their whole force; and the world has no thought to bestow. Simplicity is all their cry ... They may see a thousand beauties obvious to the eye; but if there lie jewels in the mine that require labour to come at, they will not dig.'[182] The emphasis, significantly, is on the efforts of discovery required to read difficult poetry, in contrast to the superficial pleasures connived in by Hill's old adversary. 'I do not think', he concludes, 'that were Milton's Paradise Lost to be now published as a new work, it would be well received.'[183]

What Richardson admired in *Paradise Lost* he practised in *Clarissa*. If the two have a resemblance (and the analogy, explicitly invited within the novel, has been a commonplace of criticism since Sarah Fielding's *Remarks*),[184] it lies above all in the demands they make on their reader. Those made by the earlier text, and their centrality to the homiletic project of its author, have been fully documented. As Stanley Fish has shown in his classic study *Surprised by Sin*, Milton drew in the poem on 'a tradition of didacticism which finds its expression in a distrust of the affective and an insistence on the intellectual involvement of the listener-pupil'; he thereby contrived for the reader 'a dialectical experience which has the advantage traditionally claimed for dialectic of involving the respondent in his own edification'. It is not by authorial precept but by the complexity of the reading experience itself that the poem instructs, Fish suggests – an experience in which the reader is brought up against a variety of difficulties, intellectual, moral and spiritual, and forced to

---

[182] To Hill, 27 October 1748, Barbauld, I, 120. It is worth noting that in a recent attempt to rehabilitate Hill's religious and descriptive poetry, Harriet Guest has explained its lack of contemporary success in very similar terms. Contrasting Hill's *Creation* with Pope's *Essay on Man*, Guest describes a poet whose recognition of the flawed and limited nature of human perspectives and perceptions leads him to eschew the clarity, assurance and authority of the Popean couplet. His poetry is cast instead in a Miltonic blank verse of peculiar opacity, which in its account of the created world works to involve the reader in kinds of difficulty and confusion more in keeping with his own view of the human condition as one at best of 'reverent uncertainty': see Guest, *A Form of Sound Words: The Religious Poetry of Christopher Smart* (Oxford, 1989), pp. 27–33.

[183] To Hill, 27 October 1748, Barbauld, I, 120. Richardson may be recalling Jonathan Richardson's *Explanatory Notes and Remarks on Milton's Paradise Lost* (1734), pp. cxliv–cxlv, which stresses the rewarding difficulty of the verse with the same emphasis on the reader's involvement, and the same imagery of effort and excavation: 'a Reader of *Milton* must be Always upon Duty ... There are no Lazy Intervals, All has been Consider'd, and Demands, and Merits Observation ... whoever will Possess His Ideas must Dig for them, and Oftentimes pretty far below the Surface. if This is call'd Obscurity let it be remembered 'tis Such a One as is Complaisant to the Reader, not Mistrusting his Ability, Care, Diligence, or the Candidness of his Temper' (pp. cxliv–cxlv, partly quoted in Stanley Fish, *Surprised by Sin: The Reader in Paradise Lost* (1967), p. 54).

[184] Milton's pervasive and complex presence in Richardson awaits full investigation, but a good starting point is provided by Gillian Beer, 'Richardson, Milton, and the Status of Evil', *Review of English Studies*, NS 19, No. 75 (1968), 261–70. See also Dustin Griffin, *Regaining Paradise: Milton and the Eighteenth Century* (Cambridge, 1986), pp. 129–32.

examine his own performance in encountering them. The poem becomes (in a phrase of Milton's own) 'not so much a teaching, as an intangling'; and in its manner of entangling it brings the reader to full awareness of the facts of the Fall, of his own complicity in it, and of his own resulting weakness and liability to error.[185]

At first sight, of course, Milton's public epic and Richardson's domestic history suggest very different preoccupations on their authors' part. Yet the Fall and its effects were at the very heart of Richardson's concerns as well, and not only at the level of a plot which overtly recapitulates Milton's subject in its account of Clarissa's fall from the Harlowe garden and her subsequent recovery, at death, of a paradise within.[186] Where Milton set out to document and account for the fallen state of the world, Richardson's ambition (rooted, as Jocelyn Harris has suggested, in seventeenth-century millennial thought) was 'to contribute, though but by his mite, to mend it'.[187] And where Milton sought (in Fish's words) to teach 'the hardest of all lessons, distrust of our own abilities and perceptions', Richardson too addressed himself to these same fallen faculties, seeking their partial repair: his novels were to 'inform the judgment' as the romances they replaced had failed to do, or again to 'inform the Understanding'.[188]

It is in this context that Fish's account of *Paradise Lost* is so very suggestive for *Clarissa*, above all in its analysis of Milton's methods of trying and testing his reader. Like Milton, Richardson had designs on the reader which must indeed be called didactic, but which involved processes very much more complex than those normally understood by the term; and like Milton he enlisted the reader's active participation to fulfil them. In further detail his strategies are quite different, but the underlying similarity remains – a similarity admirably suggested in Johannes Stinstra's description to Richardson of the novels as 'mazes and labyrinths, which perplex your common readers'.[189] His method in *Clarissa*, far more than is usually supposed, is to make reading not simple but problematic; and his expectation is that the reader's activity in addressing the resulting difficulties will itself be a source of instruction. If the novel really is to enhance his competence in concerns the title-page calls '*The most* Important ... *of* Private LIFE', after all, it is not enough merely to give lectures on the difficulties and dangers of the world, in the manner of a conduct book: versions of these same difficulties and dangers must be epitomised, and actually experienced, in the very business of reading. Again, if the novel is

---

[185] Fish, *Surprised by Sin*, pp. 7n., 49, 21.   [186] See below, pp. 111–14, 208–9.

[187] Jocelyn Harris, *Samuel Richardson* (Cambridge, 1987), pp. 1–2; Richardson to J. B. de Freval, 21 January 1751, Carroll, p. 175.

[188] Fish, *Surprised by Sin*, p. 22; *Sentiments*, p. 70; *Hints of Prefaces*, p. 8.

[189] Stinstra to Richardson, 24 December 1753, Slattery, p. 63.

indeed to inform the judgment and the understanding, as Richardson expected, it can do so most effectively to the extent that it first taxes them. Accordingly, *Clarissa* comprises (as the postscript explains) 'a variety of incidents sufficient to excite Attention, and those so conducted as to keep the Reader always awake' (VII, 432; p. 1499); and in the attentiveness and wakefulness thereby cultivated it will equip him for his life in the world. Its usefulness will derive not from any bare message but from the process of striving for it, a process which demands from the reader the most strenuous efforts of interpretation and adjudication, of mind and moral sense – a process which demands, in effect, that he educate himself.

Interestingly, Richardson has left several demonstrations of how his ideal reader (the 'attentive reader' to whom he often alludes in footnotes and letters) might cope with the characteristic difficulties of his work. A simple example comes in *Clarissa*'s concluding letter (a report of Lovelace's duel with Morden by the servant De la Tour), to which he provided an elaborate gloss in response to Edward Moore's expression of regret that he had not been 'a little more minute about the Death of Lovelace'. The ending, for Moore, was too opaque and ambiguous, and represented a failure on Richardson's part to seal the novel in morally absolute terms. 'The triumphant Death of Clarissa needed a more particular Contrast here than in the Deaths of Belton and Sinclair', he wrote, suggesting that this more explicit (and hence instructive) contrast might more effectively have been enforced from the pen of a narrator better placed than a mere servant to give an intimate, detailed account of Lovelace's death and (in particular) remorse. 'He should have given Belford an account of his own Remorses after the Duel; or if that had been improper (wounded as he was), Morden might have visited him privately, and have written the Account himself – In short, any one might have done it but a Servant.'[190]

The offending letter itself is at first sight one of the novel's most straightforward, as though Richardson had indeed sought to rid his closing pages of narrative complication and make his message clear: the relative detachment of the narrator (a travelling valet engaged by Lovelace only weeks earlier) removes the usual motives for misrepresentation, and seems to promise, at last, a genuine objectivity. His complete ignorance of the reason for Lovelace's tour (even Clarissa's name means nothing to him) and his occasional baffled resort to a vocabulary of supposition and seeming perhaps suggest that he may not be fully competent to digest and explain the material he conveys; but such deficiencies can easily be remedied by the knowing reader, or so one would assume. In the reading Richardson now expounds, however, there begins to emerge a hidden subtext to the letter. First considering the possibility of using another

---

[190] Moore to Richardson, 23 December 1748, FM XV, 2, f.20.

narrator, he systematically rules out all available alternatives, incidentally noting how the report might vary from writer to writer. The duellists themselves he discounts primarily on grounds of plausibility; 'Mowbray wd. have given a Brutal or Farcical acct.'; Tourville would have been too partial in Lovelace's favour. De la Tour, in consequence, is the only option; but his narrative too has its own predispositions, and must be read with care. Here, as hitherto, one must keep in mind the rhetorical situation of the narrator, in particular by remembering that De la Tour, as Lovelace's servant, is unlikely to be quite so perfectly impartial as might at first appear. His narrative too will be distorted under the pressures of allegiance, most obviously in the enthusiasm with which he couches praise or blame: 'every praise of Morden from a Servant of Lovelace was praise indeed to Morden', Richardson suggests; 'and every half hint to the disadvantage of Lovelace a whole one'.[191]

Having indicated this basic reading strategy, Richardson then goes on to demonstrate that the narrative does indeed work, as Moore wanted it to work, to Lovelace's detriment, but that it does so with such reticence as to require the reader to complete the process himself. It is 'given in *Character*', he reminds Moore, 'and ... with circumstances of *great Terror*, if duly attended to'.[192] These circumstances, however, are largely obscured by the narrator's mediation of events; Richardson therefore seeks in his analysis to recover them, bringing to the surface various pieces of evidence, skirted or suppressed by De la Tour, which show Lovelace's despairing awareness of his own reprobacy, a corresponding degree of physical suffering, and the likelihood that he was tormented in his dying hours by a remorseful vision of Clarissa. Underlying all these points is his suggestion that the narrator, mindful of his readers (not only Belford but also Lovelace's kin), is deliberately playing down the extent of his master's agony. The letter's most explicit indication that it is marked by such ellipses comes in De la Tour's remark: 'His few last words I must not omit, as they shew an ultimate composure; which may administer some consolation to his honourable friends' (VII, 415; p. 1487). Phrased as it is, the sentence raises the issues of both selection (what, then, *must* De la Tour omit?) and motivation (to what extent might the desire to console displace a desire to transcribe that elusive '*whole* truth'?) Accordingly, Richardson dwells on and seeks to undermine the sentence in question, notably by alleging a basic disparity between telling and showing in 'The *Ultimate Composure* mentioned by De la Tour, rather mentioned to comfort his surviving Friends than appearing to have reason to suppose it to be so, from his subsequent description of his last Agonies'.[193] Richardson's suggestion, in effect, is that narrative evaluation is here grossly misleading,

---

[191] To Moore, [December 1748–January 1749], Carroll, p. 119.   [192] Carroll, p. 120.
[193] Carroll, p. 121.

and that the event described can only be assumed to have been greatly at odds with De la Tour's explanation of it. Lovelace's last words in fact give the lie to 'ultimate composure', and reveal in his death a horror all the more chilling for the narrator's failure to see it; and in this way the report presents a more striking contrast to Clarissa's death even than the violent and distracted ends to which, ever the melodramatist, Moore had wished it to conform. For Richardson, it could achieve its unique effects only by implication; and the imaginative process by which the reader might resolve the odds between event and explanation was itself of great importance. By these standards the letter could not be replaced by a more authoritative, clarifying account, and in subsequent editions it survived largely unchanged. Room remained for Moore's misreading; room too for an unsettling sense of simultaneous distance and immediacy, of the horror of a death that cannot quite be fathomed and becomes all the more disquieting for the mundane particularity and the pedantic impercipience of its report.

It might of course be objected that Richardson's response to Moore's complaint begs as many questions as it answers – in particular the question of how, given the insufficiency of the narrative itself, any one conjectural reading constructed from it can claim to be definitive, or any more legitimately restorative than the next. Richardson himself, in fact, is ready to jest about the indeterminacy of De la Tour's report, for example in the slightly gothic business of Lovelace's vision (seemingly, but only seemingly, of Clarissa): 'I leave it to the Reader to suppose it the ghost of Miss Betterton, of his French Countess, or of whom he pleases, or to attribute it to his delirium', he teases Moore.[194] But his playful tolerance of interpretative variety in this trivial (and uncontentious) case does little to contain a larger problem posed by the relatively determinate expectations he elsewhere maintains about the proper response to De la Tour's unreliable narrative. By vesting with the reader responsibility for the construction of meaning while also retaining certain (albeit flexible) intentions about the meanings to be thus constructed, Richardson treads a precarious path; for in the act of reading, dutiful recovery can easily drift towards unlicensed invention, responsible liberty towards wilful autonomy. Here Richardson's reliance on the reader's co-operative role stops short of the happy intimation of poststructuralist theories of reading one might be tempted to detect, for he was rarely prepared to embrace to the full any notion of interpretative free play: there is always, if not a single 'correct' interpretation at which the reader is expected to arrive, then at most a limited range of possible responses within which he is to remain confined. Richardson seems, indeed, to envisage a hypothetical reader of very much the kind

---

[194] Carroll, p. 121.

posited in the reception aesthetics of Wolfgang Iser (a theorist much indebted to Richardson's contemporaries, it is worth noting, for his basic arguments, his supporting examples, and many of his theory's most successful practical applications).[195] The reader Richardson seeks, when in his most prescriptive moods, is no free agent but rather a careful subordinate prepared to work his way obediently through the text, filling in its gaps and indeterminacies in response to the text's internal signals and thereby realising a set of meanings which in the last resort remains authorially governed. Yet such ideal processes as this (as Iser's critics themselves have pointed out)[196] are subject to inevitable interference. The many different experiences, mentalities, predispositions and idiosyncrasies of individual readers in the world can only lead them away from the route of the ideal 'attentive' reader. Once Richardson moves from the explicit to the implicit, in consequence, and in his own words 'leave[s] it to the Reader to suppose [what] he pleases', he opens the way to an unruly plurality of conflicting interpretations.

The objections of poststructuralist critics, then, retain an undeniable force, and it would be futile to attempt a complete reconciliation between Richardson's own ideal of 'attentive' reading and theories of textuality in which meaning is relocated in the reader alone. There can, nonetheless, be little doubt about the centrality of textual indeterminacy and readerly creativity to his project for the reader's education. His last novel, *Sir Charles Grandison*, gives the method its freest rein. Here, in a narrative geared to register the subtlest resonances of human interaction on the finely tuned sensibilities of its principals, his interests do indeed move in discernibly Jamesian directions; and it was above all in what he called *Grandison*'s 'delicate' (as opposed to *Clarissa*'s 'critical') situations that he was prepared to show his readers a degree of licence impossible to square with any picture of unyielding didactic control. At the same time he gave, in a remarkable series of letters to Lady Bradshaigh (by 1753–4 perhaps the closest epistolary confidante he had ever had), an account of his purposes and methods which must rank as the most original, intimate and detailed to have survived from his pen. Indeed, there is good evidence that he himself saw this correspondence as the nearest existing approach to the

---

[195] See Iser's most concise and influential theoretical statement, 'Indeterminacy and the Reader's Response in Prose Fiction', in *Aspects of Narrative*, ed. J. Hillis Miller (New York, 1971), pp. 1–45; reprinted in *Prospecting: From Reader Response to Literary Anthropology* (Baltimore, 1989), pp. 3–30. Both Fielding and Sterne are regularly cited in this essay, as they are in his fuller theoretical work *The Act of Reading* (Baltimore, 1978). See also his related readings of Fielding and Smollett in *The Implied Reader: Patterns of Communication in Prose Fiction from Bunyan to Beckett* (Baltimore, 1974), and his reading of Sterne in *Laurence Sterne: Tristram Shandy* (Cambridge, 1988).

[196] See, in particular, Fish's review of *The Act of Reading*, 'Why No One's Afraid of Wolfgang Iser', *Diacritics*, 11 (1981), 2–13; reprinted in *Doing What Comes Naturally: Change, Rhetoric, and the Practice of Theory in Literary and Legal Studies* (Oxford, 1989), pp. 68–86.

definitive statement on the novels he hoped, late in life, to leave behind: in a letter of 1757 he quotes one reader's remark that 'it wd. make the best Commentary that cd. be written on the History of Clarissa', and diffidently asks Lady Bradshaigh 'whether a Critique on these Pieces [i.e. *Clarissa* and *Grandison*] might not be contracted *anonymously* from our Correspondence, if it wd. make yr. Ladiship easier'.[197] (Presumably the promise of anonymity failed to make her easier, for she seems to have ignored the suggestion.)

Constraints of space forbid a full analysis here of the intricate series of cruxes and dilemmas which, in the novel in question, Richardson requires his characters and readers to negotiate. Something of *Grandison*'s complexity can be seen from Sylvia Kasey Marks's *Sir Charles Grandison: The Compleat Conduct Book*, to date the only published monograph to focus exclusively on the novel.[198] However, Marks's anxiety to place *Grandison* in the tradition of the prescriptive conduct book (as opposed to the closely related yet far more flexible and exploratory tradition of casuistry) leads her to neglect the profound ethical indeterminacy of the novel, in which characters are presented not as perfect exemplars of right conduct but rather as anxious analysts of their own vexed situations – situations that can never be reduced to black and white, and consistently fail to yield a set of unequivocal imperatives to be obeyed. It was this more problematic dimension that Richardson himself chose to stress in his letters about the novel, to other readers as well as to Lady Bradshaigh: 'the whole piece abounds, and was intended to abound, with situations that should give occasion for debate, or different ways of thinking', he wrote to Hester Mulso. 'And it is but fair that every one should choose his or her party.'[199] In such passages his commitment to the interpretative liberty of the reader is unmistakable. Far from seeking to impose a particular response or judgment, he presents himself as a writer who leaves such matters open, as though it is through the mental exercise of reading and debate that the reader will best learn, and not through any passive reception of simple detachable lessons.

Similar emphases are more fully made in the Bradshaigh correspondence itself, where Richardson's explanations hover intriguingly between ideas of control and release. He continues to protest impatiently that his readers are guilty of 'inattention'; that they are 'not enough used to this way of writing, to the moment' to read it competently; that they neglect a basic principle of interpretation, 'that in the minutiae lie often the unfoldings of the Story, as well as of the heart'; and that, above all, they will read

---

[197] To Lady Bradshaigh, 19 November 1757, Carroll, pp. 336, 337.
[198] Sylvia Kasey Marks, *Sir Charles Grandison: The Compleat Conduct Book* (Lewisburg, 1986). See also Jocelyn Harris's detailed account of the novel and its surrounding debates, '*Sir Charles Grandison* and the Little Senate: The Relation between Samuel Richardson's Correspondence and His Last Novel' (diss., London, 1968).
[199] To Hester Mulso, 21 August 1754, Carroll, p. 311.

only *once*.[200] At the same time, however, he also stresses the value of
openness and authorial silence, characteristics that foster each reader's
vicarious entanglement in the ethical entanglements of the characters, so
that the novel becomes a kind of interpretative assault-course on which to
practise before returning, newly equipped, to the fray of life. In contriving
the novel's dilemmas he has left it, he says, 'to my Sovereign Judges the
Readers, to agree as well as they can, which to blame, which to acquit'.
Having done so, moreover, he not only expects but welcomes an intelligent
diversity of response: 'Thank Heaven, I find not often two of the same
Mind, in relation to the more delicate Circumstances', he goes on.[201] And
in perhaps the most striking passage of all he explicitly confers on the
reader at least part of the authorial prerogative: 'Something also must be
left to the Reader to make out', he explains, before returning again to the
theme:

> The undecided Events are sufficiently pointed out to the Reader, to whom, in this
> Sort of Writing, something, as I have hinted, should be left to make out or debate
> upon. The whole Story abounds with Situations and Circumstances debatable. It
> is not an unartful Management to interest the Readers so much in the Story, as to
> make them differ in Opinion as to the Capital Articles, and by Leading one, to
> espouse one, another, another, Opinion, make them all, if not Authors, Car-
> vers.[202]

A 'Carver' is one who carves, or figuratively 'he that chooses for himself'[203] – exactly the operation Richardson is so often thought, in his
intention at least, to have denied.

Even here, of course, there survives a considerable sense of authorial
control, while a residual expectation that the free interpretative choices
made by readers will nonetheless coincide with specific interpretations
favoured by the author himself can occasionally be seen to resurface.
When Richardson talks, for example, of having 'play'd the Rogue with my
Readers; intending to make them think now one way, now another, of the
very same Characters',[204] he is not authorising them to judge at whim, but
asking them instead to participate in a determinate, though complex and
variable, sequence of prestructured responses. Yet there remains, for all
that, a consistent recognition in *Grandison* itself and in Richardson's

---

200 To Lady Bradshaigh, 14 February 1754, Carroll, p. 289.
201 To Lady Bradshaigh, 8 February 1754, Carroll, p. 280.
202 To Lady Bradshaigh, 25 February 1754, FM XI, f.87. Carroll, p. 296, suggests 'Carpers'. The
   MS, however, clearly reads 'Carvers', an archaism in the eighteenth century but frequent in
   seventeenth-century writers such as Joseph Hall (whose casuistry Richardson knew). See
   Hall, *Resolutions and Decisions of Divers Practicall Cases of Conscience* (1649), p. 375, and *The
   Remedy of Discontentment* (1652), p. 39; also Elizabeth Bergen Brophy, 'A Richardson Letter:
   "Carpers" or "Carvers"?', *Notes & Queries*, NS 25 (1978), 44–5.
203 Johnson, *Dictionary*, 'Carver'.
204 To Lady Bradshaigh, 12 November 1753, Carroll, p. 248.

discussions of it that it is neither the author alone nor the reader alone who governs the meaning of the text: the two must participate, jointly and equally, in its construction. By the time of the novel's end, indeed, Richardson had become ready to arrange a strikingly direct enactment of the unusual equality between author and reader everywhere sustained by his narrative method, and left the text quite literally incomplete. Instead of settling the matter of Clementina's marriage, he printed a pamphlet cleverly designed to merge the imaginative world with the real by calculating that the plot comes down to the present time and, instead of ending in 'some great and decisive event', should be thought of as continuing in silent parallel with the reader's own life. As the reader continues to live, he should therefore consider how the novel's protagonists might continue to live, and in particular how Clementina, in response to the conflicting exigencies of sentiment, conscience and duty, might choose between wedlock and the veil. 'Do you think ... I have not been very complaisant to my Readers to leave to them the decision of this important article?', he asks in a pamphlet printed for distribution after publication of the final volume.[205] Such playful gambits are not of course unique. In *Tom Jones* Fielding leaves a lacuna of twelve years, asking the reader to employ his sagacity 'by filling up these vacant Spaces of Time with his own Conjectures'; while in a famous later example Sterne's *Tristram Shandy* leaves the reader a blank page to draw on in place of the description of Widow Wadman he finds himself unable to supply: 'Sit down, Sir', Tristram urges, 'paint her to your own mind –.'[206] In the case of *Grandison*, however, Richardson's own abdication involved the very crisis and climax of what in any event was a far less whimsical text, and his readers could not easily let it pass. They proved reluctant to take up the challenge, however, and continued to press for an additional volume, doubtless hoping for something like the gratifying certainties provided two years later by the author of a narrative redaction of *Grandison* who takes it upon himself to reassure readers that a year later Sir Charles 'had the pleasure to find the Lady *Clementina* perfectly recovered from the disorder of her mind, and to be present at her marriage with the Count of *Belvidere*.[207] Richardson himself was prepared to offer no such satisfaction, however, and in eventual frustration he responded to continuing requests by taking the gesture of making his readers almost authors to its logical extreme, attempting to persuade them not merely to imagine but actually to *write* the continuation. He himself would be the mere co-ordinator of their activities, as he

---

[205] *Copy of a Letter to a Lady, Who Was Solicitous for an Additional Volume to the History of Sir Charles Grandison* (1754), in *Grandison*, III, 470; III, 468.

[206] *Tom Jones*, I, 116; *The Life and Opinions of Tristram Shandy, Gentleman*, ed. Ian Campbell Ross (Oxford, 1983), p. 376.

[207] *The Paths of Virtue Delineated; or, The History in Miniature of the Celebrated Pamela, Clarissa Harlowe, and Sir Charles Grandison* (1756), p. 232.

explains the plan to Lady Bradshaigh: 'It is this: That every one of my Correspondents, at his or her own Choice, assume one of the surviving Characters in the Story, and write in it; and that ... I shall pick and choose, alter, connect, and accommodate, till I have completed from them, the requested Volume.'[208] Lady Bradshaigh was to be Charlotte, Elizabeth Carter Mrs Shirley, Susanna Highmore Harriet, and Hester Mulso (who seems to have done most to scuttle the project) the unlucky Clementina. Had it gone ahead, readers themselves would have collaborated in completing the novel in the most literal imaginable sense: *Sir Charles Grandison*, and the career of its author, could not have reached a more appropriate close.

It is in *Clarissa*, however, where the much higher moral and political stakes of the work inhibited such playful attitudes, that the relations between formal indeterminacy, the reader's role and authorial instruction are at their most critical and vexed. Here the most frequently alleged case in which Richardson fails to control the reception of the novel, thereby jeopardising the simple didactic project he is assumed to have set in train, comes with the depiction of Lovelace, most notably in the prominence the novel gives to Lovelace's narrative. In both *Pamela* and *Grandison*, the libertine protagonists Mr B. and Sir Hargrave exist only in the hostile medium of their intended victims' letters, and as a result they rarely threaten to usurp the reader's sympathies. Lovelace, however, sets against Clarissa's narrative an alternative and more winning account of his own character and actions, and it is largely through this formal difference that he is able (as he notoriously does) to transcend his allotted role as scapegoat and devil. Richardson, as is well known, fought repeated battles against the resulting complications of allegiance in many readers, which he did indeed see, in certain contexts, as a significant threat to his claims for the morality of the novel. Yet it is equally possible to find him defending Lovelace ('Have you read Lovelace's Bad, and not his Good?' he rebukes Moore on one occasion),[209] a fact that says much about the intricacy of his plan. The plan depends, to be sure, on eliciting a series of responses from the reader which will culminate in reprobation; but it also envisages a series complex and flexible enough to leave room as well for a strong initial sympathy. Richardson's 'attentive' reader in the end must condemn Lovelace, and indeed may do so from the very start. But the reader who begins in sympathy and admiration has by no means overturned the novel's moral programme, and in fact can easily be seen as the more ideal participant within it than one for whom condemnation is immediate and easy. After all, a reader who first experiences (and perhaps

[208] To Lady Bradshaigh, 30 May 1754, Carroll, p. 306. A letter by Lady Bradshaigh as Charlotte survives on FM XI, ff. 116–19. See also the account given of the episode by Eaves and Kimpel, *Biography*, pp. 412–13.
[209] To Moore, 3 October 1748, Carroll, p. 89.

embraces) the delusions of attractive evil, only to be required after the rape to conquer his initial response as a matter of deliberate effort, will undergo a form of dramatic instruction unavailable to his more hostile counterpart; and such an experience will hardly fail to encourage within him a heightened awareness not only of the dangers represented in Lovelace but also of his own susceptibility to them. In this respect, the depiction of Lovelace is no simple case in which Richardson's didactic concerns are defeated by conflicting mimetic concerns, or by his scrupulous adherence to the Christian axiom that evil will attract and beguile. It constitutes instead a peculiarly dramatic warning, which works by exposing the reader to literary versions of a danger he may also encounter in the more perilous medium of life itself, leading him to develop, through the process, new capacities of vigilance, resistance and self-consciousness.

Samuel Johnson was one of the first to attribute such power to Richardson's new genre: 'the great Use of Books, is that of participating without Labour or Hazard the Experience of others', he writes in a chapter contributed by him to Lennox's *Female Quixote*, praising Richardson by contrast with the escapist romance of earlier generations.[210] And in his better-known essay on the topic in the *Rambler* he more explicitly links this process of vicarious participation with the Richardsonian novel, a genre he praises for involving the reader in kinds of protected literary experience through which to learn. 'The purpose of these writings is surely not only to show mankind, but to provide that they may be seen hereafter with less hazard', he writes:

to teach the means of avoiding the snares which are laid by Treachery for Innocence, without infusing any wish for that superiority with which the betrayer flatters his vanity; to give the power of counteracting fraud, without the temptation to practise it; to initiate youth by mock encounters in the art of necessary defence, and to increase prudence without impairing virtue.[211]

As well as depicting the world with new fidelity the Richardsonian novel educates its reader the better to live within it, Johnson insists, the 'mock encounters' of reading being of a kind to prepare him for his real encounters beyond. The novel is not just a representation but an experience, his suggestion is; and the experience will fortify.

Clarissa's first instalment offers the reader one very striking 'mock encounter' of this kind, coming at a point where, early in the action, Clarissa and Anna themselves misread Lovelace. While staying at an inn near Harlowe Place, Lovelace finds his attention drawn to the daughter of

---

[210] Charlotte Lennox, *The Female Quixote*, ed. Margaret Dalziel (1970), p. 372. Johnson's authorship of this passage remains conjectural, but the evidence is very strong: see Dalziel's note, pp. 414–15n. For Richardson's own involvement in *The Female Quixote* and the novel's relation to *Clarissa*, see Duncan Isles's appendix to the same edition.

[211] *Rambler*, III, 22–3 (No. 4, 31 March 1750).

the house – 'the only flower of fragrance', he says, 'that has blown in this vicinage for ten years past; or will for ten years to come' (I, 230; p. 162). He decides, however, to leave the girl, whom he calls 'my Rose-bud', be. The letter in which he describes the episode (only his second) reveals an intriguing mixture of motives. He presents his forbearance as a function at once of pride, policy and his adherence to rakish convention: Rosebud's grandmother has pleaded with him to spare her, a gratifying approach he calls 'the right way with me'; his whereabouts might be discovered by the Harlowes, in which case any scandal would offer a handle against him; while he is enjoined by the rake's code 'never to ruin a poor girl, whose simplicity and innocence was all she had to trust to'. Richardson, however, buries these deliberate reasonings (which may in any case be written merely to please or provoke Belford, whose attitudes remain at this stage an unknown quantity) beneath a wash of sentiment. Lovelace rarely anticipates the Man of Feeling, but in this case the dialogue between cynicism and tenderness, for all its irony of tone, is unusually equal. He even makes up his Rosebud's dowry.

After an interval long enough for these details to have been over-shadowed by the increasingly convoluted struggles and debates at Harlowe Place, the episode returns to view in a letter to Clarissa from Anna, who gives a new and far more hostile version of events. Her outraged report, in fact, is at odds with Lovelace's on every point, describing the 'abominable wretch's behaviour and baseness' in the affair (II, 145; p. 284), and alleging in particular his probable seduction of the girl. Clarissa fulminates at his villainy in response; but not for long. Having met Rosebud, Anna is forced in her next letter to acquit Lovelace of her charges, and learns even of his generosity in the matter of Rosebud's dowry. 'Mr. Lovelace comes out with so much advantage from this inquiry', she grudgingly concludes, 'that were there the least room for it, I should suspect the whole to be a plot set on foot to wash a blackmoor white' (II, 151; p. 287).

Where Richardson's own strategies are concerned, there is an important sense in which it is exactly that. At this point in the text not only Clarissa but also many readers begin to see Lovelace as a man of benevolence and decency – led astray by the rakish spirits of youth, perhaps, but essentially good at heart. Only later is the incaution of their responses clearly revealed; but however understandable the mistake is it still brings with it, in the case of each, serious and far-reaching consequences. When Clarissa thinks that Lovelace had seduced Rosebud she refuses to open a letter he has sent her, but when reassured of his innocence and selflessness she decides instead to read it, is drawn again into the clandestine correspon-dence, and thereby takes another fateful step towards her father's garden door. And though the novel's reader runs no such practical danger, he too is at the top of a slippery slope; for the reader who admires Lovelace's generosity and restraint at this point has already started on the course of misreading which brought some, even after the rape, to advocate marriage between Lovelace and Clarissa as the novel's proper conclusion.[212] To do so, obviously enough, was to subvert the novel's moral scheme, which insists in the end on the impossibility of union between its two antagonists. Yet the sense of Lovelace's attractiveness experienced by many readers at this early stage is not in itself illegitimate, unforeseen or at odds with 'attentive' reading. Indeed, the text clearly invites its reader to share Clarissa's perception of Lovelace's seeming benevolence, and thus also to share, in what ultimately will prove an educative way, a part at least of her error. Richardson's comments on the subject betray irritation not at this initial blindness to Lovelace's danger, but at the failure of readers at later points to recognise and correct their error. He designedly left room for them, he told Lady Bradshaigh, to 'find out what was worthy and agreeable in Lovelace', but at the same time he insisted that those who ended by pleading Lovelace's cause had failed to resist this discovery: 'But little did I think at the time that those Qualities (politically rather than from Principle exerted as some of them evidently were, particularly in his Behaviour to his Rosebud) would have given Women of Virtue and Honour such a liking to him.'[213] The episode had offered the reader a kind of temptation, an exemplary 'mock encounter' with evil's allure; and clearly some, rather than returning to examine their own initial unguardedness, had instead become too wedded to the errors by which they were expected to learn. Others, however, were more vigilant. In particular, Richardson applauded David Graham's perception that Lovelace 'makes to himself a comparative Merit ... for sparing his Rose-bud; though his Inducements to do so, were first, as you well observe, the Sacrifice he made by it to a graven Idol, *The Pride of his own Heart*; and next, and principally the View he had to promote by this Sacrifice of his libidinous Desires, his grand Plot against a more favourite Object'.[214]

As these letters reveal, Richardson remained uneasily tolerant of interpretative variety even in this most critical case: in the first instalment at least, attraction and rejection are equally available options, each of which can be accommodated within his larger strategy. Both letters were written after publication had been completed, however, and they already display a shift away from the complexity and indeterminacy that mark the writing of the first edition. Alarmed that the reluctance of some readers to abandon their initial sympathies had persisted to the novel's end, Richardson seems now to be retracting at least a part of that complexity. His

---

[212] See below, pp. 204–6.
[213] To Lady Bradshaigh, 15 December 1748, Carroll, pp. 112–13.
[214] To Graham, 3 May 1750, Carroll, pp. 157–8.

explanations simplify the Rosebud episode by reading it almost exclusively in terms of Lovelace's passing and rather obscure remark that 'a report in my favour from simplicities so amiable may establish me' (I, 230; p. 162) – hardly a conclusive proof that he planned the whole affair simply as a ruse to 'promote ... his grand Plot', and only one among many items of potentially conflicting evidence. As in many of his letters, Richardson here begins to offer bathetic, if not flagrantly tendentious, explanations of his own text. Yet for all his evident irritation he resisted the urge to simplify the passage in *Clarissa*'s revised third edition, and intervened only to the extent of adding a pair of footnotes in which the reader is invited to measure his own (and Clarissa's) response against the vigilance of the editor's voice. 'This explanation is the more necessary to be given', one note announces, 'as several of our Readers (thro' want of due attention) have attributed to Mr. Lovelace, on his behaviour to his Rosebud, a greater merit than was due to him; and moreover imagined, that it was improbable, that a man, who was capable of acting so generously (as they supposed) in this instance, should be guilty of any *atrocious* vileness.'[215]

For a more measured and generous account we may return to David Graham, a reader Richardson himself saw as an exemplary expositor of the text. He had displayed 'so perfect a Mastery of the Story' and entered 'with so much Spirit into the principal Design of the Work', Richardson wrote;[216] and his reading is indeed cogent in the account it gives of the complex demands of admiration and condemnation involved in Lovelace's portrayal. 'One objection to Mr. Lovelace's general character is, that you have made him too lovely to become the object of our indignation', Graham begins by acknowledging: readers 'must be so captivated with the picture you have drawn of him, that they will be more likely to regret his punishment, than acquiesce in the justice of it.' This, however, is a charge for which Graham has little time, and in the following paragraphs he argues instead for the efficacy and indeed the necessity of that attractiveness within the novel's larger scheme – a scheme in which Richardson 'hath furnish'd an Antidote against so dangerous a poison, and taught us to distinguish the brightness of real worth, from the superficial glare of accidental merit'. Like an antidote, the text allows us to experience something of the poison directly, and thereby requires us to develop in resistance our own remedial powers. As Graham goes on:

One of the most engaging moral qualities that appears in Mr. Lovelace, is his generosity; and this, I doubt not, hath with many, atoned for his numberless vices: For most people, weigh Actions of Beneficence in the gross, without examining, whether the motives that gave rise to them were pure or no; and whether the same Actions of two persons might not be calculated to serve ends widely different: Let

---

[215] *Clarissa*, 3rd edn (1751; rpt. New York, 1990), II, 158n.
[216] 13 May 1750, Carroll, p. 159.

us examine his Behaviour to his *Rosebud*; a piece of generosity that I suppose is the greatest favourite with a reader: He tells us 'He spared her;' a condescension like that of a Highwayman, who sometimes restores to a distressed traveller, part of the property he hath extorted from him ... Of much the same leaven is his Sincerity and Frankness of Disposition, which if duly scann'd wou'd turn out a more refined hypocrisy: but besides; allowing it to be genuine, how desperately absurd is it for a Man to value himself upon a few scatter'd instances of integrity, while he is plotting to undermine the foundations of all laws, divine and human!

Evidently Graham himself has little trouble with Lovelace; but as he also suggests, those who do have trouble will also experience a forceful dramatic lesson. By requiring the reader to acknowledge and correct the impression made on him by what, in the light of the rape, reappear as merely 'a few scatter'd instances of integrity', Richardson 'hath put us upon our guard against the approaches of an enemy'. The experience of such a reader, in which admiration must in the end be conquered by a deliberate and willed severity, will equip him to negotiate with safety the like encounter in life: the text impresses 'a conviction that ought in reason to counterpose the weight of a temptation' – all the more effectively, the hint is, for having first presented its mock temptation with such appeal and force.[217]

Again, the analogy with Milton is hard to avoid. For Sarah Fielding too, a similar dramatic warning to the one described by Graham could be detected, and in her analysis the comparison with *Paradise Lost* is made explicit. Events subsequent to the Rosebud affair would alert the reader to his own initial failure to detect 'the Mask of Virtue', she suggests, thereby instilling within him a new readiness to 'judge of a Man upon the whole, and not from any one single Action'.[218] 'The Behaviour of *Lovelace* to his Rosebud must strike every one, at first View, with Admiration and Esteem for him', she writes; 'but when his Character comes to blaze in its full Light, it is very apparent that his Pride preserved his Rosebud, as well as it destroyed *Clarissa*; like *Milton's Satan*, he could for a Time cloath himself like an Angel of Light, even to the Deception of *Uriel*.'[219]

In later criticism the comparison has persisted between these two great tempters – tempters not only of other characters but also of unwary readers. Yet there remains one vitally important difference between the kind of cautionary 'mock encounter' engineered by Richardson and Milton's alternative ways of educating and fortifying the reader. Common to both is a method of experiential teaching in which, free of risking the same calamitous results, the reader is encouraged to share in and learn from the error of a fictional character. As Fish's study shows, however,

---

[217] Graham to Richardson, 22 April 1750, FM XV, 2, ff. 83–4.
[218] *Remarks on Clarissa*, p. 36.
[219] *Ibid.*, p. 35.

Milton's reader is always subject (albeit retrospectively) to the control and reproof of the poem's epic voice. He may, like Uriel, be temporarily deceived by the blandishments of Satanic rhetoric; but he will always be brought, explicitly, to an awareness of his own mistake. By contrast, Richardson at first offers no such external guidance, and even in later editions the cautionary editorial footnotes in which he sought to recover at least some control over interpretation are few and (in a text of thousands of pages) very far between. His method, instead, is to leave the reader to make sense for himself of a uniquely complex text. His writing withholds any detached authorial discourse in which interpretations and judgments are made clear; but in so doing it invokes in the reader the remedial efforts of 'making out', 'carving', 'judging', 'debating', 'thinking' in 'different ways' that he described to Lady Bradshaigh. By these means the reader is confronted with a task that is unquestionably strenuous and challenging, but by no means unwitting on Richardson's part, and by no means necessarily subversive. Indeed, it is precisely by first absenting himself, thereby allowing the exercise of reading its fullest and freest rein, that Richardson most convincingly fulfils his claims to educate. By involving the reader, on the page, in problems of interpretation, response and judgment analogous to those he must confront in the world beyond, the novels inform his capacity to make sense of that world and to conduct his life within it.

The demands made on a reader expected to reach his own understanding of the text by the independent exercise of his own faculties and powers are admirably evoked in the most famous contemporary essay on Richardson, Diderot's 'Eloge'. The essay is wide in its range; but its emphasis falls, recurrently, on the creative role of the reader, for whom the Richardson whose death it mourns, though repeatedly addressed, is in reality no more than an absence. 'Richardson n'est plus'; and his death is a matter not only of recent biographical fact, but a condition also of his apparently 'found' works, which as collections of letters exchanged between the participants in their stories betray the presence of no controlling author. A unique air of reality results, bringing about in turn a close affinity between the reader's response to Richardson's work and his response to the world itself. One reads the epistolary novel not as a fiction but as a collection of documents from life, possessed of all the same urgency, uncertainty and fascination; and in the minds of readers drawn into the controversies of each text the distinction between novel and world breaks down:

J'ai entendu disputer sur la conduite de ses personnages, comme sur des événements réels; louer, blâmer Paméla, Clarisse, Grandisson, comme des personnages vivants qu'on aurait connus, et auxquels on aurait pris le plus grand intérêt.

Quelqu'un d'étranger à la lecture qui avait précédé et qui avait amené la conversation, se serait imaginé, à la vérité et à la chaleur de l'entretien, qu'il s'agissait d'un voisin, d'un parent, d'un ami, d'un frère, d'une sœur.[220]

For all this emphasis on sociability and debate, however, there is an extraordinary solipsism about the 'Eloge', as though in the business of reading Richardson all contact with the phenomenal world is suspended or displaced. In his encounter with the text, Diderot loses a sense not only of the author's presence but also of the very company in which the communal act of reading has taken place: 'A la fin, il me sembla tout à coup que j'étais resté seul.' He is drawn instead into the text, almost as a participant within it. 'O Richardson!', he exclaims, 'on prend, malgré qu'on en ait, un rôle dans tes ouvrages, on se mêle à la conversation, on approuve, on blâme, on admire, on s'irrite, on s'indigne.' At every point, the novel exacts from him a close and rigorous involvement, demanding efforts of understanding, judgment and decision. It is for him alone to encounter and deal with its various kinds of opacity and instability: he must wrestle, for example, with the complex characterisation of Lovelace, and the resulting need to choose between strong conflicting impressions, 'aimer ou détester ce démon'. Such struggles, however, bring with them their own reward; for having read, as Diderot puts it, 'je sentais que j'avais acquis de l'expérience'.[221]

As in the case of Johnson's 'mock encounter', we return to the idea of novels which elicit in the reader interpretative activities analogous to those demanded by life itself, and which in so doing exercise and inform his ability to make sense thereafter of his own experience in the world. Diderot finds a memorable image for the intensity of these demands, and their consequences for a reader:

Une idée qui m'est venue quelquefois en rêvant aux ouvrages de Richardson, c'est que j'avais acheté un vieux château; qu'en visitant un jour ses appartements, j'avais aperçu dans un angle une armoire qu'on n'avait pas ouverte depuis longtemps, et que, l'ayant enfoncée, j'y avais trouvé pêle-mêle les lettres de Clarisse et de Paméla. Après en avoir lu quelques-unes, avec quel empressement ne les aurais-je pas rangées par ordre de dates! Quel chagrin n'aurais-je pas ressenti, s'il y avait eu quelque lacune entre elles! Croit-on que j'eusse souffert qu'une main téméraire (j'ai presque dit sacrilège) en eût supprimé une ligne?[222]

Diderot develops this image of a reader who discovers and orders for himself the basic matter of the novels to introduce an attack on the 'main téméraire' of Prévost, whose abridged translation he saw as an attenuation of Richardson's work.[223] Alongside this local purpose, however, the

[220] 'Eloge de Richardson', in Œuvres esthétiques, ed. Paul Vernière (Paris, 1960), pp. 41, 37.

[221] Ibid., pp. 31, 30, 45, 30.   [222] Ibid., p. 36.

[223] A list of Prévost's principal omissions, together with a translation of his note on each occasion, is contained in Richardson's manuscripts (FM XV, 2, ff. 62–72). For further details see Frank Howard Wilcox, 'Prévost's Translations of Richardson's Novels', University of California

passage has a larger representative force. Richardson has himself ordered the letters in this basic chronological sense, of course, but he has done so in such a way as to efface himself and transfer to the reader many further and more challenging tasks of organisation and interpretation. Without authorial guidance, the reader must make his own sense of the complexities and indeterminacies, ellipses and controversies of the texts with which he is confronted; but in encountering these difficulties he will sound, and perhaps enhance, his own capacity to order and judge the endlessly diffusive impressions of reality itself. This reader (Richardson's 'Carver'), and the difficulties posed him in a novel written, literally, for his benefit, are the subjects of the following chapters.

Publications in Modern Philology, 12, No. 5 (1927), 341–411; François Jost, 'Prévost traducteur de Richardson', in *Expression, Communication, Language*, ed. Ronald G. Popperwell (1973), pp. 297–300; Robert J. Frail, 'The British Connection: The Abbé Prévost and the Translations of the Novels of Samuel Richardson' (diss., Columbia, 1985); Thomas O. Beebee, *Clarissa on the Continent: Translation and Seduction* (University Park, Pennsylvania, 1990), esp. pp. 9–13, 64–71.

2

Casuistry in *Clarissa*
The first instalment, December 1747

On ne peut assurément se défendre d'estimer beaucoup, et même de respecter l'héroïne de ce roman; et cependant Clarisse a fait à peu près la plus grande faute qu'une fille puisse faire, puisqu'elle a fui de la maison paternelle avec son séducteur.

Laclos, 'Des Femmes et de leur éducation'[1]

Richardson and casuistry

Clarissa is not the only book about freedom and authority to date from 1748. In the same year, Richardson read in manuscript

'A Dialogue between a Father and a Daughter,' very sprightly; a little sprinkling of something better in it, but very sparingly sprinkled; as if the author were afraid, that his mind should be thought as antique as his body. – Calculated to reconcile fatherly authority with filial obedience: (so he says.) – But I think, to level the former, and throw down distinction.

His complaints to the dialogue's author, Colley Cibber, were no less frank, focusing in particular on the undutiful character of the daughter. At Speaker Onslow's suggestion he even began a written critique. He pursued it, however, no further than the opening page of the manuscript, and despite Cibber's willingness to alter two or three passages ('but', he complained, '... not for the better') he could not be persuaded to continue. Instead he envisaged a more formal, ventriloquised response, to be produced should Cibber publish. 'If he does', he told Sarah Wescomb, 'I had a good mind that Miss Howe (who is pert enough of conscience to her mamma; Clarissa you know is dead) should answer it.'[2]

When the piece appeared, within the year, as *The Lady's Lecture, A Theatrical Dialogue, between Sir Charles Easy and His Mariageable Daughter. Being an Attempt To Engage Obedience by Filial Liberty*, it showed little evidence of Cibber's two or three Richardsonian alterations. It is perhaps

---

[1] *Œuvres complètes*, p. 440.
[2] To Susanna Highmore, 2 August 1748, Barbauld, II, 204–5; to Sarah Wescomb, [late August 1748], Barbauld, III, 318.

in deference to Richardson that the preface makes two significant caveats, against the grain of the text to follow: '*the paternal Authority ought never to throw the Reins of Government upon the Neck of its Children*', it warns, while the specific case of Sir Charles and his daughter Kitty offers only '*a reasonable Exception*' to the usual rules, there being '*very few in the same Situation of Life who can have an equal Claim*' to the liberties assumed by the latter.[3] But little of the same strictness or caution is displayed in the dialogue itself, which in the bland and spurious resolution to which it brings its central crux amply demonstrates the grounds of Richardson's dislike. In Cibber's hands, the debate between his two interlocutors on the role of each in settling the daughter's marriage remains at a level of vague abstraction, and no serious conflict of interest is allowed to rear its head. A carefree spirit of compromise prevails, Sir Charles granting his daughter a 'negative Favour' and Kitty responding by granting 'a negative Preliminary': he 'will never recommend ... a great Estate with a great Coxcomb', while she 'will never engage in a Promise to any Man' without first consulting her father. The bargain leaves Sir Charles to celebrate that 'our Difference is dissolv'd into a mutual Trust', and he concludes with a characteristic moral: 'There is no making Life easy, Child, but where Power and Obedience are as willing to give as to take.'[4]

This reconciliation between 'Power' and 'Obedience' is so easily won, of course, only because there has never been any prospect of collision: since the instinctive priority of each party is to observe (though without defining) the other's 'natural Right', Cibber has no need to adjudicate in the last resort between parental demands for obedience and filial demands for choice. As a result, his dialogue only skirts the vexed problem it explicitly claims to tackle, offering a solution entirely dependent for its success on the '*mutual Benevolence*' and '*Harmony of Hearts*' peculiar to his chosen characters.[5] By addressing in the glib language of sentimental comedy a set of questions more normally associated with the stricter codes and gloomier assumptions of religious conduct literature, Cibber's work in fact had solved nothing.

There is no evidence to suggest that Richardson's formal refutation of *The Lady's Lecture* was ever taken further, and it is perhaps surprising that the work engaged his attention at all. Part of the explanation must lie in the peculiar amplitude of Cibber's father/daughter theme – a theme of obvious centrality in patriarchal ideology, and thus of an importance that goes far beyond the merely domestic sphere. There is, however, a more straightforward explanation too. For *The Lady's Lecture* was very clearly Cibber's reply to the first instalment of *Clarissa*, published in the closing weeks of the previous year and known to Cibber in earlier manuscript

---

[3] *The Lady's Lecture, A Theatrical Dialogue* (1748), C–Cv.   [4] *Ibid*., pp. 40–1, 43.
[5] *Ibid*., pp. 39, C4, C4v.

versions. The two writers had privately debated the theme of paternal authority in the novel, taking very different positions;[6] and Richardson can have been little enamoured of this more public attempt to 'reconcile', in 43 pages, a problem he had himself insisted, in two large volumes, to be fraught with difficulty and contradiction.

Much has been written on the place of Richardson's writings in relation to the literature of conduct.[7] Not only did he contribute directly to the genre in *The Apprentice's Vade Mecum* (1734) and the conjectural *Duties of Wives to Husbands*,[8] approaching it again in *A Collection of ... Moral and Instructive Sentiments* (1755): he often presented his novels in similar terms, boasting to one correspondent that Edward Young had called *Clarissa* '*The Whole Duty of a Woman*' (a reference to the popular seventeenth-century manual, *The Whole Duty of Man*), and suggesting to another that she align the novel on her shelves with the classics of the genre, Bayly's *Practice of Piety* and Taylor's *Holy Living* and *Holy Dying*.[9] To many of his contemporaries he seemed, like these writers, to describe a complete ethical system by which the reader might measure his conduct in every station and every eventuality of life. David Graham found in each of *Clarissa*'s 'different situations' one 'grand rule of morality; which seems to consist in an unreserved obedience to the divine will: In which, as in a fix'd point, all the duties resulting from the several relations of social life, like lines drawn in a circle, so as not to interfere with each other, should ultimately center'.[10] For Philip Skelton, likewise, *Clarissa* was 'a System of religious and moral Precepts and Examples' and *Grandison* 'a living system of manners';[11] Smollett found in the works 'a sublime system of ethics'.[12] At the end of his career, Richardson was happy to promote precisely this idea of his writing as a compendious and functional *œuvre*, pointing out to a reader who had complained at his failure to treat suicide in *Grandison* that

[6] The letters do not survive but are alluded to by a Mr Bennet or Bennett, who also participated in the debate: see his undated letter to Richardson, FM, XV, 3, f.10.

[7] The most useful modern analyses are by Rita Goldberg, *Sex and Enlightenment: Women in Richardson and Diderot* (Cambridge, 1984), pp. 24–65, and Sylvia Kasey Marks, *Sir Charles Grandison: The Compleat Conduct Book* (Lewisburg, 1986). For other sources see Goldberg's note, p. 211 (note 3).

[8] 'A large single sheet relative to the Married State, intituled, "The Duties of Wives to Husbands"', is included in the list of Richardson's writings given by John Nichols in his *Biographical and Literary Anecdotes of William Bowyer* (1782), p. 306: see Eaves and Kimpel, *Biography*, p. 50.

[9] To Frances Grainger, 21 December 1749, Carroll, p. 141; to Lady Bradshaigh, 15 December 1748, Carroll, p. 117.

[10] To Richardson, 22 April 1750, FM, XV, 2, f.83.

[11] Quoted in *Hints of Prefaces*, pp. 7–8; 'From Mr. Skelton, as published in the Irish News-Papers', FM, XV, 4, f.45.

[12] *Continuation of the Complete History of England* (1761), quoted by Eaves and Kimpel, *Biography*, p. 510.

he had done so in *Pamela* and *Clarissa*, and that the volume of *Sentiments* abstracted from the three would demonstrate 'that there are not many of the material articles that may be of use for the conduct of life and manners unattended to in one or other of them; so that all together they complete one plan'.[13]

Here Richardson appears most conspicuously in the garb of the bourgeois moralist and teacher, sternly enforcing the most cherished precepts and practices of his class. Yet he knew that rules for conduct could not always be lucid or unequivocal, and that the radiating lines of David Graham's circle would sometimes, troublingly, collide. It is at such points, where daily life appears to deny the validity of laws and the efficacy of systems, that his novels are typically located. It is here too that his place in the tradition of conduct literature is at its most interesting – at points where the appropriate analogue for his writing is not so much *Holy Living* as Taylor's more tentative return to the same issues in *Ductor Dubitantium*. This latter work represents the more troubled and exploratory strain of the tradition known as casuistry, which rather than laying down structures of invariable rules instead examines their practical limitations. Casuistry starts from a recognition that system-building is a precarious enterprise, and takes as its special field particular instances in which the automatic application of rules appears most questionable. It assumes that ethical problems are best solved by detailed analysis of their own peculiar circumstances, acknowledging the value of (and taking its terms of reference from) schematic moral codes of the sort outlined in *The Whole Duty of Man*, but testing their injunctions in cases where their scope or meaning becomes obscure. As defined in the *Oxford English Dictionary*, it is 'that part of Ethics which resolves cases of conscience, applying the general rules of religion and morality to particular instances in which "circumstances alter cases", or in which there appears to be a conflict of duties. Often (and perhaps originally) applied to a quibbling or evasive way of dealing with difficult cases of duty; sophistry'.

These last phrases point to the equivocal terms in which casuistry has been viewed since the time at least of Pascal's famous attack on its Jesuit practitioners in *Lettres provinciales* (1656–7).[14] Johnson comments on this double face in the *Rambler*, where he writes that 'though casuistical knowledge be useful in proper hands, yet it ought by no means to be carelessly exposed, since most will use it rather to lull than awaken their own consciences; and the threads of reasoning, on which truth is suspended, are frequently drawn to such subtility, that common eyes cannot

---

[13] To Mark Hildesley, 21 February 1755, Barbauld, V, 132.
[14] See Albert R. Jonsen and Stephen Toulmin, *The Abuse of Casuistry: A History of Moral Reasoning* (Berkeley and Los Angeles, 1988), pp. 231–49.

perceive, and common sensibility cannot feel them'.[15] The same double-
ness is more fully seen in the work of Defoe, to which (as G. A. Starr has
demonstrated) casuistry is central. In Defoe's conduct manuals, casuistry
is the faithful servant of the ethical system from which it begins, stepping
in where necessary to patch up the system's gaps and demonstrate its
efficacy even where circumstances seem to resist the simplicity of imperatives. *The Family Instructor*, for example, legislates by casuistical testing, 'to
shew that even in these extraordinary Cases, the Husband ought not to
omit his Duty; intimating, that if not in these Cases, certainly not in Cases
less difficult, and consequently in no Case at all':[16] in such analyses, the
system's more general applicability can be confirmed. Defoe's novels,
however, give a more complicated sense of the inadequacies of rigid codes,
and their casuistical repudiation of the schematic has unsettling implications. As each narrator records his or her passage through what Starr
calls the 'ethical no-man's-land' of the novels, experience becomes a battle
of contrary impulses and imperatives, exacting perpetual vigilance, constant adaptability and an unflagging sense of moral adventure.[17] In the
hands of a Moll or a Roxana, furthermore, the ethical suppleness of the
casuist often modulates into more questionable forms of self-acquittal:
their ingenious adjustments of received notions of duty to their own
aberrant situations bring the Pascalian charge of sophistry and cavilling
inescapably to mind.

Richardson once wrote of his own anxiety to 'argue for the right, or
against the wrong, with some strictness, in order to settle the boundaries
between right and wrong'.[18] He valued casuistry, rigorously employed, as
a means of untangling the lines of duty crossed by special circumstance;
but he did so with a view to reasserting these all-important 'boundaries',
not to conniving in their breach. Casuistry's antinomian potential was as
alarming to him as it was to Johnson, and he remained anxiously aware of
its tendency to degenerate into evasive quibblings, the extenuation of
transgression, and a sinister dismantling of ethical structures. There is no
record of his response to Defoe's novels; but he was almost obsessively
quick, as a reader of memoirs written in a similar vein, to censure any hint
of casuistical palliation. When a rash of mildly scabrous autobiographies
and apologies appeared around 1750, he singled out for criticism Constantia Phillips (who, as Lady Bradshaigh concurred, 'endeavours to
throw a veil over many blamable actions, which, nevertheless, circumstances make plainly appear as they are') and Lady Vane (for 'presuming to

---

[15] *Rambler*, III, 73 (no. 13, 1 May 1750), partly quoted by G. A. Starr, *Defoe and Casuistry*
   (Princeton, 1971), p. 2. See also Johnson's ironic use of the term 'casuist' in an earlier paper:
   Rambler, III, 55 (No. 10, 21 April 1750).
[16] *The Family Instructor*, 4th edn (1741), II, iv.   [17] Starr, *Defoe and Casuistry*, p. vii.
[18] To Susanna Highmore, [1753–4?], Barbauld, II, 221.

attempt to clear her *Heart*, and to find gentle Fault only with her *Head*, in
the Perpetration of the highest Acts of Infidelity').[19] When a critique of
Phillips by Sarah Chapone publicly exposed her ability 'so to dazle the
Understanding, that it does not instantly perceive the many Evasions,
Misrepresentations, and Inconsistencies, that run through the Whole', he
warmly praised the author for detecting 'the Fallaciousness ... of a *Woman*
of so popular, tho' infamous a Character'.[20]

Explicit references to casuistry in *Clarissa* show similar suspicions. As
Starr notes, Lovelace epitomises casuistry *in malo*: he draws on its methods
to justify the unjustifiable, stifle his own conscience and divert the objections of his reader Belford – who after the rape invokes the familiar
Pascalian idea of evasive casuistry to accuse him of 'jesuitical qualifyings'
(V, 356; p. 958). Only pages later, Lovelace seems to confirm the allegation by insisting, in evasive mitigation of the rape, that no seducer can cast
the first stone: 'Thou art, surely, casuist good enough to know ... that the
sin of seducing a credulous and easy girl, is as great as that of bringing to
your lure an incredulous and watchful one' (VI, 2; p. 970). Clarissa
herself is a more conscientious exponent of the technique, but she too finds
herself succumbing to its hazards at certain points. 'I am a very bad
casuist', she writes, attempting to assess Anna's entitlement to correspond
with her against maternal command; 'and the pleasure I take in writing to
you ... may make me ... very partial to my own wishes' (III, 209; p. 482).
The particular case raised here, though repeatedly discussed, is never
definitively resolved, and the correspondence continues: both participants
are able to take comfort that Hickman, 'who pretends to a little casuistry
in such nice matters', gives Anna's disobedience his sanction (III, 332;
p. 548).

Richardson's most detailed and telling reference to casuistry concerns a
more serious matter than this, however, and is one in which the whole
casuistical enterprise is travestied. The episode in question comes where
Lovelace tricks the Hampstead women into connivance with his plan to
recapture Clarissa by discussing his quarrel with her as a novel variant of a
classic case of conscience, that of conflicting vows. In this 'unheard-of
case' (V, 47; p. 786), he and Clarissa are married but she has committed
him, pending reconciliation with her family, to a vow of celibacy – a vow
which, 'in her notion, is binding' (V, 46; p. 786). May he not now, he asks,
'insist upon her absolving me from this abominable oath?' (V, 50; p. 788).
His adroit presentation of the case wins from his audience a judgment in

[19] Lady Bradshaigh to Richardson, [early November 1749?], Barbauld, IV, 280; Richardson to
Sarah Chapone, 6 December 1750, FM, XII, 2, f.7. The references are to *An Apology for the
Conduct of Mrs. T. C. Phillips* (1748–9) and to Lady Vane's *Memoirs of a Lady of Quality* (shortly
to be published as chapter 88 of Smollett's *Adventures of Peregrine Pickle* (1751)).

[20] [Sarah Chapone], *Remarks on Mrs. Muilman's Letter to the Right Honourable the Earl of Chesterfield*,
(1750), p. 56; Richardson to Chapone, 19 October 1750, FM, XII, 2, f.6.

which the perils of careless analysis are exemplified to devastating effect. By neglecting to question the good faith of the querist, the women wrongly conclude that, as 'Miss Rawlins learnedly said, playing with her fan, a casuist would give it, that the matrimonial vow ought to supersede any other obligation' (V, 50; p. 788). They judge in Lovelace's favour, and thus unwittingly deliver Clarissa up to the far more brutal ways of 'insisting' that her rapist has in mind.

For all these implied reservations on Richardson's part, nonetheless, as strong a case can be made for the influence of traditional casuistry on his fiction as for its influence on Defoe's, albeit a case very different in pattern. In the first place, there is evidence in his correspondence of a familiarity not only with the typical concerns and procedures of case-divinity, but also with particular analyses recorded by major seventeenth-century exponents such as Joseph Hall.[21] Furthermore, he dealt as printer with a variety of works to which casuistry is central – an indication of both acquaintance and interest, given his own complaint that he 'seldom read but as a Printer' and his bibliographer's judgment that the output of his press substantially reflects his personal concerns and commitments.[22] Notable examples are Defoe's *New Family Instructor* and part of *Religious Courtship*, printed by Richardson in 1727 and 1729, as well as *Fifteen Sermons upon Social Duties* (1744) by Patrick Delany, a friend of both his and Jonathan Swift's.[23] Casuistry also emerges in less predictable contexts, such as his own adaptation of Sir Roger L'Estrange's *Æsop*, in which a casuistical twist is given to many fables: one even becomes 'a kind of a Dog-case of conscience'.[24]

Another work in the same category is Aaron Hill's bi-weekly *Plain Dealer*, which Richardson printed in its collected edition of 1730 and probably also in its original numbers of 1724–5.[25] In this journal Hill and his collaborator William Bond adopted the question and answer device pioneered in journalism by John Dunton's *Athenian Gazette; or, Casuisticall Mercury* (1690–7), which had specialised in the resolution of cases of conscience posed in readers' letters.[26] The method foreshadows Richardson's use of casuistry in the novel, in terms of both form and content: each problem is presented by means of a letter, usually from the perplexed (and probably fictive) protagonist of the case, while particular emphasis is placed on cases of courtship and marriage. In one early number, 'Dorothy Plain' poises the convoluted case of a son who, having married without

---

[21] See below, p. 121.

[22] Richardson to Hill, 2 April 1743, Carroll, p. 59; William M. Sale, *Samuel Richardson: Master Printer* (Ithaca, 1950), p. 3.

[23] Sale, *Master Printer*, pp. 162–3, 165.   [24] *Æsop's Fables* (1740), p. 73.

[25] Eaves and Kimpel, *Biography*, pp. 37–40; Sale, *Master Printer*, p. 179.

[26] See G. A. Starr, 'From Casuistry to Fiction: The Importance of the *Athenian Mercury*', *Journal of the History of Ideas*, 27 (1967), 17–32; also *Defoe and Casuistry*, pp. 8–27.

paternal knowledge, now finds that his father has arranged a more advantageous match: he is therefore faced with the inevitability of breaching his duty to either his wife or his parent, and must choose the lesser evil. In response, Hill's 'Plain Dealer' vindicates a child's right to choose, concludes that he is exempted from obeying his father as the case stands, and goes on to moralise that 'if his Parents think, that he sins against Prudence in chusing a slender Fortune, all the World will judge, that they would sin against Justice, if, forcing his Inclinations, they make him Wretched, under Pretence of making him Rich'.[27] Later the 'Plain Dealer' returns to the same theme in response to the letter of a querist 'compelled by his avaricious Parents to marry a wealthy but insupportable stale Maid'. Again, he takes the opportunity to excoriate parents who force their children's inclinations: 'Using Authority in such a Case, turns the most Indulgent of Fathers, into an insupportable Tyrant, who by one inconsiderate Decree ... dooms his own Child to the most doleful Imprisonment for Life.'[28] A third paper discusses another 'pretty nice' case, in which an heiress's parents forbid her to marry a poor lawyer, prompting a further tirade against 'the Tyranny of an Avaritious Parent ... who would no more part with his Daughter, than his Land, to any but the *best Purchaser*'.[29]

The journal's most interesting paper on this matrimonial theme claims to throw new light on it by pointing to the culpability of a party 'who has, hitherto, been look'd on as most Innocent, and deserving Pity'. The case is posed by 'Amanda', who laments 'the Persecution She undergoes from a hated Suitor, who is authorized to be her Tormentor'. She protests, in particular, at the 'Ungenerous Unreasonableness of such Perseverance, and the unhappy Fruits of a Man's insisting to make a Wife of a Person to whom he is odious'. Beyond the usual attack on parental compulsion, the force of her complaint falls on the Solmes-like admirer who, 'when her Refusal has drawn down the Resentment of her Parents, lays it, all, on his *Excess of Love*', and thereby escapes censure despite his ultimate responsibility for the family breach. Her defence is to challenge the sincerity of this love, on the grounds that 'the real Lover knows not how to *Offend*. – His Happiness must rise, and fall, with *Hers*, who inspir'd his Passion. – But if, on the contrary, His Desires run *Counter* to her Happiness, It is not *Love*; it is *Brutality*!' The words anticipate Clarissa's complaint against Solmes that 'Love, that deserves the name, seeks the satisfaction of the beloved object, more than its own' (II, 115; p. 268); while in Amanda's summing-up further intimations of the situation at Harlowe Place are hard to miss. 'This', she concludes,

[27] *Plain Dealer* (1730), I, 341 (No. 40, 7 August 1724).
[28] *Ibid.*, I, I i 8; I, 397 (No. 47, 31 August 1724).
[29] *Ibid.*, II, 375; II, 376 (No. 102, 12 March 1725).

... is *my own* Misfortune, to be miserably haunted, by the Man, whose Sight is Odious to me; One, whom no Words can convince! No Denials satisfie! No affronts affect! Insensible of my Uneasiness; and Indefatigable, in creating it! – I wou'd fly him, but I cannot, unless I wou'd fly my Friends too, and my Parents: Nor have I any *Intimate* left, whom his Diligence, and Insinuations, have not made his Own.[30]

Hill's, of course, is a debased casuistry, as close to the modern agony-page as to *Ductor Dubitantium*. The *Plain Dealer* lacks both the meticulous deliberation borrowed by Dunton and the Athenians from seventeenth-century case-divinity and the dialectical element common to the casuistry of Defoe and Richardson: typically, Hill simply endorses the querist, and exempts him from whatever law stands in opposition to the sentimental-ist's arbiter, love. Yet this shift of emphasis from answer to question and from analysis to feeling, a defect in traditional terms, also brings with it marked literary advantages: in Hill's hands, detailed presentation of the specifics of a case (required by casuistry, which addresses itself precisely to the contingent) and presentation, moreover, in first-person epistolary form begin to spice the debate on duties with the urgencies of psychologi-cal and circumstantial realism. When in *Familiar Letters* Richardson turned to this genre himself, he was able to develop the novelistic potential inherent in this mingling of casuistical content and epistolary form. By devoting the same attention to the reply as to the question, he also succeeded in restoring more careful (and very much more severe) forms of analysis.

Like the *Plain Dealer*, *Familiar Letters* is by no means exclusively casuisti-cal; but a related desire to test received ethical precepts in specific or unusual cases is very clearly a dominant impulse in the work. Richardson presents the work's division into fictive case-studies as an attempt 'to describe properly, and recommend strongly, the social and relative duties; and to place them in such practical lights, that the letters may serve for rules to think and act by, as well as forms to write after': these emphases on the application of theory to the quotidian, and on the need to supplement rules for conduct with rules for analysis, are typically casuistical. Typically casuistical too is the work's preoccupation with the staple themes of the seventeenth-century divines: it endeavours, for example, 'to set forth, in a variety of cases ... the inconveniencies attending unsuitable marriages', a subject which characteristically involves conflicts of duties or strong argu-ments for evading or suspending a duty.[31] Repeatedly, the convoluted problems of these matrimonial cases take *Familiar Letters* beyond the simpler project of exemplifying a predetermined duty, to address the difficulties which arise where imperatives seem at odds.

Second marriages are a particular concern, exhaustively treated: the

[30] *Ibid.*, II, 69; II, K k 4v; II, 70; II, 70–1; II, 71 (No. 66, 6 November 1724).
[31] *Familiar Letters*, pp. xxvii, xxviii.

table of contents lists letters 'To a rich Widow Lady with Children, dissuading her from marrying a Widower of meaner Degree, who has Children also', 'To a Gentleman of Fortune, who has Children, dissuading him from a Second Marriage with a Lady much younger than himself', 'Against a Second Marriage, where there are Children on *both* Sides'.[32] In this sequence Richardson sinks the querist's letter, leaving both statement and resolution of each case to a respondent who weighs the conflicting duties and impulses involved. Despite this suppression, however, the querist's presence is felt, in that the resolution emerges in part through a sceptical reading of his or her initial statement of the case. One typical response challenges the querist's motives for soliciting the resolution: does he request it in order to establish the right course, it asks, or does his letter merely seek endorsement of inclination, 'a kind of justification or excuse for what you ... are, perhaps, already resolved upon?' Another clarifies the problem it addresses by detecting a conflict of duties which the querist has tried, jesuitically, to present as in harmony, while concealing his true motive: the response redefines his stated inclination 'to give your *children* a *mother*, instead of the good one they have lost' with the rebuke that, 'in plain *English*, you should have said, *yourself* a *wife*, to supply your *own loss*' – a gambit that prepares the way for a stern resolution against remarriage.

In such cases, Richardson's evident suspicion of any resort to casuistry coexists with an affirmation of the technique's usefulness; for although these resolutions consistently conclude that each querist's representations are insufficient to exempt him from a prior duty to his children, Richardson is far from denying the casuistical axiom that circumstances alter cases. Instead it is the failure of the particular circumstances in question, when scrutinised, to provide adequate grounds for exemption that dictates each decision. Thus the writer of this last letter, though forbidding remarriage, is able to envisage exonerating circumstances (of financial need) in which his verdict would be reversed. 'The lesser evil, in this case, is to be chosen', he rules. 'But this is not your case.'[33]

Of greatest interest in relation to *Clarissa* are two more fully dramatised cases. Letters 91–3 address the classic matrimonial crux of a dispute between father and daughter over the choice of husband; but instead of having the daughter put her case to a third party (as in the *Athenian Mercury* or *Plain Dealer*) Richardson presents it in an exchange between the two disputants, a device which enables him to view the case more clearly in its contrasting sets of terms. In dissenting from her father's choice, the daughter bases her case on the prospective husband's age, her lack of affection and the likelihood that a dissonant marriage will result in 'evil consequences'; she agrees to obey her father, however, should her argu-

<hr>

[32] *Ibid.*, pp. xxxv, xxxviii, referring to Letters 94, 140, 142. See also Letters 141, 143, 147, 148.
[33] *Ibid.*, pp. 171, 175, 178.

ment fail to dissuade him. In his reply (which Richardson distinguishes as *'urgently enforcing, but not compelling, her Compliance'*) the father maintains his position – that he has his daughter's wellbeing at heart, is a more experienced judge, and has hit on a worthy suitor; and that the objection to age is 'surmountable', and should be conquered 'to *oblige her father'*.[34] If she cannot surmount it, however, he will not insist. Both characters thus show themselves to be caught between desire and obligation, aware that duty enjoins them to act against their own will; and a distinctly novelistic sense of individual consciousness emerges from each writer's attempts to articulate the dilemma, and to persuade the other to accept the validity of his or her plea. Here, however, the exemplary reasonableness of both parties enables Richardson to avoid the problems latent in an ethical system which forbids the parent to compel his child but refuses to waive the child's duties of obedience if he *does* compel her.[35] A similar manoeuvre is made in a later exchange between the engaged parties of a case (Letters 133–6), which this time picks up Hill's theme of a suitor whose attentions, unwanted by their object but encouraged by her family, have led to family breach. Impressed by the daughter's statement, the suitor agrees to become 'a *party* against *myself'* and withdraws his suit – though it is significant that he will persist if her affections are not already engaged.[36] Both sequences narrowly evade cruxes to which *Clarissa* would return.

As these examples indicate, the links between *Familiar Letters* and the novels are very direct, and involve matters of technique as well as theme. As the perplexed querists of *Familiar Letters* make themselves known by their casuistical self-presentations, so Richardson's characters exist for the reader not simply as actors within the narrated world but first as reporters of it, very often specifically as casuists concerned to determine or justify their own choices and conduct. His plots, moreover, draw heavily on the same staple cruxes, to such an extent that his entire output might well be accounted for in terms of the casuistical treatment of carefully contrived and varied cases of conscience, *Pamela* addressing the major cases inherent in the relative duties of masters and servants, *Pamela II* doing the same for husbands and wives, *Clarissa* for parents and children, and *Grandison* for almost anyone (but emphasising the classic case of marriage between Protestant and Catholic, to which Defoe had devoted much of *Religious Courtship*).[37] Such an account would do much to explain Richardson's idea

34 *Ibid.*, pp. 118, 119, 120.
35 For the underlying principle, see *Sentiments*, p. 118: 'In reciprocal Duties, the failure on one side justifies not a failure on the other.'
36 *Familiar Letters*, pp. 160–1. For comparison, see *Plain Dealer*, II, 69–77, and *Clarissa*, I, 224–7; pp. 159–60.
37 See Starr, *Defoe and Casuistry*, pp. 43–7. On the comprehensiveness of *Grandison*'s plan, see Marks, *Sir Charles Grandison* (which, however, presents Richardson as concerned with the provision of examples for imitation, not with the casuistical elaboration of vexed cases).

that the novels 'complete one plan'. It is in their narrative structure, however, that the novels most interestingly develop the potential of casuistry. The casuistical recognition that right conduct is rarely a straightforward or unequivocal matter is brilliantly expressed in the multiple epistolary form of *Clarissa* and *Grandison* – a form which allows for examination of each case from every possible point of view, and pits the contending positions of the interested parties against one another in epistolary debate. This pattern is most thoroughly used in the opening instalment of *Clarissa*, where narrative becomes doubly casuistical, both in the positive sense of addressing particular dilemmas by analysis of their distinctive circumstances, and also in the negative sense of employing what Jeremy Taylor had called 'tricks and devices to dance upon the ropes'.[38] The effect is disconcerting: ethical codes, if not completely in abeyance, are subject to continual question; and while verdicts proliferate with giddying abundance none remains uncontested or wins the status of objectivity. Clarissa's case remains open, and the onus of resolution is thrown instead on the reader, who must weigh the protagonists' rival formulations of the case, remaining alert to the recurrent drift from legitimate qualification to evasion and extenuation, and assessing the validity of each in relation to the particular injunction it seeks to privilege, adjust or discard.

Richardson's calculated stimulation of actual debate vividly illustrates the extent to which the activities of the reader, rather than simply the words on the page, are the true end-point of his project. Novel-reading is today a solitary activity: we forget that it was once a social practice (as in the household of Catherine Talbot, who wrote of *Clarissa*'s first instalment that 'we only read it en famille, and at set hours, and all the rest of the day we talked of it').[39] Yet when Richardson spoke of leaving his readers 'something ... to make out or debate upon', and of seeking to 'give occasion for debate, or different ways of thinking',[40] he meant it quite literally. He expected casuistical debate to continue outside the pages of each novel and pass into the reader's social life; and he left, in his letters and occasional printed interventions such as the *Answer to a Letter from a Friend, who had Objected to Sir Charles Grandison's Offer to Allow his Daughters ... to be Educated Roman-Catholics* (1754), copious evidence of the terms in which such debates might be conducted.[41] The problems of paternal

---

[38] The phrase is from *Ductor Dubitantium*, quoted by Camille Wells Slights, *The Casuistical Tradition in Shakespeare, Donne, Herbert and Milton* (Princeton, 1981), p. 33.

[39] To Elizabeth Carter, 28 December 1747, *A Series of Letters between Mrs. Elizabeth Carter and Mrs. Catherine Talbot* (1809), I, 244.

[40] To Lady Bradshaigh, 25 February 1754, Carroll, p. 296; to Hester Mulso, 21 August 1754, Carroll, p. 311.

[41] Reprinted in *Grandison*, III, 470–3. The combination of casuistical dexterity and religious toleration in Sir Charles' narrative was too much for one reader: 'one would imagine', he

authority and filial liberty posed by the opening instalment of *Clarissa* proved the most intractable and resonant of all these fictive occasions, and prompted the most spirited exchanges. Richardson held prolonged debates on the subject with (among others) Susanna Highmore (1749), Frances Grainger (1749–50), Hester Mulso (1750–1) and Sarah Chapone (1752), and allowed the debates to proliferate by circulating the correspondences among other potential participants: the debate with Sarah Chapone, for example, grew out of the Mulso letters.[42] His own formidable contribution to this correspondence (his first letter ran to '13 close Pages', the second weighed in at 39)[43] is now lost; but the scope and seriousness of the debate is clear enough from Mulso's three letters, which bring to bear citations from an array of moralists, jurists and political theorists, from Hall and Allestree on Richardson's side, by way of Grotius and Pufendorf, to Algernon Sidney and Locke on her own.[44]

As the list suggests, much is at stake at Harlowe Place. Yet for modern readers, who are likely to find no more in *Clarissa*'s first instalment than an unambiguously hideous case of oppression, the import and vexedness of its problems are hard to grasp. By the turn of the eighteenth century, in fact, this aspect of the novel was already becoming inexplicable. In 1790 Catharine Macaulay complained at the heroine's adherence to 'some very whimsical notions which she has entertained of duty and propriety of conduct', and blamed her failure to 'defend herself against [her father's] unjust resentment, by asserting her rights to an independent fortune left to her by an indulgent grandfather'. Seventeen years later the editor of Mulso's letters on *Clarissa* had to apologise not (as Richardson would have expected) for their liberalism but for their severity, stressing that 'they were written more than half a century ago; a period wherein many parents seemed really to suppose that parental authority extended to a right to control the affections, as well as to regulate the actions of their children; and ... addressed to a person, who, both in his public writings, and ... in his private character, carried these notions to the most rigid extreme'.[45] In changing ideological conditions, it would seem, *Clarissa*'s mainspring had already snapped. But for Richardson's first readers the case at Harlowe Place could not have been more finely balanced or more highly charged.

wrote, 'while the good Author slept, some insinuating J[e]suit had penned this part' (Anon. to Richardson, c. 26 December 1753, FM, XV, 3, f.25).

[42] See Chapone to Richardson, [March 1752], FM, XII, 2, f.54.

[43] John Mulso to Gilbert White, 13 December 1750, *The Letters to Gilbert White of Selborne*, ed. Rashleigh Holt-White (1907), p. 45.

[44] See Mulso's 'Letters on Filial Obedience', *The Posthumous Works of Mrs. Chapone*, 2 vols. (1807), II, 27–143.

[45] Catharine Macaulay Graham, *Letters on Education* (1790), p. 146; *Posthumous Works of Mrs. Chapone*, I, vii.

Parents, children and the ethics of relative duty

Something of this missing context can be recovered by a brief analysis of the basic code from which the novel begins – a code to which Richardson referred when writing in *Familiar Letters* of 'the social and relative duties',[46] and to which Clarissa also alludes when she discusses the meanings of love 'in all the *relative*, in all the *social*, and . . . in all our *superior* duties' (I, 181; p. 135). The ethical system they invoke received its definitive outline in William Fleetwood's influential *Relative Duties of Parents and Children, Husbands and Wives, Masters and Servants* (1705), which modernised (and slightly liberalised) for the eighteenth century the religious conduct literature of the seventeenth. Richardson quotes Fleetwood's work in his correspondence,[47] and he also encouraged and printed a close (though less moderate) imitation of it, Patrick Delany's *Fifteen Sermons upon Social Duties* (1744), later expanded as *Twenty Sermons on Social Duties, and Their Opposite Vices* (1747). Taken together, Fleetwood and Delany provide a useful measure against which to read *Clarissa*'s early action, the heroine's conduct and the casuistical exchanges in which the whole affair is disputed and described. As well as delineating recognised norms of conduct in similar cases, both writers dwell (in ways very relevant to the novel) on the larger implications also inherent in the conflict of parent with child.

Fleetwood's principal advance on his forebears, in his attempt to build their various ethical precepts into a single coherent system, is to shift emphasis from the individual's relations with God to his relations in society. '*The Design of Christianity is to make People happy* in this *World, as well as in* another', he reports; '*and the way it takes to do this, is to make them good and virtuous whilst they live, by the discharge of all the Relations they stand in to each other, whether Natural, Civil, or Contracted, i.e. by performing their Duty to their Neighbour.*' Not only the rectitude of the individual but the social order as a whole is guaranteed by this fundamental duty, and in this sense Fleetwood's analysis of Christian ethics is at root a political enterprise. Religion, he insists, works 'to secure the Duties of all Relations to each other, from want of which proceed all the mischiefs in the World'. If not the opium of the people, it is very clearly the vinculum of the commonwealth: 'It binds the Natural and Civil Duties upon all related, and concern'd, with strong and strict Commands of God.'[48]

In detailing this harmonious structure of commands, Fleetwood begins from the simple axiom, often repeated, 'that there is no Relation in the World, either Natural, or Civil and agreed upon, but there is a Reciprocal duty obliging each Party'. Whether in a state of authority, equality, or

---

[46] *Familiar Letters*, p. xxvii.   [47] See Richardson to Chapone, 2 March 1752, Carroll, p. 205.
[48] *The Relative Duties of Parents and Children, Husbands and Wives, Masters and Servants* (1705), pp. A2–A2v, 120, 163.

subjection, the individual both owes to and expects from his fellows the exercise of specific duties: human relations thus constitute a vast web of reciprocal obligation and indebtedness, uniting all men, on the domestic and civil scale alike, in an intricate system of mutually beneficial conduct. For all this intricacy, however, the system is one which sees all communities as organised by direct extension of the principles governing family life, and thus as intimate and manageable; so that in concentrating on the domestic categories of his title Fleetwood does not limit his scope so much as offer the family as a model for all society. When Clarissa exclaims that 'the world is but one great family', and complains at the Harlowe preference for 'relationship remembred against relationship forgot' (I, 46; p. 62), she echoes this emphasis on the concentric structure of family and world, and insists, like Fleetwood, that a failure to extend the practice of relative duties beyond (or to exercise it properly within) the family impairs the larger whole. Patrick Delany too urges that 'the law of GOD considers mankind as members of one great community; and therefore every member of this community is our Neighbour, that is, one to whom we owe all the duties of a social creature'.[49]

The family is of practical as well as paradigmatic significance, of course. As well as exemplifying in miniature the system of relative duties, it also serves as the unit which first instructs in, and thereafter unceasingly requires, their observance. Of the 'particular engagements and obligations, absolutely necessary to the order and well-being of society', writes Delany, '. . . the Duty of Children to Parents, hath justly obtained the first place: because all our other duties to mankind begin and are founded here. It is from a right deference to the authority and institutions of parents, that we learn to become good men, good neighbours, good friends, and good subjects, as well as good sons. In one word, it is here we ordinarily learn all the offices of a social and rational creature, in our whole commerce with mankind.'[50] Familial harmony at once epitomises and guarantees civil harmony: the institutions and relations of the family, accordingly, are placed by Fleetwood and Delany at the very heart of the national wellbeing, not only for their representative value but because an aggregate of orderly families will form, and perpetuate, the orderly society they seek.

It might be added that the more specific, unspoken reasons are at work here as well, given the family's function of controlling the transmission of property and blood.[51] 'Confusion of progeny constitutes the essence of the crime', Johnson declares of the most obvious breach in the duties of husbands and wives, adultery, while one of Richardson's model letter-

[49] Fleetwood, *Relative Duties*, p. 86; Delany, *Fifteen Sermons upon Social Duties* (1744), p. 140.
[50] Delany, *Social Duties*, pp. 140–1.
[51] See Tony Tanner, *Adultery in the Novel: Contract and Transgression* (Baltimore, 1979), pp. 3–18.

writers makes the point in more nakedly economic terms when she warns her daughter that 'a *naughty wife* often makes the children of *another man* heirs of her husband's estate and fortune, in injury of his *own children* or *family*'.[52] In marriage cases lineage and wealth are guaranteed by divine commandment, the suggestion is, and jeopardised in its transgression – and as much by a child's breach of the fifth commandment as by a spouse's of the seventh. One jurist writing shortly after *Clarissa*'s publication found it 'entirely against the public Utility that in an Affair of so great Import-ance as Marriage is, Children should contract such Family-Alliances without the Consent of their Parents, and beget Heirs to them against their Approbation and Will'.[53] Fleetwood and Delany leave these economic concerns largely implicit, however, or subsume them in a more generalised preoccupation with social order. Their basic anxieties are better illus-trated by a cautionary tale in Defoe's *Family Instructor*, in which a parent's failure in his duty to catechise his children leads inexorably to the violent dissolution of family bonds. As the children approach adulthood they openly challenge the 'Patriarchal' Authority' of their father, the family disintegrates into 'refractory rebellious Branches', and the text pursues to their ruinous ends the rebels' disorderly lives.[54]

In these contexts the insistence of both writers on the primacy of paternal authority is easy to understand; for in the hierarchy they describe the father both maintains familial order and symbolises the political and divine authorities of the world beyond. As a model of society, the family must have its head; and this head must epitomise (and indeed is formally vested with) the larger powers of King and God. Human life is thus organised around three related and complementary structures of auth-ority, a point both writers are repeatedly at pains to stress. Fleetwood notes that 'to shew us, how fit it is, to comply with and obey our Parents, God calls himself throughout the Holy Scriptures our *Father*, and from that Title and Relation calls for our obedience'; for Delany, parents are no less than God's 'substitutes upon earth'.[55] And both are quite as emphatic about the political significance of the father's role. Delany writes that 'all government, as it is originally derived from paternal authority, is in truth no otherwise to be considered, than as an enlargement of that authority', and he reiterates the analogy in the very organisation of his work, moving at last beyond domestic relations to conclude with a discourse on 'The mutual Duty of Prince and People: Preached on the Anniversary of the Martyrdom of King CHARLES I'.[56] The father stands in the same relation to

[52] *Boswell's Life of Johnson*, II, 55–6; *Familiar Letters*, p. 63.
[53] Henry Gally, *Some Considerations upon Clandestine Marriages*, 2nd edn (1750), p. 54.
[54] *The Family Instructor*, 15th edn (1761), I, 140; I, 273.
[55] Fleetwood, *Relative Duties*, p. 27; Delany, *Social Duties*, p. 141.
[56] Delany, *Social Duties*, pp. 142, xvi.

his children, Delany suggests, as the divinely ordained ruler to his people, so that any breach of filial duty carries the most sinister political connotations. Fleetwood's Whig principles produce the more pragmatic judgment that the filial duties are 'exceedingly useful to many good purposes in publick Government, and therefore all States and Kingdoms have taken care to secure them': disobedient children, he adds, 'will never make good Citizens and Subjects to the Commonwealth'. There is little need for such rationalisation in Delany's eyes, however, and he takes a gloomy relish in citing Chinese ways of nipping civil disorder in the bud: 'If a son should presume to mock a parent, or lay violent hands upon him, the whole country is alarmed, and the judgment reserved for the Emperor himself: the magistrates of the place are turned out; and all the neighbourhood threatened, as having given countenance to so infernal a temper.'[57]

Clearly enough, the implications of filial disobedience reach far; for as Delany puts it 'the same spirit that is restive to the authority of the parent, will in time be refractory to that of the magistrate, and rebellious even to that of Almighty GOD'. Implicitly, the relation between parents and children, more even than the bond of marriage, becomes the single most important social institution, while the disobedience of children replaces the adultery of spouses as the most corrosive threat. Delany, indeed, dispatches the marital duties in two discourses, and devotes six to paternal authority and its requirements. In this analysis, both he and Fleetwood are initially concerned to lay down a single general rule – that parental commands must invariably be obeyed, except where they unmistakably contravene a higher authority. Fleetwood offers exemption only where the laws of God or the land explicitly interpose; Delany is still stricter, insisting that filial obedience has 'no limitation or reserve', except in the case of a command against divine law: 'in that case, and in that only, the child's obedience is to be dispensed with; in all others, to be steadily and uniformly exacted, without admitting the least debate or hesitation.'[58] Both, however, take pains to put a rational case for their strictness, basing it on the likely disposition of parents to act in their children's interests, and on the worldly experience which equips them, better than children themselves, for the task. Children should obey in any event; but there is a concern in both writers to show that it is self-interest, as well as blind duty, that requires this obedience. The wisdom and love of parents, writes Fleetwood, ensure that 'they never command them to do any thing, but the doing it tends to the Children's Advantage'. A child is therefore wise to obey even in cases of disinclination, simply because of the great likelihood that the parent's command is judicious: children will see, he continues,

---

[57] Fleetwood, *Relative Duties*, pp. 17, 11; Delany, *Social Duties*, pp. 150–1. Delany's immediate source for the Chinese anecdote is probably the *Spectator* (No. 189, 6 October 1711).
[58] Delany, *Social Duties*, p. 111.

'that however unacceptable some Commands of Parents may for the present be, yet it is better to yield to them, than to indulge to their own humours; and that the United Wisdom and Experience of the whole World is a safer bottom to proceed upon, than any present longing'. Delany again sees less need to rationalise or justify, but he nods in the same direction by reminding children that obedience 'is also enjoined by the dictates of reason; forasmuch as parents are our natural superiors; and because they are better judges and directors ... from the advantage of more years and experience'.[59]

So far, so good. But both Fleetwood and Delany must eventually confront the possibility of parental fallibility, as well as the intricacy of a social life which will continually throw up cases where general rules seem, if not inapplicable, then at least inadequate or unclear. In its prescriptions, the entire structure of relative duties depends wholly for its pretensions to 'reason' and 'justice' on the sense and goodwill of the parties concerned, and in particular of superiors, whose commands are in theory binding. Human authority, however, cannot be perfect; and so the system must cater for its lapses. One simple way of doing so comes in the three-part hierarchy of authority described above, in which the parental must cede to the divine authority, and (more arguably) to that of the state. Beyond this, however, no firm precepts are available; and the system must enter the darker waters of casuistry. '*To make these Discourses more useful*', Fleetwood announces, '*there is something* Casuistical *in most of them, and such Rules ... laid down, as will enable a Man of tolerable Judgment, and honest Mind, to determine safely, in most cases that ordinarily happen in Humane Life.*' Some strain of contradiction is inevitable here, however, since casuistry's role is not to make rules but to test them in cases so particular and involved that only limited scope for generalisation can exist. Fleetwood's tone therefore becomes more tentative as he moves from a homily on the duty of obedience 'to consider some of the Cases, in which, the Children plead exemption from this Command; and to lay down such Rules as may, most probably, secure the Duty of Children, and the just Authority of Parents'.[60]

Both *Relative Duties* and *Social Duties* turn at this stage to the same test case, which Fleetwood reckons 'the most common case, and the most necessary to be considered', and Delany finds 'of more importance ... than any other in life' – the case of filial disobedience in the settlement of marriage.[61] The case is of such significance because it presents the system of relative duties with, in theoretical terms, its nicest challenge, and because (for reasons outlined above) its stakes are high enough to threaten

---

[59] Fleetwood, *Relative Duties*, pp. 23, 25; Delany, *Social Duties*, p. 152.
[60] Fleetwood, *Relative Duties*, pp. A3–A3v, 29.
[61] *Ibid.*, p. 40; Delany, *Social Duties*, p. 153.

the all-important familial structures on which society itself is based. On both counts it was a preoccupation of the period, and there is no better illustration of its importance in the minds of Richardson's contemporaries than its entry into the political agenda in a prolonged national debate which culminated in Hardwicke's Marriage Act of 1753. The Act amounted to a powerful legal intervention on the side of parental authority, by ruling clandestine marriages void: it thereby attempted to curtail an evil which (according to one commentator) had reached such dimensions that 'no less than six Thousand clandestine Marriages a Year' were performed at a single London chapel, Keith's, which specialised in the 'illicit Trade'.[62] Richardson himself welcomed the Act, and even speculated that his correspondence on *Clarissa* with Hester Mulso may have influenced it, having 'obtained the notice of those who brought in and carried through a bill, which should, by a national law, establish the parental authority, so violently attacked by a young lady, who is admired by all that know her'. Far-fetched though it seems, the claim is not impossible, given Richardson's network of parliamentary contacts and his habit of circulating his correspondences: 'Things done in private', he added, to strengthen the hint, 'have sometimes ... been proclaimed on the house-top.'[63]

Consensus on the extent of parental authority over the marriage of children, however, is hard to find, and here the contract theory that informs Fleetwood's thinking and the divine-right theory beneath Delany's pull the two in significantly different directions. (In its political echoings, indeed, the difference between the two bears comparison with the more exaggerated disputes on parental authority in *Tom Jones*, in which the Tory legitimist Squire Western rails at the disobedience of Sophia while his Whig sister blames him in turn for failing to govern with consent.)[64] For both writers, the issue is simple enough if all parties concerned obey the injunctions of relative duties: the ideal is 'that both the Parents and the Children might choose, *i.e.* that each should approve the others choice: And that, as *Homer* says of *Penelope*, she might be bestowed by her *Father*, upon whom *she* pleas'd ... and when that comes to pass, the Authority of Parents, and the Duty of Children are both secur'd and

---

[62] *A Letter to the Public: Containing the Substance of What Hath Been Offered in the Late Debates ... upon the Subject of the Act of Parliament, for the Better Preventing of Clandestine Marriages* (1753), p. 6.

[63] To Elizabeth Carter, 17 August 1753, *Monthly Magazine*, 33 (1812), 541. John Mulso reported that 'several great men as the Bp of London, the Speaker &c:' had read his sister's correspondence with Richardson (*Letters to Gilbert White*, p. 45); perhaps Hardwicke was another. Certainly, Richardson had links with Hardwicke's eldest son, Philip Yorke. In 1750, he visited Philip Yorke's London house and discussed his plans for *Grandison*, and his *Clarissa* papers include a warm letter of thanks from Yorke for an advance copy of the final instalment. He also printed for Hardwicke's second son, Charles. See Eaves and Kimpel, *Biography*, p. 369; Philip Yorke to Richardson, 1 December 1748, FM, XV, 2, f.14; Sale, *Master Printer*, p. 216.

[64] See *Tom Jones*, I, 335–7.

reconcil'd'. But reconciliation is unlikely to be so happily contrived in every case; and having insisted on the child's duty to obey Fleetwood finds here the strongest argument for filial dissent. He puts it forcefully, stressing the personal misery entailed in a loveless marriage as well as the threat of familial dissension. His concern, however, is not to establish filial independence so much as to redouble the obligation on parents to exercise with care their entitlement to command. They should 'urge not their Authority too far, in constraining their Children to marry, not only where there is no visible Aversion, but where there is great likelyhood that there will not be a good Agreement'.[65]

This injunction, however, only papers over a yawning crack. Though Fleetwood concedes that filial liberty is 'in nothing so necessary as in Marriage', he is unable to give unequivocal sanction to disobedience, and instead places the onus entirely on parents to exercise their power with leniency. He draws a distinction between the case of refusing to marry where commanded and that of actually marrying where forbidden; but he refuses to sanction either act, conceding only that disobedience in the first case is 'much more pardonable and pittiable' than disobedience in the second. Instead he acknowledges that he has entered an indeterminate realm, in which emerges the troubling ambiguity of the term 'relative' (which now seems to mean not only 'reciprocal' but also 'variable'). In these cases, he notes, 'there is so much to be said on both sides, and so many things to be considered particularly on each, that it is neither safe nor true, to affirm, that all Parents in all cases have a right to the compliance and obedience of their Children; or that all Children are at liberty to marry and dispose of themselves, without their Parents; for neither of these Propositions are unexceptionably true'.[66] Parents must therefore be 'cautious and sparing how they lay such commands upon' their children; children 'are to obey as far as possibly they can'; but no sure measure offers for the determination of right conduct by one party in the event of wrong conduct by the other. Instead Fleetwood concludes, lamely, by grasping for an ideal of judicious objectivity. His last resort is to direct children for resolution of any case to impartial but properly strict neighbours: the child may disobey, he hesitantly suggests, when 'those who would be glad that Children should obey their Parents, may see it reasonable they should *not* be obeyed in these Particulars'.[67]

For all his emphasis on filial duty, Fleetwood's was by contemporary standards an advanced position. Even the liberal jurist who saw no theoretical basis for filial obedience in marriage cases was prepared to acknowledge its practical usefulness, and tempered his attack on Fleetwood by conceding that 'though as a *Casuist* he is defective, yet as a *popular*

[65] Fleetwood, *Relative Duties*, pp. 55, 45.   [66] *Ibid.*, pp. 44, 50, 53.
[67] *Ibid.*, pp. 49–50, 55, 54.

Preacher he may well be excused. For it may be more necessary for common Use, in such Cases, to press Obedience in Children, than to shew the Limits of the Parents Power.'[68] For most commentators, however, Fleetwood had done not too little but far too much to show the limits of parental power, and Delany found him intolerably lenient. Where Fleetwood had found in the marriage problem the strongest possible case for filial resistance, he finds instead the most necessary case for unqualified obedience. His concern, in consequence, is not to lay down rules for special cases, but simply to stress the awful consequences of misconduct. Indeed, he recognises a command against God as the only legitimate reason for exemption, and thus regards parental commands to marry or not to marry particular individuals as problematic only because of the higher stakes involved: the child's duty remains invariable. There is, as a result, an unresolved tension in his dictum that 'as perfect obedience is required of the children, parents should be very cautious in their commands', and a startling severity in his insistence that 'as long as children continue a part of their parents family, (which must be till they think fit to dispose otherwise of them) they are absolutely in their parents power, and have no more right to dispose of themselves, than they have to dispose of the parents fortune, or inheritance, or any of their goods'. Whether the parent observes or neglects his 'should', it would seem, has no bearing on the child's 'must'; and so it is to tragedy, not casuistry, that Delany looks for resolution of the subject. 'It were infinitely better', he concludes, 'that perverse children should actually die in the disappointment of their inclinations, than that they should make both themselves, and their parents, for ever miserable, by an unfortunate and undutiful marriage.'[69]

The father's house

Richardson was printing *Fifteen Sermons upon Social Duties* as he drafted *Clarissa*;[70] and the links between the conduct manual and a novel 'Comprehending [as its title-page proclaims] *The most* Important Concerns *of* Private LIFE. And particularly shewing, The DISTRESSES that may attend the Misconduct Both of PARENTS and CHILDREN, In Relation to MARRIAGE',[71] are evident enough. Delany himself recognised them on reading *Clarissa*, and from his pen the commonplace comparison between novel and sermon acquires special force: 'He pities himself, and his own

---

[68] Henry Stebbing, *A Dissertation on the Power of States to Deny Civil Protection to the Marriages of Minors Made without the Consent of their Parents or Guardians* (1755), p. 17.

[69] Delany, *Social Duties*, pp. 134, 153, 156.

[70] The link is noted in A. D. McKillop, *Samuel Richardson: Printer and Novelist* (Chapel Hill, 1936), p. 135; on the dating of *Clarissa*'s composition, see Eaves and Kimpel, 'The Composition of *Clarissa* and its Revision before Publication', *PMLA*, 83 (1968), 416–18.

[71] *Clarissa*, title-page (observing the typography of 1747–8).

sermons', as he announced in the postscript to a letter from his wife Mary
Delany, by comparison with 'a Work which he scruples not to declare ...
the most Valuable of any his Age has produced'.[72] Here at least few could
contest Delany's sense of priorities. Yet it is from these 'pitiable' sermons
and the tradition in which they were written that *Clarissa* takes its sense of
the critical importance, both literally and as a paradigm, of the father–
daughter theme. The conflict of the first instalment, with its calamitous
breakdown in the harmonious patterns of life at Harlowe Place, draws for
its significance on Fleetwood's and Delany's sense of the centrality of
familial concord to the wellbeing of the entire social edifice – on the sense
in which, as one petitioner for the Marriage Act was to put it, 'the Peace
and good Order of Society depend upon the Peace and good Order of
private Families'.[73] The novel amplifies its father–daughter theme,
moreover, by a method of analogy which echoes the three-part hierarchy
of relations posited in their writings as the mainstay of social coherence:
the text is shot through by a series of mythic and historical parallels, in
which the rebellion of child against parent comes to reiterate, ominously,
the rebellions of man against God and of people against King. And
Richardson concentrates all the urgency of their analyses in the endlessly
resonant spatial image that presides over the novel – the image of the
father's house.[74]

Shortly before Clarissa's flight from Harlowe Place, one of the first
edition's rare explanatory footnotes cites the following formulation from
the Patriarchal Law:

Ver.3. *If a woman vow a vow unto the Lord, and bind herself by a bond, being in her father's
house in her youth;*

4. *And her father hear her vow, and her bond wherewith she hath bound her soul, and her
father shall hold his peace at her; then all her vows shall stand, and every bond wherewith she
hath bound her soul shall stand.*

5. *But if her father disallow her in the day that he heareth; not any of her vows or of her
bonds wherewith she hath bound her soul shall stand: And the Lord shall forgive her because
her father disallowed her.*   (II, 289; p. 361; quoting Numbers 30)

The text is a key authority in casuistical discussions of filial duty,[75] and its
implications, as Richardson's note draws them out, reach far beyond the
specific case to which Clarissa has applied it (that of her entitlement to

---

[72] Patrick Delany's postscript, Mary Delany to Richardson, 25 January 1748/9, FM XV, 2, f.13.

[73] Gally, *Some Considerations upon Clandestine Marriages*, pp. 25–6. In the year of the Marriage Act,
Harriet Byron can be found expressing just this view: 'that families are little communities ...
and that they help to make up worthily, and to secure, the great community, of which they are
so many miniatures' (*Grandison*, I, 25).

[74] See Tony Tanner's reading of the same topos in Rousseau's *La Nouvelle Héloïse* (*Adultery in the
Novel*, pp. 120–33), to which I am indebted.

[75] See, for example, Delany, *Social Duties* p. 153; [Allestree], *The Whole Duty of Man* (1659),
p. 291; [Allestree], *The Ladies Calling* (Oxford, 1673), p. 160; Hall, *Resolutions and Decisions of*

withdraw her undertaking to Lovelace that she will elope). Unlike men and widows, who are 'subject to no other domestic authority', the daughter is subject not directly to the authority of God but first, as though by delegation, to that of the father. Where the vows of widows and men are therefore 'indispensable', the note suggests, the daughter's relations with God are mediated at every point by her relations with her father, so that her power to commit herself to any course of action depends always on the assent of this more immediate authority. If her father chooses, her most solemn vow may therefore be rendered 'of no force'. ('This right of the parent is so undoubted, that we find God himself gives way to it', writes the author of *The Ladies Calling*).[76] Within the father's house, we are again reminded, unwavering obedience is enjoined.

The consciousness of *'being in her father's house in her youth'* in this severe sense underlies Clarissa's own analyses of events at Harlowe Place. 'Nothing but the last extremity shall make me abandon my father's house', she tells Anna (II, 68; p. 243). Caught between a recognition of daughterly obligations and the fear of a 'last extremity' (compulsion in marriage) which in her mind will relieve her of these obligations, her words here explicitly reserve for herself what might be called a right of resistance. But as this 'last extremity' becomes an imminent prospect she renounces all claims to autonomy, reasoning herself out of her resolution to elope with reference to Numbers, and thereby acknowledging the divinely sanctioned authority of those 'who, according to the Old Law, have a right of absolving or confirming a child's promise' (II, 289; p. 361). By setting her conduct against the rigours of the Mosaic dispensation, she endeavours to restore to herself her identity as the exemplary child, whose acquiescence in the paternal will is properly undiscriminating. Yet within days she has fled with Lovelace from the father's house, the very fault for which the conduct books reserve their sternest tones. 'And if Children who are under Age', writes Fleetwood, 'and wholly in their Fathers Custody and Power, and part of his House and Family, will venture to engage themselves, without the consent, or against the commands of their Parents . . . they will be guilty of sinful Disobedience, and must seek the forgiveness they will want both at Gods and their Parents Hands.'[77] Clarissa has transgressed, and in the fullest sense: by disobeying her father's will and leaving her father's house, she has crossed or *passed beyond* its bounds[78] as

---

Divers Practicall Cases of Conscience (1649), p. 379; [Steele, ed.?], *The Ladies Library* (1714), II, 5. Richardson refers again to the text in a letter to Frances Grainger, 29 March 1750, Carroll, p. 155.

[76] *The Ladies Calling*, p. 160.   [77] Fleetwood, *Relative Duties*, p. 56.

[78] See Johnson's *Dictionary*, in which the primary meaning of 'To Transgress', 'To pass over; to pass beyond', leads into the secondary meaning 'To violate; to break', or more specifically 'To offend by violating a law'.

both a physical and an ethical realm. The rest of the novel will trace her
efforts to atone.

Thus Harlowe Place is not only the literal setting of Clarissa's case of
conscience but an image of peculiar resonance, rich in its implications
about the rights and wrongs of that case. For Tony Tanner, the father's
house stands as both ethical imperative and dramatic space, 'the very
architecture of prohibition and interdiction'. More recently, Janet Butler
has placed emphasis not on the house itself but on its territorial extension,
the father's garden, bringing together Richardson's scattered but significant information about the Harlowe estate to explore the messages it
discloses about Clarissa and her family alike.[79] Though the house is the
scene of Clarissa's most direct confrontations with the authority of her
father it is in the garden, as Butler points out, that in her transactions with
Lovelace she most actively contravenes it. In combination these two
associated settings are carefully used by Richardson to inform and complicate the reader's judgment of the action staged within them.

All parties are implicated by the connotations of their environment, not
least the father himself. On turning to the specific details of the Harlowe
estate one rapidly sees, for example, that this particular father's house is no
Paradise Hall or Prior Park, in both of which the flourishing, open, and
'natural' landscape all around is used by Fielding to attest the benevolence
of its occupant.[80] 'As is the Gardener, so is the Garden', runs an
eighteenth-century commonplace;[81] and in a period as self-conscious as
this about gardens and their meanings ('Poetry, Painting, and Gardening,
or the Science of Landscape' being, in Horace Walpole's words, 'Three
Sisters', alike in their capacity to signify)[82] the scene at Harlowe Place
arouses little confidence in the mind of its owner or in the likely form in
which his authority will be exercised. Particularly significant here are

[79] Tanner, *Adultery in the Novel*, p. 103; Janet Butler, 'The Garden: Early Symbol of Clarissa's
Complicity', *Studies in English Literature 1500–1900*, 24 (1984), 527–44. Much of the following
argument pursues a line similar to Butler's, but takes issue with her assumptions that
Richardson planned the garden simply as a socio-economic indicator, that its Biblical associations are intuitive only, and that his conscious intention, subverted by these associations, was
to uphold Clarissa's blamelessness. Richardson's allusions to the Fall are deliberate and
insistent, I would suggest, and contribute to a sense of Clarissa's imperfection that is central to
the novel's plan.

[80] See *Tom Jones*, I, 42–3; II, 612–13.

[81] Thomas Fuller, *Gnomologia* (1732), quoted by Maynard Mack, *The Garden and the City:
Retirement and Politics in the Later Poetry of Pope, 1731–1743* (Toronto, 1969), p. 4. For Catherine
Talbot, Richardson's own garden was just such a projection of personality, in this case
denoting a bizarrely obsessive benevolence: 'His Villa is fitted up in the same Style his Books
are writ', she wrote on visiting Parson's Green. 'Every Minute detail attended to, yet every one
with a view to its being useful or pleasing. Not an inch in his Garden unimproved or
unadorned, his very Poultry made happy by fifty neat little Contrivances' (quoted by Eaves
and Kimpel, *Biography*, pp. 496–7).

[82] *Satirical Poems by William Mason with Notes by Horace Walpole*, ed. Paget Toynbee (Oxford,
1926), p. 43.

Lovelace's sneer that Harlowe Place, 'like Versailles . . . is sprung up from a dunghil, within every elderly person's remembrance' (I, 229; p. 161), and his subsequent description of its 'rambling, Dutch-taste garden' (I, 234; p. 164). The house is in the first place a grandiose statement of ambition, its very name being, as Anna adds, a 'piece of affectation' (II, 11; p. 211). It marks the hubristic attempt of a parvenu family to stamp its identity on the landscape, and it is also of course a central gambit in their 'darling view . . . of *raising a family*' (I, 72; p. 77) – the project, of which Clarissa is so directly a victim, to win money, land and a peerage for the son and heir. It is a Timon's Villa, conspicuous in its display of wealth and power; and as at Timon's Villa (where 'Grove nods at Grove, each Alley has a Brother', and 'The suff'ring eye inverted Nature sees')[83] the display is made above all in the rigid formality of its grounds. Here the 'Dutch-taste garden' is a clever touch, the vogue for formal gardens on the Dutch model being (as Butler observes) long outmoded at the time of writing, and at best safely conventional at even the earliest date (1721) at which *Clarissa* could conceivably be set.[84] The garden's style thus suggests the eager but ill-aimed conformity of the arriviste. There is also a hint of ingratiation, of currying favour, for the Dutch-taste garden was imported originally as a statement of allegiance to the new regime established at the deposition of James II. As Francis Coventry complained, 'The mournful family of Yews came over with the house of Orange; the sombre taste of Holland grew into vogue, and strait canals, rectilineal walks, and rows of clipt ever-greens were all the mode.'[85]

These, however, are minor points, quietly implied. What the Dutch style of the garden most obviously signifies, and with greatest relevance to Clarissa's case, is the restraint of nature, both human and vegetal, by rigid patterns and rules. At a time when Opposition grandees like Burlington at Chiswick and Cobham at Stowe could expect the naturalistic landscaping of their parks to be read, in its very boundlessness and informality, as a declaration of political principle, and when writers as diverse as Thomson, Pope and Addison could turn instinctively to the same analogy ('a spa-

---

[83] Pope, *Epistle to Burlington*, in *Epistles to Several Persons*, ed. F. W. Bateson, *The Twickenham Edition of the Poems of Alexander Pope*, III, ii, 2nd edn (1961), lines 117, 119.

[84] On the dating of *Clarissa*'s action see the introduction to Ross's edition (Harmondsworth, 1985), p. 23; Eaves and Kimpel, *Biography*, p. 239; Arthur Sherbo, 'Time and Place in Richardson's *Clarissa*', *Boston University Studies in English*, 3 (1957), 139–46.

[85] *The World* (1755–7), I, 120 (No. 15, 12 April 1753). The Revolution was 'an aera as remarkable in the annals of GARDENING as in those of government; but far less auspicious in the former instance', Coventry writes. '. . . It was the compliment which England paid her new sovereign, to wear the dress of a Dutch morass . . . [G]ood whigs distinguished their loyalty by fetching their plans from the same country which had the honour of producing their king . . . and it would probably have been then esteemed as great a mark of disaffection to have laid out ground differently from the true Belgic model, as it would be now to wear a white rose on the tenth of June.'

cious Horison is an Image of Liberty', wrote Addison),[86] the very different
meaning of the Harlowe garden would be hard to miss. With its high yew
hedges (II, 37; p. 225), its filbert walks (II, 225; p. 327), its artificial
cascades (II, 142; p. 283) and its ubiquitous gloomy ivy (II, 119–20;
p. 271), the estate combines strong suggestions of darkness, of entanglement, and above all of repressive control. In gardens of this kind, as
Horace Walpole complained, 'the sheers were applied to the lovely wild-
ness of form with which nature has distinguished each species of tree',[87]
and in this particular garden Clarissa too is subject to the same denial of
nature and liberty – not just immured or hedged in, but herself stunted, as
we might say, or checked in her growth. (Eventually, of course, she defines
herself by an image of yet more brutally damaged nature, her coffin
bearing as an emblem 'a white lily snapt short off, and just falling from the
stalk': VII, 130; p. 1306.) This same idea of nature repressed and liberty
denied is reinforced by the analogy with Versailles, for the radiating
avenues and regimented topiary of Le Nôtre's garden were nothing if not a
statement of dominion and authoritarian power, indeed of autocracy, and
were widely perceived as such.[88]

In these contexts, Richardson's few hints encode a wealth of meaning
about Clarissa's father's house. The details of the estate bring with them
connotations of ambition, authoritarianism and constraint of a kind perfectly encapsulated in Horace Walpole's diatribe against the formal
garden: 'in the hands of ostentatious wealth', he writes, '[art] became the
means of opposing nature; and the more it traversed the march of the
latter, the more nobility thought its power was demonstrated'.[89] Osten-
tation, opposition to nature, power: where in Richardson's later novel an
informal landscape of just the kind that Horace Walpole was to promote in
place of this has very different moral implications (Harriet finds the
gardens of Grandison Hall 'as boundless as the mind of the owner, and as
free and open as his countenance'),[90] the same analogy between garden

---

[86] *Spectator*, ed. Donald F. Bond (Oxford, 1965), III, 541 (No. 412, 23 June 1712). On the
political connotations of landscape in the period see John Dixon Hunt, *The Figure in the
Landscape: Poetry, Painting and Gardening during the Eighteenth Century* (Baltimore, 1976), p. 63;
Edward Malins, *English Landscaping and Literature, 1660–1840* (1966), pp. 16–17; Kimerly
Rorschach, *The Early Georgian Landscape Garden* (New Haven, 1983), p. 6. The classic literary
source here is again the *Epistle to Burlington*. which in its various oppositions and associations
provides the best available gloss to Richardson's own treatment of gardens throughout his
work.

[87] *The History of the Modern Taste in Gardening* (1771), in Isabel Wakelin Chase, *Horace Walpole:
Gardenist* (Princeton, 1943), p. 11.

[88] See Malins, *English Landscaping and Literature*, p. 5. Thomson, in particular, plays on the link
between formal gardening and oppressive government in France, in Book V of *Liberty*: see
Hunt, *The Figure in the Landscape*, p. 63.

[89] *Modern Taste in Gardening*, p. 10.

[90] *Grandison*, III, 272. See also the ensuing description of the estate, in which the hedges and walls
of Harlowe Place are allowed no place: 'the whole being bounded only by sunk fences, the eye

and gardener at Harlowe Place leads us to expect only meanness and repression. The one exception comes in those parts of the estate for which Clarissa herself is responsible, the poultry-yard and the dairy-house, where nurture replaces display as the governing priority, and where Clarissa is able to remind herself of what the Harlowes forget – that estates are not dominions but 'stewardships' (I, 124; p. 104).

That, however, is not to say that the garden image is any more to Clarissa's advantage than to her father's. Rather the reverse; for among all the wealth of associations and connotations suggested by the garden in the culture of the day one more than any other was fundamental. Above all, the garden was an image of its lost original – the first garden, where mankind lives in happiness before the Fall. When Elizabeth Montagu visited Stowe in 1744 the landscape gave her 'the best idea of Paradise that can be', while for Horace Walpole Hagley and Stourhead called to mind nothing so much as the description of Eden given by Milton in Book IV of *Paradise Lost*.[91] Even less fashionably 'natural' gardens could be invested with the same association: Edward Young solicited it by inscribing his garden at Welwyn with a text from Genesis ('*Ambulantes in horto audierunt vocem Dei*'), while it amused Horace Walpole to think that for a Frenchman 'the garden of Eden ... was something approaching to that of Versailles'.[92] The memory of Eden, it would seem, was inherent in the very idea of the garden, whatever its style; and the link is one to which Richardson was alive in both *Clarissa* and *Grandison*. In the later novel it has a simple use: the garden of Grandison Hall is directly modelled on Milton's description of the prelapsarian landscape,[93] thereby helping to define the house, for Harriet and Lucy, as a paradisal scene. *Clarissa*, however, makes more ominous use of the garden–paradise analogy, echoing not the visual details of Milton's Eden so much as the action staged within it, the 'first disobedience' which 'Brought death into the world, and all our woe'.[94] Here the emphasis, in other words, is not on Paradise itself but on its loss – an emphasis which makes the faults of Clarissa's father pale beside the implications of her own behaviour.

When, in response to Lovelace's congratulations on her escape from 'your cruel and gloomy father's house' (III, 39; p. 392), she retorts that she 'would give the world ... to have been still in my father's house,

is carried to views that have no bounds'. Sir Charles, we also learn, 'thinks it a kind of impiety to fell a tree' (III, 273).

[91] To the Duchess of Portland, 9 August 1944, quoted by George Clarke, 'Grecian Taste and Gothic Virtue: Lord Cobham's Gardening Programme and Its Iconography', *Apollo* (June 1973), 568; Walpole, *Modern Taste in Gardening*, pp. 14–15.

[92] Quoted by Mack, *The Garden and the City*, p. 25; Walpole, *Modern Taste in Gardening*, p. 7.

[93] See Dustin Griffin, *Regaining Paradise: Milton and the Eighteenth Century* (Cambridge, 1986), p. 132.

[94] *Paradise Lost*, Book I, lines 1, 3.

whatever had been my usage' (III, 35; p. 390), it is this analogy that comes to the fore: retrospectively and from beyond, the father's house appears a forfeited paradise, from which she is 'miserably fallen' (III, 202; p. 479). 'O That I were as in the months past . . . As I was in the days when the Almighty was yet with me! When I *was in my father's house*!' she later laments (adapting Job) in one of her meditations;[95] in the strictly spiritual terms of her last writings, it is a locus of righteousness and bliss, a place of the strongest religious connotations. These connotations became most emphatic when she plays on the double sense of 'father's house' in her allegorical letter to Lovelace, in which she sets out 'with all diligence for my father's house . . . overjoyed with the assurance of a thorough recon-ciliation, thro' the interposition of a dear blessed friend' (VII, 17; p. 1233) – an allusion to her penitential progress from the paradise lost of the father's house within the world to the paradise regained of the father's house beyond it. In this context, when she reproaches herself and Lovelace at St Albans for recriminating 'like the first pair, I, at least, driven out of my paradise' (III, 41; p. 393), she is wrong only in the role she gives to Lovelace (who likens himself, more aptly, to 'the grand tempter': III, 306; p. 534). Her lapse repeats the Fall.

Richardson plots the stages of this fall with precision. Before Lovelace's admission to Harlowe Place, Clarissa lives in paradisal harmony with her family, attentive to the duties of her state and the happy recipient of 'everybody's love, and good opinion' (I, 5; p. 41). At first her dealings with Lovelace seem reconcilable with these duties, to the extent that she can even ask James and Bella, when they challenge her to forbid Love-lace's visits, 'what authority I had to take such a step in my father's house' (I, 21; p. 49). When parental sanction is withdrawn and she is ordered to marry Solmes, however, she finds herself in direct opposition to the paternal will, and is confined to areas which confirm her ambivalent status within the house. Excluded from its communal parts and denied partici-pation in the social life of the family, she divides her time between two peripheral places. One is her closet, which, though formally a part of the house, constitutes her private domain within it, a locus of privacy and withdrawal.[96] (After the elopement, it is 'nailed up, as if it were not a part of the house': III, 260; p. 509.) The other is the ivy bower, 'a place, that from a girl, the young Lady delighted in' (II, 271; p. 351), but a place

---

[95] *Meditations Collected from the Sacred Books* (1750), pp. 12–13. The contents of this volume, supposedly written by Clarissa between her rape and her death, were probably included in one of the novel's pre-publication states. Richardson seems then to have intended to publish the book as a supplement to the novel, but he eventually restricted it to a private circulation. For details see Keymer, 'Richardson's *Meditations*: Clarissa's *Clarissa*', in *Samuel Richardson: Tercen-tenary Essays*, ed. Margaret Anne Doody and Peter Sabor (Cambridge, 1989), pp. 89–109.

[96] On the implications of the house's internal spaces see Christina Marsden Gillis, *The Paradox of Privacy: Epistolary Form in Clarissa* (Gainesville, 1984), pp. 21–34.

located perilously close to the garden's edge. Allowed 'the liberty of the garden' (I, 156; p. 122), she resorts repeatedly to a part which in its very situation mingles the sense of paradise with foreboding of its loss.

Her activities mark the same process of alienation. She meets with Lovelace in another part of the garden 'remote from the dwelling-house' (I, 234; p. 164) and undertakes a clandestine correspondence which is, as Anna notes, 'a great point gain'd' by him at her father's expense: 'What an intimacy does this beget for the lover! – How is it distancing the parent!', Anna warns (I, 61; p. 71). Such intimacy with the tempter and distance from the father are dangerous indeed; for in Lovelace's manipulation of the correspondence to beguile and seduce her, and ultimately to draw her beyond the walls of Harlowe Place, it becomes clear that Clarissa's apple is an epistolary one. (It can be no coincidence that on one occasion she imagines herself 'bit by a viper' on reaching for one of Lovelace's hidden letters: II, 166; p. 295.)[97] As the correspondence continues she finds herself 'more and more intangled' (I, 148; p. 117), lured into trespass by what one reader called the 'Veil of Bravery' in which Lovelace shrouds his designs: 'there, if a Person is deceiv'd', he went on, 'it must be analogous to the simplicity of the Dove being over-reach'd by y^c subtlety of the Serpent'.[98]

The drama of epistolary beguilement culminates at the borders of the Harlowe garden, where its Dutch fashioning degenerates into a sinister neglect. The contrast is sharp. On the inside of the garden door, Clarissa's bower gives on to 'a pretty variegated landscape of wood, water, and hilly country; which had pleased her so much, that she had drawn it' (II, 271; p. 351). Immediately beyond the door, however, lies the haunted coppice, a 'pathless and lonesome' place where oaklings are strangled by over-grown ivy and mistletoe, where 'owls, ravens, and other ominous birds' haunt the air, and where the only sign of civilisation is the ruin of an old chapel (I, 273; p. 352). It is a wilderness of the Harlowes' own making, than which 'nowhere is more bye and unfrequented' – a place in which Clarissa will be alone, unguided, and (with the disguised Lovelace skulking 'like a thief about these lonely walls': III, 11; p. 377) imperilled. The walls, moreover, are beginning to disintegrate, a detail which further reinforces the novel's sense of the father's crumbling authority. It could not be more apt that their loose bricks provide the place in which the clandestine letters are exchanged, so that 'but a brick wall, of a few inches thick' (II, 104 ; p. 263) separates Clarissa on the inside and Lovelace on the outside as she deposits her letters. When he surprises her as she visits the spot, throwing open his greatcoat in a gesture which, when repeated at

---

[97] Richardson took particular care to make this suggestion: the printed text reads 'bit by a scorpion', and is corrected by an erratum note at the end of the volume (II, 309).

[98] R. Smith to Richardson, [Autumn 1747], FM XV, 2, f.87.

Hampstead, prompts him to recall 'the devil in Milton' (V, 21; p. 772),
her immediate reaction is to lament 'the sin of a prohibited correspondence' (I, 236; p. 165). As Satan charms Eve in the scene from *Paradise
Lost* alluded to in the Hampstead passage,[99] however, so Lovelace allays
her fears adroitly enough to make her persist, calamitously, in her epistolary 'sin'.

Having at last resolved to elope, she arranges to meet him 'by the ivy
summer-house, or in it . . . and would unbolt the door, that he might come
in by his own key' (II, 104; p. 262): as in the correspondence, she is forced
by Lovelace to incriminate herself, to share responsibility for his intrusion
into the garden and her own departure from it. She revokes the promise,
but ends nonetheless in the same transgression: she is drawn through the
garden door and into the haunted coppice, image and precursor of the
'wilderness of doubt and error' into which she later finds herself cast by
this 'one devious step at setting out' (III, 365; p. 566). 'All amaze and
confusion' (III, 16; p. 380), she begins her journey from the lost garden
into this more exacting medium, which she sees metaphorically as one of
'fens and quagmires' (III, 365; p. 566), and which Richardson gives the
literal shape of London, 'that great, wicked town' (II, 240; p. 335). For all
the involuntariness of her 'devious step' into this wilderness, however,
there could be no greater mark of her reprobacy. Not only has she failed to
behave as a daughter *'being in her father's house in her youth'* should: she has
eloped from it, flouting her own express view of 'the leaving my father's
house, without his consent, [as] one of the most inexcusable actions I could
be guilty of' (II, 67; p. 242). By leaving the father's house in such a way,
'the fugitive daughter' (III, 2; p. 372) has committed the greatest crime,
and has entered in the same instant on its punishment, pursued by
paternal malediction. 'You might have spared your heavy curse', she later
exclaims, in apostrophe to her father, 'had you known how I have been
punished, ever since my swerving feet led me out of your garden-doors to
meet this man!' (IV, 156; p. 650).

The Fall is the most sustained and direct analogy provided for the
calamity at Harlowe Place; but like the theorists of relative duties Richardson finds political as well as theological overtones in the conflict
between father and child. Such analogies, of course, were not unique to
Fleetwood and Delany, and had been fixed in the eighteenth-century
mind by the vying political theories of Filmer's *Patriarcha* (1680), Algernon
Sidney's *Discourses Concerning Government* (1698) and Locke's *Two Treatises*
(1690).[100] To Richardson, they were almost instinctive: one need only

---

[99] See Gillian Beer's commentary on the passage, 'Richardson, Milton, and the Status of Evil',
Review of English Studies, NS 19, No. 75 (1968), p. 268.

[100] On Filmer's patriarchalism and its early critics, see G. J. Schochet, *Patriarchalism in Political
Thought* (Oxford, 1973), pp. 115–267.

recall his response to the 'dissolv'd Difference' of Cibber's *Lady's Lecture*, when he wrote of authority 'level[led]' and distinction 'throw[n] down', to detect larger anxieties welling beneath his consideration of the literal subject. His correspondence on *Clarissa* makes such analogies more explicit. In particular, the debate with Hester Mulso draws recurrently on political theory, and by its close has modulated into a parallel discussion of domestic and political principle. 'Shall the child think itself at liberty, whenever it is *disobliged*, to disobey, or the subject to rebel?', Richardson challenges her at one point; at another, 'suppose the parent or the king exert his authority to the grievance of the child, or the subject; who is to be judge of the reasonableness or unreasonableness of the exertion?'[101] Elsewhere he describes families which break down the structures of parental authority as 'Levellers'.[102]

This last term echoes the theme of Delany's concluding discourse, a 30 January sermon which looks back to the English Revolution for a monitory example of the chaos produced by the misconduct of both ruler and ruled. Combining a divine-right ideology with an apparently sincere commitment to the post-1689 Establishment,[103] Delany's analysis recommends moderation on either side for the sake of social peace, but again chooses to place greatest stress on the duties of the subordinate partner. Kings are 'of divine appointment', Delany writes, yet they have an obligation always to exert this divinely sanctioned power in their subjects' best interests. It is therefore essential that they 'guard against the influence of evil advisers; forasmuch as all such naturally tend to pervert and warp them from the ways of justice, and consequently to sap the only foundation upon which their power is built'.[104] In this context, Charles I is adduced as an example not of autocratic excess (though Delany half-heartedly acknowledges that he was 'bred under maxims of government ill suited to the genius of his people'). Rather, his fault is merely one of injudicious delegation. He is acquitted 'of all tyrannous and oppressive intentions towards his people; as well as of the guilt of that black and unnatural rebellion', blame instead being displaced (conveniently for Delany's divine-right position) towards his corrupt advisers. Charles was 'misled . . . by counsels of an evil tendency, to suffer the beginning of his reign to be blemished with a conduct ill befitting his true character', and it was through this mistake alone that the way was opened to civil war and its inevitable sequel, the illegitimate usurpation of worse rulers, 'more arbitrary and cruel tyrants'.[105] Still more significant as an apology for Charles,

---

[101] Mulso to Richardson, 3 January 1750/1 (quoting his last), *Posthumous Works of Mrs. Chapone*, II, 93–4, II, 93.

[102] Richardson to Frances Grainger, 22 January 1749/50, Carroll, p. 145.

[103] On the tenability of this position, see J. C. D. Clark, *English Society, 1688–1832: Ideology, Social Structure and Political Practice during the Ancien Régime* (Cambridge, 1985), pp. 121–41.

[104] Delany, *Social Duties*, pp. 318, 303–4.   [105] *Ibid.*, pp. 306, 308, 306, 310.

however, is the eagerness with which the greatest blame for these disasters
(and any like them) is thrown on the subjects themselves: Delany censures
'the perverse obstinacy, and restive refusals of his people to his most just,
and reasonable, and necessary demands', dwells luridly on the national
chaos and desolation which followed their 'execrable rebellion', identifies
Charles's execution as an act of 'parricide', and concludes with a related
attack on the 'too fashionable republican principles' of the present. (Such
principles, he suggests, 'under the pretence of more zeal for liberty, would
draw us again into double thraldom' – though a double thraldom, this
time, not of puritan dictatorship but of 'popery and arbitrary power'.)[106]
Throughout the whole calamity, the only exemplars of right conduct to be
found are the principled royalists who to their own great cost kept faith
with an authority they were, for all its failings, required to obey – 'those
noble patriots, who adhered to their royal master *King Charles the First* in
all his misfortunes'.[107]

Clarissa's only direct allusions to the 'parricide' of which Delany writes
here are passing remarks, in later instalments, of little obvious importance.
In one, Lovelace irreverently mocks his own lapse 'into the old dismal
thirtieth of January strain' (V, 272; p. 911); in the other, he likens his own
abuse of power to that of Cromwell ('as Cromwell said, if it must be my
head, or the king's': III, 57; p. 402). Yet in the structure of its plot the
novel follows a pattern closely related to the one Delany describes, while
also bringing to bear on events a language that is explicitly political.
Lovelace certainly is, as his allusion to Cromwell hints, a tyrant who
turns to his own advantage a dispute between ruler and ruled. More
important, Clarissa herself is not only, as outlined above, 'fallen': she is
also 'a rebel child' (I, 215; p. 154), her opposition to the authority of her
father raising echoes not only of man's first disobedience but also of this
later revolt.

Recent criticism has begun to recognise some such political dimension,
in which the heroine's predicament comes to reflect a larger pattern in the
theory or history of government. Jocelyn Harris has identified Clarissa as
'a Lockian woman in a household of Filmerian men', while Angus Ross
has suggested an analogy between the conduct of James Harlowe junior
and that of Charles's son James II, whose moves towards autocracy
precipitated the resistance of subjects in favour of a rival power. Looking
forward to a third revolution, Jay Fliegelman has shown how Clarissa's
reluctant rebellion could seem to epitomise for American readers after
1776 the turbulent birth of their own nation, while also carrying (for one
at least) a reactionary warning. 'Democracy is Lovelace and the people

---

[106] *Ibid.*, pp. 308, 316, 315, 317, 317. On the topical implication of this analysis, see below,
pp. 168–9.
[107] Delany, *Social Duties*, p. 316.

are Clarissa', wrote John Adams in 1804: 'The artful villain will pursue the innocent lovely girl to her ruin and her death.'[108] Nor was this appropriation of *Clarissa* entirely without foundation; for the novel's seeming anticipation of the American future emerges directly from its hints at the English past.

A remark of Anna's defines the problem: 'If the boundaries of the Three Estates that constitute our Political Union were not known, and occasionally asserted, what would become of each? The two branches of the Legislature would encroach upon each other; and the Executive power would swallow up both' (II, 132; p. 277). Here history provides a precedent, not only in the actions of James II but also in those of his father. Delany himself recognises the provocation caused by Charles's frequent dissolutions of Parliament, and he warns in particular against dissension between the legislative branches, the Houses of Lords and Commons. Yet the boundaries between these three estates can be worryingly indeterminate; occasional assertions can look more like transgressions; and political union is as likely to be exploded as cemented by the contentions that result. In this view, Clarissa's case is just that of the third estate, the English commons who saw in Charles's claims to royal prerogative a violation of the liberty which was their birthright.[109] It is suggestive here that the territorial 'estate' bequeathed to Clarissa by her late grandfather seems also to confer on her a birthright of just this political kind, a point her own habit of referring to the estate as 'the independency bequeathed me' (I, 79; p. 80) keeps in view. If the estate does indeed represent such a birthright, however, it is one she is reluctant to claim in full. As the advocate of autonomy, Anna has urged her to retain her estate and independency, believing (as Clarissa writes) 'that I should not make a bad use of the power willed me' (I, 123; p. 104). She herself prefers to enter a kind of Lockian contract, however, in which she resigns it to her father. 'All young creatures, thought I, more or less, covet independency; but those who wish most for it, are seldom the fittest to be trusted either with the government of themselves, or with power over others', she adds (I, 124; p. 104).

So long as the father proves himself the fittest to be trusted with government and power, all will be well. Clarissa recognises the theoretical

---

108 Harris, *Samuel Richardson*, p. 52; *Clarissa*, ed. Ross (Harmondsworth, 1985), p. 19; Jay Fliegelman, *Prodigals and Pilgrims: The American Revolution against Patriarchal Authority* (Cambridge, 1982), p. 237 (see also pp. 83–9). See also the astute remarks made about *Clarissa* in James T. Boulton, 'Arbitrary Power: An Eighteenth-Century Obsession', *Studies in Burke and His Time*, 9, No. 3 (1968), 917–19.

109 On ideas of birthright, natural right and ancient liberty in the mid-seventeenth century, see Christopher Hill, 'The Norman Yoke', in *Puritanism and Revolution* (1958), pp. 50–122; J. G. A. Pocock, *The Ancient Constitution and the Feudal Law: A Study of English Historical Thought in the Seventeenth Century*, 2nd edn (Cambridge, 1987), esp. pp. 318–21; Richard Tuck, *Natural Rights Theories: Their Origin and Development* (Cambridge, 1979), esp. pp. 143–55.

supremacy of paternal authority, and having left Harlowe Place she acknowledges her violation of 'the authority I ought to have been bound by' (III, 19; p. 381). Earlier, she recognises a father's right to restrain a child under his government, 'to prevent a headstrong child, as a good prince would wish to do disaffected subjects, from running into rebellion, and so forfeiting everything!' (I, 51; p. 65). The sad reality, however, is that her own father shares King Charles's fatal faults. Richardson's initial sketch of the father's character identifies him as '*despotic, absolute*' and '*arbitrary*' (I, ix; p. 37), while in reply to an early review of the novel he acknowledges him to be 'a gloomy and implacable tyrant', who 'made her opposition to his will, in a point so interesting to herself, a crime'.[110] It is Clarissa's predicament that, despite all this, she cannot challenge his authority. 'Another would call your father a tyrant, if you will not: All the world indeed would' (I, 176; p. 133), insists Anna, going on to protest in a later letter at his 'tyrant word AUTHORITY' (II, 60; p. 239). Lovelace too accuses him of 'an arbitrariness that had few examples even in the families of princes' (I, 241; p. 168), and later calls him, with obvious resonance, '*old prerogative Harlowe*' (V, 205; p. 873). But Clarissa herself must be more circumspect. 'My duty will not permit me so far to suppose my father arbitrary, as to make a plea of that arbitrariness to you' (I, 107; p. 95), she tells her mother.

She can, however, protest more freely at her father's second and more serious fault. Like Charles, he has improperly delegated his power to 'evil advisers', thereby compromising his natural authority. It is a significant feature of the instalment, indeed, that Clarissa's father is so remarkably absent from it, and that his authority over her is often mediated, or perhaps usurped, by his son and his elder daughter. Here the political analogy is most strongly hinted when Clarissa detects contentions within the family and likens them to 'the intrigues and plots carried on by undermining courtiers against one another' (I, 83; p. 82), or when she lays emphasis on her mother's inadvertent use of the word '*caballing*' to describe James's conferences with Bella (I, 30; p. 54). The analogy is implicit throughout, however, and in its light the influence of James comes to appear a sinister distortion of the proper structures of power. Though at first warned 'that he must not expect to rule in every thing' (I, 34; p. 56), James soon assumes effective government. Clarissa notes with anxiety that reference is continually made to him 'previous to any resolution taken by his superiors, whose will ought to be his', and that 'my papa himself, generally so absolute, constantly pays [deference] to him' (I, 31; p. 54). The third edition strengthens her complaint: 'My Brother is not my Sovereign.'[111]

---

[110] Haller, 'A Critical Account of *Clarissa*', in *Novel and Romance*, ed. Williams, p. 137n. (footnotes by Richardson).

[111] *Clarissa*, 3rd edn (1751; rpt. New York, 1990), I, 307.

Clarissa's dilemma, then, is this: she has placed her grandfather's bequest, 'that independence to which his will has intitled me' (I, 34; p. 56), under the protection of a higher authority, only to see that authority become a tyranny, falling as it does under the malign influence of caballing advisers who themselves have no natural entitlement to her obedience. In resisting the cabal, however, she necessarily finds herself 'in a state of actual rebellion' (I, 242; p. 168) against legitimate government as well – against parents determined to reassert their authority 'over the rebel who of late, has so ingratefully struggled to throw it off' (II, 32; p. 223). Her rebellion is even thought to threaten her father's life: as Clarissa herself reports, 'he hoped, that I, who had been supposed to have contributed to the lengthening of his *father*'s life, would not, by my disobedience, shorten *his*' (I, 133; p. 109).

Looking forward to later instalments, the analogy might go still further. 'I value my freedom and independency too much, if my friends will but leave me to my own judgement, to give them up to a man so uncontroulable, and who shews me beforehand, what I have to expect from him, were I in his power', protests Clarissa (II, 155; p. 290). Yet in the end she does indeed throw herself into Lovelace's power, subjecting herself to a rule crueller still than that of the Harlowes, and uncomfortably reminiscent of what Delany detects in the historical example of the Protectorate – 'the tyranny of an *usurper*'.[112] The reviewer who picked up on the analogy begun by Lovelace himself, calling him 'the Cromwell of women',[113] may well have seen as much. A self-styled protector who offers to free Clarissa 'from ungenerous and base oppression' (III, 39; p. 392), Lovelace does no more than exchange this oppression for his own: having drawn her away from her father's house, he thwarts her yearning for 'a tolerable state of independence' (III, 72; p. 409), and instead subjects her to his own tyrannical rule. She is one who 'allows herself to be overcome, and in a state of obligation . . . to her new protector' (III, 51; p. 398), later realising that 'the man who ought to be my protector . . . adds to my apprehensions' (IV, 1–2; p. 566), and longing too late for 'reconciliation with my *real*, not my *Judas*-protector' (IV, 308; p. 732). The term is insistently used, most ironically in the last letter before the rape, when Clarissa's exclamation 'Whom have I for a protector!' meets Lovelace's reply '*I* will be your protector, my dearest love!' (V, 221; p. 882). But from the very outset the political implication is clear: on leaving her father's house Clarissa soon wonders whether she has 'only escaped from one confinement to another' (III, 42; p. 393), and though initially unaware of her imprisonment she eventually begins to attempt experimental sorties from Sinclair's house to

[112] Delany, p. 308.
[113] 'The Characters of Prevot, Le Sage, Richardson, Fielding, and Rousseau', *Gentleman's Magazine*, 40 (1770), in *Novel and Romance*, ed. Williams, p. 275.

'know whether I am at liberty' (IV, 27; p. 581). After the rape (a familiar enough metaphor for the depredations of a tyrant)[114] it is horribly clear that she is not. Lovelace lamely acknowledges that her treatment has 'the face of an arbitrary and illegal imposition' (V, 348; p. 953); for Clarissa, it is a denial of 'the freedom which is my birthright as an English subject' (V, 314; p. 934).

Clarissa, of course, is no allegory. As Pat Rogers has noted, Richardson's novels draw on an unending series of historical, mythic and literary allusions, none of which carries the weight of firm and complete equivalence.[115] The point is particularly relevant to the novel's political dimension, where, rather than encoding one specific history to the exclusion of all others, Richardson quietly suggests the applicability to both past and present of Clarissa's lurch from one tyranny to the next.[116] In any case, *Clarissa*'s hints at the two calamities described here, Fall and rebellion, can only be lost in the insistence of the literal *History of a Young Lady* with which the reader is in the first place confronted. One may talk, however, of amplification, and see that the reader entangled in Clarissa's domestic dilemma is also entangled, however subliminally, in these larger associated cruxes. In contemplating the conflict of child with father, the reader also contemplates the conflict of people with prince and the conflict of man with God. A kind of conflation is at work, confirming Clarissa's resistance to 'authorities so sacred' (III, 4; p. 373) and her subsequent flight from her father's house as the paradigmatic act of transgression.

Seeming just: Clarissa as narrator

Richardson's own final judgment of Clarissa's case is hard to assess. That these larger implications do little to strengthen her cause, however, is strongly suggested by the anxiety of his response to Milton (whose *Paradise Lost* can of course be seen to hint at similar parallels between rebellions against God and against King).[117] He took a misogynistic view of the Fall, finding in Eve's transgression 'a strong Argument against Womens independency', and in *Grandison* he was prepared to speculate that his good man, avoiding the crime of Milton's Adam, 'would have done *his own duty* . . . and left it to the Almighty, if such had been his pleasure, to have

---

114 See below, pp. 175–6.
115 *Times Literary Supplement*, No. 4426 (29 January–4 February 1988), 117.
116 Contemporary applications are considered below, pp. 168–76.
117 Analogies between Milton's epic and the political experience of the 1640s are most fully explored in Christopher Hill, *Milton and the English Revolution* (1977), pp. 341–412, and Jackie DiSalvo, *War of Titans: Blake's Critique of Milton and the Politics of Religion* (Pittsburgh, 1983). See also the more modest case made by Mary Ann Radzinowicz, 'The Politics of *Paradise Lost*', in *Politics of Discourse: The Literature and History of Seventeenth-Century England*, ed. Kevin Sharpe and Steven N. Zwicker (Berkeley and Los Angeles, 1987), pp. 204–29.

annihilated his first Eve, and given him a second'.[118] Earlier he had been
ready enough to endorse Aaron Hill's condemnation of Milton's pamph-
leteering in the Parliamentary cause for its 'licentious Independency' and
'pulling down Authority', while his few direct references to the civil wars
focus in particular on 'the anarchy introduced by them', praise the 'wise
and healing measures' urged by the moderate royalist Sir Thomas Roe,
and blame the 'serious Mischiefs' of the period above all on 'ye Leaders
among the Round-Heads'.[119] Richardson's instinctive authoritarianism
and his fear of insurrection are clear enough too from what survives of his
correspondence with Hester Mulso, in which it is Mulso who is the
Lockian, while Richardson devotes much of his effort to the castigation of
'PUZZLING LOCKE': so far as can be gathered from Mulso's reply he even
steals Locke's clothes to do so, turning a distinctly Lockian argument on
linguistic abuse back in criticism of the *Two Treatises* to win an acknowledgment from Mulso that a key paragraph, if not wilfully obfuscating, is
at the very least 'carelessly expressed'.[120] It is clear from the Mulso
correspondence, moreover, that on the literal matter of filial obedience in
marriage cases he found Fleetwood's half-case for exemption too lenient,
and had turned instead to the seventeenth century to cite the sterner
authority of Joseph Hall – who, Mulso objected, 'would reduce me to the
condition of an Indian skreen, and allow my father to item me amongst his
goods and chattels, and put me up to sale for the highest bidder'.[121] At one
point in the correspondence at least, he was undoubtedly making the case
for forced marriages.[122]

It is clear, then, that as an Eve, as a rebel, and more straightforwardly
as a child who resists parental commands, Clarissa represents much to
which Richardson was instinctively hostile. There is reason enough,
indeed, to credit an apocryphal report recorded by Mme de Staël. 'On
demandait à Richardson pourquoi il avait rendu Clarisse si malheureuse:

---

[118] To Sarah Chapone, 18 April 1752, Carroll, p. 208; *Grandison*, II, 609.
[119] Hill to Richardson, 29 May 1738, FM XIII, 2, ff.14, 15; *Æsop's Fables*, p. vi; preface to *The
Negotiations of Sir Thomas Roe* (1740); Richardson to Astræa and Minerva Hill, 4 August 1749,
Carroll, p. 128.
[120] Mulso to Richardson, 3 January 1750/1, *Posthumous Works of Mrs. Chapone*, II, 106; II, 107
(referring to Locke, *Two Treatises of Government*, Book II, paragraph 55).
[121] 3 January 1750/1, *Posthumous Works of Mrs. Chapone*, II, 91: see also Mulso's complaint that
'fathers are taught by Bishop Hall, (I don't love that Bishop Hall, why did you quote him?)
and the author of the Whole Duty of Man, to consider their children as their *goods and chattels*,
things which they have as much right to dispose of as their own limbs' (II, 102). Richardson
had evidently cited Hall's *Resolutions and Decisions* (1649), which deals with cases of both
compulsion and prohibition: Hall insists that the child 'ought no more to be exempted from
the parents power of disposing, then the very lims of his owne body', that marriage cases
offer no exemption from the duty to obey '*in all things*', and that a failure to obey is 'no better
then a kind of domestique rebellion' – a phrase, in 1649, of some weight (*Resolutions and
Decisions of Divers Practicall Cases of Conscience* (1649), pp. 377, 425, 426).
[122] See Mulso to Richardson, 10 November 1750, *Posthumous Works of Mrs. Chapone*, II, 57.

C'est, répondit-il, *parce que je n'ai jamais pu lui pardonner d'avoir quitté la maison de son père.*'[123] Yet Richardson's thinking was never single in direction. Caught between equal and potentially opposite allegiances to patriarchal authority and individual liberty, and combining an evident horror at the implications of Clarissa's transgression with an almost idolatrous attachment to the transgressor herself, he found her case simply insoluble. Throughout his correspondence he sedulously avoided giving a conclusive ruling, and the most that Hester Mulso could draw from him in defence of Clarissa was an ambiguous acknowledgment that her case 'stands by itself' and entitles no daughter 'to plead her example for *non-compliance*, till they have *her reasons*'.[124] There is one fixed principle underlying all his analyses of the case, however, and it is one which made unqualified support for his heroine's position almost entirely impossible. He took from Fleetwood (and never tired of repeating) the basic principle that 'the want of duty on one side, justifies not the non-performance of it on the other, where there is a reciprocal duty':[125] no matter how unjust the command, it would seem, the duty to obey remains. Mulso's response was to challenge him with the immediate implications of the ruling for *Clarissa*, asking: 'Must [children] then pay the same obedience to cruel tyrants as they would do to kind and indulgent parents?'[126] Richardson's reply does not survive, but it was almost certainly evasive. Had a simple answer been to hand, the novel might not have been written; at any rate, there would have been little more to it than a grim fable on the perils of self-determination of the sort sketched out above.

There is, of course, much more. The text does not outline a straight-forward thesis, either authoritarian or libertarian, but instead voices and explores both contrary extremes, finding rights and wrongs on either side, and preferring investigation to pronouncement. It involves Clarissa in an impossible case in which she can be neither wholly right nor wholly wrong, and analyses it from every side, without ever endorsing any one participant's conduct or narrative position. In this respect, traditional conduct literature did more than simply define Richardson's subject and impress on him its importance. It also provided a method and a language in which the subject could be addressed – not in the blunt schematisations of moral fable, but in the subtle and endlessly modulating discriminations of casuistry. Having first developed in his plot the crux identified by Fleetwood and Delany as inherently the most recalcitrant case in social relations, to which existing ethical norms and injunctions are simply

[123] 'Quelques réflexions sur le but moral de *Delphine*', *Œuvres complètes* (Brussels, 1820), V, vii.
[124] Mulso to Richardson, 3 January 1750/1 (quoting Richardson's last), *Posthumous Works of Mrs. Chapone*, II, 135.
[125] Mulso to Richardson, 3 January 1750/1 (quoting Richardson's last), *Posthumous Works of Mrs. Chapone*, II, 93; see also *Sentiments*, pp. 118, 257; Carroll, pp. 144, 201.
[126] *Posthumous Works of Mrs. Chapone*, II, 93.

inadequate, Richardson then relays the problem in its full difficulty by communicating it from every angle in a series of letters organised in terms of contending casuistical positions. He thereby finds in the multiple epistolary form, with its withholding of a secure, objective viewpoint, a formal analogue for Fleetwood's emphasis on the indeterminacy of the problem; and by entrusting his narrative to the unreliable ruminations, justifications, accusations and persuasions of the engaged parties he only redoubles its vexedness. The result is not to instruct the reader in the answer to a problem which Richardson himself found unanswerable, and about which he is, as a novelist, quite literally equivocal. It is instead to put the problem to the reader in such a way as to enact the troubling unavailability of resolution, offering with one hand and withdrawing with the other the fullest range of conceivable responses and answers.

Clarissa herself maintains, of course, that 'there is a *right* and *wrong* in every thing, let people put what glosses they please upon their actions' (II, 156; p. 290): experience is a lucid enough text, she suggests, and carries with it its own indelible meanings. The novel's first instalment strains her credo to breaking-point, however. The retrospective irony that she makes the point to forbid herself a '*wrong*' action (elopement) she will within days have claimed an entitlement to perform is enough to discredit her assumptions. In the face of conflicting imperatives, right and wrong are not so easily distinguished, least of all by an engaged party: moral distinctions seem perilously relative or provisional, and the glosses of all concerned, Clarissa included, are vitiated by self-partiality. For more certain resolution one might turn, as Fleetwood recommends in such cases, to 'wise and unconcerned Persons' in the neighbourhood who possess 'a competent and reasonable information of the whole Proceedings'.[127] Yet Richardson denies the novel any such resolving presence. No controlling authorial voice rises above the babble of fictive voices, which remain, with varying degrees of stridency, obstinately partisan. Clarissa looks for resolution to Mrs Norton and Dr Lewen, but their presences are elusive and their decisions evasive; Colonel Morden is continually expected but never arrives. And while 'information' is copious enough, whether it is 'competent and reasonable' is more questionable. As Richardson writes, 'the first and second Volumes ... are chiefly taken up with the Altercations between Clarissa and ... her Family', and 'those Altercations are the Foundation of the whole' (VII, 431; pp. 1498–9): altercation consumes story, so that the instalment is less a rehearsal of events than an acrimonious debate about them. At the dramatic level of scenes in which Clarissa and the Harlowes argue their case, at an inner epistolary level of letters exchanged within the family, and at the outer epistolary level of Clarissa's

---

[127] Fleetwood, *Relative Duties*, p. 56; quoted by Richardson to Sarah Chapone, 2 March 1752, Carroll, p. 205.

correspondence with Anna (the basic narrative medium of the instalment), altercation is always the organising principle. No information is
unconfused by glossing or unsusceptible to challenge, and the boundaries
of right and wrong are almost impossibly blurred.

To analyse every turn of the debates between Clarissa and the Harlowes, or of the dialogue between Clarissa and Anna in which they are
subsumed, would be an interminable task. Richardson wrote of embroiling his heroine in 'the most trying and arduous Cases',[128] and his design
precluded brevity: the debates are complex, intricate and, written as they
are 'to the Moment', they continually modulate to take account of shifting
circumstances. Yet there is a certain stasis about them too, reverting as
they always do to the deadlock of paternal authority against filial independence that underlies each new modification of the case. The instalment is a
painfully insistent reiteration of this basic conflict: as Clarissa asks herself
at one point in the argument, 'And what was this ... but ringing my
changes upon the same bells, and neither receding nor advancing one
tittle?' (I, 289; p. 193). In its essentials her situation or story remains the
same, while altercation, dramatic and epistolary, proliferates endlessly
around it.

Writing is thus no mere vehicle of story but the novel's basic substance,
and a substance that must be handled with care. The problem now is not
simply that the letter may be more a mask than a casement, but that in the
hands of Clarissa and her antagonists it increasingly resembles a weapon.
At one stage, indeed, Clarissa proposes settling the case before 'an impartial moderator' by a formal literary encounter strongly reminiscent of the
duels in which the novel begins and ends – 'the facts to be stated, and
agreed upon by both; and the decision to be given, according to the force
of the arguments each shall produce in support of their side of the
question' (II, 41; pp. 227–8). Letters are repeatedly seen as instruments of
force or aggression (a point explicit in James's image for Clarissa's arsenal
of rhetorical devices as her 'female quiver'), and each one is carefully
fashioned to its purpose. The novel's frequent allusions to the prominence
of epistolary activity in the lives of its characters, though sometimes
dismissed as tactless apologies for a convention better left unmentioned, in
fact keep usefully in view how very deliberate this process of fashioning
always is. Quite apart from the sheer prolixity of the exchanges, almost
every letter is written at least twice. Clarissa sends Anna draft versions of
her carefully worded missives to the Harlowes, and finds its noteworthy on
a rare occasion when a letter is a 'first draft, struck off without blot or
erazure' (II, 42; p. 228). To the Harlowes she paints a different picture, as
in a letter she disingenuously calls 'this unguarded scrawl' (II, 95; p. 258);

---

[128] To Hill, 26 January 1746/7, Carroll, p. 83.

but their fear of her literary dexterity is not allayed. Instead they forbid her to 'correspond with *any*body out of the house' (I, 46; p. 63), and eventually they search her closet to confiscate the very materials of writing. Their principal fear, however, is at the effect of her linguistic powers on themselves. When she protests her duty and kneels, Mrs Harlowe detects a beguiling discrepancy between her rhetoric of word and gesture and her actual disposition: 'If words were duty, Clarissa Harlowe would be the dutifullest child breathing', she complains: '... Limbs so supple; Will so stubborn!' (I, 121; p. 103). Later Bella protests at her 'silver tongue' with the accusation 'that I next-to-bewitch'd people, by my insinuating address' (I, 290; p. 194), and Clarissa is denied personal access to the family. The debate continues mainly by letter, but this too is soon curtailed, James citing her 'knack at letter-writing' to explain his threat to return unopened her next, 'for I won't argue with your perverseness in so plain a case' (I, 228; p. 161). The trend is continued when her parents forbid her to write to them and send back her letters unread or torn, and when Uncle Harlowe, finding the unguarded scrawl 'too artful for me' (II, 100; p. 260), follows suit. Those letters they do read they consciously resist, employing a form of rhetorical analysis suggestively described in Clarissa's report that 'my brother has taken my letter all in pieces' (II, 31; p. 222). Uncle Antony's citation of Proverbs 18.17 (*'He that is first in his own cause, saith the wise man, seemeth just: But his neighbour cometh, and searcheth him'*), and his threat to Clarissa to 'be your *neighbour*, for I will search your heart to the bottom; that is to say, if your letter be written from your heart', are made on just such an occasion. Before beginning the 'search', moreover, Antony acknowledges its difficulty: 'Yet do I know what a task I have undertaken, because of the knack you are noted for at writing' (I, 215; p. 154).

For Terry Castle, these recurrent challenges to Clarissa's words are marks simply of her 'linguistic oppression' at Harlowe Place, as though in this case it is only reading, and never writing, that deforms.[129] Yet the complaints of the Harlowes are too insistent not to have force, if only as a reminder that Clarissa, like everybody else, is pleading a cause when she writes, and in her narrative to Anna as well as in the more obviously casuistical exchanges with her family. In this case, allegations against her come from more detached and objective sources, as when Mrs Howe reproaches Anna for judging too hastily on the basis of Clarissa's narrative: 'You have heard but one side; and that there is *more* to be said is plain, by your reading to me, but parts of her letters', she complains (I, 175; p. 132). All Clarissa's readers in fact criticise her writing in one way or another, and the reason they do so is at least in part that there is something

---

[129] *Clarissa's Ciphers*, p. 62.

significantly wrong with it – that there *is* always, as Mrs Howe says, '*more to be said*'. And the same, of course, applies to all Clarissa's disputants as well: their reports and arguments can only be compromised by their stake in the matter they debate.

Thus when Clarissa announces that 'it is a good rule to *give* WORDS *the hearing, but to form our judgements* ... *by* DEEDS ONLY' (II, 161; p. 293), few will fail to agree. Yet at the same time the reader faces the predicament that deeds in the novel are always hidden behind words, or rather that arrangements of words are the only deeds of which there is a clear view. The result is that, like Solomon's neighbour, the reader too must search before, like Fleetwood's neighbour, he can judge. In the absence of objectivity the balance of the case comes to depend entirely on how it is put, and the reader must measure for himself the contrasting vocabularies brought to bear upon it – vocabularies distilled to their essential terms by a fictive reader in Sarah Fielding's *Remarks on Clarissa*, who notes of Clarissa's conduct: 'they call it Obstinacy; she calls it Resolution'.[130] The lexical tug-of-war recorded in the text centres on precisely such words, each participant doggedly striving to redefine the position of the other: 'what I call *steadiness* is attributed to stubbornness, to obstinacy, to prepossession, by those who have a right to put what interpretation they please upon my conduct', laments Clarissa (I, 127; p. 106). In her letter to Antony she sets out her own alternative case, careful to anticipate all objections and to choose words in which her conduct will appear justifiable. 'It is not obstinacy I am governed by', she insists: 'It is aversion; an aversion I cannot overcome' (I, 214; p. 153). The 'search' with which Antony responds rebuffs her argument point by point, paying careful attention to the language of her most 'censurable passages' (I, 222; p. 157) in order to redefine her conduct as unjustifiable: 'in defence of a father's authority' he sets himself to 'beat down all the arguments a rebel child ... can bring, in behalf of her obstinacy' (I, 215; p. 154). Later Clarissa and Aunt Hervey spar with the same sets of terms: her aunt challenges her 'romantic picture of a forced marriage' as 'a fine description of your own obstinacy'; Clarissa insists on the validity of her distinction 'between obstinacy and aversion'; *Supposed* aversion may owe its rise to *real* obstinacy', replies the aunt (II, 216; p. 322). The jockeying is typical, and its outcome vital to the plausibility of each opposing case.

It might of course be maintained that the task of choosing between these two clashing terminologies is easy enough. Yet although the Harlowes can hardly be thought uncompromised in their behaviour, their contention that Clarissa herself is unjustified carries considerable force. Their position is simple enough: they uphold the fixity of patriarchal law, and they

---

[130] *Remarks on Clarissa*, p. 5.

dismiss all casuistry as illegitimate evasion. Clarissa, they contend, is 'debating about an absolute duty' (I, 103; p. 91). Continually, they present the issue as the simplest of conflicts: 'it is *my* authority you defy', her father reminds her (I, 162; p. 125); 'it was always my notion, that children should not dispute their parents authority', writes Antony (I, 220; p. 157). The position has the sanction of orthodoxy, and the Harlowes are authorised by the strict tradition that runs from Joseph Hall to Patrick Delany to argue that implicit obedience is more rather than less necessary in 'the most important concern' of marriage. When Clarissa pleads the dutifulness of her past life, her mother insists that her previous conduct is immaterial when compared with the case before them. 'Now that you are grown up to marriageable years, is the test', she maintains (I, 106; p. 95), to be echoed later by Aunt Hervey's remark that 'there was no article so proper for parents to govern in, as This of marriage' (I, 260; p. 178). Their conclusion is that Clarissa's duty is a wholly straightforward matter: she must overcome her disinclination and marry Solmes. 'I ask nothing of you but what is in your power to comply with, and what it is your duty to comply with', her father insists (I, 49; p. 64).

While instructing children to obey absolutely, however, even the severest authorities also instruct parents not to compel. Consequently, the Harlowes find it easier to condemn Clarissa than to justify themselves. The more lenient members of the family at least see the need to do so, and they draw on a range of standard gambits in defence of their position. Aunt Hervey, for example, justifies compulsion on the grounds that 'many a young creature has thought she could not love a man, with whom she has afterwards been very happy' (I, 303; p. 201). She also reminds Clarissa, in case of unhappiness, 'what great consolation you will have on one hand, if you pursue your parents advice, that you did so; what mortification on the other, that, by following your own, you have no-body to blame but yourself' (II, 246; p. 338).[131] But the family's principal resort to casuistry comes with the use they make of Lovelace's involvement – a circumstance that enables Mrs Harlowe to lament 'that just when the time arrived which should crown all their wishes, she should stand in the way of her own happiness, and her parents comfort, and ... give suspicions to her anxious friends, that she would become the property of a vile rake and libertine, who ... had actually embrued his hands in her brother's blood' (I, 132; p. 109). By alluding to these circumstances, they are able to define

---

131 Both arguments are endorsed by more objective voices: Mrs Howe regards herself as living confirmation of the first argument (II, 232; p. 330), while Mrs Norton puts the second (I, 2653; p. 180). To Hester Mulso's consternation, Richardson even used them himself: 'I did not expect from Mr. Richardson to have heard any excuses, any palliatives for their sordid, base way of thinking; I did not expect to hear from HIM that "daughters many times have reason to wish that they *had been* prevailed on"' (10 November 1750, *Posthumous Works of Mrs. Chapone*, II, 57).

their conduct as actually protective of Clarissa, 'while the man who was so obnoxious to every-body remain'd unmarry'd, and while he *buzz'd* about' (I, 111; p. 97). They thereby explain the remission of a right to which Clarissa might otherwise be entitled: as James puts it, less judiciously than his mother, 'the liberty of *refusing* ... is deny'd you, because we are all sensible, that the liberty of *choosing*, to every one's dislike, must follow ... And what must that child be who prefers the Rake to a Father?' (II, 33; p. 223).

These repeated invocations of paternal authority make Clarissa's position very hard to maintain. For all their cruelty and cupidity (and it is a reflection not on Clarissa but on her family that their surname so strongly hints at the exchange of flesh for money), the Harlowes have a solid foundation for their case. It is a sign of the strength of that case in contemporary eyes that at least one reader gave it his guarded support. In a letter indexed by Richardson under the heading 'M^r: Bennett, justifying ye Harlowes',[132] the reader in question alludes with approval to a suggestion of Colley Cibber's, who seems to have urged Richardson to tip the scales in Clarissa's favour by denying the Harlowes the opportunity to justify themselves with reference to Lovelace's threat. 'If Lovelace appear'd to all the Family a Sober well bred man ... then the Family wou'd be condemn'd, and Cla: almost applauded', Bennett writes. As the novel stands, however, it appears that 'the Father is *almost*, if not quite, justify'd: And that Cla: will be absolutely condemned'. 'Wou'd not You think Yourself Justify'd in endeavour.^{g} to *force* Your Daughter to marry Solmes, rather than, risque her being snap'd up by a Lovelace, knowing the latter to be an avow'd Libertine?', he asks. There is no reason to depend on Clarissa's offer to remain single:

did She not correspond with Lovelace before Solmes made any offers? was not Lovelace permitted to address her before the Rencounter between the Brother and Him? did She not at that time countenance his Addresses? and can it be *depend[ed] on* that She Cou'd guard against the insinuations of such an Intriguer who had doubtless made some impression on her, or She wou'd not have enter'd into a Literary Cor[respondence with him?]

It is not enough, Bennett adds, simply to accuse the father of avarice, or to dismiss his objections to Lovelace's libertinism as 'a pretence to hide his true Reason ... for who can pretend to say the *Rencounter* was not his inducement for breaking off the Match ...? – I believe such an Affair in any Family wou'd put an end to all intended Alliances.'[133]

[132] FM XV, 3, f.2.
[133] Bennett to Richardson, [1746–7?], FM XV, 3, f.10. Bennett's letter is a useful reminder of how very easy it would have been for Richardson to put Clarissa unequivocally in the right. Cibber and Bennett were not the only readers to urge such a change: Aaron Hill made a similar argument late in 1746, and actually included the change in his MS 'Specimen of NEW

Other defences of the Harlowes were also possible. Richardson himself sometimes credited them with genuine concern for Clarissa's wellbeing, and even persuaded Hester Mulso to grant (though somewhat grudgingly) 'that when they bade her be *guilty* and *miserable*, they did not understand the import of their words, and thought they bade her be happy. And this, though it aggravates their *absurdity*, lessens their *guilt*.'[134] In such contexts, it is clear that Clarissa has much to contend with in her arguments, all the more since she too accepts the basic tenets of the Harlowe case. Like them, she rehearses a number of principles from Fleetwood and Delany, for example that 'parents have great advantage in every eye over the child, if she dispute their pleasure in the disposing of her ... Since out of twenty instances perhaps two could not be produced, where *they* were not in the right, the *child* in the wrong' (II, 53; p. 235). In particular, she stresses the double bind of the relative duties system, 'that whether or not the parent do his duty by the child, the child cannot be exempted from doing hers to him' (II, 53; p. 235). As she has already pointed out, this is a condition (if accepted) that forces her to be reconciled to suffering: 'were we perfect', she tells Anna, '... we could not be happy in this life, unless those with whom we have to deal (those, more especially, who have any controul upon us), were govern'd by the same principles' (I, 127; p. 106). Perfection, in fact, would make unhappiness *more* likely; for to win the world's admiration for her 'blind duty and will-less resignation', as Anna writes, Clarissa must marry Solmes (I, 90; p. 86). Since she will not, while also wishing to appear not to transgress, her letters face a hard uphill struggle: they must account for her resistance to an authority to which, as she acknowledges, she should as a rule defer.

To do this, Clarissa seizes on a loophole recognised by Fleetwood, that 'if the Parent offer what the Child cannot possibly assent to ... refusal ... will not fall under the head of sinful Disobedience'.[135] The task of her narrative, consequently, is to prove not that she *will not*, but that she *cannot* obey. 'I am sorry my case is so circumstanced, that I *cannot* comply', as she tells Anna: '... it would be my duty to do so, if I could' (I, 180; p. 135). One method by which she seeks to stress this impossibility is by narrating

CLARISSA' (1746), a sample abridgment of the novel's opening pages written at Richardson's request. In particular, Hill's MS improves Lovelace's behaviour in the duel to make him 'generous', 'reluctant' and 'Tender' ('The Specimen of NEW CLARISSA', FM XIII, 3, f.70), thereby weakening the Harlowes' objection to Clarissa's intimacy with a man they are able to present, in Richardson's version, as her brother's violent assailant. 'The Affection of the Sister would by this seem juster, and less Blameable, than now', Hill urged: '... As it is now, the Family's Resentment, may be thought more just, then *her Affection* for a Man who openly avows his hatred of, and triump[h]s over, her Relations, with a Vein of Scorn that ought to shake her Inclination to converse with him' (23 October 1746, FM XIII, 3, f.60). It can only be assumed that simplifications of this sort had no part in Richardson's scheme.

[134] To Richardson, 10 November 1750, *Posthumous Works of Mrs. Chapone*, II, 74.
[135] Fleetwood, *Relative Duties*, pp. 55–6.

in such a way as to attribute all responsibility for her own actions directly to the Harlowes themselves. Her characteristic images of helplessness, and in particular of being entangled or impelled, work just such an effect. 'Thus ... has my brother got me into his snares', she writes, 'and I, like a poor silly bird, the more I struggle, am the more intangled' (I, 151; p. 119): choice, she thus implies, is unavailable. The language of impulsion too emerges at an early stage (Letter 8, for example, opens with 'They drive on here at a furious rate', I, 43; p. 61), and becomes a persuasive means of disowning responsibility for her own actions, or even her emotions. One letter expresses 'vexation, to be driven to such streights and difficulties ... as oblige me to answer letters' from Lovelace (I, 166; p. 128); another, more self-consciously, entertains the possibility that 'my particularly unhappy situation *had* driven (or *led* me, if you please,) into a liking of the man' (I, 274; p. 185). She is 'driven to and fro, like a feather in the wind, at the pleasure of the rash, the selfish and the headstrong'; and it is the drivers, not the driven, who must take responsibility for where she blows: 'I have not an option, altho' my ruin ... may be the dreadful consequence of the steps taken', she concludes (II, 228; p. 329). Here a judiciously impersonal construction avoids the need to attribute blame to anyone in particular, but elsewhere she is more explicit. Her concern is only 'to avoid the extremities, which nevertheless I pray to God they do not at last force me upon' (I, 311; p. 205): her elopement, in short, will be the family's crime. She is quite deliberate about this meaning. 'Whatever course I shall be *permitted* or be *forced* to steer, I must be considered, as a person out of her own direction', she insists, opening a long nautical metaphor in which she is kept from port 'by the foaming billows of a brother's and sister's envy; and by the raging winds of a supposed invaded authority' (II, 138; pp. 280–1).

Passive constructions and images of helplessness, however, can only be an embellishment of Clarissa's basic strategy, which is to claim exemption from the duty to obey on rigorously casuistical grounds. One moment where her writing sets most purposefully about this task comes in Letter 13, where she doubles back on herself to narrate recent events for a second time, but now with a new gloss: the letter is 'a kind of supplement' to her previous account, she writes, which will go 'a little backward' 'in order to set this matter in a clear light' (I, 71–2; p. 76). The long retrospective narrative that follows replaces her previous assumptions about her family's motives (hostility to libertinism on her parents' part, college-begun antipathy on James's, slighted love on Bella's) with the single, clear motive of avarice, a motive she 'now find[s] ... plain upon recollection' (I, 78; p. 80). Their purpose in arranging her marriage to Solmes is now not to keep her from Lovelace, as she had begun by supposing, but to increase their own wealth, status and power. Although on this issue she never allows herself the trenchant sarcasm of Hester Mulso (who wrote to Richardson of 'mere Smithfield bargains, so much ready money for so much land, and my daughter flung in into the bargain'),[136] what she calls 'the family fault' becomes her litany from this point on, repeatedly invoked as the crucial flaw in the case against her. It is not simply that she can thus discredit her parents' motives, since that alone would not exonerate disobedience: more significant is her claim that to accept the wealth of Solmes's family would make her a party to theft. When she turns her attention to the Harlowes' enthusiasm for Solmes's 'noble settlements' (I, 80; p. 81), examining the meanings obscured by the adjective 'noble', she presses this latter point: 'And should I not be as culpable, do you think, in my acceptance of such unjust settlements, as he in the offer of them ...?' (I, 81; p. 81). With this argument, that she 'ought not to be the instrument to deprive Mr. Solmes's relations of their natural rights' (I, 126; p. 105), she feels her way, tenuously, towards an exemption explicitly recognised by Fleetwood – that 'if Parents should be so wickedly inclin'd, as to command their Children ... to Steal' the children 'are not at liberty to obey'.[137]

More orthodox as a claim for exemption is her contention that marriage to Solmes would be dishonest, in that it would involve a breach of vows. The point begins as a variation on the rejected argument from aversion, and is first made in a letter which asks Bella, 'will it be *just*, will it be *honest*, to marry a man I cannot endure?' (I, 188; p. 139). Before long it has developed into a full-fledged case for non-compliance. 'I cannot *honestly* be his', she tells her parents. 'Had I a slighter notion of the matrimonial duty than I have, perhaps I might. But ... my *heart* is less concerned in this matter than my *soul*; my *temporal*, perhaps, than my *future* good' (II, 29; p. 221). Later she envisages an inescapably sinful life with Solmes, 'every day ... rising to witness to some new breach of an Altar-vow'd duty!' (II, 64; p. 241). The argument gets her nowhere with her family, of course, but it considerably strengthens her position in the novel's great debate, and was seized on by several readers. Hester Mulso found in it a conclusive vindication of Clarissa's position: the marriage, she wrote, 'would not only have plunged her into misery but guilt; a guilt no less black than that of solemn perjury before the altar of God'. Sarah Chapone used the same phrase, being unconvinced 'that either of the contracting Parties can escape the Guilt of Solemn Perjury, provided they marry a Man or Woman whom they do not at that Time love and honour'.[138] Love being involuntary, it would seem, Clarissa *cannot* marry Solmes, since in so doing

---

[136] 3 January 1750/1, *Posthumous Works of Mrs. Chapone*, II, 122.

[137] Fleetwood, *Relative Duties*, p. 30.

[138] To Richardson, 12 October 1750, *Posthumous Works of Mrs. Chapone*, II, 32; Sarah Chapone to Richardson, [March 1752], FM XII, 2, f.47.

she would make dishonest vows and thereby breach the higher duty to
God – and as Fleetwood explains, parental commands do not bind
children 'to do, what God forbids'. Fleetwood adds the proviso, however,
that 'the Command of God must be plain and evident; it must not be a
doubtful and disputed thing; but full as certain, as that obedience is due to
the Commands of Parents'[139] – a point that makes Clarissa's plea more
questionable than either of these readers assumed. The divine command
supposedly flouted by any vow to love Solmes was indeed doubtful,
Richardson replied: 'the promise of the wife to *love* and *honour* her
husband, implies no more than that she will *endeavour* to love and honour
him', he maintained, and so could insist that his correspondents withdraw
the term 'perjury'.[140] Again Clarissa's case seems to have teetered, in his
eyes at least, on the brink of jesuitry.

These are just some of the lines of argument developed by Clarissa in her
efforts to determine her own conduct and convince her family, Anna, and
(by extension) the reader of its rectitude. At other times, of course, her
narrative comes closer to the 'dramatic' style described by Mark Kinkead-
Weekes, seeming to efface its own deliberateness and put the reader in
immediate (or unmediated) possession of each represented scene. Yet even
at these most dramatic moments her letters never quite let us forget her
own activities as a writer: indeed, Clarissa's dramatic techniques, with all
her emphases and interjections, often make a very direct contribution to
the larger business of self-justification, working in tandem with the casuistical strategies more explicitly shown in discursive passages elsewhere.
This characteristic complication of scenic presentation by casuistry is well
illustrated by Letter 20, in which Clarissa, having been anxious to 'plead
for a palliation to *myself* of my mamma's sufferings on *my* account' (I, 127;
p. 106), interrupts a scene at the crucial point where her mother has
implored her to obey 'as well for *her* sake, as *mine*' (I, 135; p. 110). The
following paragraph details the inner reasonings with which Clarissa
responds, carefully leading the reader through her conflicting feelings and
thoughts before culminating in a speech of respectful refusal. First she
describes her anxiety to oblige her mother if she *can*: 'Affected by my
mamma's goodness to me, and by that part of her argument which related
to her own peace', she reports, '. . . I could not but wish it were possible for
me to obey.' The following two sentences delay the introduction of the
counter-argument, and stress Clarissa's internal conflict: she 'paused,
hesitated, consider'd', aware of her mother's suspense. But in the next
sentence (which occupies almost a page of the original edition) she then
'recollect[s]' at least seven distinct reasons for exemption, drawing on

[139] Fleetwood, *Relative Duties*, p. 30.
[140] Mulso to Richardson, 10 November 1750 (quoting Richardson's last), *Posthumous Works of Mrs. Chapone*, I, 65–6; see also Carroll, p. 204.

natural law, divine law, expediency and sentiment to build the case for refusal. She thus prepares the reader to understand her ensuing refusal, and the rest of the scene, in terms of 'all these reflections, which are ever present with me, crouding upon my remembrance' (I, 135–6; pp. 110–11).

Set pieces of this sort, for all the sympathy they enlist, must also elicit a degree of scepticism: they are never quite as artless as Clarissa alleges them to be. Sometimes, moreover, even the illusion of artlessness vanishes. One of the most disquieting moments in her narrative comes where the desire to put forward a watertight case seems to displace completely the scrupulous concern stated in her opening letter to 'recite facts only'. By the time of Letter 29 her sole purpose is to forestall the Harlowe position that aversion may be overcome, and she now proposes to do so by setting the case on a new foot. Since (as she explains to Anna) 'they have grounded their principal argument for my compliance with their will upon my acknow- legements that my heart is free' (I, 182; p. 136), she decides to withdraw all such acknowledgments, thereby invalidating their position. 'Facts' figure little in her reasoning now: all that matters is the strength of the case. But the ruse, of course, backfires, as Clarissa later reports: 'The declaration, that my heart was *free*, afforded them an argument to prove obstinacy and perverseness upon me; since it could be nothing else that govern'd me in my opposition to their wills, if I had no particular esteem for another man: And now, that I have given them reason (in order to obviate this argument) to suppose that I *have* a preference to another, they are resolved to carry their schemes into execution as soon as possible' (I, 257–8; pp. 176–7). The ruse also backfires, however, in what ultimately is a more important sense; for the abrupt shift here in Clarissa's presentation of the case strongly raises the possibility that her casuistical practices are, if not absolutely cosmetic, then at least more immediately concerned with influencing her readers than with representing the truth. If her reports of her own inner life can be inverted simply for the purpose of trying out a new argument, how can the reader ever know the authentic state of that life?

Richardson gives focus to such suspicions in the letters of Anna, whose correspondence with Clarissa recapitulates, on a large scale, the question and answer pattern of traditional casuistry: Clarissa is the querist, posing her case and in so doing soliciting both advice and endorsement; Anna, at once sceptical and sympathetic, is her respondent. That is not to say that Anna provides an authentically Richardsonian perspective, for hers is much the most liberal voice in the debate (with the possible exception of Dolly Hervey, who in Clarissa's case would 'have Mr. Lovelace out-of-hand, and take up her own estate': II, 192; p. 309). But Anna does at least provide (as a respondent should) a careful, fair and critical reading of the

terms in which the case has been put – and she does it to troubling effect.
Just as Bella finds in Clarissa's conduct a '*well-acted* indifference' towards
Lovelace (I, 15; p. 46), so Anna finds the same processes at work in her
narrative, and challenges her that love, rather than the dutifulness in
terms of which she represents her own actions, is the real determinant of
her conduct. She detects not the expected unbosoming of the familiar style
but a veiling, and dwells on suspect and evasive passages with such
insistence that Clarissa herself is forced to acknowledge their vulnerability:
'I cannot tell what turn my mind has taken, to dictate so oddly to my pen'
(I, 63; p. 72), she writes when accused of incipient love. It is here that
Anna first makes her remark that 'a stander-by is often a better judge of
the game than those that play' (I, 60; p. 70): her careful analyses of
Clarissa's letters tease new and subversive meanings from them, and
provide a model for the reader's own activity.[141] Initially, Anna assumes
that the letters merely reveal inclinations of which Clarissa herself is
unconscious, and she urges her to return, more vigilantly, to 'a close
examination into the true springs and grounds of this your *generosity* to that
happy man' (I, 62; p. 71). Increasingly, however, she comes to suspect a
more deliberate unreliability. When Clarissa formally withdraws the
acknowledgment that her heart is free she alleges 'a reason for this
change of style, which you have not thought fit to give me', and again
offers to demonstrate ways in which the letters betray her emotional
entanglement: 'it is a point out of all doubt, from fifty places in your
letters, were I to labour the proof' (I, 251–2; p. 173).

The implications of her charge are devastating. Instead of candidly
revealing her heart, it would seem, Clarissa's narrative is misleading, and
perhaps designedly so. For Anna, indeed, her reports only become reliable
at the very point where Clarissa herself, in confessing her preference for
Lovelace, presents them as least sincere. Drawing directly on the conventional language of the familiar letter, Anna censures such dissimulation,
demands 'nothing less than the knowlege of the inmost recesses of your
heart', and singles out the particular phrases in which these recesses are
instead obscured as 'overt-acts of treason' against their friendship (I, 253;
p. 174). Clarissa defends herself with her usual objection, 'I wrote my
heart' (I, 256; p. 176); but she does so in terms that only lend weight to
Anna's allegation. When she talks of keeping in mind as she writes 'what it

---

[141] The love-question was of course a principal feature of debate, its indeterminacy carefully
contrived by Richardson. When urged by Hill to make her 'in downright Love' he preferred
to 'have it imputed to her ... by her penetrating Friend, (and then a Reader will be ready
enough to believe it, the *more* ready, for her not owning it, or being blind to it herself)' (FM
XIII, 3, f.59; Carroll, p. 72). Readers proved all too ready to do so, with the result that by
1751 Richardson was defensively insisting that she was '*in Liking* only' (3rd edn (1751; rpt.
New York, 1990), VIII, 290). '*In love* she certainly was – I cannot allow it was only liking',
protested Mary Delany (24 April 1751, Barbauld, IV, 37).

became a person of my sex and character to *be* and to *do* ... where the imputed love is thought an undutiful, and therefore a criminal, passion', or of her 'desire of appearing ... the person I ought to be; had I no other view in it, but to merit the continuance of your good opinion' (I, 257; p. 176), she inspires little confidence. Her letters seem determined not by 'reality' but by the self-image she prefers to project, and they are based on a model of daughterly exemplariness that is increasingly at odds with her actual state. At such points her narrative seems doubly a fiction – not the expected undressing of the familiar letter but an anxious construction, addressed to the good opinion of her reader, of the person she ought to be.

As the instalment reaches its climax in the question of Clarissa's entitlement to elope, this habit of always preferring something to truth has serious consequences. Confirming her appointment with Lovelace, she writes that she has 'no way to avoid the determin'd resolution of my friends in behalf of Mr. Solmes; but by abandoning this house by his assistance' (II, 269; p. 350) – a strong plea in defence of her intention, if so. Yet this statement, which more or less summarises her explanations of the previous fifty pages, is also one of her most questionable. Even her staunchest advocates in Richardson's circle recognised it as such, and exposed its neglect of at least two other (and preferable) ways of avoiding marriage to Solmes. Aaron Hill found the argument specious and compromising, on the grounds that a forced wedding is a technical impossibility. 'A Woman of her Sense and Spirit', he wrote, 'could not fail to know, that only to with-hold her own Consent upon the Question when the Minister should ask it ... would invalidate the whole confederated Plot against her.'[142] Even if flying her father's house were necessary, moreover, elopement with Lovelace is not the only option. Initially Clarissa is anxious to escape only to the Howes, as 'a protection I could more *reputably* fly to, than to That of any other person' (II, 224; p. 327). In the absence of Mrs Howe's consent, however, she refuses to accept Anna's help, lamely arguing that her elopement with Lovelace will save Anna 'the trouble of procuring for me a vehicle; as well as the suspicion from your mamma of contributing to my escape' (II, 254; p. 342). By now one can hardly miss the suggestion of dissimulation. The reasons given for refusing Anna's help, the novel hints, may be no more than a smokescreen behind which lies a very different reason for preferring that of Lovelace – as Anna gently puts it, 'a latent, un-owned inclination, which balancing, or *preponderating* rather, made the issue of the alternative ... sit more lightly upon the excuser's mind than she cared to own' (II, 279; p. 358). For Aaron Hill, the implications were intolerable: 'she must never suffer even a Thought,

---

[142] To Richardson, 23 January 1747, FM XIII, 3, f.84.

of meeting Lovelace, privately, with whatsoever Purpose, or on what Pretence soever. – She must be *betrayed* into the Act of meeting him', he expostulated. Richardson should remove the problem of Mrs Howe's refusal, so that Clarissa might fall innocently into Lovelace's hands by the agency of a bribed servant of the Howes: thus her conduct 'wd. stand justified, even to the severest Prude's Examination'.[143] Lady Bradshaigh reached the same conclusion. Where Anna offers to assist Clarissa's escape herself, she wrote in the margin of her copy: 'This conveyance should have been procured and no appointment made with Lovelace, then would she have been wholly blameless.'[144]

'I did not want her to be wholly blameless', wrote Richardson beneath Lady Bradshaigh's remark. In seeking to polarise the rights and wrongs of Clarissa's case, both she and Hill had misread his scheme. Hill even went on to remind Richardson that 'where Example and Instruction are in View, too strong an Error in the *Moral* Conduct of the Party, the Instruction is to be derived from, absolutely cuts off the Effect, expected from it'.[145] What he failed to see was that Richardson's 'Instruction' was not to be derived from a banal exemplariness of this kind. Troublingly, Clarissa is *not* wholly blameless: 'she is not in all respects a perfect character', as Richardson insists even in the edition of 1751, which in general revises the text in Clarissa's favour.[146] From the perspective of the final letters, indeed, her scrupulous casuistry throughout the preceding volumes seems little more than a decoy, barely relevant to a case that more and more resembles one of amorous elopement. In the end Clarissa appears of course to elope only involuntarily, having resolved 'to suspend, for the present, my intention of leaving my father's house' (II, 292; p. 362-3) – though having also resolved, on more dubious grounds, to keep her appointment with Lovelace at the garden gate in order to tell him so. Her retraction, however, is a reassurance (and an ambiguous one at that) which Richardson originally withheld from the reader for several months. At the end of the first instalment Clarissa seems to have changed her mind yet again, and to have reverted to her plan to elope. The second volume ends with her confession of having done 'an inexcusable thing' (II, 307; p. 370), and with Anna's baffled response: 'Observe, my dear, that I don't blame *you* by all this – your relations only are in fault! – Yet how you came to change your mind, is the surprising thing! –' (II, 308; p. 371).

---

143 To Richardson, 9 February 1746/7, FM XIII, 3, ff. 90, 91.

144 Quoted by Samuel Crompton, 'Richardson's *Clarissa* Annotated', *Notes & Queries*, 5th Series, 8 (1877), 101-2. The copy in question is now at Princeton, and will be more fully described by Margaret Anne Doody in a forthcoming issue of the *Princeton University Library Chronicle*; see also Bernard Quaritch's 1987 sale catalogue, *Samuel Richardson, Jane Austen: The Complete Novels and a Play*.

145 To Richardson, 9 February 1747, FM XIII, 3, f.92.

146 *Clarissa*, 3rd edn (1751; rpt. New York, 1990), I, vii.

Beyond casuistry

There can be little doubt that by the mid-eighteenth century casuistry had had its day.[147] For Pope in 1714, 'Dry'd Butterflies, and Tomes of Casuistry' were comparable images of redundancy, belonging already 'to the Lunar Sphere, / Since all things lost on Earth, are treasur'd there'.[148] Others would have dissented, but the tradition in which Hall and Taylor had worked was never matched by later generations, and technical casuistry survived more as a literary form than as a living practice. The casuistical manual, moreover, had always been an anomaly; for if circumstances alter cases then no resolution can have any wider application than to the specific case resolved. Adam Smith sounded the death-knell in his *Theory of Moral Sentiments* (1759), where he insists that such books have no useful part to play in moral philosophy, and 'ought to be rejected altogether'. In part he argues from the Pascalian position that books of cases 'teach us to chicane with our own consciences, and by their vain subtilties serve to authorise innumerable evasive refinements with regard to the most essential articles of our duty'. But he also saw the insufficiency, for practical purposes, of casuistry's reliance on the particular:

> what would hold good in any one case would scarce do so exactly in any other, and what constitutes the propriety and happiness of behaviour varies in every case with the smallest variety of situation. Books of casuistry, therefore ... could be of little use to one who should consult them upon occasion, even supposing their decisions to be just; because, notwithstanding the multitude of cases collected in them, yet upon account of the still greater variety of possible circumstances, it is a chance, if among all those cases there be found one exactly parallel to that under consideration. One, who is really anxious to do his duty, must be very weak, if he can imagine that he has much occasion for them.[149]

Such books can, in consequence, be no substitute for the individual conscience, which must be diligently cultivated as the source of all moral choice. 'It is only by consulting this judge within', Smith writes earlier, 'that we can ever see what relates to ourselves in its proper shape and dimensions; or that we can ever make any proper comparison between our own interests and those of other people'. Yet to judge with genuine impartiality, he also insists, great imaginative efforts are required, and the conscience must go beyond the self: 'Before we can make any proper comparison of those opposite interests, we must change our position. We must view them, neither from our own place nor yet from his, neither with

[147] See Slights, *Casuistical Tradition*, pp. 9–10; Jonsen and Toulmin, *Abuse of Casuistry*, pp. 275–8.

[148] *The Rape of the Lock and Other Poems*, ed. Geoffrey Tillotson, *Twickenham Edition*, II, 3rd edn (1962), Canto V, lines 122, 113–14.

[149] Smith, *The Theory of Moral Sentiments*, ed. D. D. Raphael and A. L. Macfie (Oxford, 1976), pp. 340, 339–40, 339.

our own eyes nor yet with his, but from the place and with the eyes of a
third person, who has no particular connexion with either, and who judges
with impartiality between us.' If it can attain this selfless place, however,
the conscience, 'the great judge and arbiter of our conduct', will guarantee
the rectitude of our lives. 'We shall stand in need of no casuistic rules to
direct our conduct.'[150]

For Smith, the novelist was uniquely equipped to foster this all-
important capacity of the conscience to transcend the individual's point of
view and cultivate his powers of imaginative association: Richardson,
Marivaux and Riccoboni, in these ways, were 'much better instructors'
than Zeno, Chrysippus and Epictetus.[151] And indeed 'the extension of our
sympathies' and the fellowly 'effort at understanding'[152] typical of the
novel in its classic period were strong impulses, already, in Richardson.
When telling Susanna Highmore of his anxiety 'to settle the boundaries
between right and wrong', he added (with some awkwardness) that 'when
they are exceeded, I believe there hardly lives the wight that allows more
than I do for unwilful failings'.[153] In *Clarissa* he solicits exactly this
response, and it is to his credit that the repressive codes that preside over
the novel are always countered by an insistence on their human implications. If Defoe's Roxana can find grounds to 'move the Pity, even of
those that abhor the Crime',[154] Clarissa herself does infinitely more to
enlist the sympathies of even her most disapproving readers: Richardson
thereby creates an involvement in her predicament through which a
hostile response becomes almost impossible. Few readers, as a result, will
fail to feel the persuasiveness of Anna's final remarks, however authoritarian in outlook or sceptical in approach. The copious tears of the novel's
first audience bear witness to the effect. They were shared not only by
romantic and indulgent readers like 'Philaretes', who can have impressed
Richardson little by writing: 'Your Clarissa is an Angel; and I could not
have borne her Family's barbarous Treatment of her with Patience, if I
had not been calmed with the Hope, that she would have met with the
Reward of her Piety and Virtue, and been happy with Lovelace at last.'[155]
Also 'such an old Fool as to weep', despite herself, was Lady Mary Wortley
Montagu, who thought Clarissa 'so faulty in her behaviour as to deserve
little Compassion'.[156] Even Patrick Delany found her predicament

---

[150] *Ibid.*, pp. 134, 135, 226–7, 227.   [151] *Ibid.*, p. 143.

[152] George Eliot, *Essays*, 2nd edn (Edinburgh, 1884), p. 235; *Middlemarch*, ed. W. J. Harvey
(Harmondsworth, 1965), p. 312.

[153] [1753–4?], Barbauld, II, 221–2.

[154] Defoe, *Roxana*, ed. Jane Jack (Oxford, 1981), p. 39.

[155] 'Philaretes' to Richardson, [early 1748], FM XV, 2, f.32.

[156] To Lady Bute, 1 March 1752, *Complete Letters of Lady Mary Wortley Montagu*, ed. Halsband, III,
8–9. 'Any Girl that runs away with a young Fellow without intending to marry him shou'd be
carry'd to Bridewell or Bedlam the next day', she adds.

'moving' and asked his wife to record that he 'agrees perfectly' with the entire contents of a letter she had written to Richardson on completing the second instalment. Significantly, the letter in question blames both parties, although the sympathies of its writer are clear: on the one hand she confesses herself 'provoked by the tyrannical Usage of the *Harlowe's*'; on the other she longs to see Clarissa rewarded, 'for surely her Disobedience hath been sufficiently chastised'.[157]

Many will feel that even the qualified severity of these last responses is best forgotten, stemming as it does from an ideology that seems to permit, if not sanction, much of the Harlowes' oppression. It is worth bearing in mind, however, that both Lady Mary Wortley Montagu and Mary Delany were more fully aware of the personal misery entailed by the code they blame Clarissa for failing to observe than we can ever be. Lady Mary confessed that the opening volumes had 'soften'd' her 'by a near resemblance of my Maiden Days', when her father, on failing to secure the desired settlement with her preferred suitor and eventual husband Edward Wortley, had attempted to force her to marry a more amenable rival.[158] Mary Delany's reading too cannot fail to have been informed by her own experience, having been compelled at the age of seventeen to marry Alexander Pendarves, a fat old man to whom she had 'an invincible aversion'.[159] Inescapably, these are not readers for whom the novel's case was a merely theoretical matter, and we cannot dismiss their criticism of Clarissa's 'faulty ... behaviour' or 'Disobedience' as lightly made. Nor should we, if only for literary reasons; for to cut through the complexities of Clarissa's case and endorse her conduct wholeheartedly, as readers detached from the ideological context of the 1740s will naturally do, is to miss much of the novel's original challenge. However reprobate the Harlowes, there is by prevailing standards much to be said on their side, and whatever Clarissa's victimisation there is much to be said against hers. The dilemma at Harlowe Place is strictly speaking insoluble, and in his method of posing it Richardson offers no easy resolutions. Recapitulated in the epistolary structure of the instalment, the ethical conflict becomes a great casuistical dispute, in which one side contends for absolute duty and the other for exemption, and in which every word is charged by its involvement in debate. Narrative itself is infected by the struggle it describes, and though the case is presented from a variety of perspectives

---

157 Mary Delany to Richardson, 18 June 1748, FM XV, 2, f.7.
158 *Complete Letters*, ed. Halsband, III, 9. The affair is described in Halsband's *Life of Lady Mary Wortley Montagu* (Oxford, 1956), pp. 10–28.
159 On Mary Delany's first marriage, see *The Autobiography and Correspondence of Mary Granville, Mrs. Delany*, ed. Lady Llanover (1861), I, 23–28; also Carol Houlihan Flynn, *Samuel Richardson: A Man of Letters* (Princeton, 1982), pp. 70–1. Oddly enough, there is no evidence to suggest that her second marriage, to Patrick Delany, was anything other than voluntary.

there exists no stable authoritative position from which it can be seen objectively and whole.

Thus Richardson seems at last to turn the casuistical tradition on its head; for where the manual of cases seeks always to untie and resolve, *Clarissa* entangles and perplexes. It is by these very means, however, that Richardson caters for the insufficiency of casuistical books more fully even than Adam Smith may have seen (and certainly more fully than the sentimentalists with whom Smith associates his name). By probing the system of relative duties at its most crucial and ambiguous points, the novel brings its reader to a problematic awareness of the vexedness of social relations, in which the absolutes of conventional ethics must finally be recognised as complex, provisional and uncertain. By inviting the reader to consider the case from the conflicting perspectives of its protagonists, it requires him in the act of reading to rehearse the changes of position, Smith's 'proper comparisons' of 'opposite interests', through which the conscience is imaginatively informed. And by using these rival perspectives to embody rival discourses or ideologies, each of which articulates one system of judgment and thought and interrogates that of the other, it also enables the reader to examine the limitations and consequences of the prevailing norms in terms of which the conscience has to work.

In this particular case, moreover, it is never an option simply to sit back and admire the text's ethical indeterminacy. *Clarissa* heightens the need to pass judgment, partly from the intense emotional involvement it commands and partly from the unique urgency and significance of its father–daughter theme, so that the reader must himself participate in Clarissa's case and move from efforts at sympathy and efforts at understanding to a perpetual effort at resolution. That effort is always inhibited, given the continual shifts of judgment involved in reading a narrative which itself shifts from viewpoint to viewpoint, repeatedly undermining its own positions and modifying the case with the introduction of new factors or the redefinition of the old. But it is the process or method of deciding that is more important than the decision itself; for in this process the reader's 'judge within' is exercised, educated and prepared. Even as Richardson draws on casuistry, in other words, he provides for its replacement in the individual mind. He offers, indeed, a form of instruction that is perhaps the aptest of all preparations for a life in which (in Jeremy Taylor's formulation) we are always 'intangled with difficult cases of conscience, insnared with passions, amazed with fears, full of cares, divided with curiosities and contradictory interests'.[160] By embroiling the reader in one such intricate case, by withholding simple answers or any uncompromised

---

[160] Jeremy Taylor, *Holy Living and Holy Dying*, ed. P. G. Stanwood, 2 vols. (Oxford, 1989), II, 47.

viewpoint from which to find such answers, and by forcing him to understand on his own initiative the situation itself and the controversies that surrounds it, *Clarissa* at once replicates this problematic world while also stimulating the faculties needed to live within it. It returns the reader from the mock experience of reading to the vexed business of living newly equipped to negotiate the world with vigilance.

3

The part of the serpent
The second instalment, April 1748

Lovelace the principal Male Character in the Celebrated Romance of Clarissa is
evidently a Copy of Rowe's Lothario in the fair Penitent this D.ʳ Johnsons owns
But adds 'that the Imitator has excell'd his original in the Moral Effect of this
Fiction Lothario w.ᵗʰ gaiety which cannot be hated & Bravery which cannot be
Despised retains too much of the Reader's Kindness, it was in the Power of
Richardson alone to teach us at once *Esteem* & Detestation.' But D.ʳ Beattie
another formidable Critic & the friend of D.ʳ Johnson is of a very different
Opinion.

'Richardson's Lovelace says he whom the Reader ought to abominate for his
Crimes is adorned wᵗʰ youth Beauty Eloquence Wit & every intellectual & bodily
accomplishment, is there not then reason to apprehend that some Readers will be
more inclined to admire the gay profligate than to fear his Punishment' – so
contentious a Science is criticism & so little reference have the opinions of the
Learned in Matters of Taste to any common Standard. –

MS note in Clarissa, 4th edn (1759), British Library[1]

Representation and disruption: two controversies

Richardson's sense of the intricacy of social relations was not always so
acute as in *Clarissa*'s first instalment. His earliest known book, *The Apprentice's Vade Mecum*, is a straightforward and rigorous conduct manual,
dealing not with the familial relations that were to preoccupy him as
novelist but with a social category of pressing importance to his activities
as Citizen and Master Printer. Written in the stern tones of the future
Master of the Stationers' Company, the *Vade Mecum* details a strict system
of rules to which the apprentice must adhere within the establishment of
his patron and the larger establishment of the City, extending its scope to
cover the realms of imagination and ideology as well as mere practice. (Its
dual endeavour, as stated in the preface, is 'to regulate the Behaviour, and

[1] I, iii, British Library, 1607/1752. According to an ownership inscription in the same hand, the
book belonged in 1763 to Eliza Rose of Kilravock, whose name survives as the chief correspondent for half a century of her cousin Henry Mackenzie. See his *Letters to Elizabeth Rose of
Kilravock*, ed. Horst W. Drescher (Edinburgh, 1967).

improve the Morals' of its readership.)[2] The work addressed (in the words of a newspaper puff) 'a Situation of inexpressible Concernment to all Degrees of Men in this Maritime and Trading Kingdom',[3] and the situation was one that Richardson found jeopardised by a variety of contemporary trends. Notable among them was the recent expansion of the London theatre. A long digression dwells anxiously on the stage's capacity to corrupt both individual and society, and the theme was pressing enough for him to return to it eighteen months later in *A Seasonable Examination of the Pleas and Pretensions of the Proprietors of, and Subscribers to, Play-houses* (1735), a vigorous critique of the disorderly forces of theatricality.[4]

There is an obvious paradox. Where Fielding began his literary career as a prolific and successful playwright, his satirical virtuosity partly provoking the notorious Licensing Act of 1737, Richardson began his as one of the stage's most articulate opponents, and did much to sustain the climate in which the Act could gain assent. Yet in the next decade the former playwright Fielding presents himself as fashioning his 'new Province of Writing' from the material not so much of drama as of epic, while it is the antitheatricalist Richardson whose 'new Manner' draws in more marked and fruitful ways on the stage tradition.[5] The dramatic sources and methods of his novels have been illuminated from many different angles,[6] but the tension within these apparently happy generic relations is rarely noted, despite the overt distrust of theatricality from which Richardson's writing begins.

Antitheatrical polemic enjoyed new life in the early eighteenth century: 'the soul of old Prynne seems to have reanimated the heaviest part of his clay', as Aaron Hill wrote in response to one particularly retrograde example first published in 1706.[7] Between Jeremy Collier's *Short View of the Immorality and Profaneness of the English Stage* (1698) and William Law's *Absolute Unlawfulness of the Stage-Entertainment Fully Demonstrated* (1726) the stage controversy was fuelled by nearly eighty known blasts and counter-

---

2 *The Apprentice's Vade Mecum* (1734), p. iii.   3 *Weekly Miscellany* (1 December 1733).
4 On Richardson's authorship of these pamphlets, see A. D. McKillop, 'Samuel Richardson's Advice to an Apprentice', *Journal of English and Germanic Philology*, 42, (1943), 40–54, and 'Richardson's Early Writings – Another Pamphlet', *Journal of English and Germanic Philology*, 53 (1954), 72–5.
5 Fielding writes of 'a new Province' (*Tom Jones*, I, 77); Richardson of 'a new Manner' (Carroll, p. 329).
6 On Richardson's dramatic sources, see especially Ira Konigsberg, *Samuel Richardson and the Dramatic Novel* (Lexington, 1968); Margaret Anne Doody, *A Natural Passion: A Study of the Novels of Samuel Richardson* (Oxford, 1974), pp. 99–127; Janet E. Aikins, 'A Plot Discover'd; or The Uses of *Venice Preserv'd* within *Clarissa*', *University of Toronto Quarterly*, 55 (1986), 219–34. On the formal links between novel and drama see Mark Kinkead-Weekes, *Samuel Richardson: Dramatic Novelist* (1973), pp. 395–461.
7 *The Prompter*, ed. William W. Appleton and Kalman A. Burnim (New York, 1966), p. 47 (No. 42, 4 April 1735), referring to a 1735 reissue of Arthur Bedford's *The Evil and Danger of Stage Plays* (1706).

blasts,[8] many of them indeed virulent enough to recall the splenetic diction of puritanism: the prejudices of the preceding century are at work even in Law's generally measured tract, which slips at one point into a rant against 'the Devil's House', 'the very Porch of Hell', and 'the Fountain-head of all Lewdness'.[9] Richardson's own interventions in the debate, however, were part of a more local movement, and they strike a distinctly modern note. He explicitly dissociates his writing from dogmatic antitheatricalism, proclaiming that he 'would not, like some narrow Minds, argue against the *Use* of any thing, because of the *Abuse* of it', and even acknowledging 'that under proper Regulations, the *Stage* may be made subservient to excellent Purposes, and be an useful Second to the *Pulpit* itself'.[10] His concern is not to launch a dogmatic assault on the inherent evils of feigning but to address, in more pragmatic terms, the narrower issue raised by these last phrases – the issue of 'proper Regulation', as it exercised the London magistracy and ultimately Parliament in the particular circumstances of the day.

In 1729 an unlicensed playhouse opened at Goodman's Fields in Whitechapel, an astutely chosen site close enough to the economic centre of the capital to draw large audiences of journeymen and apprentices, but technically beyond the jurisdiction of the City authorities. The City reacted with anger and alarm. An open letter to the Lord Mayor detailed the detrimental effect of play-going on the conduct of the workforce, among whom it fostered 'Notions of Greatness and Pleasure, unfit for their Employments and Stations'; 'Tradelove' wrote to the *Weekly Miscellany*, predicting the disruption of City life by 'innumerable Riots and Disorders'; Sir John Hawkins, years later, lamented the displacement of 'useful manufacturers and industrious artificers' by taverns and brothels, and recalled the anxiety of the remaining merchants on seeing 'the seats of industry hold forth allurements to vice and debauchery'.[11] Early moves at suppression were beaten off by the theatre's proprietor, however, and by the mid-1730s Goodman's Fields seemed not only to be securely established but to have set a dangerous precedent for the proliferation of other non-patent houses about the margins of the City. Renewed and more concerted action was inevitable, and in 1735 a proposal to build another theatre at St Martin's le Grand was met by a parliamentary Bill 'for Restraining the Number of Houses for Playing of Interludes, and for the

[8] See Sister Rose Anthony, *The Jeremy Collier Stage Controversy, 1698–1726* (New York, 1937), pp. 300–7.

[9] *The Absolute Unlawfulness of the Stage-Entertainment Fully Demonstrated* (1726), pp. 15–16.

[10] *Vade Mecum*, p. 9.

[11] [Bishop Francis Hare?], *A Letter to the Right Honourable Sir Richard Brocas, Lord Mayor of London* (1730), quoted by Jonas A. Barish, *The Antitheatrical Prejudice* (Berkeley and Los Angeles, 1981), p. 241; *Weekly Miscellany* (8 March 1735); Hawkins, *The Life of Samuel Johnson, LL.D.*, 2nd edn (1787), pp. 73, 74.

better Regulating Common Players of Interludes'. The Bill was introduced in March by Sir John Barnard, an Independent Whig of mercantile
and dissenting background (with whom Richardson had both professional
and political links),[12] and it was vigorously supported by his London
constituents. Readings were punctuated by representations to the
Commons from City groups, typified by a petition from the Lord Mayor
and Aldermen which censures Goodmans' Fields as 'a great Encouragement to Vice, Debauchery, and Corruption of Youth, to the lessening of
Industry, and the great Prejudice of Trade': prompt and firm action is
urged against what the Bill itself describes as 'this great and growing
Evil'.[13]

Richardson participated in this movement as a polemicist for the City
interest, articulating in cogent form the complaints of his fellow tradesmen
and developing from their prejudices and fears a coherent rhetoric of civic
antitheatricalism. Though beginning as a gloss on the apprentice's inden-
ture addressed specifically to youth, the *Vade Mecum* takes the opportunity
of the clause 'Not to haunt *Play-houses*' to build an attack on the theatre
that is also a more widely addressed call for parliamentary action.[14] When
action was forthcoming Richardson issued a second edition of the work,
calling particular attention in advertisements to its antitheatrical passages. At the same time he returned to the fray with *A Seasonable Examination*, which endorses 'the Bill now under Consideration of the Legislature'
and attacks the representations of the Goodman's Fields lobby.[15] Both
critiques are thus closely tied to particular circumstances and interests,
while also growing directly from the larger regulatory purposes and social
theories outlined in the *Vade Mecum* as a whole. It is in this context that
Richardson's antitheatricalism is best understood.

Central to the rhetoric of the *Vade Mecum* and *A Seasonable Examination*
are the terms 'City' and 'Commonwealth', which in the repeated usage of
both tracts acquire special resonance. 'Commonwealth' is a key term in
the work (among others) of Locke, who uses it to describe the origin and
function of civil society as an edifice erected to guarantee the security of

[12] See William M. Sale, Jr, *Samuel Richardson: Master Printer*, pp. 39, 57, 149; T. C. D. Eaves and
B. D. Kimpel, *Samuel Richardson: A Biography*, p. 31.
[13] *Journals of the House of Commons*, 22 (1732–7), 470; *A Bill for Restraining the Number of Houses for
Playing of Interludes, and for the Better Regulating Common Players of Interludes* (1735). p. 2. On the
Goodman's Fields affair and the background to Barnard's Bill, see the introduction and
calendar in *The London Stage, 1660–1800, Part 3 (1729–1747)*, ed. Arthur H. Scouten (Carbondale, 1961); Vincent J. Liesenfeld, *The Licensing Act of 1737* (Madison, 1984), pp. 15–16, 23–59;
Robert D. Hume, *Henry Fielding and the London Theatre, 1728–1737* (Oxford, 1988), pp. 39–44,
192–9.
[14] *Vade Mecum*, p. 9.
[15] *A Seasonable Examination of the Pleas and Pretensions of the Proprietors of, and Subscribers to, Play-houses*
(1735), p. 5. The second edition of the *Vade Mecum* was advertised in the *Weekly Miscellany* on
26 April 1735, and *A Seasonable Examination* on 3 May 1735.

covenanting parties: in the *Two Treatises* the Commonwealth exists for the preservation of its members' 'Lives, Liberties and Estates', and it achieves this end by the institution of government and laws.[16] These meanings are clearly at work in Richardson, but he is also anxious to stress that systems other than the legislative and executive have a role in binding the Commonwealth. Consequently, he emphasises the particular importance of the City – a term signifying not simply 'a large collection of houses and inhabitants'[17] but more specifically the ancient and commercial centre of London, locus of the economic systems from which the wider community draws in the first place its sustenance, and ultimately its stability and power. The City is the vital organ of the Commonwealth, which as a whole 'owes its Support, and the Figure it makes abroad, intirely to Trade'. And within the City the apprentice's situation in particular is '*of very high Importance to the Good of the Community ... Since it is from this Source, that the most numerous and most useful Members of the Commonwealth are derived; on whose Industry and Labour the Welfare of the Whole almost intirely depends*'. The conduct of these members could hardly be a more critical matter. They are 'the most useful Underwheels of the Commonwealth, that keep the great Machine of Trade and Manufacture going'; if they fail, the implication is, the Machine stops. In setting out to regulate the apprentice's conduct, and to instil in him moral and religious principles which will ultimately make such regulation a purely internalised matter, Richardson therefore seeks to secure the 'weal' of society as a whole – its prosperity, health and cohesion.[18]

Richardson's image of the 'great Machine' is undeniably disturbing, suggesting as it does that his concern for the moral welfare of the apprentice is cynical at root. To keep the individual within the bounds of religion and morality, after all, is also to keep him to the grindstone. Yet the apprentice of whom Richardson writes is no ordinary cog in the machine. In the radically capitalist Commonwealth of the *Vade Mecum* he takes over the role of Plato's young guardian, his instruction not only guaranteeing the present vitality of trade, but also preparing for his future responsibilities as a Citizen one '*who when he comes to be Master, in his Turn, may contribute to amend the Age*'. The *Vade Mecum*'s purpose, accordingly, is to confirm the apprentice in the patterns of thought and conduct proper to these important roles, future as well as present, and to forbid anything likely to

---

[16] *Two Treatises of Government*, ed. Peter Laslett (Cambridge, 1960), p. 368. On the more immediate implications of the term, see Caroline Robbins, *The Eighteenth-Century Commonwealthman* (Cambridge, Mass., 1959).

[17] Johnson, *Dictionary*, 'City'. On the meanings invested by Richardson in London's two rival poles, the City and the Town, see Edward Copeland, 'Remapping London: *Clarissa* and the Woman at the Window', in *Samuel Richardson: Tercentenary Essays*, ed. Margaret Anne Doody and Peter Sabor (Cambridge, 1989), pp. 51–69.

[18] *Vade Mecum*, pp. 11, vi, 18–19.

interfere with them. Trade, Richardson insists, 'can never prosper, if the *whole* Mind and Application be not ingross'd by them, preferably to any other Considerations'.[19] For the apprentice and future burgher, vocational commitment is paramount: nothing must divert him from the single-minded pursuit of his calling.

Richardson's objection to the theatre is that it constitutes just such a diversion, and one that has an almost overwhelming power. To an extent his argument simply rehearses the complaints with which, during the reading of Barnard's Bill, the House of Commons was wearyingly besieged. He worries at truancy, for example, and is concerned too at hostile representations of the cit (caustically citing the convention by which 'to make a Cuckold of a rich Citizen, is a masterly Part of the Plot'). There is more to these superficially banal objections, however, than meets the eye. The lost hours at the playhouse portend the theatre's larger tendency to undermine the vocational commitment of apprentices, and the mockery of burghers is only its most obvious way of doing so, 'at best teaching them to despise the Station of Life, to which ... they are inevitably destin'd'.[20] These are but simple instances of a profoundly disruptive power, the theatre's capacity to disengage the mind from the constraints of the quotidian, to open it on new and seductive realms of experience, and to release its most disorderly desires. For the theatre possesses the most dangerous and hypnotic allure: 'the glittering, the dazling Scene' will transport the apprentice's imagination beyond the mundane reality of his calling, and will undermine the dour commitment necessary for its fulfilment.[21] Verbs of distraction and disintegration recur with ominous frequency: in *A Seasonable Examination* the theatres 'amuse the *Eye* and the *Ear*, and intoxicate, thro' them, the *Understanding*'; in the *Vade Mecum* the apprentice's mind 'must be seduc'd and misled, must be relaxed and unbent' by spectacles of a kind to 'detach' or 'unhinge' him from his proper concerns. One extreme passage details the stages of a process by which he comes 'to sit loose to those narrow Ties to which his Business necessarily binds him', the sober realities of the City banished from a mind instead transfixed by the circean illusions of the stage.[22]

Yet these imaginative dislocations form only a part of the theatre's threat; for the fantasies which so compellingly undermine the sense of identity proper to the apprentice are not simply irrelevant to his social role but directly inimical to it. With its characteristic glorification of the malefactor, the theatre not only diverts the spectator from his calling but actually turns him against the moral consensus on which society rests. Richardson is hard enough on Restoration drama, singling out for criticism the 'odious and detestable Characters' of Congreve, and finding in its

[19] *Ibid.*, pp. v, 14.   [20] *Ibid.*, pp. 11, 17–18.   [21] *Ibid.*, p. 11.
[22] *Seasonable Examination*, p. 19; *Vade Mecum*, pp. 17, 13, 14, 13.

whole corpus 'at the very best, How the *Heroes* of Antiquity courted near 2000 Years ago' and 'how the People in *high Life* confound all Distinctions of Right and Wrong'.[23] Worse even than Restoration libertinism, however, is the flagrant criminality of the modern stage, in which characters mimic the most delinquent elements in society while plots dwell illicitly on their transgressions. *A Seasonable Examination* inveighs against the theatre's preoccupation with 'the vile Rogueries of an Harlequin *Shepherd*, the Villanies of *Newgate* and *Bridewell*, a detestable *Mackheath*' and the like, and the *Vade Mecum* defines the objection more clearly. The theatrical representation of criminality is at best equivocal, uncontrolled by didactic reprobation; more often, it is blatantly subversive. The Newgate heroes are exhibited 'not for the Sake of Poetical Justice, in their *Execution*, but to divert the Audience by their *Tricks* and *Escapes*; and if they have been brought to Justice at last, it has been in such a Manner, as to move the Pity of the Audience for them'. Instead of celebrating the proper victory of justice over crime, the stage mounts a flagitious inversion of the two terms: 'the vilest Actions of the vilest Miscreants', instead of appearing in their properly vile colours, become occasions of a carnivalesque pleasure, even of instruction in cozenage.[24]

In combination, these factors are fatal. The allurements of the stage first seize the apprentice's mind, in ways that can only unsettle his adherence to his own vocation; and in distracting, to compound the evil, they also corrupt, engaging his sympathies to the cause of deviancy and fomenting his most unruly impulses. Here Richardson is at his closest to mainstream antitheatricalism, which contends that whatever imitates the passions is in danger also of unleashing them: in Law's formulation, the stage 'applies to the Corruption of our Nature ... awakens our disorder'd Passions', and so 'fatally undo[es] all that Religion has done'.[25] For Richardson, mimetic representation has just this ruinous power, a power fascinating enough to overwhelm all but the most vigilant: he sees the stage 'impudently propagating, by heighten'd Action and Scenical Example, to an *underbred* and *unwary* Audience, Fornication, Adultery, Rapes, and Murders', and thereby turning society's most useful members into potentially disruptive enemies. Here the question of individual morality for its own sake pales in significance: Richardson's strictures, much more than those of Collier and Law, go far beyond the state of the spectator's soul. Instead they emerge from considering the theatre within the context of City and Commonwealth, and from a pressing fear of social disintegration. Richardson is relatively unconcerned, for example, by playhouses at 'the gay End of the Town', whose fashionable audiences take no part in the all-important

[23] *Vade Mecum*, p. 12; *Seasonable Examination*, p. 15.
[24] *Seasonable Examination*, p. 15; *Vade Mecum*, pp. 13, 18.
[25] *The Absolute Unlawfulness of the Stage-Entertainment Fully Demonstrated*, pp. 4, 5.

processes of economic life. But when they invade the vital organ of the Commonwealth his response changes. 'They must be of pernicious Consequence when set up in the City, or in those Confines of it, where the People of Industry generally inhabit': here the results of individual corruption are immediate and severe. The *Vade Mecum* concludes its antitheatrical digression in a protest that 'the Civil Power and City-Magistracy have been ... brav'd and insulted' by the erection of a playhouse 'but just remov'd out of the Liberties of the City, to avoid the Cognizance of the Magistrates of this excellently well-govern'd Corporation'. *A Seasonable Examination* lingers with similar anxiety over the wording of the St Martin's le Grand proposal, that 'the said Ground is *out of the City*, and yet very near the *Heart of it*'. Being out of the City, the playhouse can flout the laws by which its order is maintained; being also near its heart, it has a lethal potential for damage. Ultimately, Richardson's suggestion is, the threat is to society itself: 'we find ourselves hastening apace into that Depravity of Manners, that prov'd the Ruin of the best constituted States and Commonwealths that ever were in Being'.[26]

The political action urged by these two tracts in fact proved abortive.[27] But Richardson's polemical efforts had more enduring results, for his engagement in the Goodman's Fields controversy developed in him a heightened sense of the functions and powers of mimesis. In neither tract does he suggest that dramatic representation necessarily tends towards social collapse: his alarm is not at any inherent malignity in the theatre, simply at a misapplication of its power. In the *Vade Mecum* he illustrates his description of the stage as 'useful Second to the *Pulpit*' with a digression in praise of Lillo's City tragedy *The London Merchant*. More significantly, *A Seasonable Examination* considers the political role of the Athenian and Roman dramatists, acknowledging that 'the Stage has been thought worthy, in old Time, to be taken immediately into the Protection of the State'.[28] In such passages can be detected the germ of Richardson's own fiction, with its elaborate designs on the reader. When, years later, he turned to the novel, he did so to reverse the depredations of the stage, recover the mimetic for its potential 'excellent Purposes', and so counter the slide into 'Depravity of Manners' which, in the hyperboles of *A Seasonable Examination*, had seemed to threaten collective ruin. This project, moreover, eventually went beyond anything that might have been expected in the 1730s from the ideological stringency of the *Vade Mecum*: regeneracy rather than mere stabilisation becomes the primary impulse of Richardson's writings until, in *Grandison*, he ends by delineating (in

---

[26] *Vade Mecum*, pp. 17, 16, 18; *Seasonable Examination*, pp. 5, 4.
[27] See Liesenfeld, *The Licensing Act of 1737*, pp. 52–9; Hume, *Henry Fielding and the London Theatre*, pp. 197–8.
[28] *Seasonable Examination*, p. 24.

Jocelyn Harris's words) a 'vision of millennial love, justice and reform'. If this work's lessons were truly learned, wrote one early reader, 'how would this world be changed, from a sink of corruption, into a paradisaisall State; our lost Eden be restord again to us'.[29]

Less fanciful contemporaries recognised Richardson's writings as in this sense political interventions, attempts to buttress and repair the 'polity' itself. In *Clarissa*, wrote one, he had 'strengthen'd the cause of Virtue, and the moral interest of Society, and is entitled to the gratitude of all good Men'; another urged him to apply as an epigraph to the text a passage from Strabo, which he rendered: 'FICTIONS have been made use of, in preference to other compositions, not only by Poëts, but, long before, by States, & Law-givers (in regard to the usefulness of them) upon considering the natural disposition of a RATIONAL ANIMAL.'[30] In verses appended to *Clarissa*'s third edition John Duncombe went so far as to suggest that the reasons which made Plato banish the poets from his ideal republic left Richardson exempt:

> Ev'n Plato, in Lyceum's awful shade,
> Th'instructive page with transport had survey'd;
> And own'd its author to have well supply'd
> The place his Laws to Homer's self deny'd.[31]

In one respect, however, the relation between the repertoire at Goodman's Fields and Richardson's own novels is less happily antithetical. At the core of his antitheatricalism is an anxiety at the vivid depiction of evil, a fear that the immediacy of access to vice offered by the stage will enlist the spectator's sympathies to criminality and disrupt his commitment to the patterns of thought and conduct by which society is bound. Yet his own novels owe their vigour (their very plots, indeed) to the same subversive presence, and are propelled forward by the illicit impulse of libertinism. The process, of course, is not unsupervised: in both *Pamela* and *Grandison*, the rake-figure exists only within the ostentatiously virtuous discourse of the heroine, and thus is at once defined and controlled by the viewpoint of his moral antagonist. (It is not irrelevant that this formal control has its counterpart in each plot, which brings the libertine to final penitence and conversion.) In *Clarissa*, however, and most markedly in the second instalment, the position is very different: unlike Mr B. and Sir Hargrave, Lovelace is also a narrator. One reviewer wrote that here

29 Jocelyn Harris, *Samuel Richardson* (Cambridge, 1987), p. 2; Thomas Newcomb to Richardson [late October 1754], FM XV, 4, ff. 39–40.
30 David Graham to Richardson, 22 April 1750, FM XV, 2, f.84; Solomon Lowe to Richardson, 18 May 1749, FM XV, 2, f.117. The passage in question is from Strabo's *Geography*, C 19 (Loeb ed., with an English translation by H. L. Jones (1917–32), I, 67). Richardson considered it seriously enough to solicit a second translation, from R. Smith (FM XV, 2, f.117).
31 *Clarissa*, 3rd edn (1751; rpt. New York, 1990), VIII, 303.

Richardson had learned from criticisms of *Pamela*, improving on the first novel's 'statue of a lover, who never speaks but by the organs of another';[32] and it is certainly true that the access to Lovelace provided by his own parallel narrative constitutes a major innovation, which from a purely formal point of view adds welcome depth and complexity. In the context of Richardson's rhetorical purposes, however, the issue is far less clear. The gesture of giving Lovelace his voice was not only innovative but hazardous, a bold experiment in intimacy with evil which gave rise to a barrage of hostile criticism, and remained significantly unrepeated in his final work. To many early critics, it seemed that to let the reader into the mind of Lovelace was not to enrich *Clarissa* but to undo it – to reduce the text to the same disruptiveness lamented by Richardson himself in the drama of the previous decade.

In its simplest form, the controversy about Lovelace deals with the legitimacy of his characterisation, in which malignity is decked out in attractive, even winning, form. As Eliza Rose saw in her playful note about the 'contentious ... Science' of criticism, the rival judgments of Johnson and Beattie mark out the area of debate. For Johnson, Richardson had created Lovelace by expanding on Rowe's Lothario,

but he has excelled his original in the moral effect of the fiction. Lothario, with gaiety which cannot be hated, and bravery which cannot be despised, retains too much of the spectator's kindness. It was in the power of Richardson alone to teach us at once esteem and detestation; to make virtuous resentment overpower all the benevolence which wit, elegance, and courage naturally excite, and to lose at last the hero in the villain.[33]

In Lovelace, the tension between realism and 'moral effect' of which Johnson had written with such anxiety in *Rambler* 4 is uniquely reconciled, it would seem: Johnson sees no need to class Lovelace among those mixed characters 'whose endowments threw a brightness on their crimes', and whose resemblance, according to the *Rambler*, 'ought to no more to be preserved, than the art of murdering without pain'.[34] Beattie, however, is less sure. He fears a capacity in Lovelace to suspend the severity proper to his conduct, and ultimately to win from the reader approval (or even imitation) of his libertinism:

when a character, like Richardson's *Lovelace*, whom the reader ought to abominate for his crimes, is adorned with youth, beauty, eloquence, wit, and every other intellectual and bodily accomplishment, it is to be feared ... that some readers will be more inclined to admire the gay profligate, than to fear his punishment.[35]

[32] Haller, 'A Critical Account of *Clarissa*', in *Novel and Romance*, ed. Williams, p. 131.
[33] *Lives of the English Poets*, II, 67.
[34] *Rambler*, III, 23 (No. 4, 31 March 1750).   [35] *Dissertations Moral and Critical*, p. 569.

By leavening iniquity with attractiveness, Richardson now seems to risk
losing the *villain* in the *hero*, thereby imperilling his own most cherished
purposes.

There was also a third corner to the debate. For every reader who found
the encounter with Lovelace dangerously alluring, others found it simply
horrifying, to the extent that Richardson was sometimes challenged as at
heart a Lovelacean himself. Beattie feared that some readers might even
fancy 'that a character so highly ornamented must have been a favourite
of the author',[36] and so indeed it proved. When the second instalment
appeared, one reader expressed amazement that 'a Gentleman of a universal good Reputation can support such a Character as Lovelace' and
urged Richardson in future to 'let us have only that Part of your Mind
which is admired by all the Good Part of the World'. Three ladies from St
Neots likewise detected in Lovelace's letters a darker side to their author,
and brushed aside Edward Moore's attempts to defend his friend: 'For it
seems I am so partial to the Man that I shut my Eyes to the Book', a letter
from Moore reports.[37] Nor was this *ad hominem* turn confined to the
fastidious English. In the endnote to *La Nouvelle Héloïse* Rousseau mounts a
thinly veiled attack on his predecessor's mind: 'Je ne saurais concevoir
quel plaisir on peut prendre à imaginer et composer le personnage d'un
scélérat, à se mettre à sa place tandis qu'on le représente, à lui prêter l'éclat
le plus imposant.'[38] Following this lead, a prudent reviewer in the *Journal
encyclopédique* chose not to accompany Diderot to the back of the cave
where, in the 'Eloge', Richardson holds a torch. First assuming that
Clarissa is simply a case in which 'le Moraliste manque son but', and that
in Lovelace 'Richardson a probablement réussi dans ce caractère au delà
de ses espérances', the reviewer soon moves towards a less tolerant view of
Richardson's deepest motives: 'concerter des entreprises d'une horreur
aussi compliquée, metter autant de réflexion dans les complots, autant de
génie dans les noirceurs, créer une âme aussi atroce ... comment peindre
un tel monstre, sans se révolter contre son ouvrage?'[39] Perhaps Lovelace is
only the image of his author, such criticisms suggest, and the moralist no
more than a pervert. For Sade, certainly, Richardson could be recon-
structed at the century's end as an essentially amoral philosopher of evil,
fascinated by human nature in all its darkest possibilities, 'tel que doivent
le rendre les modifications du vice, et toutes les secousses des passions'.[40]

The link between Lovelace's first-person narration and the perilous
vividness of portrayal detected by all these witnesses is rarely made in

---

[36] *Ibid.*, p. 569.
[37] Anon. to Richardson, 20 May 1748, FM XV, 2, ff.5–6; Moore to Richardson, 1 October 1748,
f.18.
[38] *La Nouvelle Héloïse*, Garnier edn (Paris, 1967), p. 568n.
[39] 'Observations sur *Clarice*', *Journal encyclopédique* (15 March 1763), pp. 66, 67.
[40] Sade, 'Idée sur les romans', in *Les Crimes de l'amour* (Brussels, 1881), p. 115.

early criticism. As the most interesting contemporary allegations make clear, however, the reader's intimacy with Lovelacean evil has its origin not so much in Richardson's perverse psyche as in his polyphonic narrative form – a form which not only gives privileged access to Lovelace's psychological 'noirceurs' but also invites the reader to experience the novel in part from a libertine stance. The point is tellingly made by Joseph Priestley, who locates the problem of Lovelace's letters not so much in their unveiling of an evil heart as in their exposure of the reader to a subversive narrative perspective. In Priestley's theory of reading (which draws directly on the associational psychology of David Hartley), some temporary suspension of one's own viewpoint and a corresponding identification with that of a narrator is inevitable in the act of reading. The mind conforms itself to what it perceives, Priestley suggests, so that 'a person, for the time, enters into, adopts, and is actuated by, the sentiments that are presented to his mind'. The principle is a general one, demonstrable in such simple sensory examples as the vicarious vertigo experienced by a man who sees another on the brink of a cliff. Its effects in the case of narrative, however, are particularly significant and insinuating, where 'the passions, sentiments, and views of those persons whose history is written so as to engage our attention, become for a time … our own passions, sentiments, and views.'[41] The final result, all too often, is an unperceived distortion of judgment.

Hence, in part, arises the difficulty of reading the history of any two rival states, or personages, with absolute indifference and impartiality. Before we were aware, we find we have entered into the sentiments, passions, and interests of the one or the other of them; and afterwards find it difficult to *change sides*, as it were; notwithstanding, in the progress of the history, we may see reason enough to be disgusted with the party we at first adopted.

Unless at pains to resist and correct what Priestley calls 'this mechanical propensity', the reader will find himself unwittingly endorsing criminal behaviour or condemning that of the just. In the case of rival states, a reader of Thucydides will find himself 'distressed to the last degree with the miscarriage of the flagrantly ambitious and unjust invasion of Sicily', for the simple reason that the historian's perspective (for all his attempts at evenhandedness) is incorrigibly Athenian.[42]

For the case of rival personages Priestley turns to *Clarissa*, which he cites to illustrate the dangers of promiscuity in the use of point of view. Writers should not engage their readers' attention to vicious characters, he contends, since any engagement of attention necessarily brings with it an

---

[41] Priestley, *A Course of Lectures on Oratory and Criticism* (1777), ed. Vincent M. Bevilacqua and Richard Murphy (Carbondale, 1965), p. 127.

[42] *Ibid.*, p. 128.

engagement of interest, against which 'a natural love for virtue is a very insufficient security'. Intimacy leads inexorably on to complicity: once interested in the character and schemes of a bad man, the reader will become, in his sympathies, confederate with him, like the reader who sanctions the imperialism of the Athenian invaders. The lesson Priestley draws is that no writer should trust to the reader's capacity to correct this corrupting influence; and he finds the lesson strikingly demonstrated in the evidence of *Clarissa*'s reception. 'Even the prudent and virtuous Mr. Richardson hath interested his reader so much in the character of *Lovelace*, in Clarissa, that ... there are few of his readers who would be displeased with the success of his base designs upon any other woman than Clarissa herself, in whose favour we have been beforehand more strongly interested.'[43] The novel is saved only because Lovelace's letters are countered within the text by the double narrative (as though Thucydides had also included a parallel Spartan account). Otherwise, Priestley suggests, the intimacy with evil induced by the letters would lure the reader into sanctioning the crimes they report.

The shift of emphasis here from personality to viewpoint is instructive. For all its inflexibility and determinism, Priestley's theory of reading enables him to shed the debilitating obsession of contemporary criticism with immoralities of character and plot, and to focus instead on the more basic questions of narrative form and perspective. What is significant, in these new terms, is not simply Lovelace's villainy or even the vividness of its portrayal, but rather the extent to which the reader's experience itself becomes unwittingly Lovelacean. In the very act of reading, it now appears, his sympathies and judgments will be beguiled.

An amusingly direct instance of the associational problem raised by Priestley's remarks comes in the recurrent charges of pornography levelled against *Clarissa* in its second instalment, and specifically against Lovelace's heated report of Clarissa's 'sweet discomposure' (IV, 294; p. 724) when awakened at Sinclair's by shouts that the house is on fire. At publication Richardson was soon embroiled in debate with readers (including some of his staunchest supporters) who wanted the fire-scene withdrawn. Forced to solicit defences from less disapproving members of his circle, he even printed and distributed a pamphlet of his own in justification of the scene. In it, he carefully distances himself from personal criticism as a writer of erotic narrative by attributing the report solely to Lovelace's character and point of view. As he wrote the letter he was merely '*personating*' a fictive narrator, he insists: 'are not the different Persons to write *in Character*? And *To the Occasion*? And if this Scene was to be described by *Lovelace*, did not the Lady's *personal* as well as intellectual Beauties, and his

---

[43] *Ibid.*, p. 129.

avowed Passion for her, *characteristically*, as I may say, require that it should be done with Warmth?'[44] His supporter Jane Collier took another tack, turning the objection to the scene back on the objectors with the chilly rebuke that 'the Reason of a Man's blaming it as being too highly painted must be from his dwelling more strongly on the Person of the lovely Sufferer, than on her Innocence and Distress'.[45] Both she and Richardson, however, are careful to avoid detailed inspection of the way the text itself dwells on Clarissa's body, resting their case instead in Lovelace's statement that he intends in reporting the scene to Belford 'to put a bound to thy roving thoughts' (IV, 290; p. 722). The thoughts of other readers continued to rove, nonetheless. '*Clarissa*'s Charms are all displayed before our Eyes, her lovely naked Bosom, and fine turn'd Limbs, exposed in the Struggling', drooled one reviewer. 'We can hardly avoid being fired with the warm Description: And imagine with *Lovelace*, that he might *hurt the tenderest and loveliest of all her Beauties*.'[46] In Lovelace's hands, the scene was incendiary indeed.

Similar allegations preoccupy another early pamphlet to concentrate its fire on the Lovelace volumes, the anonymous *Critical Remarks on Sir Charles Grandison, Clarissa and Pamela. Enquiring, Whether they have a Tendency to corrupt or improve the Public Taste and Morals* (1754). 'The hearts of men are very corruptible, especially where there is an incitement from a natural passion', its writer pronounces, and censures Richardson for playing to the most transgressive impulses of his readers. Lovelace's narrative is singled out for criticism as one which not only directs attention to an illicit subject but also applies to it a flagrantly criminal gloss – notably in the 'luscious' description of Clarissa in the fire-scene, which will leave only readers of 'a very philosophical constitution' unmoved. A wittily mock-heroic passage follows, outlining 'the natural catastrophe of a serious perusal of the fire-adventure': 'the passions of the reader being now raised, his next business is to satisfy them', and he 'sallies forth, fully bent to enjoy Clarissa in imagination'. He eventually settles, bathetically, for a Dorcas Wykes instead.[47]

Critical Remarks, however, is no prudish critique of licentiousness, but draws knowingly on the commonplace pornography charge as a way of bringing Richardson's pretensions to social usefulness under focused scrutiny. In enquiring whether the novels will 'corrupt or improve', in fact, the pamphlet turns very much the substance of Richardson's antitheatrical case back in criticism of his own subsequent practice, and ends in the same

---

[44] Eaves and Kimpel, 'An Unpublished Pamphlet by Samuel Richardson', pp. 404, 405.
[45] Collier to Richardson, 9 July 1749, FM XV, 2, f.9.
[46] [Francis Plummer], *A Candid Examination of the History of Sir Charles Grandison*, 3rd edn (1755), pp. 24–5.
[47] *Critical Remarks on Sir Charles Grandison, Clarissa, and Pamela* (1754), ed. A. D. McKillop, Augustan Reprint Society No. 21 (Los Angeles, 1950), pp. 41, 46–7.

allegation of a socially disruptive effect. For its writer, chastity is the primary social virtue because of its capacity to maintain the integrity of families, and promiscuity is correspondingly the primary vice: chastity works 'to keep these separate and distinct, to prevent them from falling into confusion, on all which the good oeconomy and internal happiness of the state much depend'; as for promiscuity, 'many undergo capital punishments daily for crimes ... much less destructive to the interests of Society'.[48] The capacity to discourage the reader from the latter vice and confirm him in the former virtue therefore provides a basic test of Richardson's wider claims; and it is a test that *Clarissa* fails. The first instalment's admirable investigation of familial discord (which if given due weight would prevent 'a vast variety of mischiefs and miseries in private life') is utterly subverted in the second, where instead of upholding the social virtues Richardson lingers ambivalently on their overthrow. In Lovelace's narrative he offers us 'a minute and circumstantial detail of the most shocking vices and villainous contrivances' and in so doing familiarises them to us, so that '*We first endure, then pity, then embrace*' Lovelace's evil.[49] Its vivid representation of transgression at once excites and informs the potential depravity of the reader's imagination, fomenting the very disorders that Richardson explicitly sets out to restrain.

Critical Remarks thus culminates in a direct refutation of Richardson's grandest claims, drawing its case to a close with reference to Platonic argument of the kind distantly suggested in the *Vade Mecum* and explicitly raised in the 1751 edition of *Clarissa*. Its conclusion is that Richardson's pretensions to applause as a guardian of society are hollow, and that his writings can only be disruptive. Citing John Duncombe's verses on Homer and Richardson, the critic not only refutes the claim made in them ('if the one ... was denied an admission into the Platonic commonwealth, the other would have been kick'd out of it with shame and disgrace'), but also goes on to ridicule Richardson's own debased notion of the ideal state. In this analysis London is no longer the 'well-govern'd and populous Metropolis' of *A Seasonable Examination*: it is 'the overgrown metropolis of a powerful Empire, and an extensive commerce', the corrupt centre of 'a monarchical and commercial state, where there is a hereditary noblesse, and a great inequality among the fortunes of the citizens' – conditions radically inimical to those of Plato's ideal.[50] *Clarissa* would be meaningless in the true Republic, in fact: it belongs in London alone, where it will stand at once as testimony and fodder to the depravity of the city's inhabitants.

Critical Remarks thus brings to completion the contemporary case against

[48] *Ibid.*, pp. 29, 31.
[49] *Ibid.*, pp. 15, 43, 41 (quoting Pope, *An Essay on Man*, Book II, line 220).
[50] *Ibid.*, pp. 53, 54; see *Seasonable Examination*, p. 11.

Clarissa, putting it in the larger political terms in which, long before the novel's composition, Richardson was already viewing the project of mimesis. From this and other sources there emerges a formidable composite objection – that in depicting with such vividness a vicious yet winning character, in organising the novel around his stratagems and plots, and in filtering large sections of it through his point of view, Richardson brings the reader to perilous intimacy and even complicity with evil, thereby subverting his own design of stabilisation and reform. In general terms, moreover, the same objections remain current. Though replacing eighteenth-century anxieties about the immediate influence of novel-reading on social conduct by a more abstract and sophisticated critique of authorial control, many of *Clarissa*'s recent critics continue to rehearse the classic moves of the Lovelace controversy. Carol Houlihan Flynn, for example, sees in Lovelace's letters the vicarious fantasy life by which we may read Richardson's psyche in its full perversity; William Beatty Warner sees in them the loose thread which need only be pulled to unravel the whole didactic structure. For all their differences, both find Lovelace a subversive and unruly presence within the text – a presence which works, more than any other, to subvert or transcend his creator's larger intentions.[51] One might even speculate that Richardson had unwittingly become a Goodman's Fields dramatist himself. By representing, like them, 'the vilest Actions of the vilest Miscreants ... in such a manner, as is far from making their Vices odious and detestable',[52] he seems to place in jeopardy his own most cherished intentions.

Tearing up fences: Lovelace as plotter

Such charges only become stronger when one turns to the details of Lovelace's portrayal. For Lovelace, unlike the Newgate heroes of Goodman's Fields, is no ordinary criminal: in ways that offer many parallels with the embattled sociology of the *Vade Mecum*, Richardson represents him as the archetypal enemy of society, the most extreme challenger of its values, identity and organisation. In its details Lovelace's definition could hardly be more hostile – something that makes his ability to escape it, or even to make the definition appealing, more problematic still.

In its very plot, *Clarissa* is a novel about the ruin of a society, in which Lovelace is cast as the primary agent of ruin. He throws in turmoil the world of Harlowe Place, and having tempted Clarissa to abandon it he tyrannises her to the point, eventually, of rape. He bears final responsibility for a catastrophe which 'depriv[es] the world' of its 'shining light'

---

[51] Carol Houlihan Flynn, *Samuel Richardson: A Man of Letters* (Princeton, 1982), pp. 196–234; Warner, *Reading Clarissa*, pp. 28–55.
[52] *Vade Mecum*, p. 18.

(VII, 333; p. 1436) and leaves its community irreparably fragmented. In developing this literal sense of Lovelace's destructive agency, Richardson draws too on many prejudices and fears widely shared in society as a whole, to invest in him a range of meanings by which his threat to Clarissa's world is amplified as a threat to the reader's own. In the terms of an ideological consensus which saw its values of 'liberty and property' guaranteed by the rule of law, a stable social order, the balanced consitution and the established church,[53] Lovelace is the ultimate bugbear. In a variety of senses, he is society's perilous 'other'.

To exchange the term 'rake' for 'libertine' is to approach this range of meanings. 'To *be* a libertine, at setting out, all compunction, all humanity, must be overcome', Colonel Morden tells Clarissa. 'To *continue* to be a libertine is to continue to be every thing vile and inhuman' (III, 361; p. 564). Strong but imprecise words: they can be glossed, however, by the four definitions of 'libertine' in Johnson's *Dictionary*, which trace the term's development and indicate the anxieties conventionally invested in it. In its original sense, the Latin *libertinus* denotes a freedman or former slave, and from this root meaning develop three distinct senses. The first is relatively neutral, even perhaps positive: a libertine is 'One unconfined; one at liberty'. But in the second this enviable state takes on more sinister implications: the libertine is 'One who lives without restraint or law'. The third sense, more ominously still, finds this lawlessness of practice matched by a similar abandonment of ideological restraint: 'One who pays no regard to the precepts of religion'. In its fullest and most subversive sense, 'libertinism' thus comes to mean 'Irreligion; licentiousness of opinions and practice'.[54] The idea is of a wholesale challenge to law, and thus to the society preserved by its rule – a challenge which moves from the transgression of particular laws to a theoretical rejection of law's very grounding as authority or constraint. 'Every thing vile and inhuman', it would seem, is everything antisocial: as David Graham recognised, when Lovelace plots against Clarissa he is also seen as 'plotting to undermine the foundations of all Laws, divine and human'.[55]

Richardson's development of these meanings owes much, paradoxically, to the stage tradition, which offered a precedent in which to express, deplore or celebrate the subversiveness of libertinism. The word 'Lovelace' is itself revealing. It first suggests the morality name 'Love-

---

[53] Richardson's political commitments, a complex and still largely unexplored matter, are touched on at various points in this chapter. For present purposes it is enough to place him (with many of his early readers) within the range of assumptions and anxieties described by H. T. Dickinson, *Liberty and Property: Political Ideology in Eighteenth-Century Britain* (1977), pp. 121–92.

[54] Johnson, *Dictionary*, 'Libertine', 'Libertinism'.

[55] To Richardson, 22 April 1750, FM XV, 2, f.84.

less',[56] identifying its bearer as one lacking in love – lacking, in other words, in the qualities of feeling and benevolence on which, in the world of sentimental comedy, harmony depends. Here Richardson's particular allusion is to Colley Cibber's *Love's Last Shift* (1696), in which the rakish Loveless resists the world of bourgeois virtue until at last reclaimed by his suffering wife, Amanda. Cibber's Loveless is a relatively anodyne figure, however, and the variant spelling inhibits the analogy even as it is raised.[57] Instead the ending '–lace' compounds this sense of a deficiency in the sentimental affections by which families are united with a sense also of the more illicit passions which disrupt them: Lovelace plays on just this meaning when he brags of entangling or binding his victims 'in the silken cords of love' (VI, 283; p. 1144). The appropriate analogue here is not the rake of comedy, who eventually acquiesces in the moral norms of society, but the more destructive rake of tragedy, who contests them absolutely. Charles Johnson's Lilloesque *Cælia* (1733) provides a relevant example in which, again, names point the link: Cælia's surname is Lovemore, her assailant's Wronglove. The analogy emerges more clearly still in the plot, in which 'a vicious young Fellow' (as the Belford-figure Bellamy summarises)

corrupted a Gentleman's Daughter of Family and Fortune ... And by many solemn Vows and Promises of Marriage, and eternal Fidelity, prevailed on her to leave her Father's House, and run away with him ... Without suffering her to make Peace with her Friends, or taking any care for her Support himself, he sent her to be exposed among Prostitutes in a common Brothel ... as if, from the Baseness of his Heart, he had received Pleasure in that unprovoked Cruelty.[58]

In his remorseless pursuit of pleasure, Wronglove's character is a striking anticipation of Lovelace's, representing a libertinism altogether uglier than that of Cibber's Loveless. Wronglove himself comes largely from stock, however: as Samuel Johnson saw, the *locus classicus* is Rowe's Lothario, who develops an aggressive philosophy of pleasure both in his determination to 'rifle the sweets' of nature 'and taste her choicest fruits, / Yet scorn to ask the lordly owners leave', and also in the power-lust with which he celebrates his 'triumph o'er Calista'.[59] Again the parallel is

---

[56] Some contemporaries, such as Fielding, used the spellings interchangeably: see his letter to Richardson, 15 October 1748, *The Criticism of Henry Fielding*, ed. Ioan Williams (1970), p. 188. On Lovelace's name see also Ian Watt, 'The Naming of Characters in Defoe, Richardson and Fielding', *Review of English Studies*, 25 (1949), 332–3.

[57] One reader even found in Richardson's tragic ending an implied critique of Cibber's indulgence towards the rake-figure: for Clarissa to forgive, he wrote, 'might have been the Character of Amanda the Wife of *Loveless*, but not of the exalted Conqueress of *Lovelace*' (R. Smith to Richardson, 3 February 1748/9, FM XV, 2, f.112).

[58] [Charles Johnson], *Cælia; or, The Perjur'd Lover* (1733), p. 49. On *Clarissa*'s debt to *Cælia*, see Konigsberg, pp. 40–5.

[59] Rowe, *The Fair Penitent*, ed. Malcolm Goldstein (1969), II ii lines 126–7; I i line 129.

invited by Richardson himself: Johnson's view of Lothario as Lovelace's 'original' is explicitly generated within *Clarissa*, where Belford compares events with the plot of *The Fair Penitent*.[60]

Lovelace had living as well as dramatic originals, of course. The stage type itself takes its origin in the empirical world, and in contemporary anxieties at the rise of aristocratic libertinism:[61] it is clear enough from Richardson's antitheatrical tracts that the *'high Life'* characters on stage who 'confound all Distinctions of Right and Wrong' are only the images of living counterparts in whom (as he elsewhere complains) 'virtue and vice change names and qualities'.[62] An eminent example of the type is John Wilmot Earl of Rochester, and in developing the idiom of Lovelace's letters Richardson may have drawn on the self-consciously libertine epistolary discourse of Rochester's correspondence (partly published in 1697), as well as on biographical accounts of his 'go[ing] about in odd shapes' (a habit which anticipates Lovelace's extravagant role-playing at Hampstead).[63] One need not suppose purely literary sources, however, especially in a rare case where Richardson acknowledges drawing, at least in part, from life.[64] Richardson nowhere identifies his model or models; but the real Dover Street had a real inhabitant known to him in Philip Duke of Wharton, widely assumed at the time to have been Lovelace's original,[65] and similarities with his character and career as delineated in the anonymous *Life* printed by Richardson after Wharton's death are striking. The vestigial case-history offered by Anna to explain Lovelace's character (in early life he was 'never ... subject to contradiction', she reports, and thus has 'never known what it was to be controuled', becoming instead 'the governor of his governors') is exactly that of Wharton, whose *'impetuous and uncontroulable'* temper is traced back to the death of his father, which *'early set him free from those Restraints which were necessary for holding him within due Bounds'*.[66] The rakish careers of both are marked by parallel events, from these lax upbringings to their obscure and ignominious deaths abroad. In Rome, for example, Wharton 'could not always keep within the Bounds of the *Italian* Gravity, and having no Employment

---

[60] See John A. Dussinger, 'Richardson and Johnson: Critical Agreement on Rowe's *The Fair Penitent*', *English Studies*, 49 (1968), 45–7.

[61] See Lawrence Stone, *The Family, Sex and Marriage in England, 1500–1800* (1977), pp. 529–36.

[62] *Seasonable Examination*, p. 15; *Sentiments*, p. 44.

[63] Gilbert Burnet, *Some Passages of the Life and Death of the Right Honourable John, Earl of Rochester* (1680), p. 28. Links with Rochester are more fully explored in two recent essays: see James Grantham Turner, 'Lovelace and the Paradoxes of Libertinism', in *Samuel Richardson: Tercentenary Essays*, ed. Margaret Anne Doody and Peter Sabor (Cambridge, 1989), pp. 70–88, and Jocelyn Harris, 'Protean Lovelace', in *Eighteenth-Century Fiction*, 2 (1990), 327–46.

[64] See Carroll, pp. 79, 103, 181.

[65] See William Seward, *Anecdotes of Distinguished Persons* (1804), II, 302.

[66] *Clarissa*, I, 67; p. 74, and III, 238; p. 498 (see also Carroll, p. 116); *The Life and Writings of Philip, Late Duke of Wharton* (1732), I, Av–A2. On Richardson's printing of the *Life*, see Sale, *Master Printer*, pp. 212, 226.

to divert and amuse his over-active Temper, he run into his usual Excesses; which being taken amiss there ... it was thought adviseable that the Duke should remove from that City'. Lovelace's Italian excesses, likewise, 'made ... those who honour'd him with their notice, give him up; and his stay both at Florence and at Rome shorter than he designed' (III, 360; p. 563). More significantly, the Wharton biography keeps in play a sense both of his winning qualities ('*Extensiveness of Wit, Liveliness of Imagination, all the Graces of a most persuasive Oratory, and an exceeding Frankness of Temper*') and of the deficiencies which lead to their misapplication ('*his Grace's active Genius and enterprizing Temper*', '*the tempestuous Winds of his headstrong Passions*') – all Lovelacean attributes. Perhaps most distinctive of all is the mercurial nature of both. Wharton's biographer confesses an inability to reconcile the contradictory aspects of his subject within 'a regular, uniform Character: This is not to be expected from the Character of the Duke of *Wharton*'. 'Who expects consistency in men of our character?', as Lovelace writes (IV, 238; p. 694).[67]

The varied sources, influences and models behind Lovelace's representation share a telling common denominator. In *The Fair Penitent* and *Cælia*, the rake-figure is guilty of more than individual degeneracy: he is the agent of a large calamity, whose actions mount a general challenge to law. The plays are similar in outline: they trace the destruction by libertinism of an initial state of familial harmony, and they show the domestic trauma to impinge on society as a whole. Loveless is tamed. But Lothario, who is 'base enough / To break through law, and spurn at sacred order', subverts both domestic and social stability: in his remarks on *The Fair Penitent* Belford is particularly alive to the disruptions which attend his seduction of Calista, noting the licentious mingling of roles by which she 'yields to marry Altamont, tho' criminal with another' (VI, 378; p. 1206). This seduction, moreover, leads directly on to a larger political turmoil: it turns the 'peaceful city' of Act II into the 'afflicted state' of Act V, precipitating civil war between factions which 'drown the voice of law in noise and anarchy'.[68] *Cælia* takes these processes less far, but this play too finds larger ramifications in its protagonist's libertinism: his behaviour constitutes 'a Crime against Society', for which he is 'answerable ... to all Mankind'.[69] Similarly, the depredations of libertines in the world itself have wider implications. A challenge to the rule of law is implicit in the catalogue of seductions, elopements, duels and routs that makes up the rake's biography. Burnet's account of Rochester's death, for example, has Rochester himself acknowledge the 'Vice and Impiety' of his former life to be 'as contrary to Humane Society, as wild Beasts let loose would be'.[70] In

---

[67] *Life and Writings of Philip, Late Duke of Wharton*, I, 20; I, Av; I, A3; I, A4; I, 14.
[68] *The Fair Penitent*, II, ii lines 69–70; II ii line 57; V i line 48; V i line 51.
[69] *Cælia*, p. 49.   [70] *Life and Death of the Right Honourable John, Earl of Rochester*, p. 125.

Wharton's case the challenge becomes overt, the practical libertinism of his youth culminating in an ostentatious renunciation of standard religious and political commitments in favour of Rome and the Pretender.

This sense of disruptiveness and enmity, already more than latent in Richardson's sources, is explicitly developed in *Clarissa*. There are times at which Lovelace seems almost comically 'other' to the City of the *Vade Mecum*, as when he dismisses the seduction and childbed-death of Miss Betterton on the grounds 'that she was but a tradesman's daughter' (III, 232; p. 495), or when he bullies Clarissa's bourgeois guardians the Smiths with complaints at 'the dignity of trade in this mercantile nation' (VI, 389; p. 1213). But Richardson also envisages a more widely applicable challenge. The plot itself is akin to that of the two plays, representing Lovelace's waywardness as a threat seen ultimately as that of anarchy. He brags of having often 'defied the civil magistrate' (V, 288; p. 920), proclaims himself 'above all law' (III, 89; p. 419), and proposes to prove it by such actions as the kidnap of Solmes (a plan which leaves Clarissa terrified at the thought of 'such defiances of the laws of society': III, 126; p. 438). Outlawry is repeatedly stressed. At one point he even considers intercepting the bearer of Clarissa's letters, holding himself 'justify'd ... to have him stript and robbed, and what money he has about him given to the poor':[71] 'the law was not made for such a man as me' (IV, 6; p. 569), he remarks. At another, Clarissa complains at his 'worse than Waltham disguises' (V, 113; p. 822), alluding with hostility to a significant instance of social unrest in the early 1720s – an instance in which the Whig establishment had invested its deepest fears of disorder and insurrection, and to which it had reacted with the notoriously draconian Black Act of 1723.[72] Asked to explain the phrase, Richardson showed little anxiety to distance himself from the Whig vilification of Blacking, depicting the Blacks as 'disorderly' and 'audacious' enemies of property and life, happily defeated by the timely interposition of law. 'They fired at many Persons in their own Houses, maimed their Cattle, broke down their Gates and Fences, cut down young Plantations of Trees, Avenues, and broke down the Heads of Fishponds ... Insomuch that the Legislature was obliged to

---

[71] Needless to say, Robin Hood did not always enjoy his present reputation: see Fielding's attack on the Roberdsmen, *An Enquiry into the Causes of the Late Increase of Robbers*, ed. Malvin R. Zirker (Oxford, 1988), p. 136.

[72] The Waltham Blacks and their suppression are the subject of E. P. Thompson's *Whigs and Hunters: The Origin of the Black Act* (Harmondsworth, 1977); for a view closer to that of the eighteenth-century establishment (including Richardson himself) see Pat Rogers, 'The Waltham Blacks and the Black Act', *Historical Journal*, 17 (1974), 465–86, and *Eighteenth-Century Encounters: Studies in Literature and Society in the Age of Walpole* (Brighton, 1985), pp. 75–92. Whether or not Richardson knew it, there were also links between Blacking and Jacobitism: see Eveline Cruickshanks and Howard Erskine-Hill, 'The Waltham Black Act and Jacobitism', *Journal of British Studies*, 24 (1985), 358–65.

Exert itself by a particular Act of Parliament.'[73] Their depredations (invoked again when Lovelace considers engaging 'a plaguy parcel' of 'blacks' to terrorise the Harlowes: V, 326; p. 941) seem to have provided him with a compelling instance of an idea which preoccupied him in his social thought in general, and in the creation of Lovelace in particular – the idea of the fence broken down, of the structures which organise society razed.

Within the novel, it is only after the rape that these wider implications are understood, as they finally are when Mrs Howe insists 'that the good of society requires, that such a beast of prey should be hunted out of it' (VI, 82; p. 1016). But Richardson was always keen to bring out the underlying threat. When a reviewer protested at the implausibility of Lovelace's conduct 'in a country so jealous of its laws and its liberty', he explicitly made the link between Lovelace's imprisonment of Clarissa and his general subversion of law and the liberties guaranteed by it, pointing out that Lovelace 'defied the laws of his country, as too many of his cast do', and citing as evidence of this defiance both his Italian crimes and his Whartonian readiness 'to become an exile from his native country for ever'.[74]

Libertinism, however, means more than simple criminality. In Johnson's definition, the libertine's transgression of law is only the practical counterpart of a more dangerous ideological licentiousness, which works not only to disregard particular laws at particular times but also to demolish their very basis, the religious and moral structures by which *all* law is underpinned. This link between the breaking down of local safeguards and the attack on larger ideological safeguards is wholly commonplace, and perhaps most memorably expressed in Boswell's petulant analogy between the '*practical* philosophers' of *The Beggar's Opera* and 'pernicious *speculative* philosophers' such as David Hume.[75] Within Richardson's circle it is most clearly seen in a short allegory of lawlessness published in 1744 by Philip Skelton, in which some freethinking Oxonians travel the road to London, their journey punctuated by Shaftesburyan effusions on the natural world to either side. Admiration soon gives way to desire, and to a challenge to the right of property: Aerius laments being 'debarred of our natural Rights and Privileges' by 'Hedges and Ditches erected here without my Consent, to shut me and Mankind out from our own', and he proposes that they leave the 'Confinement and Restraint' of the road to 'trace out a free and generous Path for themselves' through the gardens and fields beyond. 'Where is the Good of thinking freely', he declares, 'if I may not act with suitable Freedom? Whilst nothing in

---

[73] Richardson to Stinstra, 2 June 1753, Slattery, pp. 43–4.
[74] Haller, 'A Critical Account of *Clarissa*', in *Novel and Romance*, ed. Williams, p. 139, 139n.
[75] *Boswell's Life of Johnson*, II, 442.

Nature ... can bound my Thoughts; must I suffer Ditches to confine my
Feet, and Locks my Hands?'[76] His companions then prepare, 'with a loud
cry of Nature and Liberty', to sweep away 'these arbitrary Fences', and
are only restrained by Polites, who reminds them that in 'the goodly State
of Nature' proposed by Aerius the lands they admire 'would in one Season
become useless and unfruitful', and force would be the only law.[77] Polites
wins the argument by convincing them of the impossibility of subsisting
out of a society, and of the necessity in such a society of the larger walls
and fences of the law – with the result that they return tamely to 'the
King's High-way', a familiar emblem of rectitude and law. Skelton's tale
thus stages the defeat of intellectual libertinism, which 'under the Pretence
of Liberty, would turn us wild into the Fields, a kind of Beast more Savage
than any other, as not sparing its own Kind, and whilst it is misled by a
false Notion of Nature, committing Things that Nature abhors'.[78] A banal
enough moral, perhaps; but the fable displays in usefully naked form an
anxiety shared equally in *Clarissa* – a fear of libertinism's capacity not
simply to breach particular laws but to break down their ideological
foundation. The same image of broken fences explicitly recurs when
Belford, first protesting that as libertines he and Lovelace have not 'got
over ... all moral obligations, as members of society' (IV, 86; p. 612), goes
on to accuse him in his treatment of Clarissa of having 'broken thro'', and
overthrown ... all the fences and boundaries of moral honesty' (IV, 88;
p. 613). As Clarissa herself puts it, he 'avows a disregard to all moral
sanctions' (III, 129; p. 439) and refuses to accept the validity of constraint
in any form: the moral is for him a meaningless category.

For Richardson, the equation between practical and intellectual libertinism was as immediate as it was for Johnson, Boswell and Skelton. Indeed,
the parallel attack on the two phenomena was almost a life's work,
beginning once more in the *Vade Mecum*, the third part of which is a
diatribe against freethinking (partly original and partly drawn from
Locke, Addison, and others). Here Richardson pays little attention to the
subtlety and variety of the period's most innovative philosophy, instead
using libertinism, deism, scepticism and infidelity as interchangeable
terms, alike in their corrosive power. The age, he writes, is 'lamentably
over-run with Atheism, Deism, and Infidelity', systems of thought he
alleges to have been engineered as a rationale for libertine conduct.
Atheism is dismissed abruptly as beyond the pale, 'the Plague of Society,
the Corrupter of Manners, and the Underminer of Property', leaving the
bulk of the analysis for the more refined infidelities of deism and scepticism, which work 'to free the Minds of Men from those *Restraints* which
the Christian Religion imposes upon their *sensual Appetites*'. Their effect,

[76] Skelton, *Truth in a Mask* (Dublin, 1744), pp. 49, 50, 51, 52.   [77] *Ibid.*, pp. 53, 52, 66, 65.
[78] *Ibid.*, pp. 73, 74.

he alleges, is to remove all moral sanctions against evil, leaving society perilously insecure of its members' '*Conformity* to those laws which preserve *Order* among Men, and hinder the World from falling into *Confusion*'. He protests in particular that 'many of our modern *Reasoners* have carry'd their Notions of *Liberty* and *Pleasure* so far, that nothing but the Civil Magistrate can secure Property, and the Persons of our *Sisters* and *Daughters* from their lewd Attempts'. The work concludes with a resounding alarm at the imminent collapse of all order: 'their Attempts can only tend to loosen and untie the Bonds of Human Society; confound the Distinctions of Right and Wrong; take away the Terrors that with-hold Evil-Doers; tear up the Fences that inclose and preserve Property; and leave the feeblest of Mankind to the Mercy of the most Potent, and perhaps the most Deprav'd'.[79]

The output of his press kept up the attack. A notable example from later years is John Leland's compendious *View of the Principal Deistical Writers* (1754–5), which rehearses the same fears that scepticism threatens 'a perversion of all public order', that without the moral laws of Christianity the civil laws become only 'feeble restraints', and that ultimately 'all the ties and bands that keep society together are in danger of being dissolved'.[80] Another example is Philip Skelton's *Deism Revealed* (1749), which, as Richardson approvingly wrote, 'scourges our infidels, sceptics, deists, &c. as well by name as works'.[81] His own novels too were widely held to be in polemic with deism, albeit less forthrightly. *A Candid Examination of the History of Sir Charles Grandison* explained his last novel as a fundamentalist counterblast to sceptical principles, finding in 'this *Christian Hero*' a challenge to Wollaston's '*Religion of Nature*' and Shaftesbury's 'Notion of the *Beauty of Virtue*'.[82] *Critical Remarks*, on the other hand, begins as a refutation of Richardson's attack on deism, attempting to turn the tables by identifying the novels themselves, rather than the philosophy they condemn, as more disruptive in effect.

A full account of the relations between scepticism and the novel would find allegiances less clearly demarcated, of course: even as Richardson explicitly condemns freethinking, his novels imply quite revolutionary attitudes towards (for example) the relativity of perceptions. Where the new philosophy emerges most explicitly in his work, however, it does so in the form of hostile caricature. In Lovelace's case he did at least resist making the caricature too blunt, as the portraitist Joseph Highmore had suggested: 'Let the Dog be an Atheist', Highmore had urged, 'or worse, if worse can be; or, at least, say nothing about his religious Sentiments;

[79] *Vade Mecum*, pp. 55, 68, 69, 70, 60, 83.
[80] John Leland, *A View of the Principal Deistical Writers*, 2 vols. (1754–5), II, 654–5.
[81] Richardson to de Freval, 21 January 1751, Barbauld, V, 275.
[82] *Candid Examination*, pp. 11, 9; see also *Critical Remarks*, pp. 8–11.

unless he is represented as an abominable Hypocrite.'[83] Highmore wanted the link between Lovelace's practices and opinions to be unmistakable. The text, however, is more evasive, in part for pragmatic reasons. It is clear from the preface's anxious denials that Lovelace and Belford are 'either Infidels or Scoffers' (the passage to which Highmore here objects) that Richardson anticipated criticism from 'such as may apprehend Hurt to the Morals of Youth from the more freely-written Letters' (I, iii–iv; p. 35). Evidently, the pressures of audience expectation inhibited him from developing the intellectual side of Lovelace's libertinism to the full. Another problem was that Clarissa could have nothing to do with an open atheist, as a second reader (taking issue with Highmore) notes: 'if ... the Editor makes use of [Highmore's] Scheme of making Lovelace an Infidel or Atheist, What will the Adviser do to secure the admirable Clarissa's Character, in entering upon Terms with such an open Profligate, when, before, she had rejected Wyerly on this very account?'[84]

Yet if Lovelace could not, for the sake of the novel's or its heroine's reputation, be made an open atheist, he could indeed be made 'an abominable Hypocrite' – a hypocrite being, as this last reader put it, one who 'may be supposed to conceal real Infidelity under a sanctimonious Appearance', where an Atheist 'discovers his Enmity to Mankind by wishing the Bonds of Society to be dissolved, and disputing the Being and Authority of the Governor of the World'.[85] What is certainly the case is that the novel itself fails to match the cautious disclaimers of its preface. Clarissa herself does indeed believe that Lovelace 'is not an infidel, an unbeliever' (IV, 246; p. 698), but the belief says more about her own credulity than about Lovelace's religious commitment – a credulity that becomes all the more obvious when, absurdly, Lovelace invokes the authority of Shaftesbury to persuade her of his own orthodoxy of belief (III, 136; p. 443). A reader, of course, may still follow Clarissa in crediting Lovelace's professions that, 'libertine as I am thought to be, I never will attempt to bring down the measures of right and wrong to the standard of my actions' (VI, 207, p. 1096), and that others are more faulty than he among those 'men of free principles' who resort to scepticism 'in order to justify to themselves their free practices; and to make a religion to their minds' (VI, 115; p. 1037). But there is good reason to follow Anna instead, who maintains that in this matter Lovelace 'is certainly a *dissembler*, odious as the sin of hypocrisy' (III, 149; p. 451), and who reads his eager professions of faith as messages to the contrary. What supports her conjecture is the fact that Lovelace also rehearses many obtrusively libertine arguments, and at points where there is no such motive for insincerity. He

---

[83] Highmore to Richardson, [Autumn 1747], FM XV, 2, f.86.
[84] R. Smith to Richardson, [Autumn 1747], FM XV, 2, f.87.
[85] R. Smith to Richardson, [Autumn 1747], FM XV, 2, ff.87–8.

quotes Mandeville on the benefits of private vice, for example (V, 161; p. 847); he questions whether women have souls (IV, 256; p. 704); he suggests that '*all human good and evil*' is '*comparative*' (IV, 286; p. 720). Most tellingly, he approves Church rituals on the grounds that 'if they answered any good end to the *many*, there was religion enough in them, or civil policy at least' (VI, 285; p. 1145). A Christian such as Richardson might agree, but he would put the point rather differently: here Lovelace gives the classic deistical rationale for religion as a hollow instrument of social control – a move disparagingly attributed, in Leland's *View*, to both Bolingbroke and Hume.[86]

This evasiveness in the matter of Lovelace's scepticism is tactically shrewd: it enables Richardson to acquit Clarissa of knowingly negotiating with an 'infidel' and himself of perpetrating an irreligious text, while tacitly tarring Lovelace with the hypocrisy popularly alleged against deism and thought to be its most subversive characteristic. (The deists, writes Skelton, 'borrow the name and cloak of Christianity, in order to attack it', successfully luring their readers from religion only by appearing to uphold it.)[87] Richardson thus points the reader towards Anna's view of Lovelace while reserving the option of Clarissa's view to allay the fears of the over-zealous. Indeed, the novel has been persuasively read by one recent critic as a direct defence of traditional Christianity 'against the most devastating of contemporary sceptical attacks – that of Mandeville' – a defence in which the two protagonists are cast as exemplars and advocates of whole ideological systems.[88] It may be adventurous to attribute to Richardson any very close reading of Mandeville (a single citation of the Mandevillean catchphrase, '*That private vices are public benefits*', hardly proves profound knowledge), but the gist of Tavor's analysis is surely right. *Clarissa* advances, literally, a fight to the death between Christian virtue and libertinism, in which libertinism is not a matter simply of dissolute conduct but brings with it a sceptical challenge to the values of Clarissa and her world. Richardson represents in Lovelace what he perceived as its full double threat, the wilful transgression of positive law coupled with a sceptical challenge to its ethical and religious foundation; and he does so, on occasion, very ingeniously. (See, for example, Letter 110, in which Lovelace takes on the manner of the empirical philosopher, setting himself to undermine the notion of virtue and prove it, experimentally, false.) We cannot expect this sceptical challenge to be fully worked out, if only because of Richardson's reluctance to read anything 'shocking

---

[86] *A View of the Principal Deistical Writers*, II, 655–6, referring to Hume, *Philosophical Essays concerning Human Understanding*, 2nd edn (1750), p. 231; Viscount Bolingbroke, *Works*, 5 vols. (1754), IV, 59–60; V, 322.

[87] Skelton, *Ophiomaches; or, Deism Revealed*, 2 vols. (1749), I, xvi.

[88] Eve Tavor, *Scepticism, Society, and the Eighteenth-Century Novel* (1987), p. 54; see also pp. 54–107.

to fundamentals'.[89] He knew only enough to see in scepticism an attenuation of religious and moral law, and in his fiction he dramatised the chaos he felt it to threaten.

From our perspective these alarms seem, at best, exaggerated. Yet in developing the third major sense of Lovelace's social subversiveness – a political sense – Richardson was by no means tilting at windmills. Political implications, of course, are already in play, since in the allegations of Richardson and the anti-deists of his circle breach of law and libertine freethinking have a corrosive social effect. On occasion, however, these implications become much more specific. Again Philip Skelton provides a cue; for Richardson's concluding alarm in the *Vade Mecum* that the ensuing collapse will leave mankind 'to the Mercy of the most Potent, and perhaps the most Deprav'd' recurs in more detail in *Deism Revealed*, which similarly culminates by considering '*Whether libertinism is of a good or evil tendency, in respect to the State*'.[90] In outline Skelton's fears recapitulate Richardson's: 'being once become irreligious and wicked, [men] immediately grow lawless', and come to acknowledge 'no government of their appetites and pleasures'. Without religion, 'the great band of society', anarchy ensues.[91] But Skelton has more specific allegations to make as well, and he sees in libertinism a conscious desire for this overthrow of government: 'our Libertines, looking on the happy freedom of our constitution as nothing, shew . . . a rank tincture of republican principles', he claims; they 'speak in terms most extravagantly panegyrical of the usurper *Cromwell*, toast his memory, and wish for such another'.[92] Anarchy, clearly, is not the end-point of the argument: the state of nature, in which men prey wantonly on one another, produces its own result, in the shape of the tyranny to which the abandonment or overthrow of law can only lead. Painting a lurid picture of the chaos of the civil war, he concludes by envisaging a repetition of the same 'infernal scenes of distraction and desolation'. He fears, too, the same final result – 'an absolute tyranny'.[93]

It has already been suggested that Richardson's novel, in which Lovelace draws Clarissa into revolt against the rule of her father and eventually subjects her to his own, mirrors just such a possibility – a possibility more explicitly described in Patrick Delany's *Social Duties*.[94] But there is at least some reason to see a more topical side to Clarissa's plight. Part of the reason is simply circumstantial. For writers of the mid-1740s, the civil war, with its associations of revolution, disorder and eventual tyranny, was no merely antiquarian concern, but could be drawn on instead to address the

---

[89] To Young, 12 December 1744, *The Correspondence of Edward Young*, ed. Henry Pettit (Oxford, 1971), p. 191. See also his somewhat limited response to Bolingbroke and Hume, 'very mischievous writers' (Barbauld, V, 109), and to Hartley (Carroll, p. 308).

[90] *Deism Revealed*, I, d3v.   [91] *Ibid.*, II, 397; II, 396.   [92] *Ibid.*, II, 398.

[93] *Ibid.*, II, 399; II, 398.

[94] See above, pp. 114–20.

most urgent political question of the day[95] – the prospect or threat of Jacobite restoration, which, as Richardson was writing *Clarissa*, became very real. As the account of the '45 added to his 1748 edition of Defoe's *Tour* recalls, the rebellion 'broke out at last with such Force, as to spread itself into *England*, and not without Reason alarmed the Inhabitants of the Metropolis'; in the Italy of *Grandison*, 'hardly any thing else was talked of ... but the progress, and supposed certainty of success, of the young invader'.[96] Delany's recollection of the civil war in *Social Duties* was in fact written in direct anticipation of such upheavals; but his intention was not, as one might at first assume, to support the hereditary claim of the Stuarts or, like Fielding's Squire Western, to propose a hostile analogy between 'Roundheads and *Hannover* Rats'.[97] Certainly, he sees Charles as a legitimate ruler unjustly overthrown; but his purpose is to undercut the parallel between the Rebellion of the 1640s and the Revolution of 1688–9 by which Jacobite historiography challenged the Hanover succession, and to establish in its place a new set of analogies, linking Charles I with George II on one side as legitimate monarchs, and the Protector with the Pretender on the other as illegitimate usurpers. His discourse on 'the mutual Duty of Prince and People' is thus an attack on the Jacobite challenge, envisaging the disasters that would attend the restoration of the very house whose first overthrow in the 1640s it begins by lamenting. Urging 'fidelity to the constitution as by law established; and to the King as supreme, and guardian of it' and writing explicitly in support of the Glorious Revolution, 'which its bitterest enemies have no way more maliciously studied to revile, than by wresting it into a parallel with the transactions of these detested times', Delany presents the republicanism of the 1640s and the Jacobitism of the 1740s as alike inimical to all that the 1689 settlement guarantees: his pressing fear is of the violent replacement of that settlement by a retrograde autocracy.[98] Skelton himself addresses the same theme in his Swiftian (indeed Orwellian) fable of government and tyranny in the states of Hierapolis and Dictatoria in *Truth in a Mask* (1744). A year later he was again warning (in language clumsily aimed at the memories of his Irish audience) that if Jacobite sympathisers, 'by the Assistance they are disposed to lend the Pretender, should enable him to now Model our Affairs, they will find themselves ... in the same condition with those, who in the Days of *Cromwell*, being unable to endure the

---

[95] See Helen W. Randall, 'The Rise and Fall of a Martyrology: Sermons on Charles I', *Huntington Library Quarterly*, 10 (1946–7), 157.

[96] *A Tour thro' the Whole Island of Great Britain*, 4th edn (1748), IV, 361; *Grandison*, II, 124. The scare referred to in the *Tour* reached its height on 6 December 1745, when news reached London of the occupation of Richardson's birthplace, Derby – 'that Day of Confusion', as Fielding called it (*The True Patriot and Related Writings*, ed. W. B. Coley (Oxford, 1987), p. 309 (No. 33, 17 June 1746); see also p. 210n.).

[97] *Tom Jones*, I, 321.   [98] Delany, *Fifteen Sermons upon Social Duties*, pp. 316, 311, 317.

Government of a good King, plotted and fought till they had given
themselves a Tyrant'.[99]

Doubtless Richardson shared something of these fears, although his
attitude to Jacobitism cannot have been uncomplicated. In 1722 one
professional rival named him a 'High Flyer', and in 1728 another
(Edmund Curll) tried to implicate him in the scandal caused by Wharton's 'treasonable' number of *Mist's Weekly Journal*.[100] Whatever the truth
of their allegations, Richardson certainly sailed close to the wind in early
professional life, notably by printing for the Atterbury camp during the
1723 treason trials: as well as Wharton's *True Briton* (1723–4), he also
printed speeches on the affair by Wharton and by Atterbury's co-
defendant Kelly, as well (after sentence had been passed) as benefit editions
of works by Atterbury and Kelly.[101] A youthful fling with Jacobitism is
therefore a possibility, although in the context of Richardson's less contentiously Opposition voting and printing of the period it is quite as likely
that he was simply one of many who mistook Wharton for what he
pretended to be – an Old Whig in opposition to the Robinocracy precisely
because it flouted the principles of 1689, not a Jacobite bent on the
reversal of these principles. After the 1720s, in any case, no evidence
survives to contest John Duncombe's testimony that Richardson's 'political principles were very different' from Wharton's.[102] In the 1730s he
had moved out of Opposition, and was voting and printing for the
Ministry while expressing explicit support for the Hanoverian régime. His
meticulous removal from his edition of *Æsop's Fables* of all Sir Roger
L'Estrange's Jacobite or absolutist applications shows his Establishment
sympathies very clearly, and while his statement that the Jacobite L'Estrange was 'certainly listed in a bad Cause as to Politics' is unemphatically
made there is no room to doubt the warmth of his 'fervent prayer', when
dedicating *The Negotiations of Sir Thomas Roe* to George II, 'that these
Nations may be always happily governed by a Prince of Your Royal
House to the End of Time'.[103] When the '45 threatened a somewhat
quicker end, his 1748 edition of Defoe's *Tour* firmly condemns 'a Rebellion
so unnatural' and warmly praises the patriotic service of Cumberland in
bringing about its defeat.[104] In *Grandison* a reference to 'the troubles, now
so happily appeased' makes clear that Richardson's good man is a loyal
Hanoverian who, 'being known to be warm in the interest of my country',
must endure the taunts of Jacobite sympathisers. Elsewhere Richardson

[99] Skelton, *Truth in a Mask*, pp. 93–109; *The Chevalier's Hopes* (Dublin, 1745), p. 21.
[100] Eaves and Kimpel, *Biography*, pp. 21, 31–5.
[101] Sale, *Master Printer*, pp. 147, 155.
[102] In John Nichols, *Literary Anecdotes of the Eighteenth Century*, 9 vols. (1812–15), IV, 580.
[103] Eaves and Kimpel, *Biography*, pp. 35–6; *Æsop's Fables*, p. vi; *The Negotiations of Sir Thomas Roe* (1740), p. iv.
[104] *A Tour thro' the Whole Island of Great Britain*, 4th edn (1748), IV, 179; IV, 361.

refers dismissively to the Chevalier as 'a certain Adventurer'.[105] Any
Jacobite allegiances he may once have had, in short, had been rejected, and
by the time of *Clarissa* he seems already to have reached the conviction,
expressed in 1755, that the Whig interest was 'ye Constitutional Interest;
ye Interest of ye Country'.[106]

Clarissa, however, is quite without the obtrusive topicality of *Tom
Jones*,[107] and any suggestion that Jacobitism might be another of the
'–isms' listed by Lovelace among his by now formidable credentials as an
enemy of society can only be made with great caution. With his 'intimates'
he frequents 'the Cocoa-tree in Pall-mall', a well-known rendezvous of
disaffected Tories (II, 14; p. 213); yet it may simply be the raffishness of
the house, not the Jacobitism of its clients, that takes him there. We are
told, indeed, that he takes no interest in political questions (albeit in
somewhat equivocal terms): he 'troubles not his head with politics', Anna
reports, 'tho' no body knows the interests of princes and courts better than
he' (I, 68; p. 74). It is certainly the case that he mentions affairs of state
only rarely. He is scornful of the 'proud senators ... induced, by presents
or subscriptions of South Sea stock, to contribute to a scheme big with
national ruin' (V, 101; p. 816); he could (but doesn't) 'expatiate upon the
benefits' that would arise from a project next his heart, '*annual Parliaments*'
(V, 205; p. 874); and he whimsically considers entering the Commons (V,
205; p. 873). Lord M. encourages him, believing in his talents 'to make a
great figure there'. Even as he encourages Lovelace, however, Lord M.
shows anxiety at his likely allegiances and conduct, praising in ambivalent
terms the powers of 'a tongue that would delude an angel', urging him not
to be 'a Malecontent', and querulously warning: 'And may St. Stephen's
fate be yours, if you wilfully do *public* mischief!' (IV, 185–7; p. 666).

Alone, none of these hints is particularly significant or damning: the
picture they paint is simply one of seigneurial disdain for the values of
Whiggery, and a nailing of colours to the mast of Patriot Opposition. In
combination, however, they do again raise the ghost of the Duke of
Wharton. Allusions to the fiasco of the South Sea Bubble as evidence of
Ministerial corruption and calls for the repeal of the Septennial Act recur
in the *True Briton*. On 10 June 1723, for example, Wharton urges the case
for '*Frequent Parliaments*', and on 18 October he anticipates Lovelace's
words by seeing the South Sea Bubble as a Trojan Horse, its belly 'big with

---

[105] *Grandison*, II, 124; to Lady Bradshaigh, 25 February 1754, Carroll, p. 296.
[106] To Thomas Edwards, 30 May 1755, FM XII, 1, f.139.
[107] On Fielding's allusions to the '45, see Peter J. Carlton, '*Tom Jones* and the '45 Once Again',
      Studies in the Novel, 20 (1988), 361–73; Thomas Cleary, 'Jacobitism in *Tom Jones*: The Basis for
      a Hypothesis', *Philological Quarterly*, 52 (1973), 239–51, and *Henry Fielding: Political Writer*
      (Waterloo, Ontario, 1984), pp. 264–72; Anthony Kearney, '*Tom Jones* and the Forty-five',
      Ariel, 4 (1973), 68–78; Ronald Paulson, *Popular and Polite Art in the Age of Hogarth and Fielding*
      (Notre Dame, 1979), pp. 190–207.

the Ruin of HONEST TROY').[108] One need not be a Jacobite to make such complaints, of course (although a later work to issue from Richardson's press does explicitly identify the call for annual parliaments as a Jacobite ploy).[109] A favourite theme of the *True Briton*, in fact, was to attack Walpole's habit of tarring all his opponents, whatever their objections, 'as Espousers of the Cause of a Popish Pretender'[110] – a plausible enough complaint, and one voiced also by Richardson's quite unimpeachable friend Speaker Onslow.[111] In Wharton's case the complaint was disingenuous, however. When the *True Briton* first appeared it may have looked like a straightforward Opposition manifesto; but by the time Richardson reprinted it in 1732 Wharton had been revealed in his true colours, and its reader could instead (as the preface notes) *'observe by what Progressions this Great Man, first setting out under the plausible Name of a* PATRIOT*'*, was *'guilty of the most lamentable Defection from the good old* English *Principles ... which throughout the Course of his Writings here collected, he pretended zealously to inculcate and recommend'*.[112] In their similarity to Wharton's, Lovelace's political remarks are thus at least potentially crypto-Jacobite, establishing a context in which Lord M.'s anxieties at his beguiling tongue and the possibility of *'public* mischief' sound ominous echoes.

One further hint keeps in view, throughout the novel, the possibility that Lovelace's resemblance to Wharton may go beyond mere libertinism. As the reader is often reminded, he is 'the swiftest short-hand writer in England' (VII, 171–2; p. 1332), and writes his letters to Belford in cipher. A clumsy attempt on Richardson's part to account for his prolixity, perhaps; but this explanation is not quite enough. Lovelace is anyway 'one of the readiest and quickest of writers' (I, 67; p. 74), a fact that makes Anna wonder 'what inducements could such a swift writer as he have, to learn short-hand?' (I, 69; p. 75). Though anxiously pondering the question, and pointing out that his subjects can hardly resemble the innocent ones of her correspondence with Clarissa, she fails to recognise the implications of her own information that Lovelace is 'a great plotter, and a great writer' (I, 23; p. 50), and that 'in the correspondence by letters which he holds, he is as secret and careful, as if it were of a treasonable nature' (I, 68; p. 74). The conjunction of plotting and cipher-writing becomes more suggestive still when Lovelace further disguises his text by the use of cant names, as when he warns Belford 'How know we into whose hands our letters may fall?' and jests that he has temporarily changed his

[108] *Life and Writings of Philip, Late Duke of Wharton*, I, 18 (*True Briton*, No. 3); II, 345 (*True Briton*, No. 40).

[109] See *Letter to a Great Man in France* (1743), an anonymous attack on Bolingbroke.

[110] *Life and Writings of Philip, Late Duke of Wharton*, II, 374 (*True Briton*, No. 42).

[111] See Brean S. Hammond, *Pope and Bolingbroke: A Study of Friendship and Influence* (Columbia, 1984), p. 131.

[112] *Life and Writings of Philip, Late Duke of Wharton*, I, A4–A4v.

name 'without an act of parliament' (III, 86; p. 417): secrecy, not speed, is evidently the important consideration. The letters are not literally treasonable, to be sure: Lovelace's plot is simply to seduce Clarissa away from her father's house and subject her to his own power. But an analogy is implied, and Richardson may well be recalling the Jacobite conspiracies and treason trials of the early 1720s, in which cant names and coded correspondence played a central part. In the extravagant terms of the Bill against Atterbury, the conspiracies would if successful have deprived the people 'of the Enjoyment of their Religion, Laws, and Liberties, involved them in Blood and Ruin, and subjected [them] to the Bondage and Oppression of *Romish* Superstition and Arbitrary Power'[113] – a fate to which Clarissa's (popery apart) comes horribly close.

These are slight hints, to be sure. But they may have been enough to suggest a political dimension to Clarissa's history at a time when (as a leading Jacobite wrote) Hanoverian laws had 'brought such a habit and spirit of dissimulation on them, that a Jacobite can never be discovered by his words. It must be his actions that decypher him.'[114] There is certainly a sense in which Lovelace's actions *do* decipher him, and at a level that moves, in the end, a step towards allegory. That sense becomes available when we turn to Fielding, rather than to the romantic retrospect of Scott or Stevenson, for our sense of what Jacobitism means: 'It is a Cause', Fielding warns, '... in which our All is concerned; our Religion, our Liberties, our Properties ... are at Stake.'[115] Above all, the perceived threat was of tyranny; and there is good reason to suppose that on this issue Richardson, like Skelton and Delany, had conflated the historical example of the Protectorate and the contemporary menace of Jacobite autocracy, finding in Lovelace's oppression of Clarissa an image of the threat exemplified by each. From this point of view, the most significant echoes of Jacobitism in the text lie not in its local hints of Whartonian

113 Quoted in [Abel Boyer], *Historical Narrative of the Tryals of Mr. George Kelly, and of Dr. Francis Atterbury* (1727), p. 99. On the Atterbury plot, see G. V. Bennett, *The Tory Crisis in Church and State, 1688–1730: The Career of Francis Atterbury Bishop of Rochester* (Oxford, 1975), pp. 223–75; on treasonable correspondence, see [Charles Yorke], *Some Considerations on the Law of Forfeiture, for High Treason*, 3rd edn (printed by Richardson in 1748). In Wharton's speech, cipher-writing and deciphering became central issues of the trial. He castigated the Bill against Atterbury for its flimsy basis in 'decyphered Letters full of Fictitious Names and Cant Words', dismissed the decoding of them as 'an Art which depends upon Conjecture', and concluded that the decipherers' readings were not objective (as they claimed) but partisan, the product of deliberate attempts 'to draw very ill-natur'd and forc'd Constructions from them' (*His Grace the Duke of Wharton's Speech in the House of Lords, on the Third Reading of the Bill To Inflict Pains and Penalties on Francis (Late) Lord Bishop of Rochester* (1723), pp. 5, 6, 19). The whole affair he later found paradigmatic of his own opponents' attempts to 'decypher *a Desire of doing Good, into a petulant Humour of doing Mischief*' (*Life and Writings*, II, A2) – attempts that were by no means wide of the mark.

114 William Macgregor of Balhaldy, quoted in Eveline Cruickshanks, *Political Untouchables: The Tories and the '45* (1979), p. 45.

115 *A Serious Address*, 2nd edn (1745), in *The True Patriot and Related Writings*, p. 313.

mischief or Atterburyan liaisons, but in the larger pattern to which these hints eventually point – a pattern in which the rape of Clarissa intimates an absolutist menace anticipated, partly realised and finally quenched as Richardson drafted and redrafted the novel.

Morris Golden has recently elucidated just such a pattern: 'some large identifications seem forced on us once we consider the grand context', he writes. Some of the identifications he goes on to detail look tenuous or indiscriminate, but others are very telling, notably the parallel between *Clarissa*'s plot and a historical situation in which 'on the throne was a family risen as recently as Richardson's young adulthood (out of a dung-heap within living memory, as Lovelace said of the Harlowes), plotted against, threatened continuously, and directly attacked by a representative of an older legitimacy while the novel was in progress'.[116] In this context, 'while political groups were jockeying for place and power and while a sinister foreign claimant seduced a party to join his attack', the tumults at Harlowe Place reflect the factionalism of the post-Walpole vacuum, 'Clarissa begins to pick up symbolic nuances of her embattled nation' and 'Lovelace [nuances] of sinister Stuart absolutist adventure'. With the Harlowes as Hanoverians, Clarissa as their people and Lovelace as the ambitious Pretender, there begins to emerge a sense in which Richardson's *History of a Young Lady* also encodes, very quietly, a history of his own times – a history which ultimately celebrates the enemy's defeat and 'the emergence of a new stability'.[117]

Further evidence might be added. It is certainly the case, for example, that Lovelace's challenge to the authority of the father-ruler has discernibly Jacobite overtones. In his first letter he complains about Clarissa's mistaken allegiances in an otherwise inexplicable language of thwarted legitimacy: 'she takes the man she calls her father ... to *be* her father ... How my heart rises at her preference of them to me, when she is convinc'd of their injustice to me!' By having her become 'mine, without condition', however, he will retrieve the situation: 'Then shall I have all the rascals, and rascalesses of the family come creeping to me: I prescribing to them; and bringing that sordidly-imperious brother to kneel at the foot-stool of my throne' (I, 198–9; p. 145). *Clarissa*, however, was probably drafted in full before the expected Jacobite incursion came, and one cannot expect the text to reiterate its precise course: there are, as Golden notes, no 'sharp outlines of allegory'.[118] Once the basic structure was in place, nonetheless, historical contingencies do seem to have informed the processes of revision. A good example is provided by the final letter of the book, in which

116 Morris Golden, 'Public Context and Imagining Self in *Clarissa*', *Studies in English Literature 1500–1900*, 25 (1985), 589.

117 *Ibid.*, 595, 589, 598.

118 *Ibid.*, 592. For dates of composition see Eaves and Kimpel, 'The Composition of *Clarissa* and Its Revision before Publication', 416–18.

Lovelace meets his Culloden in 'a little lone valley' (VII, 411; p. 1485). In the narrative of De la Tour (a name which itself has Jacobite associations),[119] Clarissa's 'Protector' now becomes De la Tour's 'dear Chevalier' (VII, 413; p. 1486), and is defeated by a man whose name (Colonel William Morden) conflates those of William Duke of Cumberland and the Brigadier Mordaunt identified in the 1748 Defoe's *Tour* as a prime actor in Cumberland's force. (After Culloden Mordaunt's spoil was the Chevalier's coach, which he reportedly announced that he would drive to London 'till it stops of its own accord at the Cocoa Tree'.)[120]

Whether the reviewer who applauded 'the honour and soldier-like behaviour of Mordaunt'[121] (*sic*) at the end of the novel took Richardson's hint and found in Lovelace's death an echo of Jacobitism's defeat remains unclear. But there are many occasions where Lovelace's words and conduct might well have put contemporaries in mind of the Jacobite menace. His declaration that he is 'above all law', for example, echoes not only the conventional libertine pose but also the Pretender's famous declaration that (as Fielding warned) he is 'above our Laws; that he will regard none of them, not the most antient, upon which the Security of every Man's Property rests, nay, even the security of their Lives'.[122] Again, Lovelace's repeated use of the word 'triumph' to describe his projected 'conquest' of Clarissa, and his exclamation '*Io Triumphe*' (IV, 354; p. 757) on discovering her at Hampstead, echo the ominous motto 'TANDEM TRIUMPHANS' with which, according to the 1748 *Tour*, the Chevalier embarked on his attempt to subject the nation to his rule.[123] Other boasts, about the bestowal of preferments, about acts of forfeiture or about his 'own imperial will and pleasure' (III, 59; p. 403), have similar implications.

The really significant analogy is structural, however, not local. Like the Jacobite bogeyman of Whig propaganda, Lovelace is precisely a tyrant, and in his obsessive desire to have Clarissa 'IN MY POWER' (III, 56; p. 401) he does very precisely involve her in the 'Blood and Ruin' feared by the opponents of Stuart restoration. In this sense, the rape of Clarissa gives a hostile and compelling explanation of rebellion and its results which at times seems to reflect on the precedent of Cromwell, at times on the threat of Jacobitism, but which ultimately is a vision quite simply of tyranny itself. In Lovelace's favourite imagery of sieges and campaigns, the analogies between sexual and military invasion and between sexual and political oppression are immediate, becoming most disquieting when after the

119 See Swift, *Gulliver's Travels*, ed. Paul Turner (Oxford, 1986), pp. 192, 353 (note 29).
120 The report was Horace Walpole's: see John Prebble, *Culloden* (Harmondsworth, 1967), p. 317.
121 'Remarks on *Eloisa*', *Critical Review*, 12 (1761), in *Novel and Romance*, ed. Williams, p. 245.
122 Fielding, *A Serious Address* (1745), in *The True Patriot and Related Writings*, p. 30.
123 *A Tour thro' the Whole Island of Great Britain*, 4th edn (1748), p. 323.

rape he laments: 'Cæsar never knew what it was to be *hyp'd* ... till he arrived at the height of his ambition: Nor did thy Lovelace know what is was to be gloomy, till he had completed his wishes upon the charming'st creature in the world, as the other did upon the most potent republic that ever existed' (V, 232; p. 888). Such analogies between rape and conquest were not unique, of course. Fielding's most brilliant work of propaganda, the nightmare of Jacobite occupation in *True Patriot* 3, uses rape as a political metaphor in just this way;[124] and Richardson had a conspicuous precedent before him in the Lucretia myth, which associates the rape of Lucretia with the tyranny of the Tarquins while also identifying it as the catalyst for their overthrow.[125] 'A less complicated villainy cost a Tarquin – But I forget what I would say again' (V, 242; p. 895), writes Clarissa after the rape. That particular gap, at least, is easy for the reader to fill.

Throwing dust: Lovelace as writer

Few will find Richardson's prejudices and fears appealing in every detail, least of all at a distance of two centuries and a half. One may even sympathise with Lovelace's protest that he has been '*manifestoed* against' (VII, 336; p. 1437): there is a sense in which, for all its complexity, *Clarissa* can indeed be seen as a manifesto, which condenses in Lovelace the perceived threats of criminal, ideological and political disruption, thereby positing a definition of evil closely tied to the particular interests of Richardson's class, time and place. Yet at the same time the manifesto is also one of a most audacious kind. Like Fielding in *Tom Jones*, Richardson could give original and exploratory expression in the form of the novel to social and political preoccupations that elsewhere seem merely common-place, and in *Clarissa* he did so by the most daring and controversial of methods. Having invested in Lovelace so many conventional anxieties, with supreme unconventionality he then (to recall Rousseau's formula-tion) put himself in Lovelace's place as he wrote, to let evil speak for itself.

Lovelace's narrative, only infrequently heard in the first instalment, comes to pre-eminence in the second instalment and dominates the opening volume of the third. In volume III Clarissa has 34 letters to his 25; in volume IV she has 11 to his 32; in volume V, which includes the rape,

---

124 See *The True Patriot and Related Writings*, p. 132. For earlier uses of the rape image by both Jacobites and Williamites see Howard Erskine-Hill, 'Literature and the Jacobite Cause: Was There a Rhetoric of Jacobitism?', in *Ideology and Conspiracy: Aspects of Jacobitism, 1689–1759*, ed. Eveline Cruickshanks (Edinburgh, 1982), pp. 49, 61–2.

125 On the political implications of the Lucretia myth, see Ian Donaldson, *The Rapes of Lucretia: A Myth and Its Transformations* (Oxford, 1982), esp. pp. 103–18. Donaldson notes that Richard-son may have known the anti-Stuart dramatisations of the myth by his friend William Duncombe (1735) and by one of *Clarissa*'s most frequently cited playwrights, Nathaniel Lee (1680), but finds no political dimension to the novel (pp. 57–82).

she has none:[126] the distribution of letters exactly reflects the shift in power towards Lovelace within the novel's world. Even in the second instalment the two narratives are by no means co-equal, however. Statistically, volumes III and IV present in unusually pure form the 'double, yet separate' narrative structure envisaged in Richardson's preface, in which the same conflict is simultaneously documented by its two principal participants. The narrative oscillates rapidly between their parallel but antagonistic reports, inviting the reader to compare the two versions, fit them together, or note their failure to fit together: the effect is disorienting, even schizophrenic. But Lovelace always has the edge. Long before the numerical decline of the fourth volume, Clarissa's letters are epistemologically disadvantaged. As soon as she leaves the Harlowe garden hers is a confused and inadequate viewpoint, and her narrative, though copious, is vitiated by its failure to understand or explain. 'Every time I see this man', she tells Anna, 'I am still at a greater loss than before what to make of him' (III, 51; p. 398). Often she can record no more than her own bafflement before an adversary 'so various, that there is no certainty that he will be next hour what he is This' (III, 170; p. 462). Her letters reveal nothing so much as the vulnerability to Lovelace's schemes to which her own incomprehension exposes her: typically, they betray an agonising discrepancy between what they tell, the wariness with which Clarissa repeatedly credits herself, and what they show, her actual inability to detect and resist the plots of her antagonist.

These failures in perception are compounded by the possibility of intentional unreliability, which grows ever more acute as her situation becomes more compromising: 'I very much fear', she warns, 'that my unhappy situation will draw me in to be guilty of evasion ... and of curvings from the plain simple truth' (III, 213; p. 484). Anna regularly accuses her of such evasions, on one occasion even wishing that she had access, for a more illuminating report, to '*his* account of the matter' (III, 240; p. 499). Other unreliabilities are less to Clarissa's disadvantage, but no less incapacitating. Lovelace himself notes her deliberate failure to report her illness (III, 277; p. 519) – a failure for which Clarissa discreetly apologises to Anna, finding it 'more friendly in me, to conceal from *you* ... that worst part of my griefs, which communication and complaint cannot relieve' (IV, 1; p. 566). In many such ways her letters fail to account for the wilderness beyond the father's house or for her own efforts to negotiate it, and the reader must turn to Lovelace's narrative for primary access to the story.

To do so is in some senses a relief. When Lovelace's letters make their brief intrusion on the first volumes, interrupting the casuistical exchanges of Clarissa, Anna and the Harlowes with an exuberant prose in which the

---

[126] These figures refer only to letters separately numbered in the text: reported or included letters are otherwise discounted.

terms of casuistry are emphatically rejected, a release from the vexed and oppressive tone of the instalment is welcome enough. In their wilful disregard of the constraints, linguistic and ethical, by which other narrators are confined, his letters are momentarily exhilarating; in the Rosebud narrative, moreover, they seem to belie the Harlowes' allegations of vindictiveness and malice, displaying instead a winning combination of wit, vigour and even benevolence. But at the same time an alarm is sounded. In the context of Clarissa's epistolary seduction, which shows in dramatic form Lovelace's use of letters to deceive and mislead, to mould readers to his purposes, his first narrative letters begin to look very different. They briefly reproduce for the reader the same capacity to beguile that makes their writer so dangerous within the novel's world.

These linguistic skills are more fully demonstrated at the opening of volume III, just when Lovelace is beginning to assume the position of dominant narrator. His letters to Clarissa in the preceding instalment are only reported, but now the processes of epistolary manipulation are directly shown. Before his narrative to Belford even begins, he writes to the servant Joseph Leman a letter that is in many ways an exaggerated, almost parodic model of that narrative. He talks of the plot to abduct Clarissa as 'a little innocent contrivance' which, regrettably, has become 'necessary' to bring about the ultimate good of 'holy wedlock' (III, 23; p. 383). He reassures Joseph that by involving himself he will become 'an happy instrument of great good to all round' (III, 26; p. 385), and takes him in completely. Instead of enabling Joseph to see Lovelace's heart with clarity, the letter makes him set aside his initial (and very proper) suspicions – a process also eased by the 'new earnest of ... future favour' enclosed by Lovelace within. 'I love your Honner for contriveing to save mischiff so well', Joseph now writes. 'I thought till I know'd your Honner, that you was verry mischevous ... But find it to be quite another thing. Your Honner, it is plane, means mighty well by every body, as far as I see' (III, 27; pp. 385–6). The nearer one gets to Lovelace, it would seem, the less it is one sees.

Similar vignettes recur. Later, Clarissa reads a letter from Thomas Doleman presenting a choice of lodgings from which, carefully watching Lovelace for signs of 'visible preference', she chooses Sinclair's (III, 187; p. 471). In scrutinising Lovelace's eyes rather than Doleman's text, however, she misdirects her vigilance. Lovelace, we soon discover, has dictated the letter himself, successfully predetermining her response simply by his arrangement of words. 'Didst thou ever read a letter more artfully couch'd than this of Tom Doleman?', he asks. 'Who could forbear smiling, to see my charmer, like a farcical dean and chapter, choose what was before chosen for her ...?' (III, 189–90; p. 472). The comedy of which Lovelace writes, however, is comedy of a peculiarly disturbing kind. By giving Doleman's letter in full and withholding Lovelace's admission until later, Richardson has invited the reader to share Clarissa's initial misreading, and so become a 'farcical dean' himself: for this reason alone, the 'smiling' Lovelace expects will be at best an uneasy response.

Experiences of this kind combine to push the reader beyond the naive theory of the letter which makes Clarissa herself so slow to resist Lovelace's epistolary manipulation. When she asks 'what are *words*, but the *body* and *dress* of *thought*? And is not the mind indicated strongly by its outward dress?' (III, 322; p. 543), her assumptions can no longer be endorsed. In Lovelace's hands words are not incarnations but contrivances, their referentiality no more than a useful illusion. It is significant, indeed, that his *actual* dress conveys only garbled messages. As Belford alleges (intensifying Lord M.'s talk of 'a tongue that would delude an angel'), he has 'a face that would deceive the devil', and his clothing, notwithstanding his own *aperçu* that 'we do but hang out a sign in our dress, of what we have in the shop of our minds', signifies something quite unlike what lies within. 'What sort of a sign must thou hand out, wert thou obliged to give us a clear idea, by it, of the furniture of *thy* mind?', Belford goes on to accuse (VI, 261; p. 1130): to take sign for body, whether the code is sartorial or linguistic, is evidently to be deceived. Aptly enough it is Antony Harlowe, the 'searcher' of Clarissa's letters in the first instalment, who is most alive to these vagaries in Lovelace's writing in the second. His own letters, he reassures Mrs Howe, will stand for his 'upright meaning; being none of your Lovelaces' (IV, 110; p. 625).

Lovelace's speeches too are crooked, in ways that the third instalment will later explain in simple binary terms. An example comes in the fraudulent casuistry used by him at Hampstead to elaborate an alternative explanation, in moral negative, of the actual case.[127] Posing to Mrs Moore as an honest barrister for whom sign and reality are on principle inseparable, he tells her: 'I never was such a sad fellow as to undertake, for the sake of a paltry fee, to make white black, and black white' (V, 17; p. 770). To Belford, in contrast, he admits to muddying these opposites: 'And as every cause has a black and a white side, I gave the worst parts of our story the gentlest turn' (V, 36; p. 780). For Clarissa, however, the disparity between her own experience and his reports is nothing less than absolute: 'Make me as black as you please. Make yourself as white as you can' (V, 112; p. 822), she protests. He does so successfully enough. Seduced by his fair words, the Hampstead women exemplify, within the text itself, Lovelace's capacity to win over his audience, unjustly, by his manner of putting the case. He exults in his superiority, as illusionist, to the realist Clarissa, whose failing is 'to neglect to cultivate the opinion of

---

[127] See above, pp. 90–1.

individuals, when the whole world is governed by appearance!' (V, 52; p. 789).

On this occasion Lovelace simply lies. Even where facts are known, however, he can persuade his audience to set aside severity by the strong appeal he makes to their other faculties. At Colonel Ambrose's ball he charms the company, converting hostility to admiration and leaving Anna vexed to see 'how pleased half the giddy fools of our Sex were with him, notwithstanding his notorious wicked character' (VI, 271; p. 1136). The most telling case, however, is that of his 'tryal', when he is arraigned by his family for his crimes to Clarissa, and by a combination of wit and dissimulation talks them out of their responsibilities as judges. He succeeds not through the merits of his case (there are few, of course), but through his manner of putting it. He attacks and undermines Clarissa's rival pleas, again raising the analogy with forensic process: 'But he must be a silly fellow who has not something to say for himself, when every cause has its black and its white side' (VI, 106; p. 1031). At the same time he leavens his rhetoric with wit, winning his audience's hearts as well as minds (as when he notes 'that my humorous undaunted way forced a smile into my service from the prim mouths of the *younger* ladies especially': VI, 107; p. 1032). The analogy between his oratorical and narrative practices is here made quite explicit, as when he abridges his report to Belford with the explanation: 'Were I to tell thee the glosses I put upon these heavy charges, what would it be, but to repeat many of the extenuating arguments I have used in my letters to thee?' (VI, 111; p. 1034). His speeches at the trial simply repeat the letters in the novel, the implication is. They share the same strategies, and they exploit to the full the same underlying advantage – that, as he elsewhere says, 'it is much better ... to tell your own story, when it *must* be known, than to have an adversary tell it for you' (VI, 116; p. 1038).

In contexts such as these the reader is scarcely encouraged to give Lovelace an impartial hearing. Although these most overt dramatisations of his rhetorical wiles are retrospective, placed in such a way as to rebuke readers for their errors rather than forearm them against them, there is reason enough even at the opening of the second instalment to approach Lovelace's letters with caution. Yet they can be very insinuating, and in their explicit priorities they do much to allay any such caution. His narrative is, above all, an entertainment. Where Clarissa writes to Anna in vexed debate on the ethics of conduct, Lovelace extends to his fellow-rake, the usual companion of his 'frolics', a vicarious participation in his intrigues. His aim is to reproduce, in literary form, the pleasures of the chase. 'Next myself, thou wilt be the happiest man in the world', he tells Belford (III, 30; p. 387), and at times it can indeed seem that his whole endeavour is to fabricate for himself and his addressee a grand amusement, to which every deed or word is in the first place a contribution. Experience is subject to double manipulation, actual and then literary. The world itself is mere 'scenery for intrigue, for strategem, for enterprize' (III, 78; p. 413); the processes of seduction are 'more truly delightful' than the long expected, long deferred 'crowning act' (IV, 94; p. 616), and must be relished accordingly – 'for never, never shall I again have such charming exercise for my invention' (IV, 200; p. 674). (Or, with ominous innuendo, 'a more illustrious subject to exercise my pen upon': III, 52; p. 399). His plot itself exists only to be written, moreover, and to serve as a 'pre-text' for the development of narrative pleasure. Like 'Julius Cæsar; who perform'd great actions by day, and wrote them down at night' (I, 67; p. 74), he reverses the usual relation between experience and writing, moulding the first to fit his desired pattern for the second. The end-point of his intrigues is always the report to which they give rise; and that report matches them by documenting a story of libertine predation in a distinctively libertine idiom. Its hallmark, again, is the rejection of constraint, above all the constraint of stability in language and signification. Words multiply licentiously, transgressively. One reviewer wrote that 'the style ... of *Lovelace* is full of new words, arbitrarily formed in his own manner, which are strongly expressive of his ideas'; others, less indulgently, complained at the corruption of the language by his 'many new-coin'd words and phrases', or even looked to Johnson 'to rescue the *English* Language from this licentious Treatment'.[128] His coinages and *double entendres* amount to a literary libertinism, a repudiation of linguistic law. He seems to claim as much when announcing himself regardless, in his writing, 'of connexion, accuracy, or of any thing, but of my own imperial will and pleasure' (III, 59; p. 403): the offence to Lockian sensibilities is linguistic now as well as political, and quite overt.

Thus both plotting and writing combine to wrest experience into conformity with the model of 'rakish annals' (V, 160; p. 846), dispelling the moral norms of Clarissa's letters and inviting the reader to observe and judge through a new lens in which considerations of pleasure take absolute priority over considerations of justice. When much later Clarissa herself reads a sample of these 'rakish annals', she sees its exclusion of all that gives her own letters meaning, and notes 'how unaffected with the sense of its own crimes, is the heart that could dictate to the pen this libertine froth!' (VI, 177; p. 1077). It takes great efforts of resistance, however, to recover any sense of these 'crimes' from a narrative in which such categories are perpetually obscured, and in which Clarissa's own story of oppression and rape is rewritten as one of erotic quest.

The transformation is abrupt. 'I will pursue my melancholy story' (III,

---

[128] Haller, 'A Critical Account of *Clarissa*', in *Novel and Romance*, ed. Williams, p. 135; *Critical Remarks*, p. 4; *Candid Examination*, p. 44 (see also p. 38).

31; p. 387), writes Clarissa early in volume III. But now her narrative is challenged and redefined, a fact clearly seen when Lovelace intercepts her letters and comments on them in order to undermine the language and assumptions from which they begin. Reading in one letter that she is *'thrown upon the wide world'*, he is wittily pedantic: 'Now I own, that Hampstead-Heath affords very pretty, and very *extensive* prospects; but 'tis not the *wide world* neither' (IV, 359; p. 760). After the rape, again, he makes similar objections to her words 'ruin' and 'undone': 'I have no patience with the pretty fools who use those strong words to describe the most transitory evil; and which a mere church-form makes none. At this rate of romancing, how many *flourishing ruins* dost thou, as well as I, know?' (V, 199; p. 869). Evidently Lovelace has his own alternative assumptions, which the reader will hesitate to endorse; but his narrative works to enforce these assumptions in a sustained and compelling way. The 'melancholy story' is displaced by 'rakish annals'; Clarissa the conscientious subject of the first is redefined as Lovelace's 'charmer' or 'goddess', the erotic object of the second; the 'elaborate and premeditated ... wickedness' of the elopement plot as described by Clarissa gives way to the 'charming exercise for my invention' described by Lovelace. Clarissa's complaint 'I am but a cypher, to give him significance, and myself pain' (IV, 2; p. 567) has been highlighted by Terry Castle as an epitome of her position in the work as a whole[129] – somewhat paradoxically, since the overall pre-eminence of Clarissa's narrative does give her the prime position of authority in the novel as a whole. But the cipher image perfectly catches her changed situation at this point, when instead of being the subject of her own text she becomes the object of Lovelace's, her 'pain' effaced to make way for his pleasure. In Lovelace's own cipher (the cryptic code of his letters to Belford, and the 'rake's code' which informs those letters) she is emptied and transposed.

His first letters emphatically set these new terms: suddenly the qualities of piety and conscience by which Clarissa defines herself are displaced by sensual images of 'the mantled cheek, the downcast eye, the silent, yet trembling lip, and the heaving bosom' (III, 100; p. 425). The language creates a new Clarissa, no longer the would-be paragon of the first instalment nor yet the Christian heroine of the third: as he found so many early critics complaining, Richardson was dicing with the ornate pornography of *Fanny Hill*.

Her emotions were more sweetly feminine, after the first moments; for then the fire of her starry eyes began to sink into a less-dazling languor. She trembled: Nor knew she how to support the agitations of a heart she had never found so ungovernable. She was even fainting, when I clasp'd her in my supporting arms.

---

[129] *Clarissa's Ciphers*, pp. 15–16.

What a precious moment That! How near, how sweetly near, the throbbing
partners!   (III, 54; p. 400)

Such passages not only ask the reader to view the story in new and
exclusively libertine terms: they also bring with them whole sets of
assumptions, even predictions. This particular description is not just
external or physical in its emphases, where Clarissa's has been internal
and moral. It tells a new story, of repressed but mutual desire. The merest
glance is required to see how blatant an anticipation it is, in its final
phrases, of Lovelace's intended 'crowning act'. The passage even explains
how that act will come about, as the necessary consummation of the
history: from Lovelace's perspective, the self-control that is central to
Clarissa's narrative will be overwhelmed by the ungovernable heart that
gains precedence in his. Similar suggestions are at work all around. Where
he sees 'the wavy ringlets of her shining hair . . . wantoning in and about a
neck that is beautiful beyond description' (III, 53; p. 399), he manages to
insinuate, in what at first seems a purely physical detail, a hint of latent
depravity – a potential in Clarissa, the expectation is, to be realised in the
pages to follow. (Once again Richardson borrows from Milton, whose
phrase 'in wanton ringlets wav'd' at once invites the innocent reading
'unrestrained', while also anticipating Eve's fall into more lascivious forms
of wantonness.)[130]
    As such passages accumulate, the meanings attached by Clarissa to her
story are gradually lost. By reformulating it in wittily salacious terms,
Lovelace calls forth an indulgent response to his depredations, and by
presenting Clarissa as herself potentially libertine and her fall as a fore-
gone conclusion he relocates the story in a reassuringly comic world where
all will be for the best. The generic shift is explicit, and is often noted: he
even proposes to write the story (as 'The Quarrelsome Lovers') in the terms of
his favourite genre (IV, 10; p. 571). Clarissa's taste is for tragedy, but
libertines, Lovelace reports, 'love not any tragedies but those in which
they themselves act the parts of tyrants and executioners; and, afraid to
trust themselves with serious and solemn reflections, run to comedies, to
laugh away the distresses they have occasioned, and to find examples of as
immoral men as themselves' (IV, 97–8; p. 618). His own comic mediation
of the story has just this effect of 'laugh[ing] away . . . distresses'. In heroic
tragedy and libertine comedy, as he sees, the same act can appear in very
different colours. His letters create precisely the latter context, in which
crime is at worst venial and reprehension is swept aside in the certainty of
eventual reconciliation. By these standards it is Clarissa who is out of step:
she, in Lovelace's paradoxical generic shift, is now the 'tyranness' (IV, 18;
p. 575).

---

[130] *Paradise Lost*, Book IV, line 306; see also Fish's commentary, *Surprised by Sin*, pp. 101–3.

These comic norms are reinforced by the ideology of his 'libertine maxims' (III, 111; p. 430), foremost among which is the certainty that 'Love *within*, and I *without*, she'll be *more* than woman ... if I succeed not' (III, 112; p. 431). Many fables are adduced to confirm them. The most remarkable is 'the simile of a bird new caught' in Letter 170, which compares a boy's imprisonment of a captive bird to Lovelace's own treatment of Clarissa, a parallel instance of 'sportive cruelty' (III, 348; p. 557). The brilliance of the analogy comes from its comic presuppositions: cruelty is not merely commonplace, a condition of 'nature' and common to the reader's own experience; it is also a merely transient evil, given the inevitability of the captive's acquiescence (and eventual pleasure) in her condition. The analogy brings with it a prediction of 'consent in struggle' and 'yielding in resistance'; the bird's limited resentment itself confirms its liberty as valueless, and the captivity as innocuous.

Hast thou not observed the charming gradations, by which the insnared volatile has been brought to bear with its new condition? How at first, refusing all sustenance, it beats and bruises itself against its wires, till it makes its gay plumage fly about, and overspread its well-secured cage ... As it gets breath, with renew'd rage, it beats and bruises again its pretty head and sides, bites the wires, and pecks at the fingers of its delighted tamer. Till at last, finding its efforts ineffectual, quite tired and breathless, it lays itself down, and pants at the bottom of the cage, seeming to bemoan its cruel fate and forfeited liberty. And after a few days ... its new habitation becomes familiar; and it hops about from perch to perch, resumes its wonted chearfulness, and every day sings a song to amuse itself, and reward its keeper.   (III, 348–9; p. 557)

Clarissa's story, Lovelace suggests, must be the same: she too will 'be brought to sing me a fine song'.

As one sees in retrospect, one of Richardson's most brilliant ironic touches is to show the ultimate resistance of the image to Lovelace's intended meaning. It begins to elude his control, eventually forcing an acknowledgment 'that I have known a bird actually starve itself, and die with grief, at its being caught and caged'.[131] At such moments, the darker implications of Clarissa's oppression return to view – but these are rare moments. More often, Lovelace's narrative works to pre-empt all qualms, inviting the reader to experience and understand the history in terms that are entirely libertine. On this matter the response of his addressee Belford is revealing. Dimly aware that the narrative works to dull objections which direct access to the events described, or even a less artful rendition, might otherwise elicit, he remarks: 'But to have aukward fellows plot, and

---

[131] Cowper wrote 'An Ode on reading Mr. Richardson's "History of Sir Charles Grandison"'. Perhaps his melancholy verses on a goldfinch 'caught and caged and starved to death' (though most immediately inspired by a real-life source) bear the mark of his reading *Clarissa*. See *Poetical Works*, ed. H. S. Milford, 4th edn, rev. Norma Russell (1971), pp. 305, 661.

commit their plots to paper, destitute of the seasonings, of the *acumen*, which is thy talent, how extremely shocking must their letters be!' (IV, 78; p. 608). Belford fails, however, to make the effort to imagine Lovelace's plots without the gloss of this '*acumen*', and instead asks him to continue to 'enliven my heavy heart by thy communications'. Far from eliciting detestation, Lovelace's letters win him to a kind of collusion in the intrigues on which his own vicarious pleasures depend, the result being that his awakening conscience is easily checked. He is hooked, and Lovelace can punish him 'by my silence, altho' I have as much pleasure in writing on this charming subject, as thou canst have in reading what I write' (IV, 82; p. 610).

Here Richardson seems to anticipate the objection that Lovelace wins complicity from his readers, to the point even of showing that Belford's response to the situation changes according to his medium of access. Belford's first remonstrance, opening 'Thou, Lovelace, hast been long the *entertainer*; I the *entertained*' (III, 242; p. 500), and entering 'professedly in [Clarissa's] behalf', at first seems to recognise and resist the beguiling power of the Lovelacean entertainment, restoring to view as it does the fact of Clarissa's oppression. Yet the analysis which follows remains wholly within the terms set by Lovelace, urging Lovelace to change course on grounds of expediency alone. (Belford even confesses that his 'inducements to this are not owing to virtue'.) His attitude changes only when he meets Clarissa face to face, rather than reading the 'Clarissa' of Lovelace's letters. Now he explains his previous attitude on the grounds that 'then I had not seen her' (III, 345; p. 555), and shifts to an explicitly moral stance. The implication, clearly, is that Lovelace's narrative is a kind of moral anaesthetic, which works to allay the response that might be expected from less evasive reports of events. Lovelace suggests as much when his accomplice Mennell responds, like Belford, with qualms 'now he has seen this angel of a woman' (IV, 6; p. 569). 'I was a fool to let either you or him see her; for ever *since* ye have both had scruples ...' (IV, 172; pp. 658–9), Lovelace later complains. His letters have lulled each reader into a lax response, which is questioned only when other ways of knowing Clarissa become available. Throughout the novel they continue to blunt Belford's moral sense, to the extent that after Clarissa's death Lovelace can accuse him of a direct complicity. As a reader of Lovelace's plots who saw no need to act against them, Belford himself has 'more guilt than merit even in this affair' (VII, 342; p. 1441).

Belford's anaesthesia foreshadows the reader's difficulty. In Lovelace's hands, quite simply, the story changes: seen from a new perspective, and under the light of new standards and priorities, it solicits new judgments. In the narrative world of 'rakish annals' the moral falls into abeyance, and becomes, if not quite forgotten, irrelevant, so that half the work of self-justification is done for Lovelace without even the need for special pleading. As Philip Skelton complained in *Deism Revealed*, the libertine has 'no other lawgiver nor governor, but himself', claims 'unbounded liberty of thought and action', and therefore has no need of casuistical shifts, legitimate or otherwise. He 'hath his casuistry within himself, and is his own Jesuit'.[132] Under the governance of 'libertine maxims' and the 'rake's code' Lovelace's narrative works in just this way, supporting his position simply by the atmosphere established when morality is replaced by pleasure as an organising principle.

Yet the claims of 'unbounded liberty' inherent in the procedure of each letter are never quite enough, and there are times at which Lovelace must also support his position in ways familiar from the first instalment (though more extreme): whenever the simple priority of pleasure or comedy seems inadequate to secure the assent of his reader, he draws on casuistry in its most flagrantly self-serving forms. Belford's eventual realisation that he is guilty of 'jesuitical qualifyings' (V, 356; p. 958) heralds Richardson's more overt warnings of this sophistry in later editions: the 1751 synopsis of the caged-bird letter, for example, alerts the reader to the writer's 'endeavours to palliate his purposes' and 'characteristic reasonings in support of his wicked designs'.[133] Thus at one point casuistry is replaced because libertinism denies the moral laws from which it starts; at another it is perverted, transformed into a series of dazzling sophistications with which Lovelace, in Belford's later phrase, 'throw[s] dust in the eyes of his judges' (VII, 114; p. 1295).

This dust-throwing is so successful because the process, in Lovelace's hands, is often almost impossible to detect. His sophistry has been likened to the extenuations of Moll Flanders, whose seeming candour is doubly disarming in that it creates an illusion of frankness under which Moll's other methods of dissimulation take cover, thereby pre-empting and attenuating the potential severity of reader response.[134] In Lovelace's case, at least one early reader saw that 'his Sincerity and Frankness of Disposition ... if duly scann'd wou'd turn out a more refined hypoc-risy',[135] and even Clarissa detects self-interest of this kind behind it: 'He is extremely ready to *own his errors*', she says, '... by this means, silencing by acknowlegment the objections he cannot answer; which may give him the praise of ingenuousness, when he can obtain no other' (I, 271; pp. 183–4). Knowing 'that his own wild pranks cannot be concealed', he 'owns just enough to palliate (because it teaches you not to be surprised at) any new one, that may come to your ears', Anna adds (II, 133; p. 278). The

---

[132] *Deism Revealed*, II, 267; II, 268; II, 290.

[133] *Clarissa*, 3rd edn (1751; rpt. New York, 1990), IV, 377.

[134] Starr, *Defoe and Casuistry*, p. 133 and note.

[135] Graham to Richardson, 22 April 1750, FM XV, 2, f.84.

illusion of frankness is itself a rhetorical gambit, a means by which Lovelace cuts the losses involved in reports of his actions and diverts the reader from awareness of the accompanying palliations. He is, Anna sees, 'cunning enough to know, that whoever accuses himself first, blunts the edge of an adversary's accusation', and 'his ingenuity is a salvo' (III, 150; p. 451). The ambiguity of a word denoting at once ingenuousness and ingeniousness catches the points to perfection.[136]

Thus Lovelace scores points by his apparent unwillingness to conceal and extenuate, while at the same time making his actual strategies of concealment and extenuation harder to detect. 'Were I to be as much in earnest in my defence, as thou art warm in my arraignment', he tells Belford, 'I could convince thee ... that tho' from my ingenuous temper ... I am so ready to accuse myself in my narrations; yet I have something to say *for* myself *to* myself, as I go along' (IV, 286; p. 720). The balance between candour and apology, however, is more unequal than Lovelace suggests; for his frequently reiterated frankness is rarely more than expedient, and on occasion it may even be set aside. 'Little, very little difference, is there', as Dr Lewen notes, '... between a *suppressed* evidence, and a *false* one' (VII, 47; p. 1252); yet concealment is always a possibility in Lovelace's letters, most obviously in the critical case of the rape. Here candour provides Lovelace with his only possible grounds for claiming praise, and Belford does indeed grant it: 'I owe to thy own communicative pen the knowlege I have of thy barbarous villainy; since thou might'st, if thou would'st, have passed it upon me for a common seduction' (V, 224; p. 884). At this point, however, Lovelace has not been as communicative as his reader believes, having withheld the detail of the drugging. 'I did not intend to tell thee of this *innocent* trick', he confesses later; '... but that I hate disingenuity ... Besides, one day or other, thou mightest, had I not confessed it, have heard of it in an aggravated manner' (V, 230; pp. 887–8). Here the extent to which it is better 'to tell your own story ... than to have an adversary tell it for you' is unmistakable; for in confessing to the crime himself Lovelace is able to present it in the most favourable possible light. His report is carefully worked. In the first place, he never directly acknowledges the use of opiates, instead taking refuge in romance images of 'the Leaden God' waving 'over her half-drowned eyes his somniferous wand' (V, 230; p. 887). Having raised the possibility of drugging while veiling it in this magical and consoling idiom, he then confirms 'that some *little* art has been made use of: But it was with a *generous* design'. From this point on, description of the drugging, and still less of the rape, is unavailable. Instead of revealing the crime in his vaunted 'ingenuous' manner, he conceals it beneath a detailing of his

---

[136] On this ambiguity in contemporary usage, see Susie I. Tucker, *Protean Shape: A Study in Eighteenth-Century Vocabulary and Usage* (1967), p. 119.

kindness in making that now given act as painless as possible. The generous design works 'to lessen the too quick sense she was likely to have of what she was to suffer' (V, 230; p. 887); indeed, Clarissa is 'beholden' to him 'that, at the expense of *my* honour, she may so justly form a plea, which will intirely salve *hers*' (V, 231; p. 888). In this account his significant action is not to violate Clarissa but to protect her from distress and shame. No longer a rapist, he is even a healer: 'Do not physicians prescribe opiates in acute cases, where the violence of the disorder would be apt to throw the patient into a fever or delirium?' (V, 244; p. 896).

In his broadside against the Dublin bookseller George Faulkner for his piracy of *Grandison*, Richardson mounts a studious rhetorical analysis of Faulkner's self-defence. Faulkner has 'slubbered over' his thieving, obscuring it by ellipsis, evasion and a 'parade' of integrity: 'Indeed you seem to be lost in the dust you raise about yourself by it', he complains.[137] Lovelace too, the thrower of dust, is a 'slubberer' of this kind: his narrative works to conceal his crime, and to set in its place a sense of something laudable. Rape is 'slubbered over' by an emphasis on the drugging; drugging itself is presented not as the enabling means of rape, but rather as a generous sugaring of a somehow inevitable pill. One might well point to analogies in the evasiveness of Defoe's narrators, as when Moll diverts attention from her theft of a child's necklace to her humane resistance of the urge to murder the child.[138] Equally, one might look back to the original 'treasonable' correspondence of the early 1720s, and to the defence of the conspirator Kelly as printed by Richardson himself. 'The *first* and most acknowledged *Art* of a *Guilty Defence*', wrote Benjamin Hoadly in criticism of Kelly's speech,

is the *Art* of perpetually avoiding *All* that is most strongly and chiefly urged against a *Man*; and of dwelling with Earnestness and Vigour only upon *That*, which either was never urged at all against *Him*, or only very faintly ... This is an *Art* indeed; the *Art* of putting out of Sight the *principal* Considerations, which ought to be always in View ... This *Proceeding* ... is the *Proceeding* of *Guilt*, and not of *Innocence*: and is no better than if a Man indicted of killing *One* Certain Man, should spend his own Breath, and the *Time* of the *Court*, in shewing that he did not kill *Another* Man, as, He was inform'd, it had been *reported* of Him abroad.[139]

Lovelace goes one better than Moll, Roxana or Kelly, however; for here it is as though the murderer blames his victim for having died. 'When all's done, Miss Clarissa Harlowe has but run the fate of a thousand others of her Sex – Only that they did not set such a romantic value upon what they call their *honour*; that's all' (V, 226–7; p. 885). Her ravings are unwarranted, 'strange effects from a cause ... so slight' (V, 232; p. 889); 'What

[137] *An Address to the Public* (1754), in *Sir Charles Grandison*, 7 vols. (1753–4), VII, 438; VII, 436.
[138] See Starr, *Defoe and Casuistry*, p. 153.
[139] *Remarks on Mr. Kelly's Late Speech ... By Britannicus* (1723), pp. 2, 3.

nonsense ... to suppose, that such a mere notional violation, as she has suffered, should be able to cut asunder the strings of life?' (V, 281; p. 916).

In this extreme case, Lovelace clearly organises his narrative to conceal rather than reveal, 'slubbering over' the plain facts of the case by omission and evasion, and losing himself in the 'dust' of extenuation. Yet the narrative of the rape only presents in conspicuous form what he has been doing, more discreetly, all along – 'putting out of Sight the *principal* Considerations', and 'dwelling with Earnestness and Vigour' on the irrelevant. In his methods of doing so, he lends his guilty defence an insinuating appeal. The pleasures of Lovelace's text, its comic assumptions, its witty suspension of virtue and morality and its jesuitical dexterity all combine to put out of sight not only his particular crimes but any way of seeing in which the concept of crime has meaning. In this sense, the central section of Richardson's moral fiction is insistently amoral. It *amuses*, in both senses of the word. It entertains; but in entertaining it misleads, distracting the reader's attention from the facts of captivity, oppression and rape as surely as Pamela distracts her pursuers in Lincolnshire, 'throwing my Petticoat and Handkerchief into the Pond to amuse them, while I got off'.[140]

Satan himself

One might conclude, with the instigators of the Lovelace controversy, that as a result of these clever epistolary manoeuvres Lovelace does indeed 'get off'. His alternative presentation of the story is radically deconstructive, it is sometimes claimed, so that his system of values (or rather, his *denial* of values) irresistibly prevails. For Warner, 'Lovelace helps to undo the matrix of truth and value through which Clarissa would have us see, know, and judge':[141] he brings about the recognition that meaning can never be drawn out of phenomena, only read into them – that the story, in effect, can as well mean what he makes it mean as what Clarissa makes it mean. And this seems to be Richardson's troubling realisation – that meaning, and most of all moral meaning, is in the end an arbitrary matter. His novel abounds in variant meanings, all of them vulnerable, and in its very form it refuses to choose between them. Instead it implies the equality of each.

The result, in this view, is an instance of self-defeat that goes far beyond a mere confusion of allegiances in relation to the novel's plot. Having set out to represent in Lovelace a sceptical challenge to all his own most cherished values – 'the Distinctions of Right and Wrong', 'the Bonds of Human Society', 'the principles of Liberty'[142] – Richardson then allows

---

[140] *Pamela*, p. 198. On the verb 'amuse' see also Wilhelm Uhrström, *Studies on the Language of Samuel Richardson* (Upsala, 1907), p. 158.

[141] *Reading Clarissa*, p. 30.   [142] *Vade Mecum*, p. 83; *Æsop's Fables*, p. xii.

the challenge to work havoc without check. Instead of reaffirming his values he enables Lovelace to oppose them with an unmatched appeal and eloquence, luring his audience in the process of reading to enter into, adopt and even perhaps endorse a world-view in which these and all such values fall victim to Lovelace's own alternative imperatives of 'will and pleasure'. Whether the cause of this disruptiveness lies in some unacknowledged resistance within Richardson himself to his own explicit commitments or merely in the vigour with which he is able to imagine and represent their overthrow, the effect remains the same: at the very heart of *Clarissa* exists a narrative voice which subverts all the more positive meanings that the novel, in more favourable conditions, might otherwise succeed in upholding.

Here, then, would seem to be the completion of Lovelace's triumph – its completion, at any rate, if the reader can be assumed to adopt a purely passive role in response to Lovelace's words. Yet this, given Richardson's own anxiety to provoke the reader into an active role as examiner, arbiter and judge, cannot be taken for granted. In its structure *Clarissa* does indeed refuse to choose between its principal narrators and antagonists, but this relativism of form is very far from meaning that choices are never made: it means simply that explicit choices are withheld by the text itself, and must be recovered or supplied by the 'Carver', 'the Reader, to whom in this Sort of Writing, something ... should be left to make out'.[143] This reader may not wholly endorse Clarissa's own perspective or position (indeed, the first instalment makes clear enough how much there is to inhibit him from doing so without reserve). But the novel also allows and in some ways actively encourages the reader to resist Lovelace's alternative – whatever its initial attractions. What is most interesting about the process is that the strongest such encouragements, when Lovelace is unmistakably revealed in the third instalment as a rapist in his conduct and as an apologist for rape in his writing, are only offered volumes after the appeal of his character and ways of seeing has initially been felt.

Here the analogy with *Paradise Lost* is again illuminating, and clearly of importance in Richardson's own thinking; for Milton's Satan is the grand example in which all the more mundane evils figured forth in Lovelace are subsumed. The analogy extends, moreover, as far as the question of reception: 'in each case unwary readers have succumbed to the attractions of intelligence, determination, and courage present in evil', as Gillian Beer notes.[144] Indeed, Blake's famous remark that Milton 'was a true Poet and of the Devil's Party without knowing it'[145] offers a precise parallel with the

[143] Richardson to Lady Bradshaigh, 25 February 1754, Carroll, p. 296.
[144] Beer, 'Richardson, Milton, and the Status of Evil', p. 270.
[145] *The Marriage of Heaven and Hell*, in *Complete Writings*, ed. Geoffrey Keynes (Oxford, 1966), p. 150.

Lovelace controversy, which in its modern form no longer castigates Richardson for lending appeal to the evil he sets out to contest, but instead applauds him as 'a true Novelist' for imaginatively transcending the constraints of his ideology. In each case, criticism detects the subversion of the text's most urgent purposes by its own artistically superior (though rhetorically inept) performance.

Yet Milton at least has had his defenders, who find in the problem of response to Satan a practical demonstration, as well as a historical account, of the human frailty which is his poem's theme. 'Milton's purpose', writes Stanley Fish, 'is to educate the reader to an awareness of his position and responsibilities as a fallen man, and to a sense of the distance which separates him from the innocence once his; Milton's method is ... to make him fall again'.[146] In this analysis, Satan's role is to tempt not only the first pair but also the reader, whose susceptibility to Satanic rhetoric becomes a measure of his own reprobacy. The result, once recognised, is to foster a new and valuable self-awareness. Instead of merely reporting Satan's appeal Milton enables it to be felt directly, opening the way to a prime instance of the mistake–correction–instruction pattern characteristic of the poem's didacticism.

By casting Lovelace as Clarissa's tempter and destroyer, Richardson begins to invite the parallel between his rake and (as Clarissa puts it) 'Satan himself' (V, 241; p. 894). He uses it, moreover, to make a typically Miltonic emphasis not only on Lovelace's evil but also on the capacity to obscure it that makes him so dangerous. At Sinclair's house, Clarissa finds in her own experience the lesson 'that form is deceitful' (IV, 65; p. 601), and after the fire-scene she asks: 'O why was the great fiend of all unchained, and permitted to assume so specious a form, and yet allowed to conceal his feet and talons ...?' (IV, 351; p. 755). This concealment becomes a recurrent motif. Lovelace himself jokes that the maid at Hampstead 'could not keep her eye from my foot; expecting, no doubt, every minute to see it discover itself to be cloven' (V, 22; p. 773); later, Anna is 'amazed' that he 'did not discover *his foot* before' (V, 183; p. 859). The most revealing such allusions, however, are those that refer specifically to the Satan of *Paradise Lost*. In the opening instalments they are often veiled, working merely by verbal or narrative echoings.[147] An example is the arresting shift in diction of Lord M.'s 'you have naturally a great deal of elocution; a tongue that would delude an angel' (IV, 187; p. 666), the semicolon marking a leap from prosaic notice of Lovelace's eloquence to an alarm at its Satanic implications which hints at the beguilement of

---

[146] *Surprised by Sin*, p. 1.
[147] See Beer, 'Richardson, Milton, and the Status of Evil', pp. 264, 266.

Uriel in Book III of *Paradise Lost*.[148] At other points these echoings are more explicit verbally, but obscure in their application. After the dinner at Sinclair's, for example, Clarissa quotes from the conference in Hell:

> – *His tongue*
> *Dropt manna, and could make the worse appear*
> *The better reason, to perplex and dash*
> *Maturest counsels; for his thoughts were low;*
> *To vice industrious: But to nobler deeds*
> *Tim'rous and slothful: – Yet he pleas'd the ear.*
>
> (III, 325; p. 545, after *Paradise Lost*, II lines 112–17)

The lines refer to the fallen angel Belial, who shares the rhetorical prowess of his master, and Clarissa applies them, with superficial aptness, to Belford. She misses the usefulness of her own analogy, however, and fails to progress from a sceptical resistance to Belford's honeyed yet paradoxically genuine words to a new awareness of Lovelace's similar but truly deceitful eloquence. Anna comes nearer the mark: 'By your account of your wretch's companions', she responds, 'I see not but they are a set of infernals, and he the Beelzebub' (III, 333; p. 549). Only in the third instalment does the analogy become exact and explicit, however, when Lovelace likens himself to 'the devil in Milton (an odd comparison tho'!)' (V, 21; p. 772). Here Richardson is no longer content to rely on the verbal and structural parallels or the veiled allusions of preceding volumes and forces the least attentive reader to perceive the 'odd comparison', thereby informing his response through the example of Milton's text.[149]

Contemporary reception attests his success. Repeatedly, readers used the analogy with Satan to perceive and explain Lovelace as a type of beguiling evil. Some grasped tentatively at the link, like the reader who told Richardson: 'But as for your Hang-Dog Lovelace, I know not well what to make of him. He is a compound of good & bad Qualitys[,] an Amphibious creature, an Original Character, not unlike the Devil in the Serpent'.[150] Others, such as the daughters of Aaron Hill, saw in Clarissa's encounter with Lovelace a dramatisation of the attractiveness of evil which could be understood (and rewritten) in openly Miltonic terms. The clumsily Miltonic diction of a verse by Urania Johnson has Lovelace

> like a Serpent, wind his wily Way;
> While fair *Clarissa*, in Heaven's Wardrobe drest,
> Surveys his glitt'ring Sides, and haughty Crest,
> Nor heeds the Poison lurking in his Breast![151]

---

[148] *Paradise Lost*, Book III, lines 682–91: this is the passage cited in Sarah Fielding, *Remarks on Clarissa*, ed. Peter Sabor, Augustan Reprint Society Nos. 231–2 (Los Angeles, 1985), p. 35.

[149] See Beer, 'Richardson, Milton and the Status of Evil', pp. 268–9.

[150] H. Morgan to Richardson, 9 August 1748, FM XV, 2, f.16.

[151] Urania Johnson, 'To the Author of *Clarissa*', FM XV, 2, f.41.

Her sisters Astræa and Minerva Hill went on to link this thematic concern with a didactic strategy, attributing to Richardson a project to warn against 'such mask'd male Savages as Lovelace' 'unexperienc'd and well-meaning Maids, whose own Hearts being innocent, can serve but to betray 'em into a belief of every Lying Likeness that looks honestly'. In explaining Richardson's method they begin to go astray, however, seeing in *Clarissa* a cautionary demonstration of evil's allure in which this 'unexperienc'd' reader, under careful authorial supervision, is fortified by a remedial textual experience and shown the dangers of evil while guarded from their appeal:

How satisfy'd a Confidence may be repos'd, by all your giddiest Scholars, in a Guide, whom modesty and Virtue call upon 'em to commit their Hands to! we are led on, (when you lead us) as our common mother was through Paradise, before her Fall ... See, whatever was adorn'd to tempt, but see it, without Levity: See every thing that had a Face to threaten; yet pass by it, without Danger.[152]

At this point the wrongheadedness of the Hills' analogy becomes clear – and not only because Eve's tour of Paradise, as a defensive exercise, is so inauspicious a precedent. More significant is the extent to which the image of being led by a guide falsifies the experience of a novel which so evidently provides its reader with no explicit guidance and instead requires him to find his own path through the text. (As Laclos was to write in a characteristically perverse passage of praise, the reader of *Clarissa* is *not* 'guidée dans sa manière de voir', the result leaving little room for the 'Confidence' of the Hills: as he concludes, 'cette lecture peut être dangereuse'.)[153] The Hills, of course, are right that Richardson's representation of attractive evil also involves a project to arm the reader against it; but they are wrong in expecting the project to take so simple a form. Richardson exposes the reader directly to the blandishments of a Satanic voice, and asks him to resist it on his own initiative; and he goes a step further than Milton by refusing to set against that voice any unequivocal form of correction. The attendant risk that the reader, bereft of authorial guidance, will respond inadequately to the challenge of being left to his own resources (free to fall, in effect) is thus severe. Seeing what is 'adorn'd to tempt', the reader may simply succumb, and commit his sympathies and judgments to Lovelace's cause: as Richardson wrote in reply to the Hills, many readers 'pity the Lovelace you are affrighted at, and call Clarissa perverse, over-delicate, and Hard-hearted'.[154]

It was precisely this possibility that preoccupied the writer of *Critical Remarks*, who foresaw readers embracing both Lovelace himself and Love-

152 Astræa and Minerva Hill to Richardson, 13 December 1748, FM XIII, 3, ff.138, 139–40.
153 Laclos, *Œuvres complètes*, p. 440.
154 To Astræa and Minerva Hill, 14 December 1748, Carroll, pp. 102–3.

lacean ways of seeing. His complaint at the depravity of the central volumes culminates in an allegation that Richardson acts 'the part of the serpent, and not only throw[s] out to men the tempting suggestions of lust and pleasure, but likewise instruct[s] the weak head and the corrupt heart in the methods how to proceed to their gratification'. He 'tempt[s] them to swallow the forbidden fruit of the tree which they were commanded not to eat; I mean the tree of the knowledge of good and evil'.[155] Now it is the reader, not Clarissa, who is Eve, left helpless before the allure of Lovelacean vice. Where the Hills had seen Lovelacean evil as perpetually subject to authorial control, the writer of *Critical Remarks* sees it as instead escaping that control: beginning as a theme represented in the text, the capacity of evil to attract and beguile spills over to become a subversive process at work in its reading. The pleasures of Lovelace's narrative seduce the heart, the suggestion is, and paralyse the head. They will make the reader fall.

Early reception offers a third way of explaining the analogy between Lovelace and Satan, however, and one that is at once more subtle and more tolerant. In Sarah Fielding's discussion of the Rosebud affair[156] it becomes possible to acknowledge Lovelace's capacity to beguile his readers while also finding in the process not a subversion of the text so much as an advancement of its purposes. Placing Lovelace's fair words within the context of a larger rhetoric, that of *Clarissa* as a whole, Sarah Fielding stresses the importance of the reader's vigilance in a text 'where the Characters must open by degrees, and the Reader's own Judgment form them from different Parts'. At first Lovelace may indeed win 'Admiration and Esteem', she writes; but after the rape a reader will see that,

like *Milton's Satan*, he could for a Time cloath himself like an Angel of Light, even to the Deception of *Uriel*.

> *For neither Man, nor Angel can discern*
> *Hypocrisie; the only Evil that walks*
> *Invisible, except to God alone,*
> *By his permissive Will, through Heaven and Earth:*
> *And oft, though Wisdom wake, Suspicion sleeps*
> *At Wisdom's Gate, and to Simplicity*
> *Resigns her Charge; while Goodness thinks no ill*
> *Where no Ill seems; which now, for once, beguiled*
> Uriel, *though Regent of the Sun, and held*
> *The sharpest-sighted Spirit of all in Heaven.*

Proud Spirits, such as *Satan's* and *Lovelace's*, require Objects of their Envy, as Food for their Malice, to compleat their Triumph and applaud their own Wickedness. From this Incident of the Rosebud, and the subsequent Behaviour of *Lovelace*, arises a Moral which can never be too often inculcated; namely, that Pride has the

---

[155] *Critical Remarks*, p. 43.   [156] Cited above, p. 81.

Art of putting on the Mask of Virtue in so many Forms, that we must judge of a Man upon the whole, and not from any one single Action.[157]

The reader comes away, by this account, with a rather banal 'Moral'; but the process of its acquisition has been more interesting. Like Clarissa and Uriel, the reader is beguiled, but unlike them may profit from the experience. Richardson has not simply told him 'that we must judge of a Man upon the whole', but has made him first misjudge and then recognise his own failure to judge, thus experiencing in himself the human susceptibility to evil with which the novel is so preoccupied. In the end, Lovelace's capacity to beguile his readers has the effect of a 'good temptation'.

The underlying suggestion is exactly that of the 'mock encounter', which Johnson was to formulate more explicitly in the *Rambler* the following year, and which also underlies his defence of Richardson in the passage cited by Eliza Rose in the epigraph to this chapter. Here Johnson's precise words are telling, stressing as they do that the process of rejecting Lovelace must involve both struggle and time. 'It was in the power of Richardson alone to teach us at once esteem and detestation', he writes; 'to make virtuous resentment *overpower* all the benevolence which wit, eloquence, and courage naturally excite, and to lose *at last* the hero in the villain'.[158] With these words Johnson takes into account, as Richardson's detractors do not, that reading is a continuing process, with possibilities within it for development or correction in response. Such an emphasis leaves room for the reader's beguilement, but identifies it as merely a stage in the larger process by which the efforts of author and reader collaborate in the final reassertion of 'virtuous resentment'. The encounter with Lovelace, in this view, may thus be salutary indeed. It re-enacts the perils of evil as both an external force and an internal impulse, exposing the reader to difficulties and dangers of the kind encountered by all those who deal with Lovelace within the novel itself, and perhaps even leading him to make the same mistakes. But in the mock world of the text the consequences of temporary failure will ultimately be beneficial, bringing the reader to experience and recognise his own vulnerability to evil, or even his own complicity in it. Such recognitions, the assumption is, can only fortify. As Richardson himself wrote: 'Temptations are sore things; but without them, we know not ourselves, nor what we are able to do.'[159]

Perhaps, in short, Richardson was closer to Milton than his detractors have recognised, both in his ambition to let us more fully 'know ourselves' and in his ways of doing so. Clearly enough, Lovelace's voice does indeed have the capacity to beguile and disrupt, not only by communicating winning qualities of the kind described by Sarah Fielding and Johnson but

---

[157] *Remarks on Clarissa*, pp. 35–6. [158] *Lives of the English Poets*, II, 67 (italics mine).
[159] *Sentiments*, p. 75.

also by offering a view of the world that is pleasurably unfettered: it invites the reader to admire his character and endorse his ways of seeing. Yet that is not the novel's only invitation; for here, as in Milton's representation of Satan, Richardson does not mislead what Sarah Fielding calls 'the Reader's own Judgment' so much as demand its activation. Like Milton, he contrives a kind of temptation designed in the end to promote self-awareness, resistance and a reassertion within the reader of all the values, moral and human, that the tempter seeks to destroy.

Where there is a difference, of course, is in the openness of Richardson's scheme. For all Johnson's talk of authorial 'power', Richardson's control over the processes of *Clarissa*'s reception is far less extensive than that of Milton, in whose hands the epic voice is always available, albeit retrospectively, to rebuke, explain or correct. Richardson does have other less explicit means of encouraging resistance to Lovelace at his disposal, which he employs, like Milton, retrospectively: in the third instalment the increasingly brutal character of Lovelace's behaviour, the more obvious speciousness of his explanations, and the growing cogency with which Belford challenges both, combine to similar effect. Yet even here, where Richardson seems to have designed to correct the more easily seduced, nothing carries the inescapable force of metalinguistic commentary. The onus remains with the reader to discover Lovelace's foot for himself, making the mock encounter contrived by the text an unpredictable and volatile process. The novel's readers remain free to 'carve' a variety of routes: the most vigilant reader will perhaps be invulnerable, even to the first Rosebud letter; Sarah Fielding's will admire Lovelace, and only after Clarissa's rape be forced to correct his response; Johnson's will be torn throughout between contradictory impulses to esteem and detestation, struggling in his mind towards the eventual victory of resentment; but a fourth reader may simply embrace all that Lovelace offers, and proceed no further down any of Richardson's envisaged paths towards repudiation.

Richardson was acutely aware of the problem. He intended, as he told Aaron Hill, that Lovelace 'should have something to say for himself to himself, tho' it could not have weight to acquit him with the rest of the World',[160] but instead found the world queuing up to acquit. Evidence of Lovelace's capacity to win readers to his cause, both intellectually and emotionally, was almost overwhelming. Many embraced Lovelacean interpretations of the conflict with Clarissa: Colley Cibber, for example, found in Letter 99 'such almost justifiable sentiments of his intended treatment of Clarissa, that scarce a libertine reader will forbear to triumph with him, over the too charming, and provoking delicacy of his

---

[160] To Hill, 10 May 1748, Carroll, p. 88.

Clarissa'.[161] Some fell into the Lovelacean view of Hickman, and took it as objective: when Lady Bradshaigh denigrated his character, Richardson was forced to announce himself 'a little mortified ... to find that you are not alone in taking his Character rather from the ludicrous Treatment of a Lovelace, whose Business it was to depreciate him ... than from a Clarissa'.[162] Other readers fell into simpler emotional responses, prompting Richardson (even before publication began) to start the processes of revision which were to culminate in the emphatic blackenings of 1749–51.[163] 'I once read to a young Lady Part of his Character, and then his End', he told Hill in October 1746, 'and upon her pitying him and wishing he had been rather made a Penitent, than to be killed, I made him still more and more odious ... leaving only some Qualities in him, laudable enough to justify her first Liking'.[164] The openness of his scheme was coming home to roost: expecting to find readers develop in themselves a resistance to this 'first Liking', he instead claimed in his tetchiest moments to have 'met with more Admirers of Lovelace than of Clarissa'.[165] Nor was cruder rewriting the only available response: 'several times as I proceeded', he later told Sarah Chapone, 'I had Thought of burning the Ms. for fear of doing Mischief by his Character.'[166]

One could hardly look for a more comprehensive admission of failure. Yet it was nothing peculiar to his own text that frustrated Richardson in these instances, only general conditions which in other cases he was happy to recognise. For the vagaries of reception experienced here only exemplify a universal phenomenon, common to Richardson, Milton and any other writer – that no text can ever wholly predetermine the responses of its reader. There is nothing very new about the perception. As William Godwin saw at the century's end, the text is a realm created but then relinquished by its author, and handed over to the will of a reader whose responses are ultimately ungovernable. Extending to the question of textual interpretation the principles of anarchism that inform his political thought, Godwin turns for illustration to a series of examples of particular relevance to *Clarissa*. *The Fair Penitent*, he suggests, can be read as 'a powerful satire upon the institutions at present existing in society relative to the female sex', but it can equally well be read as a confirmation of these institutions, in which the duty of women 'to devote themselves in all things to the will of their fathers and husbands' is unyieldingly enforced. *Paradise*

---

[161] Cibber to Richardson, 30 March 1748, Barbauld, II, 168 (referring to *Clarissa*, III, 52; p. 399).

[162] To Lady Bradshaigh, [1749–50?], Carroll, p. 168.

[163] See Kinkead-Weekes, '*Clarissa* Restored?', *Review of English Studies*, NS 10, No. 38 (1959), 156–64.

[164] To Hill, 29 October 1746, Carroll, pp. 73–4.

[165] To Frances Grainger, 21 December 1749, Carroll, p. 141.

[166] To Sarah Chapone, 25 March 1751, Carroll, p. 181.

Lost, though conceived 'To justify the ways of God to men', may equally well 'inspire nothing but hatred' towards the deity. And in Richardson's own case 'it would not perhaps be adventurous to affirm that more readers have wished to resemble Lovelace, than have wished to resemble Grandison'. All writers are in the same boat, where intention and execution count in the end for little, Godwin suggests: the meanings with which readers depart depend ultimately on these readers alone, 'and will be various according to the various tempers and habits of the persons by whom the work is considered'.[167]

Theories of textuality and histories of reception combine to confirm Godwin's vision of hermeneutic anarchy. But *Clarissa* offers one intriguing complication. By monitoring reception as he wrote and revised, and by publishing the novel in three widely spaced instalments, Richardson gave himself an unusual opportunity to reassert his own authority over readers, and to intervene in the processes of interpretation. It is not simply that he could prepare in the third instalment a retrospective clarification of what in the second had been obscure. Serial publication also gave him the flexibility to revise the instalment, before publication, in light of evidence of how its predecessors had been read. He was able, in other words, to respond to response – and so he did. Having published the Lovelace volumes in April 1748, he told Aaron Hill in May that 'one half of the sequel must be new written',[168] and was ready to publish the rewritten continuation only in December. *Clarissa* is thus marked by the history of its own reception, what follows the second instalment being no ordinary continuation of the text but in many ways a riposte.

[167] William Godwin, *The Enquirer* (Dublin, 1797), pp. 136–7, 135, 135, 137.
[168] 10 May 1748, Carroll, p. 87.

4

Forensic realism
The third instalment, December 1748

I think ye Author a Person of refind understanding, but that he has Needlessly spun out his Book to an extravagant Prolixity – & which he would scarce have done, had he not been a *Printer* too as well as an *Author*. Nothing but *Fact* could authorize so much particularity, and indeed not *that*; but in a Court of Justice – Shenstone to Lady Luxborough, 23 March 1749/50, on reading *Clarissa*[1]

Providence, anti-Providence and the instability of justice

In the late seventeenth century and for much of the eighteenth, Shakespeare's *King Lear* was supplanted by Nahum Tate's notorious revision of the play, which brought it into conformity with contemporary desires and expectations by '*making the Tale conclude in a Success to the innocent distrest Persons*'.[2] The apocalyptic original was barely tolerable to the audiences of Richardson's day, who (as one of Tate's modern editors notes) were 'more interested in thickening the walls than in being shown the nearness of chaos'.[3] Edward Moore felt 'no other Passion than Terror' at the play, Joseph Warton found it 'painted with circumstances too savage and unnatural', and John Dennis complained that the deaths of Cordelia and Lear 'call the Government of Providence into Question':[4] all three typify the climate of taste and opinion in which Tate's more consoling version could hold the stage. Even Johnson, who saw in the original a demonstration 'that villany is never at a stop, that crimes lead to crimes, and at last terminate in ruin', was unprepared to see the demonstration pursued to its catastrophe in Shakespeare's fifth act, which he found 'contrary to the natural ideas of justice, [and] to the hope of the reader'.[5] When judged

---

[1] *Letters of William Shenstone*, ed. Duncan Mallam (Minneapolis, 1939), pp. 199–200.
[2] Tate, *The History of King Lear* (1681), in *Five Restoration Adaptations of Shakespeare*, ed. Christopher Spencer (Urbana, 1965), p. 203.
[3] Spencer, *Five Restoration Adaptations*, p. 23.
[4] Moore to Richardson, 23 December 1748, FM XV, 2, f. 21; *The Adventurer*, 3rd edn (1756), IV, 148; Dennis, *An Essay on the Genius and Writings of Shakespear* (1712), p. 10.
[5] *Johnson on Shakespeare*, ed. Arthur Sherbo, intr. Bertrand H. Bronson, *The Yale Edition of the Works of Samuel Johnson*, VII–VIII (New Haven, 1968), VIII, 704.

by its capacity to satisfy the emotional and ideological needs of an
eighteenth-century audience, Shakespeare's play was a non-starter. In
Tate's conclusion, however, a less troubling world is on offer. Here Gloster
is able to celebrate 'the King's blest Restauration', Cordelia can rejoice
'Then there are Gods, and Vertue is their Care', while Edgar finds in the
action an example fit to

> convince the World
> (Whatever Storms of Fortune are decreed)
> That Truth and Vertue shall at last succeed.[6]

Such reassurances had an evident and compelling appeal.

There were, of course, dissenting voices. Addison's was one, protesting
at Tate's debasement of the play 'according to the chymerical Notion of
poetical Justice'. (His complaint had little immediate influence, however,
perhaps because neutralised by John Dennis's claim that he made it only
to adjust expectations in favour of his own *Cato*.)[7] Another such voice was
Richardson's. The postscript to *Clarissa* quotes Addison's remarks and
adds a footnote attributing the prejudice against Shakespeare to 'false
Delicacy or affected Tenderness': Garrick is urged ('*now* seems to be the
time') to restore the original to the stage (VII, 428n.; p. 1497). Yet
Richardson too, like Addison, had ulterior motives of his own. By 1751 the
note had served its purpose and was withdrawn; but in December 1748,
when *Clarissa*'s closing instalment first appeared, his allusion to the alternative endings of Shakespeare and Tate was very pointed. In citing the
Lear debate he had raised a telling precedent against which to measure the
last great controversy surrounding his own work – whether it should end,
likewise, in ruin or in success.

It is easy to mock the proponents of an alternative ending to *Clarissa*, as
Richardson himself gently did when describing the pseudonymous letters
he had received from readers who, 'enamoured, as they declare, with the
principal Character, are warmly solicitous to have her *happy*' (VII, 425;
p. 1495). Yet Richardson himself could hardly have done more to foster
the confusion between fictive and real that gave rise to these interventions.
One need not argue that his official pose as merely the editor of genuine
letters was taken literally to see that what he called 'that kind of Historical
Faith which Fiction itself is generally read with, tho' we know it to be
Fiction'[8] could in this case involve readers intimately enough to prompt
their Quixotic pleas. *Clarissa*'s 'reality effect' is peculiarly strong: the
narration of events by the protagonists themselves, the simultaneity of
narrative and event posited by the epistolary form, and the famous

---

[6] Tate, *The History of King Lear*, V vi line 119; V vi line 97; V vi lines 159–61.
[7] *Spectator*, I, 170 (No. 40, 16 April 1711); see *Johnson on Shakespeare*, VIII, 704.
[8] To William Warburton, 19 April 1748, Carroll, p. 85.

particularity and prolixity of Richardson's writing all combine to close the gap between the world of the novel and that of the reader's own experience. Mary Delany found it 'impossible to think it a Fiction',[9] and indeed few literary representations can ever have seemed so real.

Suspense was another factor, which again arose in part from Richardson's prolixity – a point suggested by Aaron Hill's praise of his 'cruel Power, of interposing such a world of charming *Bars*, between the Lady's Fate ... and the Reader's longing Expectation'.[10] And for *Clarissa*'s first readers both realism and suspense were uniquely exaggerated by the circumstances of publication, which quite precisely slowed reading time down in step with narrated time, and twice interrupted the novel at critical and uncertain points. The three instalments were published in December 1747 and April and December 1748,[11] thus keeping pace with fictive events dated between 10 January and 7 December of a single year; while the two breaks between instalments coincided with Clarissa's two escapes, from Harlowe Place and from 'Dover Street', in each case leaving the outcome unsettled and 'the Passions' (as one reader complained) 'so raised ... as by no Means to be satisfied, till the Catastrophe shews whether Vice or Virtue is to prevail'.[12] To separate the instalments so widely was to withhold such satisfaction – something Richardson again planned to do by issuing *Grandison* 'at three several times; because there are some few Surprises in different Parts of it, which, were the Catastrophe known, would be lessen'd, and take off the Ardor of ... Readers'.[13] By such methods he could make fictive events assume a dimension in readers' minds commonly reserved for the real, and enhance their involvement accordingly.

Readers reacted, beneath their banter, with evident resentment. After the first instalment Mary Heylin accused Richardson 'of Cruelty in raising our Expectations to the highest Pitch of Woman's Curiosity and Impatience, and then unkindly leaving us in Suspense'. After the second Mary Delany complained: 'But ... now you have interested me so strongly for the unhappy and deserving Clarissa, will you have the Cruelty to leave me long in the anxious State I am in for her?'[14] Others sought to resolve their anxieties, at least temporarily, by continuing the suspended story in their own imaginations. In effect (as Richardson told Elizabeth Carter) he had 'left everyone at liberty to form a catastrophe of their own',[15] so that indi-

---

9 To Richardson, 25 January 1748/9, FM XV, 2, f. 13.
10 To Richardson, [1745–6], FM XIII, 3, f. 37.
11 William M. Sale, *Samuel Richardson: A Bibliographical Record of his Literary Career with Historical Notes* (New Haven, 1936), p. 48.
12 Anon. to Richardson, 20 May 1748, FM XV, 2, f. 6.
13 To Alexis Claude Clairaut, 5 July 1753, Carroll, pp. 236–7.
14 Mary Heylin to Richardson, 24 November 1747, FM XV, 2, f. 3; Mary Delany to Richardson, 18 June 1748, FM XV, 2, f. 7.
15 17 December 1748, Carroll, p. 117.

vidual readers could usurp him, in their own minds, as authors of Clarissa's future. But not, of course, for long. By dispelling their imagined catastrophes and killing Clarissa, Richardson was able in response to involve them in a dramatic lesson, a mock encounter with death felt all the more keenly by those who had entertained elaborate projects for the heroine's future happiness. To lose her, for these most involved of readers, was to lose a friend to whose mortality they had remained complacently blind. 'Philaretes' suspected the tragic conclusion in advance, and complained that he would 'read the Account of her Death with as much Anguish of Mind, as I should feel at the Loss of my dearest Friend'. 'Belfour' (pen name, at the time, of the still secretive Lady Bradshaigh) pleaded 'the joy I had promised myself from a happy catastrophe'. For both, Clarissa's death was little less than a bereavement.[16]

Intercessions of this kind, however, could carry little weight with an author who had carefully prepared for his readers just this shock, intending his work 'to make those think of Death who endeavour all they can to banish it from their Thoughts'.[17] In their imagined continuations, 'Philaretes' and Lady Bradshaigh clearly had endeavoured to 'banish' death. By giving them rein to do so and then drawing it sharply in, Richardson had contrived in return what he saw as an instructive trauma (and one so acute that both, initially, refused to read on). To Lady Bradshaigh, who rebuked him for preferring 'to give joy only to the ill-natured reader, and heave the compassionate breast with tears for irremediable woes',[18] he was quite explicit about his purposes. He had indeed planned to give his readers pain, he told her, but in the benevolent manner instead of the good physician: he did it 'to arm them against the most affecting Changes' of life, and to prepare them 'by remote Instances, to support ourselves under real Affliction, when it comes to our Turn to suffer such'.[19] He would have 'lost [his] Aim' had she *not* been pained – the aim of this smaller pain being, ultimately, to fortify against a greater. 'My Story is designed to strengthen the tender Mind, and to enable the worthy Heart to bear up against the Calamities of Life', he wrote.[20] Clarissa's death was to be a form of inoculation, or a form of remedial surgery: as Joseph Spence put it, the 'Pangs' suffered by readers 'should be looked upon like the Incisions made by a kind Surgeon . . . who gives them only out of Humanity, and to save his Patients'.[21]

Remarkable testimonies survive of the response to Clarissa's death.

[16] 'Philaretes' to Richardson, [early 1748?], FM XV, 2, f. 32; Lady Bradshaigh to Richardson, [early December 1748], Barbauld, IV, 215.
[17] To Hill, 12 July 1749, Carroll, p. 126.
[18] To Richardson, 10 October 1748, Barbauld, IV, 178.
[19] To Lady Bradshaigh, 15 December 1748, Carroll, pp. 110, 111.
[20] To Lady Bradshaigh, 26 October 1748, Carroll, p. 97; 15 December 1748, Carroll, p. 116.
[21] Quoted in *Hints of Prefaces*, p. 10.

Mary Delany, who after the second instalment had looked forward with 'Impatience to see her meet with a Reward to her Virtue', described to Richardson how she was 'almost broken-hearted at some Passages, and raised above this World in others ... By turns we read it, and many Times were obliged to throw down the Book, unable to proceed.'[22] Joseph Highmore's daughter Susanna reported a similar experience. Where Anna views Clarissa's corpse,

I laid down the Book, and felt for some Moments I verily think as much Affliction as such a Friend in real Life so circumstanc'd could feel ... I see, I hear, I feel the same, and am for the present as unhappy, as if it were all true ... and when I slept, I dream'd of them, and again saw their Distress, as my own Imagination represented it, not as a Fiction ... [W]e none of us could read aloud the affecting Scenes we met with; but each read to ourselves, and in separate Apartments wept –.[23]

Still more extreme was the case of Lady Bradshaigh who, having 'expected to suffer, but not to that degree I have suffered', found herself interrupting every third line of the deathbed scenes with renewed bouts of tears. The tears pursued her even when the book was closed: 'My spirits are strangely seized, my sleep is disturbed; waking in the night, I burst into a passion of crying; so I did at breakfast this morning, and just now again.'[24]

It might be objected that this collective lament was no more than a shallow emotional ritual, by which Richardson's readers, knowingly, could demonstrate and confirm their participation in some larger community of the feeling heart.[25] Yet what is most striking about the responses recorded here is not the characteristic self-congratulation of sentimentalism but rather their bitterness and violence: the overthrow of language by tears, the disintegration of the family reading party and the disruption of domestic routine reported by these readers indicate not so much a celebration of shared values as a painful challenge to them. In this respect Richardson's practice is as reminiscent of the seventeenth-century divine as of the eighteenth-century sentimentalist: rather than foster a Rousseauvian festival of tears he played, quite dispassionately, on the sensibilities of his readers, and forced them to look death in the eye. Tears were only the initial response to a challenge that ultimately required more deliberate efforts at remedy. 'You will hardly believe what pains I have taken to reconcile myself to the death of Clarissa, and to your catastrophe', wrote Lady Bradshaigh as she battled to draw the benefit of her mock bereavement.[26] Others passed more readily from the lament at Clarissa's death to a resolution to imitate it. 'I could scarce forbear wishing myself so

[22] To Richardson, 18 June 1748, FM XV, 2, f. 7; 25 January 1748/9, FM XV, 2, f. 13.
[23] To Richardson, 2 January 1748/9, FM XV, 2, f. 12.
[24] To Richardson, 11 January 1749, Barbauld, IV, 240; IV, 242.
[25] On emotional ritual in Richardson see Janet Todd, *Sensibility: An Introduction* (1986), esp. p. 83.
[26] To Richardson, 11 January 1749, Barbauld, IV, 243.

circumstanced, in the Agonies of instant Death', wrote Patrick Delany, now eloquent (not to say reckless) in his praise of the penitent heroine: 'God in his Mercy grant I may, when it shall please him to call me.'[27] The Sussex shopkeeper Thomas Turner wished for 'grace to lead my life in such a manner as my exit may in some respect be like that divine creature's'.[28] And Sarah Chapone, her epistolary voice weak and distraught only days after her husband's death, reported that during his final weeks the couple had returned, in preparation, to *Clarissa*: 'Clarissa's Death took such a possession of his mind, that he frequently spoke of it to me afterwards', she told Richardson, 'and I thought had an happy influence on his own Conduct when soon after, he came into the like trying Circumstances.'[29] As well as preparing readers to bear the deaths of their kin, the novel, it seems, could prepare them to undergo their own – 'to die', in an arresting phrase of Edward Young's, 'with safety and comfort'.[30]

This effort to reactivate the themes and methods of *Holy Dying* was not the only reason for Clarissa's death, however. The need to familiarise and exemplify was certainly of great importance to Richardson: justifying the ending, he told Lady Bradshaigh that he had himself been 'attacked' by 'no less than Eleven concerning Deaths' within two years; while one of his last literary acts was to suggest the inclusion in Young's *Conjectures upon Original Composition* (1759) of a passage recommending the emulation of Addison's pious end.[31] But there were also more immediate reasons for *Clarissa*'s insistence on calamity. Readers like Lady Bradshaigh had sought not only a continued life for Clarissa but also her marriage to Lovelace, and in this sense the clamour for happy resolution marked something more sinister than a flight from the reality of death. It also marked a Lovelacean response to the text, a naive acquiescence in the logic and standards of Lovelace's position that far exceeded Richardson's own readiness to tolerate (and at times embrace) interpretative variation. To marry the two antagonists as these readers proposed would have been to deny all meaning to the novel's basic struggle, and to fall in with Lovelace's own convenient explanations of his tyrannical conduct and claims. The theological and political metaphors at work in the text are enough to make clear the impossibility, for Richardson, of so doing. Obviously enough, Clarissa cannot compound with the tempter who has lured her from her paradise, or with the usurper who has drawn her into rebellion. To do so

[27] Delany's postscript, Mary Delany to Richardson, 25 January 1748/9, FM XV, 2, f. 13.
[28] *The Diary of Thomas Turner, 1754–1765*, ed. David Vaisey (Oxford, 1985), p. 32.
[29] To Richardson, 20 June 1759, FM XIII, 1, f. 155.
[30] To Richardson, 3 January 1758, *The Correspondence of Edward Young*, ed. Henry Pettit (Oxford, 1971), p. 467; see also Richardson's reply, p. 468.
[31] To Lady Bradshaigh, 15 December 1748, Carroll, p. 110; see Eaves and Kimpel, *Biography*, pp. 434–5.

would be, in terms recurrent in the text, to '*sanctify*' (VI, 278; p. 1141) or 'legitimate' (V, 282; p. 916) his depredations – to reduce to nothing, in effect, the moral, spiritual and social conflicts condensed within the novel. Even at the most literal level the happy ending would necessarily mean a kind of capitulation. For Clarissa to solicit 'with Tears, and upon her Knees', as some readers blamed her for failing to do, 'the only means upon Earth of recovering her Honour from the Stain of Violation',[32] would represent an unacceptably indulgent response to Lovelace's crime. Richardson's refusal to make such compromises, in defiance of the normative view (expressed by these same readers) that 'the Wounds of a Lady's Honour admit of no Cure but Marriage',[33] shows how far his thinking had progressed beyond *Pamela*'s wishful resolutions.

Thus when Lady Bradshaigh conceded that she could not 'help being fond of Lovelace' and protested at the construction of a character 'so wicked, and yet so agreeable', Richardson's response was a renewed attack on readers who had failed to detect Lovelace's dust-throwing. Their laxity had 'convinced me of the Necessity of such a Catastrophe as I have made', he wrote.[34] This catastrophe, in which the option of death prevails over the option of marriage, was a dramatic refutation of all Lovelace's assumptions about the veniality of his crimes, and of all his predictions of Clarissa's acquiescence – assumptions and predictions evidently embraced by many. In the 1751 postscript Richardson was quite explicit in linking the desire for a happy ending with the adoption of a Lovelacean interpretation of the history as a whole, pointing out that readers who had urged a comic resolution of the novel's struggle did so 'almost in the words of Lovelace, who was supported in his taste by all the women at Mrs. Sinclair's, and by Sinclair herself'.[35] To insist instead on an absolute incompatibility between Clarissa, Lovelace and all that each of them embodies was to admonish readers for their failure to resist Lovelace's fair words; and the rebuke was accepted by many. Fielding expected readers to be weaned from Lovelace by the final instalment, telling Richardson (on reading the fifth volume) that now 'his former Admirers must lose all Regard for him ... and as this Regard Ceases, Compassion for Clarissa rises in the same Proportion'.[36] Lady Bradshaigh reacted in just this way, Lovelace's representation in the third instalment forcing her to review and amend her response in the preceding two. 'Did I ever wish Clarissa to marry Lovelace?', she wrote in her copy. 'How I hate

[32] Reported by Edward Moore to Richardson, 1 October 1748, FM XV, 2, f. 17.

[33] Moore to Richardson, 1 October 1748, FM XV, 2, f. 17.

[34] Lady Bradshaigh to Richardson, 10 October 1748, Barbauld, IV, 180; Richardson to Lady Bradshaigh, 26 October 1748, Carroll, p. 92.

[35] *Clarissa*, 3rd edn (1751; rpt. New York, 1990), VIII, 278.

[36] To Richardson, 15 October 1748, *The Criticism of Henry Fielding*, ed. Williams, p. 188.

myself for it.'[37] In the closing volumes she at last recognised that Clarissa
and Lovelace were antagonists, and that their antagonism could not be
collapsed.

For all her spirit and wit, Lady Bradshaigh was above all a woman of
sentiment, and it was the immediacy of her own involvement in the
particular fate of characters to whom she had become attached that
moved her to intervene. Yet the happy ending was also urged, at one stage
or another, by figures of the greater stature of Fielding himself, James
Thomson, George Lyttleton and Colley Cibber,[38] a fact suggesting that
this impulse finally went beyond mere sentimental participation (though
the distresses of Cibber at least were naive enough for Lætitia Pilkington to
wonder whether, were *Clarissa* staged, 'he would not, like Don Quixote,
rise up in wrath and rescue the lady from the hands of her violater').[39] At
root, the difference between such readers and Richardson was ideological
in character. For the ending they hoped to forestall violated one of the
most cherished conventions of eighteenth-century letters – the notion of a
harmonious universe guaranteed by a benign Providence, which appears
in various forms in the work of at least three of these four readers[40] and is
underpinned by the confident theology of the day. The special intervention of God was a recurrent theme of the latitudinarian divines, for whom
the world was superintended by an active and just deity. 'Poor and
unarmed innocence and virtue is usually protected, and, sometimes,
rewarded in this world, and domineering and outrageous wickedness is
very often remarkably checked and chastised', wrote Tillotson. 'All which
instances of God's providence ... are ... an effectual declaration of that
goodness which governs all things, and of God's kind care of the affairs and
concernments of men.'[41] A comparable optimism underlies the conclusion
to Thomson's *The Seasons*, in which the many disorders and tribulations
encountered in the poem as a whole are resolved into a resonant affirmation of '*the great eternal Scheme* / Involving All, and in a *perfect Whole* /
Uniting'.[42] And it is a '*great eternal Scheme*' of just this kind that is celebrated
in the novels of Fielding, in which a harmoniously governed world
rewards the faith that characters such as Parson Adams place in 'the

---

[37] The Lady Bradshaigh *Clarissa*, V, 378, as reproduced in Bernard Quaritch's 1987 sale-catalo-
gue, *Samuel Richardson, Jane Austen: The Complete Novels and a Play.*

[38] Richardson to Hill, 7 November 1748, Carroll, p. 99. To Johannes Stinstra, Richardson later
singled out Fielding as 'a zealous Contender for the Piece ending, as it is called, happily'
(Slattery, pp. 33–4).

[39] To Richardson, 29 June 1745, Barbauld, II, 129.

[40] For Richardson, Lyttleton was the obvious exception, and he confessed himself puzzled to hear
objections to Clarissa's death from a writer whose own work embodied a recognition 'that
there cannot be an Exemption from Calamity here below' (Carroll, p. 100).

[41] Quoted by James Louis Fortuna, '*The Unsearchable Wisdom of God': A Study of Providence in
Richardson's Pamela* (Gainesville, 1980), p. 55.

[42] *The Seasons*, ed. James Sambrook (Oxford, 1981), p. 252 ('Winter', lines 1046–8).

Dispensations of Providence; being thoroughly assured, that all the Misfortunes, how great soever, which happen to the Righteous, happen to them for their own Good'.[43]

Clarissa's frustration of these confident assumptions about the prevalence of order and justice within the world is most clearly seen by comparison with *Tom Jones*. Here Fielding is concerned, like Richardson, with the fate of virtue in the world (albeit a virtue very different in definition), and he shares with Richardson a method of amplification by which his hero's fate can be seen in part to reflect the larger conditions of society and humanity in general. Here the similarity ends, however; for Fielding is at variance with Richardson in his readiness to locate his hero in a providential world where Tom is guided, protected and ultimately restored to fortune by a chain of happenings closely associated in the text with the work of a superintending power. Tom's personal fate implies larger endorsements, moreover. After his expulsion from 'Paradise Hall' and his subsequent wanderings (when '*The World*, as *Milton* phrases it, *lay all before him*; and *Jones*, no more than *Adam*, had any Man to whom he might resort for Comfort or Assistance'),[44] the hero's final providential rehabilitation suggests the fortune not only of a single man but of mankind itself, optimistically affirming the hope of postlapsarian regeneration.[45] In the context of the '45, more particularly, his eventual confirmation as Allworthy's recognised heir can also be seen as a political gesture in which the defeat of Jacobite usurpation and the final triumph of the post-Revolutionary order are celebrated and included within this larger pattern.[46] With such analogies, the novel hints at the beneficent government of Providence not only in the individual life but in the largest realms of politics and human history, extending into fiction the readiness of Fielding's journals to attribute such events such as the defeat of the '45 to 'GOD, the Deliverer of Nations' and to deny the more general proposition 'that this vast regular Frame of the Universe, and all the artful and cunning Machines therein were the Effects of Chance, of an irregular Dance of Atoms'.[47] The same optimistic determinism is reiterated in the novel's very form, the intricate yet harmonious structure of which acts as image and emblem of a world where (as Martin Battestin writes) 'a just and benign, all-knowing and all-powerful Intelligence ... orders and directs the affairs

[43] *Joseph Andrews and Shamela*, p. 237.   [44] *Tom Jones*, I, 331.

[45] See William W. Combs, 'The Return to Paradise Hall: An Essay on *Tom Jones*', *South Atlantic Quarterly*, 67 (1968), 435–6; J. Paul Hunter, *Occasional Form: Henry Fielding and the Chains of Circumstance* (Baltimore, 1975), pp. 187–9.

[46] See Kearney, '*Tom Jones* and the Forty-five'; Thomas E. Maresca, *Epic to Novel* (Ohio, 1974), pp. 213–16; Hunter, *Occasional Form*, pp. 185–6.

[47] *True Patriot*, ed. Coley, p. 274 (No. 26, 22–9 April 1746); *Champion* (22 January 1740), quoted by Martin C. Battestin, *The Providence of Wit: Aspects of Form in Augustan Literature and the Arts* (Oxford, 1974), p. 160.

of men toward a last, just close'.[48] Even when one takes into account the
countervailing strain of irony in which so much of Fielding's work is
couched, there remains a powerful sense in which the novel at once
articulates and satisfies its audience's desire for order, justice and completion.

   Clarissa, however, offers little of the same satisfaction: to look similarly
for some confident implicit theology in the discontinuous and antithetical
form of the novel, or simply in the hardships of its plot, is to find a less
happy picture. *Pamela* had of course observed the notion of divine superintendence, albeit in ambivalent terms: the novel's naive providentialism
must be attributed in the first place to Pamela alone,[49] but an editorial
voice does eventually join her in celebrating 'the Power of Providence' to
reward innocence within the world, 'and that, too, at a time when all
human Prospects seem to fail'.[50] Richardson, however, withdrew this
passage in 1742,[51] and thereafter alluded to his heroine's deliverance in
much more guarded terms.[52] In later work he preferred to present providential interventions as at best irregular; and the resulting contrast
between the worlds of *Pamela* and *Clarissa* is very great. *Clarissa*'s world is
chaos, one 'in which *innocent* and *benevolent* spirits are sure to be considered
as *aliens*, and to be made sufferers, by the *genuine sons* and *daughters of that
earth*' (VI, 87; p. 1020). There remain occasional hints of supernatural
movements, so that even Lovelace suspects 'something ... strangely retri-
butive' at work in the baroque deaths of his abettors (VII, 321; p. 1428);
but during Clarissa's lifetime providential intervention of any benignly
practical kind is conspicuously withheld. Divine justice is irregular, if not
entirely suspended, and life must be viewed as no better than a 'state of
temptation and tryal, of doubt and uncertainty' (VII, 241; p. 1377), the
duty of the Christian being not to expect present reward but to 'submit ...
to the dispensation with patience and resignation' (VI, 21; p. 980) – even,
as here, to the death.

   Richardson most forthrightly described this alternative 'dispensation' in
the revised postscript of 1751, perhaps in response to the publication in
1749 of *Tom Jones*. The relevant passage hits in general at the wishful
providentialism of his contemporaries: 'And shall man, presuming to alter
the common course of nature, and, so far as he is able, to elude the tenure
by which frail mortality indispensably holds, imagine, that he can make a
better dispensation; and by calling it *Poetical Justice*, indirectly reflect on
the *Divine?*'[53] 'The tenure by which frail mortality indispensably holds', of

[48] *The Providence of Wit*, p. 145; see also Aubrey Williams, 'Interpositions of Providence and the
   Design of Fielding's Novels', *South Atlantic Quarterly*, 70 (1971), 265–86.
[49] See above, pp. 21–3.   [50] *Pamela*, pp. 410–11.
[51] Eaves and Kimpel, 'Richardson's Revisions of *Pamela*', *Studies in Bibliography*, 20 (1967), 69.
[52] See *Grandison*, I, 3.   [53] *Clarissa*, 3rd edn (1751, rpt. New York, 1990), VIII, 288.

course, is the legacy of the Fall ('the curse upon us all': VI, 164; p. 1069), when mankind forfeited its right to absolute justice and exposed itself instead to 'the common course of nature', with all its vagaries; and Richardson is radically at odds with Fielding in his refusal to 'elude' these results. Though more reticent in its politics than *Tom Jones*, *Clarissa* is much more explicit, and more problematic, in its theodicy. The novel makes similar allusions to the grand sweep of human history, opening with Clarissa's fall from the 'paradise' of her father's house and tracing her perils and sufferings through the 'wilderness' beyond it. But Richardson's emphasis is very different, falling on isolation and adversity, not on guidance and care, and insisting always on the ascendancy of evil in the world. Like Adam and Eve, Clarissa is pursued from her paradise by a father's curse, which echoes the curses of Genesis 3 by condemning her to punishment at her tempter's hands (III, 259; p. 509). Like Job (Job being 'a Representative of Mankind in general', 'groaning under the spiritual Bondage of *Satan*, and waiting for their *Redemption* of it'),[54] she finds the curse fulfilled when Lovelace subjects her to 'the severest trials', as he recalls Satan did Job (III, 109; p. 430). There is thus a sense in which Clarissa, following these Biblical types, becomes 'a Representative of Mankind in general': her condition is that of humanity itself, labouring under the curse of the Fall and striving through adversity for redemption. She becomes, in her allegorical letter, a 'poor penitent', 'setting out with all diligence for my father's house' and 'overjoyed with the assurance of a thorough reconciliation, thro' the interposition of a dear blessed friend' (VII, 17; p. 1233) – the friend being (as Lovelace fails to perceive) the interceding Christ. Her progress is paradigmatic; and with these promises of restoration to a 'father's house' or paradise beyond the grave, and with the manifestation in the heroine's mind of certain forms of divine 'interposition', *Clarissa* clearly shares with *Tom Jones* a common concern to define the nature of a divine scheme.[55] But Richardson's *deus absconditus* is very unlike Fielding's benign intelligence, and the difference points in *Clarissa* to troubling conclusions – that the Fall demands in atonement perpetual struggle in a hostile world, and is only expiated by death.

In this context, one sees that in the end Richardson's insistence on *Clarissa*'s death went beyond the need to familiarise readers with mortality or to complete the repudiation of Lovelace: all forms of happy ending were now unavailable, simply because the just apportioning of reward and punishment within the world was for Richardson a false expectation. Thus when Cibber threw down his copy of *Clarissa* and refused to read another

54 William Worthington, *An Essay on the Scheme and Conduct, Procedure and Extent of Man's Redemption* (1743), pp. 494–6.
55 See Mary Poovey, 'Journeys from This World to the Next: The Providential Promise in *Clarissa* and *Tom Jones*', *ELH*, 43 (1976), 300–15.

line, declaring 'that he should no longer believe Providence, or eternal Wisdom, or Goodness governed the world, if merit, innocence, and beauty were to be so destroyed',[56] he had (for once) got the point. To deny the happy ending was to contest the comfortable ideology of the '*great eternal Scheme*', and to insist instead on a traditionally Christian view of global disorder. Clarissa's allegorical letter and Lovelace's 'unwilling' death point to the posthumous recompenses of a future state in which (as Belford tells Lovelace) 'thou wilt certainly meet with thy punishment ... as she will her reward' (VI, 171; p. 1073). But the world itself remains troublingly arbitrary in its dispensations, and fraught with injustice. Given the confidence of *Tom Jones*, *The Seasons* and even *Love's Last Shift*, it is easy to see why their authors resisted an ending which instead alleged the destructiveness of evil, the absence of providential care, and Richardson's version of the skull beneath the skin, the coffin in the bedchamber. By suggesting that the novel's conflicts be brought to just resolution, they were averting their gaze from the hostility of its represented world. By sticking to his guns, Richardson prevented them from doing so – or left them only the petulant means of escape that Cibber seemingly took.

While offending these 'Augustans', however, *Clarissa*'s published ending pleased readers less disposed to accept the primacy of order and harmony within the world. In the *Spectator* paper cited in the postscript, Addison had attacked poetic justice as both irreligious and empirically invalid, untrue to a world in which 'Good and Evil happen alike to all Men'.[57] It was to this idea that Richardson's supporters referred. For Philip Skelton, almost all novels except *Clarissa* were 'planned upon an atheistical footing', denying the Christian view of 'life, at the best, as a state of vanity and vexation of spirit'. For John Channing, 'the desire of having your piece end happily (as 'tis called) will ever be the test of a wrong head, and a vain mind' – vain in neglecting the reality of injustice and adversity, and in failing to look beyond it.[58] The most interesting such statement comes in a three-cornered debate on *Clarissa* and the nature of Providence conducted early in 1749 between John Duncombe, George Jeffreys and Joseph Highmore. Duncombe suggested in the first place that 'such subjects tend to impeach the justice of Providence'. Jeffreys replied that Providence manifestly was *not* just, within the world at least ('We must account, in the best manner we can, for the dark dispensations of Providence recorded in history'); but he was at one with Duncombe in thinking that literature at least should paper over its cracks. 'Those dispensations which confirm some atheists, make others, puzzle the wise, and shock the good, can answer no desirable end in books', he insisted, and they should

---

[56] Lætitia Pilkington to Richardson, 29 June 1745, Barbauld, II, 128.   [57] *Spectator*, I, 169.
[58] Skelton, *Complete Works*, ed. Robert Lynam, 6 vols. (1824), VI, 248; Channing to Richardson, 31 October 1748, Barbauld, II, 334.

have been avoided in *Clarissa*. Richardson was only acquitted when Highmore instead persuaded the two correspondents that in faithfully representing the vagaries of the fallen world rather than resorting to a wishful providentialism, *Clarissa* was more rather than less Christian. 'Perhaps Clarissa's is the "best manner" of accounting for them', he wrote in reference to Jeffreys's 'dark dispensations'.[59] There were indeed reasons for attributing to *Clarissa* an explanatory force of this kind. Instead of skirting the problem, habitually evaded by eighteenth-century writers, of providential inequality, the novel directly addresses it, urging an older, bleaker theology in place of the usual bland assertions of cosmic harmony and beneficence. Richardson himself often repeated this explanation, citing both religion and experience in his support. Where Addison objected to Tate's 'Poetical Justice' he amplified the phrase to read 'Poetical (*or, as we may say, Anti-Providential*) Justice', calling on a definition of Providence very unlike Fielding's (VII, 428; p. 1497). When Lady Bradshaigh protested at his 'crime' in leaving 'vice triumphant, and virtue depressed', he explained that 'a writer who follows Nature and pretends to keep the Christian System in his Eye, cannot make a Heaven in this World for his Favourites; or represent this Life otherwise than as a State of Probation'.[60]

William Warburton, author of the preface to *Clarissa*'s second instalment and a subtler theologian than many of his contemporaries, wholeheartedly agreed. Like Richardson, Warburton was not above the occasional invocation of supernatural care: the deity weighs in like an Olympian at Troy in his account of Culloden, for example, which Cumberland wins 'under the manifest Guidance of Providence'.[61] But in his monumental *Divine Legation of Moses Demonstrated* (1738–41) Warburton insisted that the equal and extraordinary Providence celebrated in the Old Testament was not a universal condition, but particular to a single phase of Jewish history. The present dispensation, by contrast, was one in which 'the affairs of men wear a form of great irregularity: the scene, that ever and anon presents itself, being of distressed virtue, and prosperous wickedness'.[62] Central to his argument was the representation of distressed virtue in the Book of Job, a text he dated to the period in which the extraordinary Providence was gradually withdrawn, and which he saw as an attempt to make sense of its breakdown. In addressing the questions '*Whether, and why, good men are unhappy, and the evil prosperous?*', the Book of

59 John Duncombe, ed., *Letters, by Several Eminent Persons Deceased*, 2nd edn, 3 vols. (1773), II, 182; II, 192; II, 211.
60 Lady Bradshaigh to Richardson, 10 October 1748, Barbauld, IV, 179; Richardson to Lady Bradshaigh, 15 December 1748, Carroll, p. 108.
61 *A Sermon Preach'd at the Thanksgiving Appointed To Be Observed the Ninth of October, for the Suppression of the Late Unnatural Rebellion* (1746), p. 12.
62 *The Divine Legation of Moses Demonstrated*, 4th edn (1764-5), I, 24.

Job worked to console the captive Jews, appeasing 'their doubts concerning God's Providence ... by an humble acquiescence under his almighty power'.[63]

Perhaps in response to Richardson's many allusions to the precedent of Job,[64] Warburton later attributed a similar project to *Clarissa*. In a letter to Richardson which appears to offer a supplementary preface for the third instalment, he sketches a defence of Clarissa's death as an event which remains true to the realities of adversity and injustice in the world, while also satisfying the belief in divine care. The novel does so, he suggests, by describing a form of interposition that avoids the supernatural, remaining as it does on an internal, spiritual plane. Clarissa is delivered as Job is delivered, but within her own mind: she suffers 'that long & terrible attack & combat on her Virtue which here so entangled her in the miseries of life that nothing could free her from or make her tryumphant over them but divine grace which now comes, like the God in the catastrophe of the Ancient fable [i.e. Job], to clear up all difficulties'. To explain this point, he goes on, will 'remove that silly objection ag^t the *too tragical* catastrophe' – an objection which arises 'both from want of sense & of religion' and neglects that 'an overflow of divine grace upon the human mind' is the ultimate happiness. 'I give you this hint that you may work up the concluding scene of her life as seraphicly as you can', he adds: 'cast over it that sunshine that may be able to dispell all the [impressions] that the foregoing had made upon minds really & not pretendly tender'.[65]

Doubtless Clarissa's death would have been seraphic enough without this 'hint', and there is no firm evidence to suggest that Richardson accepted the offer of a further preface. The postscript is theologically very close to Warburton, however, and it may at least have been influenced by him. Its tone is very Warburtonian when it rails against those who 'propagate another Sort of Dispensation ... than that with which God, by Revelation, teaches us, he has thought fit to exercise Mankind; whom, placing here only in a State of *Probation*, he hath so intermingled Good and Evil, as to necessitate them to look forward for a more equal Distribution of both' (VII, 425–6; p. 1495).

There is, then, a coherent theological basis to *Clarissa*'s ending, and one

[63] *Divine Legation*, V, 22; V, 61.

[64] On *Clarissa*'s use of Job see Robert A. Erickson, '"Written in the Heart": *Clarissa* and Scripture', *Eighteenth-Century Fiction*, 2, No. 1 (1989), 17–52; Keymer, 'Richardson's *Meditations*: Clarissa's *Clarissa*'.

[65] To Richardson, 25 April 1748, Barbauld, VI, facsimile page. It might be added that Warburton saw grace in *Clarissa*, which 'clear[s] up all difficulties', as an improvement on 'the God in the catastrophe of the Ancient fable'. In the *Divine Legation*, he had complained that in Job 'the Interposition was no more than a piece of poetical Machinery', and 'clears up *no* difficulties' (V, 22–3; my italics).

more rather than less in keeping with traditional Christian thought than the kind of optimistic affirmation desired by the likes of Colley Cibber. Yet for all that, the disinclination of readers to do as the postscript recommends and simply 'look forward' is understandable enough. To an audience accustomed to the straightforward reinforcement or satisfaction of ideological assumptions and emotional needs that was a primary function of the pre-Richardsonian novel,[66] the contrariness of *Clarissa* was disturbing throughout, but most of all in its final volumes. Even after publication, when the impossibility of marriage and the necessity of Clarissa's death were generally recognised, readers continued to resist the ending and tried to reassert, in their readings and rewritings of the text, some transcendent principle of coherence. In the end they could accept the '*too tragical*' fact of death; but many could never accept the '*too tragical*' implications of a world ungoverned by moral resolution – a world of which Clarissa's undeserved fate was merely a local symptom. The novel's denial of what Frank Kermode has called 'the sense of an ending', that final gratifying resolution which lends a retrospective completeness and meaning to lives and texts,[67] seemed intolerable; and most intolerable of all was the absence of visible justice. Many readers were equally troubled in this regard by the nature of *Lovelace*'s death, in which justice is neither formally recognised nor formally done. James Beattie lamented 'that the punishment of Lovelace is a death, not of infamy, according to our notions, but rather of honour; which surely he did not deserve: and that the immediate cause of it is, not his wickedness, but some inferiority to his antagonist in the use of the small sword'. (Beattie's solution to the problem would have involved 'a series of mortifications, leading him gradually down to infamy, ruin, and despair, or producing by probable means an exemplary repentance' thus bringing to the novel a satisfying moral coherence.)[68] The same anxiety takes vivid and intriguing form in Pierre Cuisin's post-revolutionary fusing of *Clarissa* and *Les Liaisons dangereuses* in *Le Bâtard de Lovelace et la fille naturelle de la Marquise de Merteuil, ou Les Mœurs vengées* (1806). Where Beattie favours unequivocal degradation or penitence, this novel proposes an exemplary punishment by means of the secular law. As Lovelace's bastard is denounced, sentenced and beheaded (his character clearly representing a degenerate aristocracy and the manner of his death clearly suggesting the revolutionary guillotine), Cuisin celebrates '*la voix de la justice, pendant quelque temps muette*', which now thunders again. '*Elle en triomphe enfin: la tête de Falselace est tranchée et tombe au milieu du plus terrible appareil des lois, et à la gloire des mœurs*

---

[66] See John J. Richetti, *Popular Fiction before Richardson: Narrative Patterns, 1700–1739* (Oxford, 1969), pp. 8–22, 262–5.
[67] See Frank Kermode, *The Sense of an Ending: Studies in the Theory of Fiction* (1967), pp. 3–31.
[68] Beattie, *Dissertations Moral and Critical* (1783), p. 569.

vengées.'[69] These were pleasures, emphatically, that Richardson had denied.

Justice and justification in Lady Echlin's ending

The fullest testimony to the 'will to justice' frustrated by *Clarissa*'s final volumes comes in an elaborate alternative ending written by Lady Bradshaigh's sister, Elizabeth Echlin. Lady Bradshaigh herself (even after she had relinquished her project of marrying Clarissa to Lovelace) plotted an alternative ending in which the rape fails, Clarissa recovers to live a single life and Lovelace, wounded by James, becomes 'a cripple, & a sincere penitent'.[70] But Lady Echlin went further, realising her own desire for a more harmonious conclusion in a lengthy manuscript pastiche of Richardson's text. In it she accepts, at least superficially, the 'tragic' ending, so that both Clarissa and Lovelace die. But she changes the circumstances completely: the rape is removed, Clarissa dies of grief while Lovelace, reformed by her example, dies a penitent, and 'will forever rejoyce in that immortal state, where smileing Angels – Exult with joy, at the conversation [*sic*] of a sinner'.[71] Reconciliation is only deferred, in such a way (as Richardson saw) that the deaths themselves lost meaning. 'If I had come into your Ladiship's Scheme, I think, I would have permitted her to live, and made her the Cause of every one's Happiness', he politely teased her, going on to suggest that Lovelace 'might have been made a Governor of one of the American Colonies', where he would enact 'Laws promotive of Religion and good Manners'.[72] For while retaining the deaths Lady Echlin had removed the conditions that gave rise to them – the conditions of a world in which evil is real and unconquerable, justice is guaranteed neither by human structures nor by supernatural intervention, and meanings remain vexed and obscure. Though keeping the external signs, she had suppressed the gloomier implications of *Clarissa*'s world – implications which, she frankly wrote, she found intolerable. She had rewritten *Clarissa* because the published ending 'serve[d] only to wound good minds', had 'agitated', 'oppresst, or distracted' her own, and was 'horribly shocking to humanity' (pp. 172–3). Clearly enough, what she called 'the woeful complicated distress attending innocence, virtue, and religion' was an affront not only to her sensibility but to her whole world-view, challenging assumptions she expected the novel instead to

---

69 Pierre Cuisin, *Le Bâtard de Lovelace et la fille naturelle de la Marquise de Merteuil, ou Les Mœurs vengées* (Paris, 1806), I, 10.

70 The Lady Bradshaigh *Clarissa*, facing VII, 432. See also Eaves and Kimpel, *Biography*, p. 234.

71 Lady Elizabeth Echlin, *An Alternative Ending to Richardson's Clarissa*, ed. Dimiter Daphinoff (Bern, 1982), p. 166. Further references to the *Alternative Ending* are given in brackets in the text.

72 To Lady Echlin, 18 February 1755, Daphinoff, pp. 177, 178.

satisfy and confirm. As well as disturbing her personally, it thereby thwarted what she took for Richardson's intended moral. 'I was sensible of the author's laudable intention, but shall ever think him mistaken in the method towards accomplishing his several great ends. Too sure I am, the good design is not effectually answered.'[73]

When Lady Echlin attempted her own rectification of this 'good design' remains unclear. She sent the manuscript to Richardson only in 1755, but probably conceived the idea on reading the final instalment in winter 1748–9 when, 'in the midst of my intolerable vexation, I endeavoured to divert my thoughts from horrible scenes by the strength of fancy'.[74] Whatever the timing, diversion of thoughts is certainly the result. The two related sources of her 'intolerable vexation', the prevalence of evil in Clarissa's world and the absence from it of a perfect and universally recognised justice, are dispelled by the classic moves of sentimentalism. First she alters Richardson's cast, countering what she presumably took for an inadvisably bleak vision of human degeneracy by introducing such worthies as Mr Friendly, Dr Christian the clergyman, Mr Carefull the surgeon and every imaginable exemplar of practical benevolence short of Mrs Bunn the baker's wife. She then sets about the plot, not only cancelling the rape but reaffirming, at many other opportunities, the comfortable principle that evil can only crumble before the resistless power of virtue. Conversions abound: no member of Lovelace's 'horrible pack of Diabolical wretches' (p. 42) can last more than a round with Clarissa before collapsing at her feet in an agony of sobbing regeneracy. 'Tomlinson was moved – he groaned – wiped tears from his eyes – and seemed to struggle for speech. he fell downe upon his knees, and said – I am an impious wretch' (p. 41). Even Lovelace, instead of committing the rape, falls into a Mackenzian fit of catatonic sensibility: 'he started – turn'd pail! a horrible distraction appear'd in his countenance; he dropt into a chair – unable to speak for many minuts' (p. 108). He soon makes up for his dumbness, however, inviting Clarissa and the now penitent Sally Martin to observe 'this once dareing – insolent – vile seducer, an humble, peniten[t,] trembling sinner' (p. 109) – a habit he persists in until silenced, mercifully, by the final stages of consumption. He also illustrates his reformation by responding to a challenge from James Harlowe with a Grandisonian lecture on 'the henious offence of Duel-fighting' (p. 151), spoiling the effect only by carelessly holding his sword at such an angle that his challenger falls on it and dies. James lasts long enough to concede that the accident was entirely his fault, however, so that nothing is left to counter Dr Christian's view of Lovelace's regeneracy as 'a great Example'

[73] Lady Echlin to Richardson, 12 August 1754, Barbauld, V, 19.
[74] Lady Echlin to Richardson, 12 August 1754, Barbauld, V, 20.

of libertinism's defeat, showing 'that, thro' devine grace, this notorious profligate, may prove an Exemplary penitent' (p. 113).

For Lady Echlin, Lovelace's conversion was a crucial affirmation of the practical supremacy of good, providing 'an instructive lesson' which 'might help to reform the Licentious, and mend the present age' (pp. 171, 172). But in *Clarissa* itself 'a most beautifull contrast is lost, if this accomplish'd Libertine be not reformed by Clarissas virtuous conversation', which in her own version 'so strongly wrought upon the mind of this once bad principle'd man, that it brought him to a just sense of his own vile inormity – he ... became a sincere convert, spent the twelve months he survived Clarissa, in imitating his dear departed; constantly observing her pious way of life, & dy'd a true penitent' (p. 172). The innate power of virtue is aided, in this, by the deity's guiding hand. Echlin remains keen to restore the fiction of an active Providence, explaining Clarissa's sufferings as the means taken by it to secure the reformation of sinners, so that various encounters which enable her to make new converts can be described as 'providential' (pp. 69, 107), the work of 'a superiour power' (p. 78). And just deserts, except in Clarissa's case, are providentially apportioned within the world. Echlin thought 'that cruel sister Arabella, & wicked Brother James shou'd haue Exemplary punishment', while Mrs Norton and Dolly Hervey 'ought to be treated according to their merit' (p. 171). James therefore dies and Bella is married off to 'a dirty, stinking, cross-leg'd prick-louse' by the name of Mr Cabbage (pp. 162–3). Clarissa's uncles settle fortunes on Miss Hervey and Mrs Norton's son, and look forward to the time when the wealthy pair 'may swing in a hammock together' (p. 143) – though not, of course, before the solemnities of 'holy matrimony' are done.

The most signal victory of justice, however, lies not in the defeat of evil and these various deserved ends, but in the consensus eventually established between all characters in their judgment of events. The triumph of virtue, by the end of Echlin's manuscript, is so luminous that all participants converge on a single coherent interpretation of the history, in which every character and event is assigned by universal consent to one of two polarised categories, black or white. Justice cannot be done in the sense of saving Clarissa; but it can be (and is) done in the sense of establishing the absolute prevalence of a single view of the story. A simple, lucid and above all an uncontested meaning is attached to Clarissa's life within the text, so that all the moral indeterminacies and cruxes of the original novel are definitively settled. Dr Christian, for example, conveniently resolves the first instalment's case of conscience, to make Clarissa 'quite guiltless' and the Harlowes 'heinously guilty' in the matter of her flight from her father's house: 'what you call a breach of Duty', he reassures her, 'was not an act of choice; for you were force'd to refuse what you cou'd not conscientiously

agree to; your compliance, in that case, wou'd be faulty – then consequently, you cannot be guilty of sinfull disobedience by not complying'
(p. 82). Lovelace abandons his palliations and instead embraces the·
language of his antagonist, incongruously praising her 'laudable
resentment' on discovering 'that I had placed her among a vile pack of
prostitutes to compass my base design' (p. 146). The only remaining
matter for dispute lies in the lengths to which each penitent will go in his
endeavour to set the record straight. Lovelace is 'impatien[t] to justify
wronged Clarissa' (p. 147) and the Harlowes too do 'all in their power to
justify, much wronged Clarissa' (p. 141), each vying with the other to do
most, by a clear and self-abasing exposition, to condemn himself. James
wins by a short head, and in his lengthy self-reproaches gives voice to
Echlin's residually Lovelacean sympathies. 'I haue been more guilty than
[Lovelace]', he declares, 'on my innocent sister's account; I was the author
of her severe trials! the principle cause of poor Clarissa's sad distress, and
cannot plead any thing in Excuse for such un-natural cruelty'
(pp. 153–4). But these are mere details. The main verdict is simple and
universally agreed, and not the least complication can cloud the blaze of
glory in which the heroine ascends. Justice may not have been perfectly
done; but it has, more importantly, been *seen*, and universally agreed.

   Had Richardson been the sentimental didact Lady Echlin took him for,
he would perhaps have advanced his 'good design' in something like this
alternative ending, with its avoidance of all vexedness, its rigidly binary
interpretations, and its easy ideological satisfaction. But he was not. He
wanted to make his reader confront all the problems, injustices and
indeterminacies collapsed by the trite consensus, the moral simplification
and the semantic closure to which she would bring the novel. In Echlin's
version he found ample evidence of her own 'Piety' and 'excellent Heart';
but he also found a wishful simplification of his text (as he made clear
when reminding her, for example, that Clarissa 'must be allowed to share
[Lovelace's] Fault, in putting herself in his Power').[75] Yet Echlin's alternative, whatever its bathos, still has its uses; for in its many evasions and
divergences it highlights the real nature of *Clarissa*'s challenge to the
reader – a challenge that requires the reader to face up to, and reach terms
with, a world devoid of providential control, infallible justice, or indeed of
any transcendent form of clarity or coherence. In representing this confused world, most disconcertingly of all, Richardson allows the same
confusion to infect the text itself. For in his own ending this troubling
denial of coherence in the end concerns not events alone but also the
interpretation of them, the meanings affixed to them within the world.
The final instalment thus carries to a logical extreme its sense of the

[75] To Lady Echlin, 18 February 1755, Daphinoff, p. 177.

postlapsarian suspension of justice: meanings, like everything else, are
fallen too, the underlying irresolution of the novel coming to involve not
only the actual outcome of Clarissa's life, but also the narrative form in
which that life is communicated to the reader, and offered up for
judgment.

Cavils about words: language, narration and the legal paradigm in Richardson's ending

As Sarah Fielding was the first to note, the interpretations and objections
of *Clarissa*'s readers are generally anticipated by the interpretations and
objections of characters in the text itself.[76] The third instalment perfectly
illustrates her point. Justice and resolution are as much the preoccupations
of Clarissa's friends as they were of the novel's first audience. Moreover,
the remedies they urge are the same: only by marriage to Lovelace or
(failing that) by formal judicial vindication, they insist, can the tribulations of her life be adequately settled. Parallels between the attitudes of
characters within the novel and those of its readers are inescapable – but
in this case whether Richardson is anticipating reader response or reacting
to it is not so easily distinguished. By exploring the possibility of alternative endings *inside* the closing volumes, he not only set the terms of the
debates that followed publication but also parodied and answered
responses of which he was aware well before his extensive final revisions in
the summer and autumn of 1748. Thus the roles of text and reception are
peculiarly intertwined. It is the text, in its final instalment, that responds
to its readers, as much as vice versa. It gives voice to their desires,
challenges the legitimacy of these desires, and eventually denies them the
comfortable resolutions they had sought – the resolutions of justice, both in
the world and on the page.

The marriage question is the novel's last great case of conscience,
exhaustively debated between Anna Howe and Lovelace's family, who
urge marriage, and Clarissa, who rejects it. Here the proponents of
marriage show themselves little more able to think beyond convention
than the readers who had been shocked at Clarissa's refusal to plead for it
herself. They present the option as a form of just reparation: Belford,
typically, thinks it 'the only medium that can be hit upon, to salve the
honour of both' (V, 378; p. 969). Yet the very insistence with which
Lovelace himself uses the term 'justice'[77] in this context is enough to
suggest its invalidity in a case where marriage would not repair the rape so
much as exonerate it. When his kinswomen insist on 'the justice due to
Miss Harlowe' he even questions the word himself, mocking their implicit

[76] *Remarks on Clarissa*, p. 41.
[77] See V, 228 (p. 886); V, 255 (p. 902); V, 263 (p. 907); V, 323 (p. 939).

view of marriage as '*an atonement for all we can do*' (VI, 118; p. 1039).
Elsewhere he asks: 'Will not the generality of the world acquit me, if I *do*
marry? And what is that injury which a *church rite* will at any time repair.
Is not *the catastrophe of every story that ends in wedlock accounted happy* . . . ?'
(V, 331; p. 944). The rebuke to readers is clear. Clarissa's letters, which
explicitly challenge the equation between marriage and justice, repeat the
point in less ironic form. To marry would be 'to *sanctify* . . . Mr. Lovelace's
repeated breaches of all moral sanctions', she says (VI, 278; p. 1141); she
will not '*creep* to the violator, and be thankful to him for doing me poor
justice' (VI, 239; p. 116).

When these illusions about the eligibility of marriage are at last stripped
away, Clarissa's adherents continue to seek other means of bringing her
case to tidy resolution, and turn instead to the option of prosecution. The
two alternatives seem far apart; yet they have a common point. Both offer
ways of settling the case unambiguously, either by bringing Clarissa and
Lovelace into union or by working out, formally, their antagonism: the
equivalence of each as a form of desirable clarification is perfectly
expressed in the Manx law cited by Anna, in which the victim of rape is
presented with a rope, a sword and a ring, and thus 'has it in her choice to
have him hanged, beheaded, or to marry him' (VI, 83; p. 1017). Dr
Lewen makes a similar link: 'the reparation of your family dishonour, now
rests in your own bosom', he tells Clarissa, 'and which only one of these
two alternatives *can* repair; to wit, either to Marry, or to prosecute him at
Law' (VII, 46; p. 1251). Accordingly, the pressure on Clarissa to marry
gradually modulates into a pressure to prosecute – a considerable demand,
since in the absence of official machinery the initiative for prosecution
normally rested at the time with the injured party, who would be termed
the 'prosecutor' and whose responsibility it would be to prepare the case,
assemble witnesses and take the lead in laying out the evidence in court.[78]

Yet it soon becomes clear that the law, like marriage, is equally flawed
as a means of doing justice. It is not simply that Clarissa might be unable
to carry through her task as prosecutor, though that is indeed a factor: as
Fielding wrote in criticism of the prevailing system, many crimes went
untried because victim-prosecutors were 'Delicate, and cannot appear in a
public Court', 'Tender-hearted, and cannot take away the Life of a Man'
or 'Necessitous, and cannot really afford the Cost' – all relevant constraints in Clarissa's case.[79] Even if willing and able to bring the case to
trial, however, she would by no means be assured of success. Instead of
definitively establishing her own innocence and Lovelace's guilt, she
suggests, a public trial would in all likelihood further confuse the two.

[78] J. M. Beattie, *Crime and the Courts in England, 1660–1800* (Oxford, 1986), p. 35.
[79] *An Enquiry into the Causes of the Late Increase of Robbers*, p. 154; see also the reasons stated in
Clarissa's letter to Dr Lewen (VI, 48–52; pp. 1252–5).

Circumstances such as her clandestine dealings with him at Harlowe Place
and her long residence at 'Dover Street' make against her; his rhetorical
powers would give him the advantage in court; and even if convicted he
has influence enough to win himself a pardon. The predictable result, in
fact, would be not his condemnation but her own: she would be 'censured
as pursuing with sanguinary views a man who offered me early all the
reparation in his power to make', and vulnerable also to the jibe 'that I
ought to take for my pains what had befallen me' (VII, 49; p. 1253). Carol
Houlihan Flynn has argued, with telling reference to eighteenth-century
rape trials, that in a real case similarly circumstanced acquittal would
indeed have been the likely outcome.[80] But internal evidence alone, given
the novel's almost Godwinian insistence on the corruptibility of law, lends
weight enough to Clarissa's qualms. The text abounds with cynical allusions to the vicissitudes and injustices of the courtroom, Lovelace ironically praising 'the *Lawyer*, who, for the sake of a paltry fee, undertakes to
whiten a black cause, and to defend it against one he knows to be good'
(V, 288–9; p. 920), while Belford uses the phrase 'the true Old Bailey
construction' (V, 376; p. 968) as an accepted synonym for the successful
imposition of a lie. And though Lovelace may be improvising when he
claims to be a Justice of the Peace (VI, 385; p. 1211), he is certainly right
that the highest legal authorities do not immediately suggest the ideal of
impartial efficiency. Lord M. and his like, he points out, are 'judges ... in
the last resort' (VII, 338; p. 1438) – Lord M. being not only a patrician
and a chauvinist but also a buffoon, his judgment rapidly and easily
clouded by his nephew's rhetorical powers. The law is clearly no more
able than marriage to make Clarissa amends, and the instincts of her
friends (as of *Clarissa*'s readers) must be thwarted. Justice appears unavailable and remains undone: Clarissa dies; Lovelace too dies unjustly, though
unjustly in another sense. He dies not by legal sentence but by duelling,
'an usurpation of the Divine prerogative' and 'an insult upon magistracy
and good government' (VII, 347; p. 1444). Instead of marking the
triumph of justice, his death completes its defeat.

In furtherance of Richardson's theological emphases, Clarissa looks to a
future state as the realm in which all will be set to rights. Yet there also
remains one less otherworldly medium in which justice may be reasserted.
In her letter to Dr Lewen, she hints at an alternative means to the
litigation he has urged as a way of establishing, within the world, her own
innocence and Lovelace's guilt. Pleas which might have procured little
advantage in the hostile environment of a public arraignment ('perhaps
bandied about, and jested profligately with') would have carried greater
weight '*out of court*, and to a *private* and *serious* audience', she suggests (VII,

[80] Flynn, *Samuel Richardson: A Man of Letters*, pp. 110–15; on the difficulty of securing convictions
for rape see also Beattie, *Crime and the Courts*, pp. 124–32.

49; p. 1253). There is, of course, one obvious means available of putting the case before 'a *private* and *serious* audience', and by now such preparations are already under way. 'Miss Howe is sollicitous to have all those letters and materials preserved, which will set my whole story in a true light', Clarissa goes on, adding that this compilation of literary evidence 'may be more efficacious ... to the end wished for, than my appearance could have been in a court of justice, pursuing a doubtful event, under the disadvantages I have mentioned' (VII, 51; pp. 1254–5). Justice may be done by a book which will imitate the processes of the courtroom, but which will also be immune to its vagaries. Like the formal prosecution which Clarissa is urged but refuses to mount, the book will gather, arrange and present all the evidence relevant to the case, accumulating the testimonies of the parties concerned and submitting them to the reader for judgment. It will be the literary equivalent of a trial.

Clarissa is not the only novel to propose analogies between its own narrative organisation and the formal processes of a trial (though it may have been the first).[81] A century later, the principal narrator and supposed editor of Wilkie Collins's *The Woman in White* introduces the novel with reference to forensic practice, presenting it as an infallible literary substitute for the fallible operations of the law. 'As the Judge might once have heard it, so the Reader shall hear it now', Walter Hartright writes:

No circumstance of importance, from the beginning to the end of the disclosure, shall be related on hearsay evidence. When the writer of these introductory lines ... happens to be more closely connected than others with the incidents to be recorded, he will describe them in his own person. When his experience fails ... his task will be continued ... by other persons who can speak to the circumstances under notice from their own knowledge, just as clearly and positively as he has spoken before them.

Thus, the story here presented will be told by more than one pen, as the story of an offence against the laws is told in Court by more than one witness – with the same object, in both cases, to present the truth always in its most direct and intelligible aspect; and to trace the course of one complete series of events, by making the persons who have been most closely connected with them, at each successive stage, relate their own experience, word for word.[82]

With this method Collins is able to unfold the ensuing mystery with an unusual effect of immediacy, placing his reader in the privileged position of a jury which gathers, from the evidence of the engaged parties, the complete facts of a case. Here, as Hartright suggests, testimony is always

---

81 For another eighteenth-century example see Robert J. Ellrich, 'The Rhetoric of *La Religieuse* and Eighteenth-Century Forensic Rhetoric', *Diderot Studies*, 3 (1961), 129–54. The close links between this novel and *Clarissa* are the subject of Rita Goldberg's *Sex and Enlightenment*, pp. 169–204, though Goldberg is concerned here not so much with narrative rhetoric as with thematic and ideological links.

82 *The Woman in White*, ed. Harvey Peter Sucksmith (Oxford, 1973), p. 1.

straightforward, the distortions of 'hearsay' are avoided, and the desired 'disclosure' becomes correspondingly more perfect and complete.

Clarissa, however, gives no such guarantee of presenting 'the truth always in its most direct and intelligible aspect'. As recent critics have stressed, the novel's internal account of its own composition is too emphatic, and too tortuous, not to bring with it more problematic implications. For Warner, the plan to compile a documentary record of Clarissa's life can be seen not as a neutral 'disclosure' of the sort described in Collins's novel, but as a rhetorical feat which overtakes even the rape as the novel's central act. 'Lovelace's violence against Clarissa', he writes, 'plants the seed for a more insidious will to power over others: Clarissa's idea for a book that will tell her story'[83] – a disconcerting overstatement, but a useful reminder at the same time of Richardson's preoccupation not only with the injustices suffered by Clarissa but also with the attempts of all concerned to define them, retributively, in words. In documenting these attempts, Richardson leaves little room for naive equations between truth, testimony and justice of the kind implied by Collins, developing the forensic analogy instead in far less comfortable ways. Warner, however, has simplified the problem. To present the book-building simply as a semantic conspiracy engineered by a vindictive Clarissa is to misrepresent her role, which remains ambiguous; for the idea of translating a life in which justice remains undone into a book in which justice may be definitively and immutably restored begins not with her but with the Howes. It begins, moreover, just as her faith in the capacity of language to provide a just or true account of the world has most evidently collapsed.

From the outset, the projected history is linked to the idea of prosecution. In a letter pressing Clarissa 'to appear in court, to do justice to herself' (VI, 82; p. 1016), Anna also urges that she formulate her plea in the more enduring form of a memoir-narrative. 'I long for the full particulars of your sad story', she tells Clarissa (VI, 83; p. 1017). But she longs, in fact, for rather more: she longs for a full definition of it. As well as reporting 'particulars', the memoir she envisages will organise and interpret them, thus delivering to the reader, ready-made, the transcendent meaning of Clarissa's life. What she proposes is the very antithesis of epistolary collage – a closed, continuous and authoritative account, clearly organised in terms of a consistent self, a coherent sequence of cause and effect, and a categorical moral gloss. It will clarify once and for all a struggle which, as Anna's hints at 'some weakness, or lurking love' on Clarissa's part suggest (VI, 82; p. 1016), might otherwise seem dangerously blurred. 'The villainy of the worst of men, and the virtue of the most excellent of women, I expect will be exemplified in it, were it to be written

[83] *Reading Clarissa*, p. 75.

in the same connected and particular manner, that you used to write to me in' (VI, 83; p. 1017). Anna's expectations are clear enough: the retrospective organisation and didactic rhetoric of the memoir will guarantee its efficacy as an alarm to the unwary and as a definitive vindication of its author. As she predicts in a later letter which again urges Clarissa to set about 'penning [her] sad story', her 'noble conduct throughout [her] trials and calamities will afford not only a shining Example to [her] Sex; but ... a fearful Warning to the inconsiderate young creatures of it' (VI, 296; p. 1152). Her view of the relations between writing and experience is wholly unproblematic. The one, in the ideal form of the connected and particular memoir, will distil, fix and infallibly convey the essential truths of the other.

Such a memoir might indeed prompt objections. But it proves impossible to write. For Clarissa herself, the activity of 'penning [a] story' and the validity of the 'connected and particular manner' as a way of making sense of the world are now less simple matters than Anna makes them. Some of the constraints inhibiting her are straightforward enough. She offers as excuses the pain of recollection, the need to devote her remaining days to spiritual preparation, and the limitations of her own knowledge of events, 'so that some material parts of my sad story must be defective, if I were to sit down to write it' (VI, 313; p. 1163). Yet there are other reasons too for the defectiveness of the proposed memoir, and for Clarissa's reluctance to resume the manner of her first letters. The mad papers written in the immediate aftermath of the rape vividly express what Terry Castle has called a 'traumatic loss of faith in articulation, and the power of the letter to render meaning'.[84] They mark a state in which coherent discourse has come to seem at once unattainable and invalid. 'What she writes she tears', reports Lovelace, 'and throws the paper in fragments under the table, either as not knowing what she does, or disliking it' (V, 233; p. 889). In every sense, discourse is ruptured. Papers are scratched through, torn or otherwise aborted; in one, punctuated largely by dashes, the familiar letter visibly collapses beneath the weight of an experience too confused and devastating to admit of explanation in the conventional, ordered syntax in which Clarissa has previously represented her life. A complete breakdown in communication is threatened. 'But how I ramble', she writes:

I sat down to say a great deal – My heart was full – I did not know what to say first – And thought, and grief, and confusion, and (O my poor head!) I cannot tell what – And thought, and grief, and confusion, came crouding so thick upon me; *one* would be first, *another* would be first, *all* would be first; so I can write nothing at all. –   (V, 234–5; p. 890)

---

[84] *Clarissa's Ciphers*, p. 121.

The fragmentation, both syntactic and material, attests a crisis in which language can no longer encompass life. Clarissa's complaint at wrongs 'beyond the power of *words to express*' (V, 251; p. 900), it would seem, is quite without hyperbole. She has (as she later tells Mrs Norton) 'neither inclination nor words' to report what has happened, and can convey in language no remotely adequate sense of her 'whole story' (VI, 32; p. 987). The extent of her suffering finally exposes the insufficiency of signs.

Nor is the difficulty confined to language alone, to the bricks and mortar of words and syntax. Clarissa's crisis of expression involves the choice of point of view as well. Her failure to reduce her experience to the linear arrangements of prose occurs simultaneously with a radical questioning of subjectivity as an organising principle, and with a new acknowledgment of its tendency to reduce the most scrupulously undertaken explanations to the level of special pleading. Having recognised the resistance of the world to 'connected and particular' rendition, she then makes the logical next step of questioning the subjective basis on which her constructions of it have previously been founded. 'But still upon *Self*, this vile, this hated *Self*!' she exclaims, in interruption of an early attempt to resume her letter-narrative: 'I will shake it off, if possible' (VI, 10; p. 974). The only valid 'penning' of her story, it seems, will be impersonal, objective and uncompromised by extenuation: otherwise, all pretensions to justice are forfeited. 'It is difficult to go out of ourselves to give a judgment against ourselves', she tells Anna; 'and yet, oftentimes, to pass a *just* judgment, we ought' (V, 360; p. 1194). But at the same time she learns that to 'shake off' or 'go out of' the self is a formal impossibility in first-person narrative – that self-regard is inherent in the very act of saying 'I'. Repeatedly, she interrupts her writing because of the distortions of subjectivity, of 'self-partiality, that strange misleader' (VI, 34; p. 987). Instead of being a judge, she discovers, the autobiographer is necessarily a *plaintiff*, a pleader of a cause. Indeed, she admits Mrs Howe's criticism of her writing that '*misfortune makes people plaintive*', lamenting that when her business is 'to repent of my failings, and not endeavour to extenuate them', she is thwarted by the tendency of '*Self*' to 'croud into' her reports (VI, 13; p. 976).

As a result, linguistic self-presentation becomes almost impossible. Quite apart from her failure to write the memoir, Clarissa's letter-narrative plays no great part in the final instalment. She continues to write letters, of course, but most are written for simple practical purposes and few are substantially descriptive. The main burden of narrative passes instead to Belford, while Clarissa devotes herself to a new literary activity, the meditation, a genre that offers some potential at least for overcoming the inadequacies of more conventional expressive forms. Her meditations, of which five are included in the novel and thirty-six were later printed by

Richardson in separate form, are collages of verses drawn mainly from
Biblical laments: as such, they provide her with a newly emphatic medium
of self-expression and one which, being private and spiritual in character,
is relatively free from the problem of 'self-partiality'. Yet even the meditations are open to challenge as simply a new rhetorical gambit. Where
Belford sees in them only Clarissa's pious endeavour 'to regulate her
vehemence by sacred precedents' (VI, 379; p. 1207), Lovelace finds them
a brilliantly contrived outlet for this vehemence, and flagrantly self-
serving: one is a 'collection of Scripture-texts drawn up in array against
me' (VI, 403; p. 1221); another is 'finely suited to her case (that is to say,
as she and you have drawn her case)' (VI, 288; p. 1147).[85]

Clarissa thus falls, effectively, into silence; and in dramatising this crisis
of expression Richardson does much to anticipate the later linguistic
investigations of *Tristram Shandy*. Sterne's attentiveness to the dilemmas set
out in the third book of Locke's *Essay Concerning Human Understanding*, 'Of
Words', is explicit: 'Well might *Locke* write a chapter upon the imperfec-
tions of words', writes Tristram at one signal instance of the interference of
what he elsewhere calls 'tall, opake words' between the understandings of
interlocutors.[86] Many passages in *Clarissa* demonstrate, however, that here
Sterne is not quite the pioneer he seems. The concerns of Locke's *Essay* are
as important to the novel's third instalment as those of the *Two Treatises*
are to the first, or those of *Some Thoughts Concerning Education* to *Pamela II*;
but where Sterne finds absurd comedy in Locke's themes Richardson
presents, for all the prolixity of his letter-writers, a tragedy of solitude,
inarticulacy and deceit. For Clarissa, gaps yawn between idea and word
and between writer and reader, making the meaningful representation or
pure communication of experience an almost impossible task. Hers is a
distinctively Lockian crisis – that of one who, sensible of the imperfection
of words, finds his thoughts 'all within his own Breast, invisible, and
hidden from others',[87] and who suffers accordingly an isolation unbridge-
able by language.

In Locke's *Essay* language is no transparent medium ideally geared for
the representation of the world and the converse of mind with mind. A
word does not signify a thing, Locke suggests, only an idea in the mind of
its employer; and since ideas must vary between individuals the pure
transmission of messages by verbal means is at best a pleasant illusion.

[85] See Keymer, 'Richardson's *Meditations*: Clarissa's *Clarissa*', pp. 91–101, 105–7.
[86] *Tristram Shandy*, ed. Ian Campbell Ross (Oxford, 1983), pp. 288, 158. See also John Traugott,
Tristram Shandy's World (Berkeley and Los Angeles, 1954), pp. 51–61; Helene Moglen, *The
Philosophical Irony of Laurence Sterne* (Gainesville, 1975), pp. 105–15; James E. Swearingen,
Reflexivity in Tristram Shandy: An Essay in Phenomenological Criticism (New Haven, 1977),
pp. 140–61. See also W. G. Day's reservations, '*Tristram Shandy*: Locke May Not Be the Key',
in *Laurence Sterne: Riddles and Mysteries*, ed. Valerie Grosvenor Myer (1984), pp. 75–83.
[87] *An Essay Concerning Human Understanding*, ed. Peter H. Nidditch (Oxford, 1975), p. 405.

Men '*often suppose their Words to stand ... for the reality of Things*', but fallaciously: they 'take Words to be the constant regular marks of agreed Notions, which in truth are no more but the voluntary and unsteady signs of their own *Ideas*'. To suppose that language can offer an unmediated representation of reality, accordingly, is to court misunderstanding: words have only a subjective reference, so that meanings become radically unstable. And since these 'unsteady signs' offer the user no certainty of producing, in the hearer's mind, ideas identical to his own, communication (which begins to fail 'when any Word does not excite in the Hearer, the same *Idea* which it stands for in the Mind of the Speaker') suffers grave and perpetual obstruction. In these ways words 'interpose themselves so much between our Understandings, and the Truth ... that like the *Medium* through which visible Objects pass, their Obscurity and Disorder does not seldom cast a mist before our Eyes, and impose upon our Understandings'.[88]

Here Locke's primary concern is with the language of philosophy; but his analyses have troubling implications for any writer concerned to represent the world of circumstances and particulars, or to reproduce in the reader's mind the fulness of his own experience – implications that Richardson explores in the passages cited above. For Clarissa herself, language is now as much a barrier as a bridge: where she begins the novel (resolving to 'recite facts only') confident of her ability to produce an objective account of the world, her efforts in the fragments to describe the rape now leave a sense only of what is 'beyond the power of *words to express*'. The torn letters vividly suggest the unavailability of any medium in which to represent with adequacy the 'full particulars' of her story, or in which to arouse in her reader's mind thoughts and feelings answerable to her own. As she nears death, the famous allegorical letter gives a measure of the resulting changes in her view (and application) of language. Instead of using the letter to inform, she now uses it (as Lovelace complains) 'to mislead and deceive' (VII, 124; p. 1301), playing on linguistic indeterminacy in a description of her imminent return to her father's house which has 'a *religious* meaning ... couched under it' (VII, 82; p. 1274) referring only to her imminent death. Paradoxically, she thus succeeds in conveying to Lovelace the message she intends him to read (that she is returning to Harlowe Place); but in so doing she relies on the capacity of language to obscure and confuse rather than represent, turning to advantage the very slippages between word and world that have largely curtailed her narrative. It is, she confesses, 'an artifice', 'only a stratagem to keep him away' (VII, 81; p. 1274); 'one would not expect, that she should set about deceiving again; more especially by the *premeditation of writing*' (VII, 74;

[88] *Ibid.*, pp. 407, 503, 476–7, 488.

p. 1269), Lovelace protests. She has ingeniously exploited 'the imperfection of words', the disjuncture between her own spiritual meaning and Lovelace's literal interpretation grimly caricaturing the Lockian dilemma, in which neither the word itself nor the idea of the speaker, but rather the mental set of the reader, controls his understanding of that word.

More serious problems are raised by Clarissa's failure to provide a neutral, impartial account of her own life – problems closer to those of the *Essay*'s following chapter (which Sterne was largely to ignore). Here Locke moves on to describe how the 'mist' cast by the imperfection of words is thickened by their abuse, 'the several *wilful Faults* ... whereby [Men] render these signs less clear and distinct in their signification, than naturally they need to be'. Like its predecessor, this chapter is concerned primarily with philosophical discourse; but in two particular cases Locke traces the abuse of words out of the academy to observe its effect in society at large. The first of these is the '*affected Obscurity*' with which men 'confound' or 'perplex' ordinary significations in order to pass off falsehood or evil on the unsuspecting reader.[89] Philosophers, Locke reports, have even obscured the distinction between opposites: 'though unlearned Men well enough understood the Words *White* and *Black, etc.* and had constant Notions of the *Ideas* signified by those Words; yet there were Philosophers found, who had learning and *subtlety* enough to prove, that *Snow* was *black*, *i.e.* to prove, that *White* was *Black*'. By such sleights, language is perverted from its proper function. It is 'employ'd to darken truth, and unsettle Peoples Rights; to raise Mists, and render unintelligible both Morality and Religion'; and the abuse is thus disruptive of society itself, of which language should be 'the great Instrument, and common Tye'. It has 'invaded the great Concernments of Humane Life and Society; obscured and perplexed the material Truths of Law and Divinity; brought Confusion, Disorder, and Uncertainty into the Affairs of Mankind; and if not destroyed, yet in great measure rendred useless, those two great Rules, Religion and Justice'.[90]

Locke's last case of abuse concerns rhetoric, which he calls an enemy of truth, a 'powerful instrument of Error and Deceit'. By employing language as a tool of persuasion rather than as a simple code to convey ideas, rhetoric can only obscure, and typically is put to just this end. 'If we would speak of Things as they are', he maintains, 'we must allow, that all the Art of Rhetorick, besides Order and Clearness, all the artificial and figurative application of Words Eloquence hath invented, are for nothing else but to insinuate wrong *Ideas*, move the Passions, and thereby mislead the Judgment; and so indeed are perfect cheat.' When these 'Arts of Fallacy' hold sway, he suggests, the mist can become impenetrable.[91]

---

[89] *Ibid.*, pp. 490, 493, 494.   [90] *Ibid.*, pp. 495, 497, 402, 496.   [91] *Ibid.*, p. 508.

In depicting the various attempts of the heroine, her allies and her adversaries to tell Clarissa's story, and in so doing to present their own roles in it to best advantage, Richardson delineates a chaos of language and signification of just this kind. 'Confusion, Disorder, and Uncertainty' are rife, the battle for possession of the word 'innocence' providing a simple example of the problem. 'Long have my ears been accustomed to such inversions of words' (V, 345; p. 951), Clarissa complains when Lovelace describes Sinclair's as an '*innocent* house'. But she herself, convinced of her guilt in fleeing her father's house, is little more able to appropriate the term: indeed, her self-justificatory letter to Mrs Norton, which appeals to God to 'vindicate my inno—', founders on exactly this word (VI, 33; p. 987). The difficulty returns with her allegorical letter. She defends the letter as 'only an innocent allegory' (VII, 117; p. 1297), but uneasily; and when Belford excuses it as 'an *innocent* artifice' she is forced to take refuge in root meanings, agreeing that it was innocent in the strict sense at least that she 'meant him no hurt' (VII, 81; p. 1274). Yet there still remains, in the juxtaposition of 'innocent' and 'artifice', a tension on which Lovelace can play. '*She*, a meek person, and a penitent, and innocent, and pious, and I know not what, who can deceive with a foot in the grave!', he complains to Belford (VII, 123; p. 1301). 'The devil ... take thee for calling this absurdity an *innocent* artifice!' (VII, 124; p. 1302).

Clarissa's anxiety about her entitlement to particular words is matched by an uneasiness at the larger rhetorical patterns of her writing – an uneasiness in which Lockian scruples are taken to their logical extreme. Where in the *Essay* rhetoric is an avoidable abuse of language, for Clarissa it becomes an inherent condition of first-person discourse, which inevitably contaminates her own. In the letter to Mrs Norton she finds her explanations lurching unavoidably towards extenuation in their selection and arrangement of words, and she is forced to curtail them: her complaint at her own misleading 'self-partiality' comes in response to a previous sentence which throws on her family the blame for 'an *accidental*, not a *premeditated* error: And which, but for them, I had never fallen into' (VI, 34; p. 987) – a judgment one might endorse, but one with which Clarissa herself is unhappy. When in a later letter to Anna the problem recurs, she proposes a radical solution. The occasion is her reply to a renewed request for the memoir, which Anna now suggests 'might be published under feigned names' (VI, 296; p. 1152). Anna is herself guilty of 'partiality', she responds, having considered events only from Clarissa's own viewpoint. Clarissa then tries to escape this viewpoint, to enable her reader to 'come into' what she calls another 'way of thinking', or to 'consider the matter in [another] light' (VI, 310; p. 1162) by imaginatively adopting the perspective of her family. She has already attempted such moves in one of the fragments, which withdraws her own previous analyses of her conduct at Harlowe Place in favour of Bella's, who 'knew me better than I knew myself' (V, 236; p. 891). But here she makes a more sustained effort to change her place. 'To judge of their resentments, and of their conduct, we must put ourselves in their situation' (VI, 310; p. 1162), she insists, proceeding to do so in a new account of events from which her usual casuistry is entirely absent. Instead she selects and emphasises terms in which the values of familial harmony appear paramount, first evoking the happiness which preceded her fall and then asking Anna to 'reverse ... this charming prospect' and consider the distresses caused by it. The reversal offers a strikingly new perspective, and points to very different conclusions. No longer are the Harlowes Clarissa's persecutors: they have become her victims. Her mother is 'made to suffer for faults she could not be guilty of' and 'robbed of that conscious merit, which the mother of hopeful children may glory in'; her brother is 'piqued to the heart of his honour, in the fall of a sister, in whom he once gloried'; her father suffers 'pangs that tear in pieces' his heart. And this new way of thinking, from the perspective of those who think Clarissa 'more in fault than themselves', makes all further self-justification hollow: 'When ... I reflect upon my fault in these strong, yet just lights, what room can there be to censure any-body but my unhappy self?' she concludes. 'And how much reason have I to say, *If I justify myself, mine own heart shall condemn me: If I say, I am perfect, it shall also prove me perverse?*' (VI, 310-12; pp. 1162–3). A literary apology, in her own words and from her own perspective, could only compromise its own intended claims.

Silence is not inevitable, however. A subjective account of the kind proposed by Anna would be inadmissibly partial in both senses of the term; but in the absence of true completeness and objectivity, justice may be done by a good second best. The rest of the letter outlines her proposal for replacing the memoir she cannot write: Belford and Anna should compile the book themselves, she suggests, drawing on the letters in their own possession. This expedient 'will answer the end wished for by your mother and you full as well; perhaps better', she tells Anna (VI, 313; p. 1163). By allowing the narrative to emerge largely from other sources, it will make Clarissa's story known, while freeing her from the compromising activity of self-extenuation: 'It will be an honour to my memory', as she puts it to Belford, 'that ... I could intrust [my story] to the relation which the destroyer of my fame and fortunes has given of it' (VI, 333; p. 1176). To Anna she makes the same point by another allusion to Job, in which the planned collection of letters is seen not as her own but as her '*adversary*'s' book, which she will bind to herself '*as a crown*' (VI, 313; p. 1164). It will still do justice as Anna defines it, however, and vindicate Clarissa's innocence. Lovelace's own letters will reveal 'the base arts of this

vile man' better than her own could do, and she has 'nothing to apprehend' from them (VI, 313; p. 1163): they do her, she believes, 'all the
justice I could wish for' (VI, 328; p. 1173).

Yet here, of course, she is unduly optimistic. She sees the inadequacy of
her own reports, but she fails to recognise that the same distortions and the
same self-serving rhetoric will be at least as great in Lovelace's. She is
cautious enough, certainly, to ask Belford for samples of his letters which
will enable her to check their veracity. But she is concerned here only with
possible errors of fact, and takes no account of the elaborate rhetorical
apparatus with which Lovelace transforms these facts. Her view of the
book's capacity to do justice is thus dangerously naive – she sounds, in fact,
like Walter Hartright, and there is her mistake. For in Richardson close
connection with the incidents recorded is no guarantee of reliability, as it
is in Collins. Quite the reverse: unreliability tends to increase in proportion with involvement, so that instead of combining in the gradual
unfolding of 'truth' *Clarissa*'s narrators are far more likely to obscure it.
Here Richardson follows through the logic of the forensic analogy as
Collins does not, presenting his narrators not as mere objective witnesses
but as plaintiffs, defendants and advocates, who may agree on the basic
facts of the case but who offer in their testimonies radically adversarial
constructions of them. *Clarissa*'s thus becomes a far more disputatious trial
than that of *The Woman in White*, closely reflecting the courtroom procedures of a period when the roles of prosecution and defence counsel
remained largely undeveloped and centre stage was held by the involved
parties themselves. (More often than not, these parties would speak
directly and continuously to the court in support of their own causes,
sometimes also examining, cross-examining and engaging in direct altercation with one another).[92] This form of trial is obviously mirrored by an
alternating narrative structure in which each narrator argues his own
cause and contests, often explicitly, that of his opponent; and what is
mirrored most importantly of all is the necessary consequence of such a
form – the inevitability that the testimony produced will be in varying
degrees self-serving. It is significant in this context that where Collins's
fictive editor Hartright sees first-person narrative as valuable simply for
being first-hand, Richardson's editor Belford begins to sense in the collec-

[92] See Beattie, *Crime and the Courts*, pp. 314–99; John H. Langbein, 'The Criminal Trial before the
Lawyers', *University of Chicago Law Review*, 45, No. 2 (1978), 263–316. Langbein's study deals
with the period 1675–1735 (towards the close of which *Clarissa* is seemingly set). Towards the
1750s, although still in a minority of cases and under strict constraints, accuser and accused
were beginning to be protected and displaced by the proxy roles of prosecution and defence
counsel (a development that may explain *Clarissa*'s hostile references to the sophisticating role
of lawyers): see Langbein's study of the 1750s, 'Shaping the Eighteenth-Century Criminal
Trial: A View from the Ryder Sources', *University of Chicago Law Review*, 50, No. 1 (1983),
1–136.

tion of narratives he will assemble a higher and more partisan charge. Though sincerely attached to Clarissa's cause and happy as editor to accept his allotted role as 'the protector of [her] memory' (VI, 333; p. 1176), he also retains a residual attachment to Lovelace's cause, finding in Clarissa's proposal a benefit for him as well. He sees that as a narrator Lovelace can be true to basic facts while still writing to his own advantage, and he reassures him that the book Clarissa envisages will thus work in his own favour too: 'thou must fare better from thy own pen, than from hers' (VI, 329; p. 1174). Belford even helps Lovelace to secure this advantage, misleading Clarissa as to the character of his narrative by changing or omitting parts of the sample letters shown to her for approval while at the same time reassuring her of 'the justice he does to your virtue in every line he writes' (VI, 330; p. 1174). Elsewhere he tells Lovelace that he should 'be glad to have the justification of her memory left to one, who, at the same time, thou mayest be assured, will treat thee, and thy actions, with all the lenity the case will admit' (VI, 350; p. 1188).

At such points the rashness of Clarissa's confidence that the book will be 'more efficacious' than formal legal proceedings can hardly be missed; for the principal obstacle, Lovelace's rhetorical skill, will be at work in either case. In book and trial alike, the antagonisms of the story told will inevitably infect its telling, as each party pleads his own cause in his own narrative. The only truly disadvantaged parties, in fact, will be the Harlowes, whose letters are few. Clarissa shows some awareness of the problem when stressing to Belford that he, as editor, 'should not think harshly of my friends [i.e. family]' (VII, 119; p. 1298). But his divided attachment to the causes of both protagonists in fact leaves little room for these third concerned parties to appear to advantage. 'Far be it from me to offer to defend [Lovelace], or even *unduly* to extenuate his crime', he tells Morden after Clarissa's death: 'But yet I must say, that the family, by their persecutions of the dear lady at first, and by their implacableness afterwards, ought, *at least*, to *share* the blame with him.' For all his air of even-handedness, the editor has his own interpretation of the story, in which the Harlowes are if anything more to blame for their obduracy than Lovelace is for the rape – for Clarissa, he adds, 'would have got over a *mere personal* injury' (VII, 344; p. 1442).

Clarissa's book thus takes shape not as a transparent exposition of facts, in which all testimonies combine in a single amplified view of the story, but as an adversarial collection of subjective versions, each vying to establish its own pre-eminence and challenging the assumptions of its rivals. Nothing could be more unlike Anna's original proposal than the adversarial collection of accusations and pleas that finally results, the accused sharing with the accuser herself the opportunities and benefits of sustained self-presentation. Yet Clarissa still persists in seeing the idea as a simple incarnation of the novel's elusive grail, 'the *whole* truth'. She leaves her life in an attempt at complete clarification, formally instituting in her will the 'compilement to be made of all that relates to my story' and describing it, in by now familiar terms, as a means 'to do my character justice' (VII, 306; p. 1418). The same urge to clarify, in fact, dominates her will as a whole, which she intends to be susceptible of one interpretation alone. She means it to forestall the 'confusion and disagreement in families' that typically arises from 'want of absolute clearness in the Testaments of departed persons'; it will also obviate 'all cavils about words' (VII, 297; p. 1412). (Belford too, in his executorship, hopes 'that there can be no room for dispute or opposition', and that the will may provide a means 'of shutting up the whole affair': VII, 296; p. 1412.) But here Richardson is at his most ironic. For the will *is* disputed; and the dispute comes in the end to concern not only the executor's disposition of Clarissa's property but also the editor's disposition of her history – the '*Lady's Legacy*' in which Clarissa's will, as to her posthumous reputation, is to be done. Possession of her effects is not the only matter in which her antagonists prove themselves (as Morden notes of James and Bella) 'true Will-disputants' (VII, 311; p. 1421): more contentiously still, they dispute Clarissa's interpretation of her past.

After her death, all parties contend to assert their own explanations of the history. In the version of Clarissa's family, Lovelace is the sole cause of the calamity. To even the relatively impartial Morden, it is he 'who occasioned this great, this extended ruin' (VII, 285; p. 1404). The family, Morden acknowledges, are to be 'pitied' – 'But how much to be cursed that abhorred Lovelace, who ... has been the sole author of a woe so complicated and extensive' (VII, 270; p. 1395). The Harlowes themselves take a still more simplified view. They too curse Lovelace as 'the author of her fall' (VII, 274; p. 1398), while James is typical in palliating his own unforgivingness: 'I thought only to reclaim a dear creature that had erred! I intended not to break her tender heart! – But it was the villainous Lovelace who did that – Not any of us!' (VII, 271; p. 1396). It is this question of obduracy that leads to a significant split in the Harlowe case, with James and Bella 'continually loading each other, by way of exonerating themselves ... with the *principal* guilt of their implacable behaviour' (VII, 418; p. 1490).

One might therefore suspect, when after the funeral the Harlowes lay claim to the executorship of the will and ask Belford to relinquish it, that their primary motive is to gain control over the book to be edited by its executor, their view being to impose their own judgments on it. Richardson nowhere explicitly ascribes this motive to them, but he does give ample evidence of the very different look the history would wear if under their control. It would cast Lovelace as the 'author' of the calamity, of course, and blame him absolutely for Clarissa's death. But it would also blame Clarissa, in ways that she, in her own letters, in part acknowledges. It would stress as a key event her meeting with Lovelace in the garden and her subsequent departure from it: to Bella this was a 'scandalous elopement' (VII, 53; p. 1256), 'a conduct, that it is a shame any young lady should justify' (VI, 229; p. 1109). To her mother too the harsher words 'sin' and 'crime' are called for, in place of Clarissa's usual terms, 'error' and 'fault': 'But for such a child as this ... to lay plots and stratagems to deceive her parents ... and to run away with a libertine; Can there be any atonement for her crime?' she has asked Mrs Norton. 'Was not her sin committed equally against warning, and the light of her own knowlege?' (VI, 302; p. 1156). Again, the Harlowe version would make much of a point tirelessly reiterated in their letters, that the prospect of a forced marriage was never real, and that when Clarissa eloped they were on the point of yielding to her aversion. It would stress, as Clarissa does in her own attempt to adopt their point of view, what Mrs Harlowe calls 'the distresses of all our family, upon the rashness and ingratitude of a child we once doated upon' (VI, 232; p. 1111). And it would repeat how wrong the family would have been to grant (again in Mrs Harlowe's words) 'the easy pardon perverse children meet with, when they have done the rashest and most rebellious thing they can do' (VI, 302; p. 1156). The story, in short, would be the same; but the details emphasised, the rhetoric employed, the causal relations proposed and the judgments made would point in quite another direction.

Illegitimate speculations, perhaps – except that elsewhere Richardson does clearly point to the link between the attempt to assume executorship of Clarissa's will and the attempt to assume editorship of her book. Lovelace too challenges Belford's executorship of the will, and he does so to contest and rewrite a history which, despite the place of his own narrative in it, he anticipates with fear. He intends to be the 'interpreter' of her will and history alike; and under his editorship its meanings will shift. To Belford he presents himself as sincere and ingenuous in his plans for the book, reassuring him that 'as no one can do her memory justice equal to myself, and I will not spare myself, who can better shew the world what she was, and what a villain he, that could use her ill?' But his next sentence shows that the presiding interpretation he envisages will have other functions as well. 'And the world shall also see', he adds, 'what implacable and unworthy parents she had' (VII, 253; p. 1385). Their guilt, and not his own, will be the dominant theme – for their 'barbarity to her, no doubt, was the *true* cause of her death' (VII, 252; p. 1384).

Despite all this, Belford retains his dual role as executor and editor and proceeds to collaborate with Anna in preparation of the book, undeterred by Lovelace's complaints that the history they compile is no unbiased revelation of truth but a work of polemic in which he is to be '*manifestoed* against' (VII, 336; p. 1437). Now, however, Lovelace's plan is not to usurp the role of editor but instead to prepare a counterblast, an alternative *Clarissa* in which all the assumptions and judgments of this '*manifesto*' will be contested and undermined. 'I have a good mind not to oppose it; and to write an answer to it, as soon as it comes forth, and exculpate myself, by throwing all the fault upon the old ones' (VII, 336–7; p. 1438), he writes. His answer will 'plead', and indeed 'prove demonstrably', that he is 'not answerable for all the extravagant and unforeseen consequences that this affair has been attended with'; and it will do so in a way already familiar from his letters, which after the rape consistently stress the Harlowes' culpability, and indeed anyone's but his own. (The tone is set at the onset of Clarissa's illness, when he cites her good health until after her escape to contend that the rape, which is 'a common case; only a little uncommonly circumstanced; that's all', cannot be its cause. Instead, 'the horrid arrest, and her gloomy father's curse, must have hurt her': VI, 211–12; p. 1099.)

The remainder of Lovelace's letter sketches out his defence, the skeleton of his 'answer', in fable form. Clarissa is now '*A*, a miser', who 'had hid a parcel of gold in a *secret place*, in order to keep it there, till he could lend it out at extravagant interest'. Lovelace is *B*, 'in such great want of this treasure, as to be unable to *live without it*'. *B*'s desire, moreover, is not unsolicited, for '*A*, the *miser*, has such an opinion of *B*, the *wanter*, that he would rather lend it to him, than to any mortal living; but yet, tho' he has *no other* use in the world for it, insists upon very unconscionable terms' (VII, 337; p. 1438). The obstacle is of *A*'s making, and leaves *B* no option: 'guessing (being an arch, penetrating fellow) where the *sweet hoard* lies, he *searches* for it, when the miser is in a *profound sleep*, finds it, and runs away with it' (VII, 337; p. 1438).

'Penetrating' is a characteristic touch; but there is more to the fable than ingenious bawdry. It is a sustained piece of exculpation in which Lovelace, by admitting to the smaller crime, can blunt the edge of larger accusations while also creating an imaginative world in which such crimes seem necessary and natural things. *B*, he acknowledges, is a thief. But Clarissa too is to blame, both for the initial suppression of her love and for setting 'so romantic a value' upon the stolen treasure that she dies at its loss. There is even a suggestion of suicide:

Suppose this same miserly *A*, on awaking, and searching for, and finding his treasure gone, takes it so much to heart, that he starves himself;

Who but himself is to blame for that? – Would either Equity, Law, or Conscience, hang *B* for a murder?   (VII, 338; p. 1438)

Reduced to this model, Lovelace suggests, the history becomes the plainest of cases: death is no '*natural* consequence' of rape, and he stands acquitted of it. Other circumstances exonerate him further, so that even the rape comes to seem a venial crime. Having stolen the treasure, after all, he relented, and even agreed to the miser's 'unconscionable terms'. 'But it would not do: The sweet miser would break her heart, and die; and how could I help it?' (VII, 339; p. 1439).

Blame for the calamity, as Lovelace envisages his defence, is thus shared not only between himself and the Harlowes but by Clarissa as well. Her death is no Christian martyrdom but rather the perverse and wilful act of one whose 'desire of revenge became stronger in her than the desire of life; and now ... is willing to die, as an event which she supposes will cut my heart-strings asunder. And still the more to be revenged puts on the Christian, and forgives me ... And what is it, but a mere *verbal* forgiveness, as ostentatiously as cruelly given with a view to magnify herself, and wound me deeper?' (VII, 194; p. 1346). Clarissa's obstinate deathwish becomes his central charge, which he uses to allege the evasiveness or even irrelevance of her own account. To Hickman, whose judgments are based entirely on Clarissa's letters to Anna, he stresses the misleading 'partiality' of these letters, and their suppression of her basic suicidal urge. He points subtly to alternative judgments, challenging not the truthfulness but the *completeness* of Clarissa's testimony – that 'tho' the lady will tell the *truth*, and nothing *but* the truth, yet, perhaps, she will not tell the *whole* truth' (VI, 206; p. 1095). What her testimony withholds, her tryst with death and what he later calls her '*Christian revenge*' (VI, 342; p. 1182), is more important than what it discloses. In other letters Clarissa's rhetorical hyperbole, as well as her evasiveness, meets with similar challenge. 'How does *she* know the requisite distinctions of the words she uses in this case?' he writes in protest at her phrase '*unprecedented wickedness*'. 'But she has heard, that the devil is black; and having a mind to make one of me, brings together, in the mortar of her wild fancy, twenty chimney-sweepers, in order to make one sootier than ordinary rise out of the dirty mass' (VI, 343; p. 1183).

Thus Richardson sketches out, as he concludes his novel, the possibility of alternative versions of its story, each of them partisan. The memoir envisaged by Anna would present an utterly polarised struggle between absolute virtue and villainy. From the self-righteous, authoritarian perspective of the Harlowes, it is they, not Clarissa, who are innocent and wronged. In the intricate, relativistic interpretation of Lovelace, he himself is '*comparatively* harmless' (VII, 336; p. 1437), '*comparatively* a very innocent man' (VI, 281; p. 1143). But these are not in fact alternatives to Clarissa's book at all, for the forensic structure of the epistolary 'compilement' incorporates something of them all. The direct efforts at justification or accusation developed in these passages only intensify processes at work in every letter in the novel, for each participant has from the start been pleading a cause and contributing, in the emphases and judgments of each report, to the positions now crystallised in his or her concluding plea. It is here that the novel's approximation to the processes of the courtroom is most disturbing in effect, its various narratives failing to converge on a single transcendent truth and instead remaining irreconcilably committed to divergent readings of events. Rather than settling her case definitively, they combine to keep it open. The book Clarissa leaves, in fact, resembles not Wilkie Collins's progressive disclosure of the hidden, but looks forward instead to that subtler Victorian product of the forensic analogy, Browning's *The Ring and the Book*, which accumulates the contending pleas of the various parties to a murder, and in so doing conveys a bafflingly multifarious vision of the case from which it starts.[93]

Clarissa's final volumes offer no escape from the resulting difficulties of interpretation, and instead bring the forensic analogy increasingly to the fore. The very verb 'To *narrate*' originally is, as Lovelace hints by reminding Belford of its Scottish derivation (VI, 95; p. 1025), a term in law, which traditionally denotes the initial statement of a case. (Thus in Giles Jacob's *New Law-Dictionary* 'Narrator' is defined as 'a Pleader or Reporter'.[94]) The implications of this original meaning are kept continually in view, Richardson once more being concerned in particular with the idea of self-serving unreliability inevitably suggested by the word's forensic roots.[95] An obvious example of 'narrative' in this suspect sense comes in the testimony of the supposedly impartial Elias Brand, who is sent by the Harlowes to establish, in the absence of reliable information, the facts of Clarissa's case ('for nothing she writes herself will be regarded': VI, 303; p. 1157). Brand's letter begins in a parade of objectivity, his first informant Mrs Smith proving so '*highly prepossessed* in [Clarissa's] *favour*' that he has discounted her evidence and turned instead to a neighbourhood gossip. The vicious insinuations of this second source serve his purposes better. On their basis he goes on to produce a thorough indictment of Clarissa's conduct, punctuating it with reports of his own distress when 'things look a little more *darkly*, than I hoped they would' and of his anxiety 'to do the lady *justice*'. Clarissa, he reports, is regularly at church; but 'nothing is more common in London, than that the frequenting of the church at morning prayers, is made the *pretence* and *cover* for *private assignations*'. She returns home, it is true, alone; but 'there is a gentleman of *no good character* (an *intimado* of Mr. Lovelace's) who is a

---

[93] See John Killham, 'Browning's "Modernity": *The Ring and the Book*, and Relativism', in *The Major Victorian Poets: Reconsiderations*, ed. Isobel Armstrong (1969), pp. 153–75.

[94] Giles Jacob, *A New Law-Dictionary*, 6th edn (1750), 'Narrator'.

[95] See, for example, *The Concise Scots Dictionary* (Aberdeen, 1985), which defines 'Narratioun' as 'the act of reporting, esp. by way of accusation, complaint or slander; a report or accusation, freq. *fals* or *wrang narratioun*, false report, misrepresentation'. 'Narrative', likewise, is 'a statement of alleged facts as the basis of a legal action, *freq. wrang* etc. *narrative*'.

constant visiter of her'. All in all, as he sums up, 'it *looketh not well*' (VII, 110–12; pp. 1292–3).

For the novel's reader, of course, this particular testimony presents no great difficulty: we know that Brand is a time-server whose obligations to the Harlowes will make him, as Clarissa laconically predicts, 'but a languid acquitter' (VI, 320; p. 1168). ('False witnesses are risen up against me', she complains more forthrightly in her book of *Meditations*.[96]) Within the world of the novel, however, Brand's misrepresentation works havoc. The Harlowes 'run away with the belief of the worst it insinuates' (VII, 106; p. 1290); only Morden treats it judiciously, 'by inquiring into her merit or demerit, and giving her cause a fair audit before condemnation' (VII, 127; p. 1304).

Elsewhere distinctions are obscurer still. The forensic analogy is again explicit in the letters which report to Belford what Lovelace calls his 'tryal for all my sins to my beloved fugitive' (VI, 97; p. 1026).[97] The language of the courtroom pervades his report, and appropriately so, for the scene follows a formal forensic pattern. In the first place he is charged, the 'indictment' being a letter from Clarissa to his kinswomen, which they read out, expecting him to answer it point by point. Instead of answering its charges, however, he first attempts to undermine its status by treating it instead as a rhetorical imposture which achieves its effects not by substance but by style. At one point in the reading he mockingly rebukes his cousin for weeping 'in the wrong place' (VI, 102; p. 1029); at another he notes 'the excellency of this lady, that in every line, as she writes on, she improves upon herself' (VI, 102; p. 1029); at a third he applauds a 'very pretty metaphor, if it wóuld but hold' (VI, 103; p. 1029). He thus weakens the foundations of Clarissa's charge, and can prepare a measured defence: 'to be required to answer piecemeal thus, without knowing what is to follow, is a cursed insnaring way of proceeding', he complains, demanding to read the letter in full 'that I may be prepared for my defence, as you are all for my arraignment' (VI, 104; p. 1030).

His next step is to make a more detailed analysis of the letter, 'looking upon it, as a lawyer upon his breviate' (VI, 104; p. 1030). Close verbal analysis enables him to turn Clarissa's arguments back against her, and to prove that while appearing to expose his faults her allegories and metaphors also work, more discreetly, to palliate her own: 'You see', he notes (having carefully reinterpreted her image of him as a 'drowning wretch' so as to condemn her for refusing to 'save' him), ' ... how pretty tinkling words run away with ears inclined to be musical!' (VI, 105; p. 1031). This basic contention that Clarissa's indictment unwittingly indicts herself lays the foundation for his own alternative plea, which he again identifies to

Belford as forensic in character: 'But he must be a silly fellow who has not
something to say for himself, when every cause has its black and its white
side. – Westminster-hall, Jack, affords every day as confident defences as
mine' (VI, 106; p. 1031).[98] The 'confident defence' in question is a
brilliant rhetorical display, featuring a range of devices to which he
occasionally alludes in technical terms, as when he describes himself
proceeding '*proleptically*, as a rhetorician would say' (VI, 105; p. 1031). He
palliates the 'black side' of the case by various extenuating arguments,
including the now familiar claim that Clarissa is 'the *only woman in the
world*, who would have made such a rout about a case that is uncommon
only from the circumstances that attend it' (VI, 107; p. 1032). The result
is to reproduce in miniature the larger pattern of the novel as a whole,
Clarissa's initial statement of her case, Lovelace's interrogation of it, and
his subsequent presentation of his own rival case serving to epitomise
(albeit schematically) the novel's basic organisation. His plea gives something close to a condensed version of his whole narrative, moreover, its
'glosses' simply reiterating (as he points out himself) the various 'extenuating arguments' already used in his letters to Belford (VI, 111; p. 1034).
This link makes the outcome of the trial scene particularly disturbing, for
after Lovelace's peroration his judges are manifestly swayed. They end not
in condemnation but in a 'kind opinion' of him, Lord M. repeating in his
favour the proverb '*That the devil is not quite so black as he is painted*' (VI, 121;
p. 1041). 'Did ever Comedy end more happily, than this long tryal?'
Lovelace exults (VI, 119; p. 1040): its result is not clarification or justice,
only the victory of the most accomplished rhetorician. The same result
recurs later, when he turns his oratorical powers on Morden and ends in
celebration of another forensic triumph: 'it is but glossing over *one* part of a
story, and omitting *another*, that will make a bad cause a good one at any
time', he tells Belford: 'What an admirable Lawyer should I have made!'
(VII, 102; p. 1287).

For jurists committed to the form of trial imitated by *Clarissa* – a form of
trial largely unmediated by counsel, and especially by counsel for the
defence – the advantage of this traditional forensic procedure lay in the
opportunity it gave to witness directly the sincerity of the parties concerned. In this system the innocent have no need of protection from
'admirable Lawyers' of the kind Lovelace mentions, for their innocence
will naturally shine through: 'every one of Common Understanding may
as properly speak to a Matter of Fact, as if he were the best Lawyer', wrote

---

[98] As the site not only of the King's Bench, Chancery and Common Pleas courts but also of
booksellers' and other shops, each court being bounded by low enclosures and open to the view
of passers-by, Westminster Hall afforded a public opportunity to watch the processes of the
courtroom at work. See Battestin, *Henry Fielding: A Life*, pp. 243–4. Recent celebrated cases in
Richardson's mind may have been the trials there of the Jacobite lords in July 1746 (Battestin,
p. 409).

one contemporary jurist, adding that 'it requires no manner of Skill to make a plain and honest Defence'. Conversely, the guilty will tend to hang themselves in their very attitude and words: 'on the other Side, the very Speech, Gesture and Countenance, and Manner of Defense of those who are Guilty, when they speak for themselves, may often help to disclose the Truth, which probably would not so well be discovered from the artificial Defense of others speaking for them'.[99] At Lovelace's trial, however, it is the victim's plea that is defeated, while the rapist's opportunity to speak for himself leads not to self-incrimination but to acquittal. The implications for the outcome of the novel's larger trial, and of the more complicated and far-reaching kinds of justice and resolution proposed within the epistolary 'compilement' by Clarissa herself, are serious indeed. Here the direct defences of the parties involved throw up a baffling range of black and white sides, good and bad causes, which threaten to deny the heroine, her friends and her readers the perfect literary justice they had sought. The history is too complex, its interaction of motivations and causes too indeterminate, the language used to describe it too imperfect and open to abuse for any such happy closure of meaning to be remotely within reach. Unrescued by God, unmarried by Lovelace, unvindicated by the law and now unjustified by narrative prose, Clarissa must leave the world deprived of the harmonious and unanimous interpretation of events without which, for Lady Echlin and others, the novel remained unresolved.

Trials of the reader's judgment

Where Richardson begins to qualify the radical indeterminacy of the final instalment is in the enhanced role, as both reader and writer, of the character he identified in his notes for a preface as central to the closing volumes – 'the reforming Belford'.[100] At the critical point of Lovelace's interview with Morden, Belford intervenes as reader of Lovelace's text to produce a vigilant critique not only of the libertine code but also of the captious rhetoric through which Lovelace palliates his conduct. The key passage in which he censures Lovelace for driving a wedge between word and world and obstructing Morden's understanding ingeniously conflates the terminology of Locke's attack on linguistic abuse – raising mists, proving white black – with the courtroom imagery of Lovelace's own letters. The conversation reported here, he concedes, 'affords a convincing proof, that there is a black and a white side to every cause: But what must the conscience of a partial whitener of his *own* cause, or blackener of

99 W. Hawkins, *A Treatise of the Pleas of the Crown* (1716–21), quoted by Langbein, 'Shaping the Eighteenth-Century Criminal Trial', 123.
100 *Hints of Prefaces*, p. 4.

another's, tell him, while he is throwing dust in the eyes of his judges, and all the time knows his own guilt?' (VII, 114; p. 1295). While granting the validity in theory of the relativism on which Lovelace depends, Belford here sets limits to it as well, feeling his way towards a distinction between legitimate complications of the history's meaning and illegitimate evasions of it. He begins to point to a middle way between the untenable moral simplicities and polarities favoured by Clarissa's most devoted adherents and the specious extenuations of her opponents – a middle way in which the possibility of an appropriately measured, complex and impartial judgment at last appears to view.

The remark gives one of several signs that Belford's own narrative, statistically predominant in the final two volumes, might even bring with it a belated escape from the problems of linguistic imperfection and abuse, and the consequent obscurity of all meaning, by which the novel has been infected throughout. Admittedly, Belford too is accused of partiality, and in the usual forensic terms. On one occasion Lovelace is outraged to find him become 'an advocate, who so much more admires his client's adversary, than his client' (VI, 322; p. 1169), and he thereafter repeatedly alludes to him as Clarissa's 'advocate'. Even she finds Belford inclined to a too undiscriminating bias in her favour. When he credits her with 'the merit of a saint, and the purity of an angel' (recurrent terms in his letters), she protests at the extravagance of his language and adds, when he pleads sincerity and politeness in his defence: 'Nothing can be polite ... that is not just' (VI, 176; p. 1076). It is significant, nonetheless, that Belford is the only narrator to be compared in the novel to a *judge*, the analogy coming at the exact point where his narrative assumes pre-eminence over the previously dominant narrative, that of Lovelace. At Clarissa's final successful escape from Sinclair's, Mowbray writes to Lovelace to report a house in turmoil, 'no-body serene but Jack Belford, who is taking minnutes of examinations, accusations, and confessions, with the significant air of a Middlesex Justice; and intends to write at large all particulars' (V, 367; p. 963). Though mocking, this account of Belford's attempts to control and order his narrative material in the manner of a 'Justice' seems also to herald what has been missing from the novel for so long, the predominance at last of a voice that is not plaintive or accusatory but genuinely judicial. Indeed, Richardson may even be mischievously promising from Belford something like the magisterial techniques of exposition, commentary and judgment developed in the novels of the most famous Middlesex Justice of all, Fielding himself.[101]

---

[101] Although Fielding's career on the Middlesex bench began only in January 1749, a month after the publication of *Clarissa*'s final instalment, his name had been entered in the Commission of the Peace for the county as early as June 1747 – something Richardson's relative closeness at the time to Fielding and his sister Sarah may well have enabled him to know: see

No such promise is fulfilled, however, for in the following volumes Belford brings to the novel only the most limited form of justice – a reductive attempt to overcome the problems of misrepresentation and partiality by a meticulous attention to the particular. The rigorous circumstantial realism of his letters fights a rearguard action against the imperfection of words, attempting to develop a neutral and exact language of description in which the hitherto yawning gap between text and world will be closed. He provides, accordingly, detailed visual descriptions of place, person and action, such as his accounts of Clarissa's prison and Sinclair's death, that are quite unlike anything else in the novel. These are the passages that, in their radical attention to the physical, underlie the praise of contemporaries who found 'no difference at all, in the impressions of things really done . . . and recollected by us – and the things we read of, in this *intellectual world*'; they also offended the more refined taste of *Clarissa*'s French translator Prévost, who did his best to excise them from his translation.[102] By now, however, mere 'particulars' are not enough, and of little help in judging or clarifying the greater complexities of the story. They can even be an impediment; for in emphasising the physical and circumstantial aspects of Clarissa's death Belford's low mimetic manner draws attention only to the most irrelevant details of it. There is something ridiculous and bathetic about his largely external descriptions of the dying Clarissa, her 'lovely skeleton' (VII, 14; p. 1231), and 'her hand, the lily not of so beautiful a white' (VI, 184; p. 1081). And the absurdity becomes inescapable at the critical point of Clarissa's death, when he attends officiously to 'the particulars of her happy exit' (VII, 216; p. 1360), even recording that 'she departed exactly at 40 minutes after 6 o'clock, as by her watch on the table' (VII, 220; p. 1363), while obtusely missing the larger significance of her final allusive words: '*It is good for me that I was afflicted!* – Words of Scripture, I suppose' (VII, 217; p. 1362). Lovelace has already drawn attention to such absurdities in Belford's prose: 'But, faith, Jack, thou art such a tragi-comical mortal, with thy leaden aspirations at one time, and thy flying hour-glasses and dreaming terrors at another, that as Prior says, *What serious is, thou turn'st to farce*' (VII, 136; p. 1309). He turns it, at any rate, to a narrowly circumstantial realism, which does no more than any other narrative to complete or perfect the reader's understanding of Clarissa's story.

Thus at the end of the novel Richardson in no way diverges from his

Battestin, *Henry Fielding*, pp. 418, 448–9. On the links between Fielding's procedures as a Middlesex Justice and his techniques as a writer of novels, see Patrick Reilly, 'Fielding's Magisterial Art', in *Henry Fielding: Justice Observed*, ed. K. G. Simpson (1985), pp. 75–100; John Bender, *Imagining the Penitentiary: Fiction and the Architecture of Mind in Eighteenth-Century England* (Chicago, 1987), chapter 6 ('Fielding and the Juridical Novel').

[102] Hill to Richardson, 5 May 1748, *Works* (1753), II, 267; Wilcox, 'Prévost's Translations of Richardson's Novels', pp. 374–7.

method of unreliable narrative: Belford's narrative simply presents a new
form of unreliability, as inadequate as its predecessors in establishing a
viewpoint from which all the complications of the history may be sorted
and understood. Even at its close the text refuses to provide an absolute
and incontestable reading of the story, leaving the reader access only, in
the novel as a whole, to an immense babble of voices endlessly disputing
the rights and wrongs of the case. When William Shenstone found in
Clarissa a prolixity appropriate only to 'a Court of Justice', and when
Hazlitt wrote that Richardson 'sets about describing every object and
transaction as if the whole had been given in on evidence by an eye-
witness',[103] both felt something of the effects of the novel's forensic
method. Richardson himself had written in defence of it 'that the Probability of all Stories told, or of Narrations given, depends upon small
Circumstances; as may be observed, that in all Tryals for Life and
Property, the Merits of the Cause are more determinable by such, than by
the greater Facts'.[104] Yet it is not in the simple copiousness of the novel's
evidence so much as in the unreliability of its presentation that Richardson's novel is most truly and brilliantly forensic. 'All the characters are on
trial in any civilized narrative', William Empson has written;[105] yet in
Clarissa above all the characters are on trial in a peculiarly direct and
immediate sense, each pleading a cause before the reader and appealing
for a favourable verdict. Each plea is compromised, of course, and some
much more than others; but each has something to be said for it, offering a
new perspective in which the same basic events take on different appearances and demand to be understood in radically different ways. Any
expectation that they may be reconciled, or that they will converge on
some single transcendent vision of the truth, remains unfulfilled. Instead –
and here is the implied completion of Richardson's forensic paradigm – it
is left to the reader to judge.

It might be argued that the reader's task in dealing with these conflicting narratives is in the end very straightforward: the voices of Clarissa's
antagonists are by now not simply compromised but utterly discredited,
and can safely be ignored. But Clarissa's viewpoint too has its own grave
deficiencies, as the final instalment makes explicit; and though few will
simply acquit Lovelace or the Harlowes many will see (many, indeed,
have recorded seeing) that there are things to be said on their side. No one
perspective alone is enough, and any full understanding of the history,
whatever the reader's instincts and sympathies, must be more than partisan. As Richardson himself wrote, 'No one can judge properly of another,

[103] Shenstone to Lady Luxborough, 23 March 1749/50, *Letters*, ed. Mallam, pp. 199–200;
Hazlitt, *Lectures on the English Comic Writers* (New York, 1845), p. 138, quoted by Watt, *Rise of
the Novel*, p. 34.
[104] *Hints of Prefaces*, p. 5.   [105] *Milton's God*, revised edn (Cambridge, 1981), p. 94.

that cannot, in imagination, be that other, when he takes the judgment-seat';[106] and his narrative method everywhere reinforces the point. It requires the reader to consider all the motives, causes, events and consequences of the history as they are understood and articulated from the varying perspectives of the contending characters, and from the varying ideologies by which these perspectives are informed – the individualist perspective of Clarissa, the authoritarian perspective of the Harlowes, the libertine perspective of Lovelace, and the diverse viewpoints of onlookers and witnesses as dissimilar as Mowbray and Mrs Norton. In its accumulation of these various testimonies, the novel makes available no simple and definitive judgments about the story it so confusingly records, and points instead to a more complex, various and vexing multivalence of meaning. 'The *whole* truth', as *Clarissa* presents it, is bafflingly diffuse.

It is tempting to conclude that Richardson was intent on bringing the reader to a radical scepticism about values and judgments, by embodying in the novel a view that right and wrong are merely our own constructions, variable according to the perspective or set of attitudes from which we start. But though the structure of his book may be relativistic, Richardson is himself no relativist. He presents, certainly, a complex and confusing world; but that presentation does not in itself mark the fulfilment of his novel's direction. It is instructive here to return to Locke, where at a later point in the *Essay* he considers the limited conditions of knowledge that obtain in the fallen world. God, he writes in his chapter 'Of Judgment',

has afforded us only the twilight, as I may so say, of *Probability*, suitable, I presume, to that State of Mediocrity and Probationership, he has been pleased to place us in here; wherein to check our over-confidence and presumption, we might by every day's Experience be made sensible of our short-sightedness and liableness to Error; the Sense whereof might be a constant Admonition to us, to spend the days of this our Pilgrimage with Industry and Care, in the search, and following of that way, which might lead us to a State of greater Perfection.[107]

Richardson gives literary form to just such a world: in *Clarissa* the theology of the novel's postscript turns out to have epistemological and moral consequences of very much the kind that Locke describes. Certainty and plainness are unavailable in the novel, and the experience of reading it is precisely calculated to make the reader sensible of his 'short-sightedness and liableness to Error'. But Richardson's concern is not just to contemplate the awful indeterminacy of human life: he has created a chaos not for its own sake but so that the reader will take on the mantle of the novel's missing judge and strive to order it himself. In his own words, he 'leave[s] it to my Sovereign Judges the Readers, to agree as well as they can, which

---

[106] *Sentiments*, p. 299.   [107] *Essay*, p. 652.

to blame, which to acquit';[108] and in so doing he taxes and exercises these readers. Where Locke identifies the faculty of judgment as a resource with which to encounter indeterminacy, so Richardson seeks to elicit in the reader just this remedial faculty, as a way of making sense first of the text, and then of the world itself. The reader, unaided, must become a judge of all the difficulties thrown up by the text, and make his own construction, in the end, of all the evidence and pleas with which he is assailed. And in responding to this challenge he will develop capacities of understanding by which, thereafter, to light his way through the actual twilit, pro-bationary state of which the novel is only a vast image.

Richardson liked to observe these processes himself. He once wrote of contriving in *Grandison* 'Trials of the Readers Judgment, Manners, Taste, Capacity', and of observing their outcome in debates about the novels: 'I have often sat by in Company, and been silently pleased with the Oppor-tunity given me, by different Arguers, of looking into the Hearts of some of them, through Windows that at other times have been close shut up.'[109] By watching his readers judge, it would seem, the silent author could judge his readers – for in the end, as his remark suggests, the reader too is on trial.

[108] To Lady Bradshaigh, 8 February 1754, Carroll, p. 280.
[109] To Lady Echlin, 10 October 1754, Carroll, pp. 315–16.

Postscript

From Samuel Johnson to Ian Watt and beyond, critics of eighteenth-century fiction have tended to cast Richardson and Fielding as polar opposites, the vying pioneers of two alternative conceptions of the nature of fiction. While not underestimating the intelligence and creativity of Fielding's response to Richardson (qualities manifested in *Shamela*, the fifth number of the *Jacobite's Journal*, Fielding's letter on reading *Clarissa*, and many passages in *Tom Jones*), this study has presented a similar picture. Fielding's moral priorities, his construction of human nature, the informing ideologies of his writing and above all the narrative rhetoric through which he supervises the reading process all announce a radical divergence from the methods and concerns of his rival (in the words of his letter to Richardson) 'for that coy Mrs. Fame'.[1] In his last novel, however, Fielding is often seen to have moved towards a more Richardsonian stance, throwing new emphasis on the detailed representation of lived experience, and pursuing with new seriousness *Tom Jones*'s more playful references to the moral and cognitive development expected to result from the reader's encounter with the text.[2] 'As Histories of this Kind', he writes in the exordium to *Amelia*, ' ... may properly be called Models of HUMAN LIFE; so by observing minutely the several Incidents which tend to the Catastrophe or Completion of the whole, and the minute Causes whence those Incidents are produced, we shall best be instructed in this most useful of all Arts, which I call the ART of LIFE.'[3] Here the novel is presented as a paradigm of experience, in which the hidden patterns of life in the world are laid bare for the reader's edification. As we read the text, the suggestion is, we also become more effectively equipped to read reality itself.

Fielding's Richardsonian turn had its limits, however, most of all in its

---

[1] Fielding to Richardson, 15 October 1748, in *The Criticism of Henry Fielding*, ed. Williams, p. 189.
[2] John Sitter, *Literary Loneliness in Mid-Eighteenth-Century England* (Ithaca, 1982), pp. 189–213; Peter Sabor, '*Amelia* and *Sir Charles Grandison*: The Convergence of Fielding and Richardson', *Wascana Review*, 17 (1982), 3–18. See also Michael McKeon, *The Origins of the English Novel, 1600–1740* (Baltimore, 1987), pp. 357–421, where McKeon's dialectical model makes possible an unusually flexible account of the novelists' partings and meetings.
[3] *Amelia*, ed. Martin C. Battestin (Oxford, 1983), p. 17.

technical aspect. In *Amelia* the work of observation and connection remains the prerogative of an objective narrator, who organises incidents and causes into the paradigmatic whole referred to here, explaining the workings of the novel's 'Model' and showing how the world might similarly be understood. By contrast, *Clarissa* fights shy of all such explanatory modes, withholding the supervision of any detached, objective or authorial discourse in which patterns and connections are made clear. It is for this reason that Richardson's novel is itself paradigmatic of the world, a 'Model of HUMAN LIFE', in a more profound and troubling sense. It recapitulates, as *Amelia* does not, the opacity or indeterminacy of experience, throwing the onus of interpretation directly on a reader left to sort out for himself the copious but recalcitrant evidence of the text. It is through this very refusal to explain, moreover, that Richardson's own claim to instruct the reader in 'the ART of LIFE' is most tellingly advanced. When Aaron Hill described the Richardsonian novel as a 'comprehensive model of mankind' which 'lead[s] *surveyors* into what has been supposed *inscrutable*, and lay[s] man *open* to his *own discovery*',[4] he not only anticipated Fielding's terms but hinted also at the dynamic role accorded to the reader in Richardson's didactic project. In the absence of authorial guidance, the reader must himself participate in the work of 'discovery', cultivating in the reading process faculties of understanding, attentiveness and judgment of precisely the kind that are required in life itself. He must make sense of the text on his own initiative, and in so doing may indeed win from the text a new capacity to make sense of the world – a new competence (in *Amelia's* terms) in 'this most useful of all Arts'.

Yet it would be misleading to end in a picture of simple antithesis between Fielding's continuing commitment to authorial explanation and Richardson's enfranchisement of the reader. With the first edition of *Amelia* and the third of *Clarissa*, both published in 1751, the two writers did indeed draw together; but the move was as much Richardson's as Fielding's. Where Fielding began to seek as his explicit end a form of instruction that was largely Richardsonian in definition, Richardson began to adopt as his enabling means a technique of explanation that was typically Fieldingesque: both converged towards a single method of didactic narration. The processes by which Richardson began to retreat from the complexity and difficulty of his own text, dismayed as he was at the apparent failure of many readers to perform their allotted role as interpreters and judges, have been thoroughly mapped out in criticism.[5] Not

---

[4] Hill to Richardson, 29 July 1741, *Works* (1753), II, 168.

[5] See Mark Kinkead-Weekes, '*Clarissa* Restored?' *Review of English Studies*, NS 10, No. 38 (1959), 156–71; William Beatty Warner, *Reading Clarissa: The Struggles of Interpretation* (New Haven, 1979), pp. 180–218; Terry Castle, *Clarissa's Ciphers: Meaning and Disruption in Richardson's Clarissa* (Ithaca, 1982), pp. 175–80. Qualifications to this hostile view of the third edition are made in Florian Stuber, 'On Original and Final Intentions, or Can There be an Authoritative

only did he overhaul the epistolary text, blackening Lovelace and whitening Clarissa so as to polarise the novel's central conflict; he also superimposed on it, in the various interventions of an editorial voice, a layer of analysis and explanation that is at once extraneous and anomalous. The 'editor' of the 1747–8 *Clarissa* is little more than a convenience to explain the provenance of the text, and his footnotes rarely do more than enable the reader, by supplying references to other pages, to make his own comparisons and checks. But in the editions of 1749 and 1751 the editor begins to double as a quasi-authorial narrator, guiding the reader's response to particular cruxes by means of new explanatory footnotes, endorsing passages in the letters themselves by typographical emphasis, and advancing in an abstract of fifty closely printed pages what seems to be presented as a definitive summary of the work. This abstract, Richardson wrote, would 'not only point out the principal Facts, and shew the Connexion of the Whole': it would also enable readers 'to form a judgment as well of the *blameable* as of the *laudable* Conduct of the principal persons'.[6] In private he added (in terms which seem to acknowledge the source of these explanations not in the complexity of the text itself but in some subsequent authorial whim) that the abstract of the novel was intended to guide 'their Understanding of it, in the Way I chose to have it understood in'. The italics would carry this work of remedial control into the very body of the text, 'to obviate as I went along, tho' covertly, such Objections as I had heard'. The footnotes would complete the process, in ways that might aptly be described with reference to Richardson's own earlier sarcasm about Pope, who 'could not trust his Works with the Vulgar, without Notes ... to tell them what he meant, and that he *had* a Meaning, in this or that Place'.[7]

It is hard to imagine a set of measures more thoroughly at odds with the original text, where narrative explanation is never detached, in person or in tense, from the conflicts of the story, and where the reader is entrusted with the final resolution of meaning. But the objection to these retrospective interventions is not simply that they work to curtail the reader's interpretative role. The analyses they advance are often crude and reductive, significantly blunting the complex text they pretend to explain in full. By 1751 Richardson was berating large sections of his audience in terms quite as extravagant as those of his diatribe against the alleged social enemies of the 1730s; and it is clear from the anxious tone of these attacks that simplification of his own work had now become an acceptable price to

Clarissa?', *TEXT*, 2 (1985), 229–44; see also the more neutral accounts of Shirley Van Marter, 'Richardson's Revisions of *Clarissa* in the Second Edition', *Studies in Bibliography*, 26 (1973), 107–32; 'Richardson's Revisions of *Clarissa* in the Third and Fourth Editions', *Studies in Bibliography*, 28 (1975), 119–52.
6 *Clarissa*, 2nd edn (1749), I, iii–iv.
7 To Hill, 12 July 1749, Carroll, pp. 126, 125; 7 November 1748, Carroll, p. 100.

pay. On Clarissa's alleged prudery he now hopes that readers 'will rather endeavour to raise their Affections to Clarissa's virtuous Standard, than by striving to impeach her Character, effectually debase, if not violently tear up, the decisive Standard of Right and Wrong'; on the question of marriage between her and Lovelace he now insists on a polarity between them which 'must for ever continue in Force, till the eternal Differences of Vice and Virtue shall coalesce, and make one putrid Mass, a Chaos in the Moral and Intellectual World'.[8] These outbursts were withheld from the printed preface of 1751, but as expressions of Richardson's private frustration their implication remains clear. In the hands of a readership of Dunces (and the echoes here of the apocalyptic conclusion to Pope's poem are hard to miss), *Clarissa*'s experimental openness had merely restored the Empire of Chaos, and must now at all costs be withdrawn. Readers had abused the liberties extended to them; the author's authority was now to regain its place.

With these gestures, Richardson ended by denying (and significantly attenuating) what is, I have argued, the most distinctive, challenging and valuable aspect of his work – its difficulty, and the intensity of the demands it makes of the reader. Richardson did then go on to write a further novel, of course, in which the reader is apparently reinstated in his former role as the arbiter of textual meaning. Indeed, it was in his letters on *Grandison* of 1753–4 that he most explicitly formulated his aesthetic of authorial reticence, central to which was the activity of readers encouraged in response to become 'if not Authors, Carvers' of the text. One might even assume that Richardson had put behind him his distress at the reception of *Clarissa*, and was pursuing his larger project undeterred. But in *Grandison*, disappointingly though by no means coincidentally, little is at stake – least of all the order or chaos of 'the Moral and Intellectual World'. Meanings are left for the reader to make out, certainly; but it would take some very ingenious re-reading indeed to make these meanings matter very much. Richardson, it is clear, was now playing safe. He would never return to investigate themes of the vexedness and urgency of *Clarissa*'s.

Even with these adjusted sights, the reception of *Grandison* seems to have brought with it only further disillusionment. Subsequently, Richardson insisted that he would not begin a new work of any kind until his two last 'were generally understood and attended to'. Instead he expressed the melancholy hope that 'when this hasty-judging world will be convinced that they have seen the *last work* of this too-voluminous writer, they will give what he has done, more of their Attention – *perhaps* – '.[9] He ended, in short, in a perception of his own failure, in retreat, and ultimately in

---

[8] *Hints of Prefaces*, pp. 13, 14.
[9] To Susanna Highmore, 31 January 1754, Carroll, p. 275; to Lady Bradshaigh, 14 February 1754, Carroll, p. 289.

silence. As these last remarks of his indicate, however, the problem lay not so much with *Clarissa* itself as with the failure of many contemporaries to rise to the challenge it had set. As Diderot wrote of the novels, 'le nombre des lecteurs qui en sentiront tout le prix ne sera jamais grand';[10] yet Richardson himself was temperamentally ill equipped to combine the demanding nature of his writing with a corresponding readiness to see it succeed only in the case of a restricted circle. Unable to shrug off the responses of readers lacking in the literary competence of generations for whom (as now) the novel has become a familiar genre, Richardson's dilemma was quite simply that of the pioneer. As reading *Clarissa* against the chequered history of its reception shows, the novel demands a fitter readership than the one it originally found – readers prepared indeed to read with 'more of their Attention'.

[10] 'Eloge', *Œuvres esthétiques*, ed. Vernière, p. 39.

Works cited

Works marked with an asterisk will shortly be reprinted in vols. IX–XI of *The Clarissa Project*, a sixteen-volume edition of *Clarissa* and related material published by AMS Press under the general editorship of Florian Stuber.

Works by Samuel Richardson

An Address to the Public (1754), in *The History of Sir Charles Grandison*, 7 vols. (1754 (pub. 1753–4)), VII, 424–42

Æsop's Fables (1740 (pub. 1739); rpt. New York, 1974)

*Answer to the Letter of a Very Reverend and Worthy Gentleman, Objecting to the Warmth of a Particular Scene in the History of Clarissa (1749), in T. C. Duncan Eaves and Ben D. Kimpel, 'An Unpublished Pamphlet by Samuel Richardson', *Philological Quarterly*, 63 (1984), 401–9

The Apprentice's Vade Mecum; or, Young Man's Pocket-Companion (1734 (pub. 1733)), ed. A. D. McKillop, Augustan Reprint Society Nos. 169–70 (Los Angeles, 1975)

Clarissa; or, The History of a Young Lady, 7 vols. (1748 (pub. 1747–8))

Clarissa, ed. Angus Ross (Harmondsworth, 1985)

Clarissa, 2nd edn, 7 vols. (1749)

Clarissa, 3rd edn, 8 vols. (1751), reprinted with an introduction by Florian Stuber, *The Clarissa Project*, I–VIII (New York, 1990)

Clarissa, 4th edn, 8 vols. (1759)

*A Collection of the Moral and Instructive Sentiments, Maxims, Cautions, Instructions, and Reflections, Contained in the Histories of Pamela, Clarissa, and Sir Charles Grandison (1755)

Familiar Letters on Important Occasions (1741), ed. Brian W. Downs (1928)

The History of Sir Charles Grandison (1753–4), ed. Jocelyn Harris, 3 vols. (1972)

*Letters and Passages Restored from the Original Manuscripts of the History of Clarissa (1751)

*Meditations Collected from the Sacred Books (1750)

Pamela; or, Virtue Rewarded (1740), ed. T. C. Duncan Eaves and Ben D. Kimpel (Boston, Mass., 1971)

Pamela, Everyman's Library edn, 2 vols. (1914)

Samuel Richardson, Clarissa: Preface, Hints of Prefaces, and Postscript, ed. R. F. Brissenden, Augustan Reprint Society No. 103 (Los Angeles, 1964)

250

A Seasonable Examination of the Pleas and Pretensions of the Proprietors of, and Subscribers to, Play-houses (1735)

*'Six Original Letters upon Duelling', *Candid Review and Literary Repository*, 1 (1765), 227–31

Richardson's correspondence

The Correspondence of Samuel Richardson, ed. Anna Lætitia Barbauld, 6 vols. (1804)

'Original Letters of Miss E. Carter and Mr. Samuel Richardson', *Monthly Magazine*, 33 (1812), 533–43

The Richardson–Stinstra Correspondence and Stinstra's Prefaces to Clarissa, ed. William C. Slattery (Carbondale, 1969)

Selected Letters of Samuel Richardson, ed. John Carroll (Oxford, 1964)

Victoria and Albert Museum, Forster Collection, 48E5–48E10 (Vols. XI–XVI)

Other primary texts

Addison, Joseph, and Richard Steele, *The Spectator*, ed. Donald F. Bond, 5 vols. (Oxford, 1965)

[Allestree, Richard], *The Ladies Calling* (Oxford, 1673)
  The Practice of Christian Graces; or, The Whole Duty of Man (1659)

Atterbury, Francis, *Maxims, Reflections and Observations, Divine, Moral and Political* (1723)

Bailey, Nathan, *An Universal Etymological Dictionary* (1721)

Barth, John, *Letters* (1979)

[Bayly, Lewis], *The Practice of Piety*, 51st edn (1714)

Beattie, James, 'On Fable and Romance', in *Dissertations Moral and Critical* (1783), pp. 503–74

A Bill for Restraining the Number of Houses for Playing of Interludes, and for the Better Regulating Common Players of Interludes (1735), reprinted in *The Stage and the Licensing Act, 1729–1739*, ed. Vincent J. Liesenfeld (New York, 1981)

Blair, Hugh, *Lectures on Rhetoric and Belles-Lettres*, 2 vols. (1783)

Blake, William, *The Marriage of Heaven and Hell*, in *Complete Writings*, ed. Geoffrey Keynes (Oxford, 1966), pp. 148–58

Bolingbroke, Henry St John, Viscount, *Works*, 5 vols. (1754)

Boswell, James, *Boswell's Life of Johnson*, ed. George Birkbeck Hill, rev. L. F. Powell, 6 vols. (Oxford, 1934–50)

[Boyer, Abel], *Historical Narrative of the Tryals of Mr. George Kelly, and of Dr. Francis Atterbury* (1727)

Browning, Robert, *The Ring and the Book*, ed. Richard D. Altick (Harmondsworth, 1971)

Burnet, Gilbert, *Some Passages of the Life and Death of the Right Honourable John, Earl of Rochester* (1680)

Carter, Elizabeth, and Catherine Talbot, *A Series of Letters between Mrs. Elizabeth Carter and Mrs. Catherine Talbot, from the Year 1741 to 1770*, 4 vols. (1809)

Chapone, Hester [Mulso], *Posthumous Works of Mrs. Chapone*, 2 vols. (1807)

[Chapone, Sarah], *Remarks on Mrs. Muilman's Letter to the Right Honourable the Earl of Chesterfield* (1750)

'The Characters of Prevot, Le Sage, Richardson, Fielding, and Rousseau', *Gentleman's Magazine*, 40 (1770), in *Novel and Romance, 1700–1800: A Documentary Record*, ed. Ioan Williams (1970), pp. 274–6

Cibber, Colley, *An Apology for the Life of Colley Cibber*, ed. B. R. S. Fone (Ann Arbor, 1968)

    The Lady's Lecture, A Theatrical Dialogue (1748)

    Love's Last Shift; or, The Fool in Fashion, in *Colley Cibber: Three Sentimental Comedies*, ed. Maureen Sullivan (New Haven, 1973), pp. 1–84

Cleland, John, *Memoirs of a Woman of Pleasure*, ed. Peter Sabor (Oxford, 1985)

Coleridge, Samuel Taylor, *Anima Poetae*, ed. Ernest Hartley Coleridge (1895)

    Biographia Literaria, ed. James Engell and W. Jackson Bate, *The Collected Works of Samuel Taylor Coleridge*, VII, 2 vols. (Princeton, 1983)

Collier, Jeremy, *A Short View of the Profaneness and Immorality of the English Stage* (1698)

Collins, William Wilkie, *The Woman in White*, ed. Harvey Peter Sucksmith (Oxford, 1973)

Cowper, William, *Poetical Works*, ed. H. S. Milford, 4th edn, rev. Norma Russell (1971)

Critical Remarks on Sir Charles Grandison, Clarissa and Pamela (1754), ed. A. D. McKillop, Augustan Reprint Society No. 21 (Los Angeles, 1950)

Cuisin, Pierre, *Le Bâtard de Lovelace et la fille naturelle de la Marquise de Merteuil, ou Les Mœurs vengées*, 4 vols. (Paris, 1806)

Defoe, Daniel, *The Family Instructor*, 2 vols., I, 15th edn (1761); II, 4th edn (1741)

    The Fortunes and Misfortunes of the Famous Moll Flanders, &c., ed. G. A. Starr (Oxford, 1981)

    A New Family Instructor, 2nd edn (1732)

    Religious Courtship, 4th edn (1735)

    Roxana, ed. Jane Jack (Oxford, 1981)

    A Tour thro' the Whole Island of Great Britain ... The Fourth Edition. With Very Great Additions, Improvements, and Corrections; Which Bring It down to the Year 1748, 4 vols. (1748)

Delany, Mary, *The Autobiography and Correspondence of Mary Granville, Mrs. Delany*, ed. Lady Llanover, 6 vols. (1861–2)

Delany, Patrick, *Fifteen Sermons upon Social Duties* (1744)

    Twenty Sermons on Social Duties, and Their Opposite Vices (1747)

Dennis, John, *An Essay on the Genius and Writings of Shakespear* (1712)

Diderot, Denis, 'Eloge de Richardson', in *Œuvres esthétiques*, ed. Paul Vernière (Paris, 1959), pp. 29–48

    La Religieuse, Garnier ed. (Paris, 1968)

Dostoevsky, Fyodor, *Poor Folk*, in *Three Short Novels by Fyodor Dostoyevsky*, trans. Constance Garnett (New York, 1960), pp. 141–273

Duncombe, John, ed., *Letters, by Several Eminent Persons Deceased*, 2nd edn, 3 vols. (1773)

Duncombe, William, *Junius Brutus, A Tragedy* (1735)

[Dunton, John, *et al.*], *The Athenian Oracle: Being an Entire Collection of All the Valuable Questions and Answers in the Old Athenian Mercuries*, 2nd edn, 3 vols. (1704)

'Easy, Sir Charles', 'A Short Character of *Clarissa*', *Gentleman's Magazine*, 18 (1748), 548–50

Echlin, Lady Elizabeth, *An Alternative Ending to Richardson's Clarissa*, ed. Dimiter Daphinoff, Schweizer Anglistische Arbeiten No. 107 (Bern, 1982)

Eliot, George, *Essays*, 2nd edn (Edinburgh, 1884)

Middlemarch, ed. W. J. Harvey (Harmondsworth, 1965)

Fielding, Henry, *Amelia*, ed. Martin C. Battestin (Oxford, 1983)

The Criticism of Henry Fielding, ed. Ioan Williams (1970)

An Enquiry into the Causes of the Late Increase of Robbers and Related Writings, ed. Malvin R. Zirker (Oxford, 1988)

The History of the Adventures of Joseph Andrews and An Apology for the Life of Mrs Shamela Andrews, ed. Douglas Brooks (1970)

The History of Tom Jones, A Foundling, ed. Martin C. Battestin and Fredson Bowers, 2 vols. (Oxford, 1974)

The Jacobite's Journal and Related Writings, ed. W. B. Coley (Oxford, 1975)

Miscellanies, Volume One, ed. Henry Knight Miller (Oxford, 1972)

The True Patriot and Related Writings, ed. W. B. Coley (Oxford, 1987)

Fielding, Sarah, *Remarks on Clarissa*, ed. Peter Sabor, Augustan Reprint Society Nos. 231–2 (Los Angeles, 1985)

Fleetwood, William, *The Relative Duties of Parents and Children, Husbands and Wives, Masters and Servants* (1705)

Forbes, Sir William, *An Account of the Life and Writings of James Beattie*, 2nd edn, 3 vols. (Edinburgh, 1807)

Gally, Henry, *Some Considerations upon Clandestine Marriages*, 2nd edn (1750), reprinted in *The Marriage Act of 1753: Four Tracts*, Garland facsimile edn (New York, 1984)

Godwin, William, *The Enquirer* (Dublin, 1797)

Graham, Catharine Macaulay, *Letters on Education* (1790)

Hall, Joseph, *The Remedy of Discontentment; or, A Treatise of Contentation* (1652)

Resolutions and Decisions of Divers Practicall Cases of Conscience (1649)

*Haller, Albrecht von, 'A Critical Account of *Clarissa*', *Gentleman's Magazine*, 19 (1749), 245–6 and 345–9, reprinted in *Novel and Romance, 1700–1800: A Documentary Record*, ed. Ioan Williams (1970), pp. 130–41

Hartley, David, *Observations on Man* (1749)

[Hawkesworth, John, *et al.*], *The Adventurer*, 3rd edn, 4 vols. (1756)

Hawkins, Sir John, *The Life of Samuel Johnson, LL.D.*, 2nd edn (1787)

[Haywood, Eliza], *Anti-Pamela; or, Feign'd Innocence Detected* (1741)

Hill, Aaron, *Works*, 4 vols. (1753)

[Hill, Aaron, and William Bond], *The Plain Dealer*, 2 vols. (1730)

[Hill, Aaron, and William Popple], *The Prompter*, ed. William W. Appleton and Kalman A. Burmin (New York, 1966)

[Hoadly, Benjamin], *Remarks on Mr. Kelly's Late Speech at the Bar of the House of Lords ... By Britannicus* (1723)

Hume, David, *Philosophical Essays Concerning Human Understanding*, 2nd edn (1750)

Jacob, Giles, *A New Law-Dictionary*, 6th edn (1750)

Johnson, Charles, *Cælia; or, The Perjur'd Lover* (1733)

Johnson, Samuel, *A Dictionary of the English Language*, 2 vols. (1755)

    Johnson on Shakespeare, ed. Arthur Sherbo, intr. Bertrand H. Bronson, *The Yale Edition of the Works of Samuel Johnson*, VII–VIII (New Haven, 1968)

    Letters, ed. R. W. Chapman, 3 vols. (Oxford, 1952)

    Lives of the English Poets, ed. George Birkbeck Hill, 3 vols. (Oxford, 1905)

    The Rambler, ed. W. J. Bate and Albrecht B. Strauss, *The Yale Edition of the Works of Samuel Johnson*, III–V (New Haven, 1969)

The Journals of the House of Commons, 20 (1722–7), 22 (1732–7)

Kelly, George, *The Speech of Mr. George Kelly. Spoke at the Bar of the House of Lords, on Thursday, the 2d of May, 1723* (1723)

Laclos, Pierre-Ambroise-François Choderlos de, *Œuvres complètes*, ed. Laurent Versini (Paris, 1979)

Law, William, *The Absolute Unlawfulness of the Stage-Entertainment Fully Demonstrated* (1726)

Lee, Nathaniel, *Lucius Junius Brutus*, ed. J. Loftis (1968)

Leland, John, *A View of the Principal Deistical Writers*, 2 vols. (1754–5)

Lennox, Charlotte, *The Female Quixote*, ed. Margaret Dalziel (1970)

L'Estrange, Sir Roger, *Fables, of Æsop and Other Eminent Mythologists* (1692)

    (trans.), *Five Love-Letters from a Nun to a Cavalier* (1678), in *The Novel in Letters: Epistolary Fiction in the Early English Novel, 1678–1740*, ed. Natascha Würzbach (Coral Gables, 1969), pp. 3–21

Letter to a Great Man in France (1743)

A Letter to the Public: Containing the Substance of What Hath Been Offered in the Late Debates upon the Subject of the Act of Parliament, for the Better Preventing of Clandestine Marriages (1753), in *The Marriage Act of 1753: Four Tracts*, Garland facsimile edn (New York, 1984)

Lillo, George, *The London Merchant*, ed. William H. McBurney (1965)

Locke, John, *An Essay Concerning Human Understanding*, ed. Peter H. Nidditch (Oxford, 1975)

    The Reasonableness of Christianity, ed. I. T. Ramsay (1958)

    Some Thoughts Concerning Education, ed. John W. and Jean S. Yolton (Oxford, 1989)

    Two Treatises of Government, ed. Peter Laslett (Cambridge, 1960)

Mackenzie, Henry, *Letters to Elizabeth Rose of Kilravock*, ed. Horst W. Drescher (Edinburgh, 1967)

    The Man of Feeling, ed. Brian Vickers (1967)

Mandeville, Bernard, *The Fable of the Bees; or, Private Vices, Publick Benefits*, ed. F. B. Kaye, 2 vols. (Oxford, 1924)

Mason, William, *Satirical Poems by William Mason with Notes by Horace Walpole*, ed. Paget Toynbee (Oxford, 1926)

Milton, John, *Paradise Lost*, in *Poetical Works*, ed. Helen Darbishire (Oxford, 1958), pp. 1–281

Montagu, Lady Mary Wortley, *Complete Letters*, ed. Robert Halsband, 3 vols. (Oxford, 1965–7)

Mulso, John, *The Letters to Gilbert White of Selborne*, ed. Rashleigh Holt-White (1907)

Nichols, John, *Biographical and Literary Anecdotes of William Bowyer* (1782)
  Literary Anecdotes of the Eighteenth Century, 9 vols. (1812–15)
'Observations sur *Clarice*', *Journal encyclopédique* (15 March 1763), 63–70
Pamela Censured, ed. Charles Batten, Jr, Augustan Reprint Society No. 175 (Los
  Angeles, 1976)
The Parallel; or, Pilkington and Philips Compared (Dublin, 1748)
Pascal, Blaise, *The Provincial Letters*, trans. A. J. Krailsheimer (Harmondsworth,
  1967)
*The Paths of Virtue Delineated; or, The History in Miniature of the Celebrated Pamela,
  Clarissa Harlowe, and Sir Charles Grandison* (1756)
Phillips, Teresia Constantia, *An Apology for the Conduct of Mrs. T. C. Phillips*, 3 vols.
  (1748–9)
A Letter Humbly Addressed to the Rt. Hon. the Earl of Chesterfield (1750)
Piozzi, Hester Lynch, *Anecdotes of the Late Samuel Johnson*, in *Johnsonian Miscellanies*,
  ed. George Birbeck Hill, 2 vols. (1897), I, 141–351
Plato, *The Republic*, trans. Desmond Lee, 2nd edn (Harmondsworth, 1974)
[Plummer, Francis], *A Candid Examination of the History of Sir Charles Grandison*, 3rd
  edn (1755)
Pope, Alexander, *A Collection of Letters, Never before Printed: Written by Alexander
  Pope, Esq; and Other Ingenious Gentlemen, to the Late Aaron Hill, Esq* (1751)
Correspondence, ed. George Sherburn, 5 vols. (Oxford, 1956)
The Dunciad, ed. James Sutherland, *The Twickenham Edition of the Poems of
  Alexander Pope*, V, 3rd edn (1963)
Epistles to Several Persons, ed. F. W. Bateson, *The Twickenham Edition of the Poems
  of Alexander Pope*, III ii, 2nd edn (1961)
The Prose Works of Alexander Pope, 1725–1744, ed. Rosemary Cowler (Oxford,
  1986)
The Rape of the Lock and Other Poems, ed. Geoffrey Tillotson, *The Twickenham
  Edition of the Poems of Alexander Pope*, II, 3rd edn (1962)
Porrett, Robert, *Clarissa; or, The Fatal Seduction* (1788)
Povey, Charles, *The Virgin in Eden*, 2nd edn (1741)
Prévost d'Exiles, Antoine François, *The History of a Fair Greek*, 2nd edn (1755)
  (trans.), *Lettres angloises, ou Histoire de Miss Clarisse Harlove*, 6 vols. ('Londres',
  1751)
Priestley, Joseph, *A Course of Lectures on Oratory and Criticism*, ed. Vincent M.
  Bevilacqua and Richard Murphy (Carbondale, 1965)
'Remarks on *Eloisa*', *Critical Review*, 12 (1761), 203–11, reprinted in *Novel and
  Romance, 1700–1800: A Documentary Record*, ed. Ioan Williams (1970),
  pp. 242–6
'Remarks on *Pamela*. By a Prude', *London Magazine*, 10 (1741), 250
Richardson, Jonathan, *Explanatory Notes and Remarks on Milton's Paradise Lost*
  (1734)
Roe, Sir Thomas, *The Negotiations of Sir Thomas Roe, in His Embassy to the Ottoman
  Porte, from the Year 1621 to 1628 Inclusive* (1740)
Rousseau, Jean-Jacques, *Julie, ou La Nouvelle Héloïse*, Garnier edn (Paris, 1967)
Rowe, Nicholas, *The Fair Penitent*, ed. Malcolm Goldstein (1969)

Sade, Donatien-Alphonse-François, Comte de, 'Idée sur les romans', in *Les Crimes de l'amour* (Brussels, 1881), pp. 97–135

Seward, William, *Anecdotes of Distinguished Persons*, 5th edn, 4 vols. (1804)

Shakespeare, William, *King Lear*, ed. Kenneth Muir (1972)

[Shaw, Peter], *The Reflector* (1750)

Shenstone, William, *Letters*, ed. Duncan Mallam (Minneapolis, 1939)

Silvester, Eusebius, *The Causes of the Present High Price of Corn and Grain, and A State of the Abuses and Impositions Practised upon the Publick in General, and the Poor in Particular, by the Millers or Meal-men* (1757)

Skelton, Philip, *The Chevalier's Hopes* (Dublin, 1745)

    Complete Works, ed. Robert Lynam, 6 vols. (1824)

    Ophiomaches; or, Deism Revealed, 2 vols. (1749)

    Truth in a Mask (Dublin, 1744)

Smith, Adam, *The Theory of Moral Sentiments*, ed. D. D. Raphael and A. L. McFie (Oxford, 1976)

Smollett, Tobias, *The Adventures of Peregrine Pickle*, ed. J. L. Clifford, rev. Paul-Gabriel Boucé (Oxford, 1983)

    The Expedition of Humphry Clinker, ed. Lewis M. Knapp (1966)

Sprat, Thomas, 'An Account of the Life and Writings of Mr. Abraham Cowley', in *Critical Essays of the Seventeenth Century*, ed. J. E. Spingarn, 3 vols. (Oxford, 1908), II, 119–46

    The History of the Royal Society, ed. Jackson I. Cope and Harold Whitmore Jones (1959)

Staël, Anne-Louise-Germaine Necker, Mme de, *Essai sur les fictions*, intr. Michel Tournier (Paris, 1979)

    De la Littérature considerée dans ses rapports avecs les institutions sociales, ed. Paul van Tieghem (Geneva, 1959)

    'Quelques réflexions sur le but moral de Delphine', *Œuvres complètes* (Brussels, 1820), V, iii–xxv

Stebbing, Henry, *A Dissertation on the Power of States to Deny Civil Protection to the Marriage of Minors Made without the Consent of Their Parents or Guardians* (1755), in *The Marriage Act of 1753: Four Tracts*, Garland facsimile edn (New York, 1984)

[Steele, Richard, ed.?], *The Ladies Library*, 3 vols. (1714)

Sterne, Laurence, *The Life and Opinions of Tristram Shandy, Gentleman*, ed. Ian Campbell Ross (Oxford, 1983)

Strabo, *The Geography*, Loeb edn, with an English translation by H. L. Jones, 8 vols. (1917–32)

Swift, Jonathan, *Gulliver's Travels*, ed. Paul Turner (Oxford, 1986)

Tate, Nahum, *The History of King Lear*, in *Five Restoration Adaptations of Shakespeare*, ed. Christopher Spencer (Urbana, 1965), pp. 201–74

Taylor, Jeremy, *Ductor Dubitantium; or, The Rule of Conscience in All Her General Measures*, 2 vols. (1660)

    Holy Living and Holy Dying, ed. P. G. Stanwood, 2 vols. (Oxford, 1989)

Thomson, James, *Liberty, The Castle of Indolence, and Other Poems*, ed. James Sambrook (Oxford, 1986)

    The Seasons, ed. James Sambrook (Oxford, 1981)

'To the Author of *Shamela*', *London Magazine*, 10 (1741), 304

Turner, Thomas, *The Diary of Thomas Turner, 1754–1765*, ed. David Vaisey (Oxford, 1985)

W—, J—, *Pamela; or, The Fair Impostor* (1744)

Walpole, Horace, *The History of the Modern Taste in Gardening* (1771), in Isabel Wakelin Chase, *Horace Walpole: Gardenist* (Princeton, 1943), pp. 1–79

Warburton, William, *The Divine Legation of Moses Demonstrated*, 4th edn, 5 vols. (1764–5)

A Sermon Preach'd at the Thanksgiving Appointed To Be Observed the Ninth of October, for the Suppression of the Late Unnatural Rebellion (1746)

[Webster, William, ed.], *The Weekly Miscellany* (1732–41)

Wharton, Philip Duke of, *His Grace the Duke of Wharton's Speech in the House of Lords, on the Third Reading of the Bill To Inflict Pains and Penalties on Francis (Late) Lord Bishop of Rochester* (1723)

The Life and Writings of Philip, Late Duke of Wharton (1732)

Whitefield, George, *A Short Account of God's Dealings with the Reverend Mr. George Whitefield* (1740)

Wilmot, John, Earl of Rochester, *Familiar Letters: Written by the Right Honourable John Late Earl of Rochester, and Several Other Persons of Honour and Quality* (1697)

Letters, ed. Jeremy Treglown (Oxford, 1980)

The World, 6 vols. (1755–7)

Worthington, *An Essay on the Scheme and Conduct, Procedure and Extent of Man's Redemption* (1743)

[Yorke, Charles], *Some Considerations on the Law of Forfeiture, for High Treason. Occasioned by a Clause, in the Late Act, for Making It Treason To Correspond with the Pretender's Sons, or Any of Their Agents*, 3rd edn (1748)

Young, Edward, *Conjectures on Original Composition* (1759)

Correspondence, ed. Henry Pettit (Oxford, 1971)

Yourcenar, Marguerite, *Alexis*, in *Œuvres romanesques* (Paris, 1982)

Secondary texts

Aikins, Janet E., 'A Plot Discover'd; or, The Uses of *Venice Preserv'd* within *Clarissa*', *University of Toronto Quarterly*, 55 (1986), 219–34

Allen, Walter, *The English Novel* (1954)

Altman, Janet Gurkin, 'Addressed and Undressed Language in *Les Liaisons dangereuses*', in *Laclos: Critical Approaches to Les Liaisons dangereuses*, ed. Lloyd R. Free (Madrid, 1978), pp. 223–57

Epistolarity: Approaches to a Form (Columbus, 1982)

Amory, Hugh, '*Shamela* as Aesopic Satire', *ELH*, 38 (1971), 239–53

Anderson, Howard, and Irvin Ehrenpreis, 'The Familier Letter in the Eighteenth Century: Some Generalizations', in *The Familiar Letter in the Eighteenth Century*, ed. Howard Anderson, Philip B. Daghlian, and Irvin Ehrenpreis (Lawrence, 1966), pp. 269–82

Anthony, Sister Rose, *The Jeremy Collier Stage Controversy, 1698–1726* (New York, 1937)

Austin, J. L., *How To Do Things with Words*, 2nd edn (Oxford, 1975)

Bakhtin, Mikhail, *Problems of Dostoevsky's Poetics*, trans. Caryl Emerson (Minneapolis, 1984)

Ball, Donald L., *Samuel Richardson's Theory of Fiction* (The Hague, 1971)

Barish, Jonas A., *The Antitheatrical Prejudice* (Berkeley and Los Angeles, 1981)

Battestin, Martin C., *The Moral Basis of Fielding's Art: A Study of Joseph Andrews* (Middletown, Conn., 1959)

   The Providence of Wit: Aspects of Form in Augustan Literature and the Arts (Oxford, 1974)

   Henry Fielding: A Life (1989)

Beattie, J. M., *Crime and the Courts in England, 1660–1800* (Oxford, 1986)

Beebee, Thomas O., *Clarissa on the Continent: Translation and Seduction* (University Park, Pennsylvania, 1990)

Beer, Gillian, 'Richardson, Milton, and the Status of Evil', *Review of English Studies*, NS 19, No. 75 (1968), 261–70

Bender, John, *Imagining the Penitentiary: Fiction and the Architecture of Mind in Eighteenth-Century England* (Chicago, 1987)

Bennett, G. V., 'Jacobitism and the Rise of Walpole', in *New Perspectives: Studies in English Thought and Society*, ed. N. McKendrick (1974), pp. 70–92

   The Tory Crisis in Church and State, 1688–1730: The Career of Francis Atterbury Bishop of Rochester (Oxford, 1975)

Black, Frank Gees, *The Epistolary Novel in the Late Eighteenth Century* (Eugene, 1940)

Booth, Wayne C., *The Rhetoric of Fiction*, 2nd edn (Chicago, 1983)

Boulton, James T., 'Arbitrary Power: An Eighteenth-Century Obsession', *Studies in Burke and His Time*, 9, No. 3 (1968), 905–26

Braudy, 'Penetration and Impenetrability in *Clarissa*', in *New Approaches to Eighteenth-Century Literature: Selected Papers from the English Institute*, ed. Phillip Harth (New York, 1974), pp. 177–206

Brophy, Elizabeth Bergen, 'A Richardson Letter: "Carpers" or "Carvers"?', *Notes & Queries*, NS 25 (1978), 44–5

   Samuel Richardson: The Triumph of Craft (Knoxville, 1974)

Butler, Janet, 'The Garden: Early Symbol of Clarissa's Complicity', *Studies in English Literature 1500–1900*, 24 (1984), 527–44

Carlton, Peter J., '*Tom Jones* and the '45 Once Again', *Studies in the Novel*, 20 (1988), 361–73

Castle, Terry, *Clarissa's Ciphers: Meaning and Disruption in Richardson's Clarissa* (Ithaca, 1982)

   Masquerade and Civilization: The Carnivalesque in Eighteenth-Century English Culture and Fiction (1986)

Clark, J. C. D., *English Society, 1688–1832: Ideology, Social Structure and Political Practice during the Ancien Régime* (Cambridge, 1985)

Clarke, George, 'Grecian Taste and Gothic Virtue: Lord Cobham's Gardening Programme and Its Iconography', *Apollo* (June, 1973), 566–71

Cleary, Thomas, *Henry Fielding: Political Writer* (Waterloo, Ontario, 1984)

   'Jacobitism in *Tom Jones*: The Basis for a Hypothesis', *Philological Quarterly*, 52 (1973), 239–51

Combs, William W., 'The Return to Paradise Hall: An Essay on *Tom Jones*', *South Atlantic Quarterly*, 67 (1968), 419–36

Connaughton, Michael E., 'Richardson's Familiar Quotations: *Clarissa* and Bysshe's *Art of English Poetry*', *Philological Quarterly*, 60 (1981), 183–95

Copeland, Edward, 'Remapping London: *Clarissa* and the Woman at the Window', in *Samuel Richardson: Tercentenary Essays*, ed. Margaret Anne Doody and Peter Sabor (Cambridge, 1989), pp. 51–69

Crompton, Samuel, 'Richardson's *Clarissa* Annotated', *Notes & Queries*, 5th Series, 8 (1877), 101–3

Cruickshanks, Eveline, *Political Untouchables: The Tories and the '45* (1979)

Cruickshanks, Eveline and Erskine-Hill, Howard, 'The Waltham Black Act and Jacobitism', *Journal of British Studies*, 24 (1985), 358–65

Culler, Jonathan, *On Deconstruction: Theory and Criticism after Structuralism* (1983)

Davis, Bertram H., *Johnson before Boswell: A Study of Sir John Hawkins' Life of Samuel Johnson* (New Haven, 1960)

Davis, Lennard J., *Factual Fictions: The Origins of the English Novel* (New York, 1983)

Day, W. G., '*Tristram Shandy*: Locke May Not Be the Key', in *Laurence Sterne: Riddles and Mysteries*, ed. Valerie Grosvenor Myer (1984), pp. 75–83

Dickinson, H. T., *Liberty and Property: Political Ideology in Eighteenth-Century Britain* (1977)

DiSalvo, Jackie, *War of Titans: Blake's Critique of Milton and the Politics of Religion* (Pittsburgh, 1983)

Donaldson, Ian, *The Rapes of Lucretia: A Myth and Its Transformations* (Oxford, 1982)

Doody, Margaret Anne, *A Natural Passion: A Study of the Novels of Samuel Richardson* (Oxford, 1974)

Dussinger, John A., 'Richardson and Johnson: Critical Agreement on Rowe's *The Fair Penitent*', *English Studies*, 49 (1968), 45–7

Eagleton, Terry, *The Rape of Clarissa: Writing, Sexuality and Class Struggle in Samuel Richardson* (Oxford, 1982)

Eaves, T. C. Duncan, and Ben. D. Kimpel, 'The Composition of *Clarissa* and Its Revision before Publication', *PMLA*, 83 (1968), 416–28

'Richardson's Revisions of *Pamela*', *Studies in Bibliography*, 20 (1967), 61–88

Samuel Richardson: A Biography (Oxford, 1971)

Ellrich, Robert, J., 'The Rhetoric of *La Religieuse* and Eighteenth-Century Forensic Rhetoric', *Diderot Studies*, 3 (1961), 129–54

Empson, William, *Milton's God*, rev. edn (Cambridge, 1981)

Erickson, Robert A., '"Written in the Heart": *Clarissa* and Scripture', *Eighteenth-Century Fiction*, 2, No. 1 (1989), 17–52

Erskine-Hill, Howard, 'Literature and the Jacobite Cause: Was There a Rhetoric of Jacobitism?', in *Ideology and Conspiracy: Aspects of Jacobitism, 1689–1759*, ed. Eveline Cruickshanks (Edinburgh, 1982), pp. 49–69

Fish, Stanley E., *Surprised by Sin: The Reader in Paradise Lost* (1967)

'Why No One's Afraid of Wolfgang Iser', *Diacritics*, 11 (1981), 2–13; reprinted in *Doing What Comes Naturally: Change, Rhetoric, and the Practice of Theory in Literary and Legal Studies* (Oxford, 1989), pp. 68–86

Fliegelman, Jay, *Prodigals and Pilgrims: The American Revolution against Patriarchal Authority* (Cambridge, 1982)

Flynn, Carol Houlihan, *Samuel Richardson: A Man of Letters* (Princeton, 1982)

Ford, Ford Madox, *The English Novel, from the Earliest Days to the Death of Joseph Conrad* (1930; rpt. Manchester, 1983)

Forster, E. M., *Aspects of the Novel* (1927)

Fortuna, James Louis, '*The Unsearchable Wisdom of God': A Study of Providence in Richardson's Pamela* (Gainesville, 1980)

Frail, Robert J., 'The British Connection: The Abbé Prévost and the Translations of the Novels of Samuel Richardson' (diss., Columbia, 1985)

Frank, Joseph, *Dostoevsky: The Seeds of Revolt, 1821–1849*, 2nd edn (Princeton, 1977)

Gillis, Christina Marsden, *The Paradox of Privacy: Epistolary Form in Clarissa* (Gainesville, 1984)

Goldberg, Rita, *Sex and Enlightenment: Women in Richardson and Diderot* (Cambridge, 1984)

Golden, Morris, 'Public Context and Imagining Self in *Clarissa*', *Studies in English Literature 1500–1900*, 25 (1985), 575–98

   Richardson's Characters (Ann Arbor, 1963)

Griffin, Dustin, *Regaining Paradise: Milton and the Eighteenth Century* (Cambridge, 1986)

Guest, Harriet, *A Form of Sound Words: The Religious Poetry of Christopher Smart* (Oxford, 1989)

Halsband, Robert, *The Life of Lady Mary Wortley Montagu* (Oxford, 1956)

Hammond, Brean S., *Pope and Bolingbroke: A Study of Friendship and Influence* (Columbia, 1984)

Harris, Jocelyn, 'Protean Lovelace', *Eighteenth-Century Fiction*, 2, No. 4 (1990), 327–46

   Samuel Richardson (Cambridge, 1987)

   '*Sir Charles Grandison* and the Little Senate: The Relation between Samuel Richardson's Correspondence and His Last Novel' (diss., London, 1968)

Hill, Christopher, 'Clarissa Harlowe and her Times', *Essays in Criticism*, 5 (1955), 315–40

   Milton and the English Revolution (1977)

   'The Norman Yoke', in *Puritanism and Revolution* (1958), pp. 50–122

Hume, Robert D., *Henry Fielding and the London Theatre, 1728–1737* (Oxford, 1988)

Hunt, John Dixon, *The Figure in the Landscape: Poetry, Painting and Gardening during the Eighteenth Century* (Baltimore, 1976)

Hunter, J. Paul, *Occasional Form: Henry Fielding and the Chains of Circumstance* (Baltimore, 1975)

Iser, Wolfgang, *The Act of Reading* (Baltimore, 1978)

   The Implied Reader: Patterns of Communication in Prose Fiction from Bunyan to Beckett (Baltimore, 1974)

   'Indeterminacy and the Reader's Response in Prose Fiction', in *Aspects of Narrative*, ed. J. Hillis Miller (New York, 1971), pp. 1–45; reprinted in *Prospecting: From Reader Response to Literary Anthropology* (Baltimore, 1989), pp. 3–30

   Laurence Sterne: Tristram Shandy (Cambridge, 1988)

Jonsen, Albert R., and Stephen Toulmin, *The Abuse of Casuistry: A History of Moral Reasoning* (Berkeley and Los Angeles, 1988)

Jost, François, 'Prévost traducteur de Richardson', in *Expression, Communication and Experience in Literature and Language*, ed. Ronald G. Popperwell (1973), pp. 297–300

'Le Roman épistolaire et la technique narrative au XVIIIe siècle', *Comparative Literature Studies*, 3 (1966), 397–427

Kearney, Anthony, '*Clarissa* and the Epistolary Form', *Essays in Criticism*, 16 (1966), 44–56

'*Tom Jones* and the Forty-five', *Ariel*, 4 (1973), 68–78

Keast, William R., 'The Two *Clarissas* in Johnson's Dictionary', *Studies in Philology*, 54 (1957), 429–39

Kermode, Frank, 'Richardson and Fielding', *Cambridge Journal*, 4 (1950–1), 106–114

The Sense of an Ending: Studies in the Theory of Fiction (1967)

Keymer, Tom, 'Richardson's *Meditations*: Clarissa's *Clarissa*', in *Samuel Richardson: Tercentenary Essays*, ed. Margaret Anne Doody and Peter Sabor (Cambridge, 1989), pp. 89–109

Killham, John, 'Browning's "Modernity": *The Ring and the Book*, and Relativism', in *The Major Victorian Poets: Reconsiderations*, ed. Isobel Armstrong (1969), pp. 153–75

Kinkead-Weekes, Mark, '*Clarissa* Restored?', *Review of English Studies*, NS 10, No. 38 (1959), 156–71

Samuel Richardson: Dramatic Novelist (1973)

Konigsberg, Ira, *Samuel Richardson and the Dramatic Novel* (Lexington, 1968)

Kreissman, Bernard, *Pamela–Shamela: A Study of the Criticisms, Burlesques, Parodies and Adaptations of Richardson's Pamela*, University of Nebraska Studies NS 22 (Lincoln, Nebr., 1960)

Langbein, John H., 'The Criminal Trial before the Lawyers', *University of Chicago Law Review*, 45, No. 2 (1978), 263–316

'Shaping the Eighteenth-Century Criminal Trial: A View from the Ryder Sources', *University of Chicago Law Review*, 50, No. 1 (1983), 1–136

Liesenfeld, Vincent J., *The Licensing Act of 1737* (Madison, 1984)

Lubbock, Percy, *The Craft of Fiction* (1921)

Mack, Maynard, *Alexander Pope: A Life* (New Haven, 1985)

The Garden and the City: Retirement and Politics in the Later Poetry of Pope, 1731–1743 (Toronto, 1969)

McKeon, Michael, *The Origins of the English Novel, 1600–1740* (Baltimore, 1987)

McKillop, A. D., 'Richardson's Early Writings: Another Pamphlet', *Journal of English and Germanic Philology*, 53 (1954), 72–5

Samuel Richardson: Printer and Novelist (Chapel Hill, 1936)

'Samuel Richardson's Advice to an Apprentice', *Journal of English and Germanic Philology*, 42 (1943), 40–54

Malins, Edward, *English Landscaping and Literature, 1660–1840* (1966)

Maresca, Thomas E., *Epic to Novel* (Ohio, 1974)

Marks, Sylvia Kasey, *Sir Charles Grandison: The Compleat Conduct Book* (Lewisburg, 1986)

Moglen, Helene, *The Philosophical Irony of Laurence Sterne* (Gainesville, 1975)

Mullan, John, *Sentiment and Sociability: The Language of Feeling in the Eighteenth Century* (Oxford, 1988)

Paulson, Ronald, *Popular and Polite Art in the Age of Hogarth and Fielding* (Notre Dame, 1979)

Perkin, M. R., *Abraham Cowley: A Bibliography* (Folkestone, 1977)

Pocock, J. G. A., *The Ancient Constitution and the Feudal Law: A Study of English Historical Thought in the Seventeenth Century*, 2nd edn (Cambridge, 1987)

Poovey, Mary, 'Journeys from This World to the Next: The Providential Promise in *Clarissa* and *Tom Jones*', *ELH*, 43 (1976), 300–15

Prebble, John, *Culloden* (Harmondsworth, 1967)

Preston, John, '*Les Liaisons dangereuses*: Epistolary Narrative and Moral Discovery', *French Studies*, 24 (1970), 23–36

  The Created Self: The Reader's Role in Eighteenth-Century Fiction (1970)

Radzinowicz, Mary Ann, 'The Politics of *Paradise Lost*', in *Politics of Discourse: The Literature and History of Seventeenth-Century England*, ed. Kevin Sharpe and Steven N. Zwicker (Berkeley and Los Angeles, 1987), pp. 204–29

Randall, Helen W., 'The Rise and Fall of a Martyrology: Sermons on Charles I', *Huntington Library Quarterly*, 10 (1946–7), 135–67

Redford, Bruce, *The Converse of the Pen: Acts of Intimacy in the Eighteenth-Century Familiar Letter* (Chicago, 1986)

Reilly, Patrick, 'Fielding's Magisterial Art', in *Henry Fielding: Justice Observed*, ed. K. G. Simpson (1985), pp. 75–100

Richetti, John J., *Popular Fiction before Richardson: Narrative Patterns, 1700–1739* (Oxford, 1969)

Robbins, Caroline, *The Eighteenth-Century Commonwealthman* (Cambridge, Mass., 1959)

Rogers, Pat, *Eighteenth-Century Encounters: Studies in Literature and Society in the Age of Walpole* (Brighton, 1985)

  'The Emerging Form', *Times Literary Supplement*, No. 4426 (29 January–4 February 1988), 116–17

  'The Waltham Blacks and the Black Act', *Historical Journal*, 17 (1974), 465–86

Rorschach, Kimerly, *The Early Georgian Landscape Garden* (New Haven, 1983)

Rosbottom, Ronald C., *Choderlos de Laclos* (Boston, Mass., 1978)

  'Dangerous Connections: A Communicational Approach to *Les Liaisons dangereuses*', in *Laclos: Critical Approaches to Les Liaisons dangereuses*, ed. Lloyd R. Free (Madrid, 1978), pp. 183–221

  'A Matter of Competence: The Relationship between Reading and Novel-Making in Eighteenth-Century France', *Studies in Eighteenth-Century Culture*, 6 (1977), 245–63

Rousset, Jean, 'Une Forme littéraire: le roman par lettres', in *Forme et signification* (Paris, 1962), pp. 65–108

  Narcisse romancier: essai sur la première personne dans le roman (Paris, 1973)

Sabor, Peter, '*Amelia* and *Sir Charles Grandison*: The Convergence of Fielding and Richardson', *Wascana Review*, 17 (1982), 3–18

Sale, William M., Jr, 'From *Pamela* to *Clarissa*', in *The Age of Johnson*, ed. Frederick W. Hilles (New Haven, 1949), pp. 127–38

Samuel Richardson: A Bibliographical Record of his Literary Career with Historical Notes (New Haven, 1936)

Samuel Richardson: Master Printer (Ithaca, 1950)

Schochet, G. J., *Patriarchalism in Political Thought* (Oxford, 1973)

Scouten, Arthur H., ed., *The London Stage, 1660–1800, Part 3 (1729–1747)*, 2 vols. (Carbondale, 1961)

Sherbo, Arthur, 'Time and Place in Richardson's *Clarissa*', *Boston University Studies in English*, 3 (1957), 139–46

Sitter, John, *Literary Loneliness in Mid-Eighteenth-Century England* (Ithaca, 1982)

Slights, Camille Wells, *The Casuistical Tradition in Shakespeare, Donne, Herbert and Milton* (Princeton, 1981)

Starr, G. A., 'From Casuistry to Fiction: The Importance of the *Athenian Mercury*', *Journal of the History of Ideas*, 27 (1967), 17–32

Defoe and Casuistry (Princeton, 1971)

Stewart, Keith, 'Towards Defining an Aesthetic for the Familiar Letter in Eighteenth-Century England', *Prose Studies*, 5 (1982), 179–92

Stone, Lawrence, *The Family, Sex and Marriage in England, 1500–1800* (1977)

Stuber, Florian, 'On Fathers and Authority in *Clarissa*', *Studies in English Literature 1500–1900*, 25 (1985), 557–74

'On Original and Final Intentions, or Can There Be an Authoritative *Clarissa*?', *TEXT*, 2 (1985), 229–44

Sutherland, James, *English Literature in the Late Seventeenth Century* (Oxford, 1969)

Swearingen, James E., *Reflexivity in Tristram Shandy: An Essay in Phenomenological Criticism* (New Haven, 1977)

Tanner, Tony, *Adultery in the Novel: Contract and Transgression* (Baltimore, 1979)

Tavor, Eve, *Scepticism, Society and the Eighteenth-Century Novel* (1987)

Thompson, E. P., *Whigs and Hunters: The Origin of the Black Act* (Harmondsworth, 1977)

Todd, Janet, *Sensibility: An Introduction* (1986)

Women's Friendship in Literature (New York, 1980)

Traugott, John, *Tristram Shandy's World* (Berkeley and Los Angeles, 1954)

Tuck, Richard, *Natural Rights Theories: Their Origin and Development* (Cambridge, 1979)

Tucker, Susie I., *Protean Shape: A Study in Eighteenth-Century Vocabulary and Usage* (1967)

Turner, James Grantham, 'Lovelace and the Paradoxes of Libertinism', in *Samuel Richardson: Tercentenary Essays*, ed. Margaret Anne Doody and Peter Sabor (Cambridge, 1989), pp. 70–88

Uhrström, Wilhelm, *Studies on the Language of Samuel Richardson* (Upsala, 1907)

Van Marter, Shirley, 'Richardson's Revisions of *Clarissa* in the Second Edition', *Studies in Bibliography*, 26 (1973), 107–32

'Richardson's Revisions of *Clarissa* in the Third and Fourth Editions', *Studies in Bibliography*, 28 (1975), 119–52

Warner, William Beatty, *Reading Clarissa: The Struggles of Interpretation* (New Haven, 1979)

Watt, Ian, 'The Naming of Characters in Defoe, Richardson and Fielding', *Review of English Studies*, 25 (1949), 322–38

The Rise of the Novel: Studies in Defoe, Richardson and Fielding (1957)

Wilcox, Frank Howard, 'Prévost's Translations of Richardson's Novels', *University of California Publications in Modern Philology*, 12, No. 5 (1927), 341–411

Williams, Aubrey, 'Interpositions of Providence and the Design of Fielding's Novels', *South Atlantic Quarterly*, 70 (1971), 265–86

Winn, James Anderson, *A Window in the Bosom: The Letters of Alexander Pope* (Hamden, 1977)

Zirker, Malvin R., Jr., 'Richardson's Correspondence: The Personal Letter as Private Experience', in *The Familiar Letter in the Eighteenth Century*, ed. Howard Anderson, Philip B. Daghlian, and Irvin Ehrenpreis (Lawrence, 1966), pp. 71–91

Index

This index lists the more significant references made in the book to individuals, texts, and a number of topics of importance to *Clarissa*. In entries for Richardson's contemporaries or near-contemporaries, italics are used to indicate passages in which particular responses to Richardson and/or *Clarissa*, or related evidence of a reader's activities, are cited or discussed.

Printed in the United Kingdom
by Lightning Source UK Ltd.
117358UKS00001B/182